Text copyright © Glynn Christian 1993
Illustrations copyright © Glynn Boyd-Harte

First Published in Great Britain in 1993 by
Good Food Retailing Publications
Stanstead Farm, 177 Stanstead Road,
Caterham, Surrey CR3 6AJ.

ISBN 0-9521942-0-1

Cover photography John Lawson
Food stylist Emma Jane Frost
Food supplied by Fratelli Camisa and Harvey and
Brockless Ltd

Printed in Great Britain by Cox and Wyman Ltd,
Reading Berkshire.
Grateful thanks to The Bromide Factory, Croydon,
Surrey, White Art, Croydon, Surrey and
TTB, London E9.

Distributed by Vine House Distribution, East Sussex.

Glynn Christian's
NEW DELICATESSEN
FOOD HANDBOOK

Illustrated by Glynn Boyd-Harte

GOOD FOOD RETAILING PUBLICATIONS

ABOUT THE AUTHOR

Glynn Christian was born in New Zealand, came to Britain in 1965 and is now one of Britain's best known food writers and TV cooks. He learned much of his ingredient knowledge as a travel writer in the early days of inclusive holidays and in 1974 opened Mr Christian's, his delicatessen on London's famous Portobello Road market.

He is best known as an entertaining and innovative TV cook for both the BBC and ITV and has now made well over 800 live broadcasts, more than any other food presenter; film series include those made on location in the eastern Mediterranean, New Zealand, California, Sri Lanka and China.

His many published books include *Fragile Paradise*, the only biography of Fletcher Christian who led the mutiny on *Bounty* in 1789; he is Glynn's great-great-great-great-grandfather.

A fellow of the Royal Geographical Society, Glynn Christian still travels widely, often lecturing aboard *QE2*, is regularly seen in on-board films for British Airways and Air New Zealand and has just begun a diploma in the Conservation of Historic Gardens, Parks and Landscapes.

Glynn Christian's
NEW DELICATESSEN
FOOD HANDBOOK

Cheeses from Switzerland, representing the superb range of traditional cheeses from
Switzerland, is delighted to be associated with the publication of
Glynn Christian's New Delicatessen Food Handbook.
This guide is essential reading for anyone who enjoys the rich variety of foods available in our
shops and provides an invaluable reference source for those whose day to day lives bring them
into contact with food.
The book is fascinating whether you read it from cover to cover or just dip in and out of
chapters, searching for an ingredient, a recipe idea or tips on what to look for when shopping.
Food is truly international and *Cheeses from Switzerland* recognizes that today we are more
eager to try fresh food ideas from all over the world. Glynn's book will help to satisfy this
curiosity – so read on!

SWITZERLAND

ACKNOWLEDGEMENTS

Thousands of people have helped to write this book, sometimes unwittingly. For the information in this book is a distillation, a collected and matured concentration of thousands of conversations and observations, of advice generously given and opinion passionately imposed.

Books, too, have been helpful, but I find many concentrate on what to do with an ingredient, rather than what it can or might do best of its own accord. The content of this one often had to be teased out of many sources before I felt I had a full overall view – for instance, it took over 20 books, five telephone calls and a trip to China to find an accurate guide to what is used to turn soymilk into tofu...

Many of those I credited for helping with the first edition of the book are now no longer in business or no longer with us, but amongst those who are, a special thanks to Kurt Weyrauch of New York who helped me with the first edition and agitated for the second. Food and Wine from France, The Italian Trade Centre, Foods from Spain, and the German food marketing organization CMA have all been a splendid support. So were Caviar House, NZ Natural Products, Billingtons Sugar, Tate & Lyle, Ryton Organic Gardens, Judy Ridgway who solved olive oil and Roz Denny who did the same for rice. Ian Lay of Accord Services helped beyond the call of duty with tea as did the Tea Council, Douwe Egberts and Andrew Knight of Andronicus Coffee Company with coffee, and Valrhona with chocolate. Pataks and Sharwoods fleshed out the Oriental side of things and Wing Yip of the eponymous Oriental supermarkets was wonderfully generous with time, advice and produce. Terry Tan helped here too and it remains impossible to write about herbs and spices without the enthusiastic support of Mike Pester of Fox's Spices. The irreplaceable Carolyn Cavele and Cathy Stuart helped with any and everything to do with Food from Britain.

My special thanks go to Bob Farrand and _Good Food Retailing_ magazine for the long, loyal friendship and support which got this edition off the ground. And of course to Maurice Johnson and Cheeses from Switzerland, whose connection with book publishing follows an eminent and ancient path; many early cookery books were published with commercial support, Mrs Beeton particularly.

And then there are the workers, editor Jenni Muir and typesetter Patrick McCarthy, who nobly worked to produce the book in record time with enormous care and regard for detail whilst continuing to assemble _Good Food Retailing_ magazine. Everyone who enjoys the book owes them a particular thank you.

THROW AWAY YOUR SHOPPING LIST

That's the way to make the most of delicatessen food.

Shopping lists selfishly focus attention only on themselves. So you don't see what is new, what is better, what is best.

The shelves of your delicatessens and specialty food stores have never offered such a fabulous range. And these days they are partnered by national and local supermarket chains in an unexpected synergy which benefits everyone. Sometimes independent shops introduce a new product which is subsequently taken up by supermarkets and offered with greater choice of quality and price; other times you might find something unexpected on, say, the cheese counter of a supermarket but go on to a specialist shop to learn more, experiment further.

And yet, not long ago a Sunday columnist defined a delicatessen as 'a newspaper shop that sells milk'. An exaggeration, certainly, but not by much. For the word delicatessen is so ill-defined it is painted up over all kinds of surprising places.

In America, where the word was popularized, a *deli* is where you go to have sandwiches made, or where you go to put together a meal that needs little further preparation. There will be hot salt beef and pastrami, smoked salmon, barrels of salt cucumbers and herrings, cheeses, and a choice of breads. Often – and New York is famed for this – the food will be largely Jewish, for originally a delicatessen was a small German-Jewish shop, a kosher food shop set up specially to cater for the hordes of young single men who could not cook for themselves. The name and style were taken to the United States in the great migrations and, like the people who accompanied them, were blended into something quite new. Yet, if you want a very special cheese, spices, something unusual in a tin, or freshly ground coffee, you do not choose a delicatessen in the United States – you find a specialty food store. The two might be combined in supermarkets, or in such New York luminaries as Balducci's, Dean and Delucca or Zabar's, but generally the European tradition of separation prevails.

The word delicatessen is not easily recognized in Europe. Sausage, cheese, pickles and farm produce are the daily fare, and not available in one store. Salami and ham come from one shop, bread from another, cheese somewhere else. The French *charcuterie* sells just pork products; for other meats and prepared dishes you must go to a *traiteur*, a *fromagerie* sells cheese. And even the small villages have a market with farm produce and home cured sausages, free range poultry and fresh fish, traditional butter and cheese, milk, eggs and cream.

A delicatessen in the United Kingdom should combine the best of all features, selling a range of fresh, unpackaged foods plus a variety of higher-class and hard-to-find specialities. It should not be confused with a health food shop, with its limited diet and vitamin supplements. A delicatessen should offer you authentic, mature farmhouse cheeses, unadulterated yoghurts, honest bread, pure ice cream, salads to go with your sliced meats, unsalted butter, quality coffees and teas, rare nuts, herbs and spices, continental sausages, dried peas and beans – and a host of little treats, simple and exotic. In fact if you scratch beneath the surface of most long-established delicatessens you will find they are an echo of the old, general grocer. My old shop, just off Portobello Road, is one of these. Within the memory of some of today's customers, the original proprietor used to boil ham, roast coffee, pack butter and age cheeses on the premises. The people behind the counter knew what they were selling, the customers knew what they were buying.

In the end, I believe you get what you deserve, and the worst of the processed foods, meats and cheeses, especially, are there simply because you bought them, perhaps knowing no better.

A great deal of modern, manufactured food is excellent, for not all progress is bad. The combination of modern refrigeration and transport systems have vastly broadened our culinary palettes in just a few years. Once combined with respect for tradition and authenticity on the part of the manufacturers, and with greater general knowledge, food will be richer for us all. You see, delicatessen food is not about smoked salmon for lunch or sausages made out of pigs' guts. It is also about knowing how to combine smoked pork with pickled cucumbers, how to improve cream cheese with a sprinkle of rose water, how to choose the proper pasta shape, or to make your own flavour of coffee.

Thus, this is a book for everyone who eats, not just for cooks. Ingredient knowledge is the key to every type of culinary enjoyment. Know your ingredients and you will never again buy something out of condition. Know your ingredients, what they can do, how, and with what and you need hardly look at a recipe book again. Know your ingredients and you will shop without shopping lists, far better armed to buy what is good, what is well-priced, seasonal or attractively priced.

Throughout the book I have given many ideas for serving and preparing. I expect you will find some bizarre, many not to your taste. This is only to be expected, for the book is not a bible, but an introduction, and discussion and disagreement about how to enjoy food is one of its most delicious condiments.

Like most of the world's greatest pleasures, the enjoyment of delicatessen food need cost you no more than you would normally spend.

I hope you find my New Delicatessen Food Handbook useful. But more than that, I hope it makes food more fascinating and more fun for you. Bon Appetit.

**Glynn Christian**

B read need only be made from flour, water and salt. Bread made without a raising agent (unleavened bread) is one of our oldest foods; even bread raised to lightness by the action of yeast was possibly discovered in Ancient Egypt. It is a simple, honest, satisfying food, yet it is a reflection on living standards in much of the western hemisphere that we should have to go to a specialty store to buy bread that *is* honest, well made and unadulterated. Bread represents such an emotive part of our heritage that it is always at the mercy of social fashion. In other parts of the world, sense has long prevailed and bread making is just as it was ten, one hundred or one thousand years ago.

In the villages, towns and cities of India, Pakistan and Bangladesh, for instance, the unleavened *chapati* and its relatives are still regularly hand-shaped and baked over open fires. The slapping sound of the dough being shaped between the palms of squatting women is an integral part of daily life. Some families may actually buy the coarse wholemeal chapati flour, but most will grind their own as they need it. Similar breads, sometimes made with flours other than wheat but also baked on griddles, are made further north. In Afghanistan the dough is rolled out to be a metre or more in diameter. Armenians make smaller, even thinner chapati-type breads and the Sardinians still make 'paper bread' in their mountain villages.

In the lands of Islam, yeast has long played a part in bread and pastry making. The most common types of bread there are flattish discs, often spiced, and the oval envelopes known widely in Europe as *pitta*. This is also common in Greece, Cyprus and has become the national bread of Israel. Eaten fresh and warm – whether Israeli, Greek or Arabic – it is perfectly delicious.

Countries of the eastern and southern Mediterranean still offer the interested tourist a chance to see a sight once familiar throughout Europe. In the tight alleyways and up the steep-stepped lanes of bazaars and medinas you will see single loaves of leavened dough being carried to a central baker. Each family identifies its loaves with its own mark, a custom which prevailed in some areas of England right up to the turn of the century.

Countries with a traditional high regard for their food forbid their flour to be tampered with, by omission or commission. This is certainly true of France and largely why the French enjoy such good breads; there is also a relative absence of large baking combines in France so the independent village baker reigns supreme. Elsewhere the story is rather different. 'Scientific' advances during the last century have changed bread making in some parts of the world more than during the previous 3,000 to 4,000 years. Reliable yeasts, better and cheaper wheat flour and ovens with controllable temperatures all coincided and caused a revolution from which upheaval recovery is still some way off.

The chemically assisted, fast-rising, sliced white loaf is marketed mainly in the United States, the United Kingdom, the Netherlands and parts of the British Commonwealth and stimulates a continuing controversy. The essential complaint is that the dough for this product is mixed, risen and baked within the hour. The gradual stretching of gluten and maturing of the dough's flavour doesn't happen; the first is achieved by extremely fast, brutally rough beating, the second is forgotten or approximated with additives. The end product, to the scientist who created it, smells right, slices like a dream, does not crumble when spread with butter and keeps well. And that, claim the manufacturers, is all bread is expected to do. The flavour seems not to matter and if it does then it must, by definition, be an acceptable flavour because everybody buys it. Not true. But, to be scrupulously fair, this type of bread is probably quite good for you, even though the long-term effects of some of the additives are unknown.

No evidence exists to support the common assumption that wholemeal bread is good for you while white bread is damaging to your health. Wholemeal bread does contain bran, however, and should offer both vitamin E and a higher proportion of minerals and trace elements than white. In practice, according to some dieticians, wholemeal bread could actually be detrimental to health. It seems we are likely to spread it more thickly with butter, jam and other good-tasting comestibles than we might white bread; arguments exist to show that such excesses are far worse for us than the suspected chemical shortcomings of white bread. Research in the United States shows that as long as the rest of the diet has a minimal proportion of high-quality protein, a white bread diet successfully supports life and encourages excellent growth in 5-15 year olds.

During the Second World War, it was thought high-extraction flour (the only type then milled) caused rickets in children. This theory is not far-fetched. Wholemeal flour contains a substance called phytic acid, which is present in the whole grain. In the bowels, this phytic acid locks itself onto valuable calcium, iron and magnesium, preventing the body from absorbing and using them. The British Government decreed that chalk, in the form of highly refined calcium carbonate, should be added to all flours other than wholemeal at a rate three times higher than daily requirements. It is still added today, for although the war-time rickets scare has passed, chalk is thought to help prevent some heart diseases.

Leavening

To leaven means to aerate dough or batter. Gas, created as a by-product of a biological or chemical action, is trapped as bubbles in dough or batter. In the heat of the oven, the gas expands even more; continued heat kills the gas-forming action and hardens the balloons formed by the gas, allowing the baked end-product to retain its risen shape.

Without yeasts we would have neither beer, wine nor bread. Yeasts are an enormous family of minute, single-celled fungi. Each is only about $\frac{1}{20}$th of a millimetre/$\frac{1}{1000}$th of an inch in diameter, and there are millions of them in the air, almost everywhere. Some are useful, some not. The most important are those that have a special aptitude to convert, by the action of their enzymes, sugar into alcohol and carbon dioxide.

The yeasts on the skins of fruits and vegetables are directly responsible for the fermentation of wines. Yeast for beer making was grown in a sweet liquid mixed with flour and potatoes, hops or both. A clever brewer's wife would try to use mainly hops with plenty of pollen upon them; she may not have known it, but these supported the strongest colonies of the yeasts she wanted.

The barm, which she kept and sold to bakers and housewives, was made and used only within the broadest of guidelines. There was no way of knowing what combination of yeasts had been cultivated or how they would perform in dough. It was this ever-changing broth of many yeasts that necessitated the long risings and provings in former times. Then, in 1850, came German or compressed yeast, made of one yeast only – *saccharomy cescerevisiae*. At last bakers had their own yeast. It worked quickly and consistently on the maltose (sugar) in flour and permanently changed the face of yeast cookery, commercial and domestic.

The new yeast went on the market under three different names: German, compressed and dried. (This has confused many people who have tried baking from old recipes: the chances are that 'dried' yeast means 'compressed' yeast.) Modern compressed yeast is often called fresh yeast. It performs consistently if it is in good condition and can be kept in the refrigerator for weeks or deep-frozen for months.

Modern (genuinely) dried yeast is much more expensive than compressed yeast but very much more easily obtainable. Dried yeast granules are twice as strong, weight for weight, as fresh yeast, eg 15g/½oz dried yeast equals 25g/1oz fresh yeast. Always use less rather than more dried yeast even if it looks ludicrously little. American recipes usually state the number of packets of yeast required; their packets hold only 7g/¼oz dried yeast, which is the same as 15g/½oz fresh yeast.

Easy-mix yeast is just what it says. It does not have to be proved or treated separately, but is mixed dry into the flour. You use the same amount as ordinary dried yeast. A boon.

Fresh yeast needs only to come into contact with warm liquid to start reproducing and creating gas and alcohol. Sugar is used for starting dried yeast but must never be added to fresh yeast as it actually enervates its strength; salt inhibits all yeasts and thus must only ever be added to the flours and not the yeast mixture – that is not a problem with Easy-mix.

If it is easy for you to buy fresh (compressed) yeast, then buy exactly the quantity you want, when you want it. If you have to store it, use the coldest part of the refrigerator. Provided the yeast was in good condition and you have bought a good-sized piece, it should last a full two weeks.

Some air circulation helps storage of yeast, so either wrap it loosely in grease-proof paper or store it in a fairly close-fitting container with a little ventilation. Keep it away from strong odours. Melon, slices of which are very often put into refrigerators unwrapped, is a particularly bad offender. There are few things that invade other foods quite so vigorously.

Even under refrigeration, yeast is prone to self-digestion which, naturally, makes it rather less potent than it might be. A clean smell, light colour and a tendency to crumble rather than collapse are clear indicators that fresh yeast is in good condition.

Those who find it difficult to obtain compressed yeast but own a freezer may safely splash out on yeast when they have the opportunity. Yeast freezes very well, and should produce excellent results for up to three months, possibly longer.

Pack the yeast in suitable sizes – say 25g/1oz batches – and seal and label it carefully. Allow frozen yeast to thaw slowly, then dissolve it in lukewarm liquid as usual.

Magical as yeast seems, all types can exceed their usefulness in bread and related baking. The action that creates gas is accompanied by other enzymic actions that ripen the flour and enhance the dough's flavour. But after a certain point the bread is said to be over-yeasted and the loaf will look and taste decidedly wrong. Bread yeast dies at a temperature of around 55°C/130°F. This is a gradual process during baking as the heat penetrates from the crust to the centre. Over-proving bread, proving in a hot place or using too much yeast, will make a loaf heavy and cause it to stale quickly.

Readers who wish to try out recipes from cookbooks printed before the advent of compressed (fresh) yeast should work backwards from the amount of flour required. For bread doughs, 25g/1oz fresh yeast is more than enough for 1.5kg/3.31lb. You can double the amount for sweet brioche-type doughs and sweet buns and cakes. The old yeasts and barms, measured by the pint or cup, contained liquid, so you may have to add extra water, milk or egg if you are adapting an old recipe and using compressed yeast instead of the old types. The method of bread making always began with a sponge, a loose, wet mixture to 'prove' the yeast was working before risking the loss of larger amounts of flour; it is not strictly necessary in these days of reliable yeasts but the extra time will give improved flavour – just as easily obtained by using as little yeast as you can and proving as long and as slowly as possible.

Babke: a Polish or Russian sponge-type cake with a dense texture baked in a deep decorative ring mold. The mixture usually incorporates some beaten egg white, so it is often described as a soufflé cake. It might be leavened with yeast or a chemical agent. Serve plain with coffee when fresh. Babke makes an excellent quick pudding or special tea time treat served with a flavoured cream, doused with syrup or liqueurs, or covered with such cream/fruit mixtures as raspberry fool. Sometimes they are available covered in chocolate.

Bagel: this yeasted, white dough bread roll is like a doughnut with a hole and varies from 8-12cm/3-5in in diameter. The ring of dough is poached in water before baking, giving the requisite tough, chewy crust. Associated with kosher food, particularly with that of New York, it is better eaten warm and is at its most famous when filled with a combination of cream cheese and smoked salmon – the lox and bagel ubiquitous for Sunday breakfast in the Big Apple. Bagels can also be bought sprinkled with caraway seeds, salt, poppy seeds or sesame seeds. Seasoned or garlic salt might be added to the dough. Even raw onion can be sprinkled on top, which bakes to a caramelized brown – not, I think, a very social breakfast choice.

Bath buns: a white bread bun, the dough of which should contain egg and milk; must have crushed lump sugar on top. Can contain lemon, chopped peel or sultanas but never currants.

Bloomers: these are the oblong, fat and rounded loaves of white bread which are always slashed diagonally and never baked in tins.

Brioches: made of a light, yeasted dough with a high proportion of egg and butter to give a cake-like texture. Sweetness is variable, but brioches are usually baked in tapering, fluted moulds, large or small, and most often eaten warm for breakfast; sometimes plaited.

Unsweetened brioches also make an elegant accompaniment to soups and other light first courses. If the centre is scooped out and replaced with a vegetable or meat purée they make a stunning savoury snack, hot or cold. A big brioche, cut into slices and toasted lightly is nice for tea; these slices can also replace toast to serve with light supper dishes such as chicken or fish with a cream sauce but again only if the brioche is not too sweet.

Brioche dough baked around a whole coarse, pork sausage is a great treat, hot or cold – Fauchon in Paris do this to salmon and serve it in slices with saffron-flavoured butter. I was eating some outside Notre Dame when a congregation spilled out. Once the Fauchon wrappings were espied literally dozens of Parisians wished me an envious *bon appetit*. So *that's* how to gain the attention of a Parisian!

My favourite way to start Christmas dinner is warm saffron-flavoured brioches served with a bowl of chilled soured cream and a pot of caviare, and it requires great Christian resolve to share, I can tell you.

Brown: this could and can mean white bread which has been coloured with caramel. Today it more often means bread made with 85 per cent extraction flour, what we used to call wheatmeal until that was forbidden; apparently this may have some colouring too. The lesson is simply not to say brown when you mean wholemeal.

Brownies: a confusing but satisfying thing for the name covers a multitude of produce. Brownies can be big, flattish and roundish cookies with a distinct chewiness and are then generally studded with nuts or chocolate. The ones I ate at the New York State Fair with dollops of crunchy peanut butter were spectacularly good. But brownies are also a type of cake baked in an oblong pan and then cut into squares; they may be moist and chewy or cake-like. Together with muffins, they have rather taken over from cheesecakes as a staple, and are just as easy to make as to buy in, which you might remember when considering the prices charged.

Ciabatta: the star of the early 90s. A flattish, long oval of white dough made with an element of olive oil; the shape is said to be reminiscent of the sole of a sloppy sort of casual slipper, but seems equally to be that of a steam-rollered bone. Ciabatta dough is made with water rather than anything milky, which encourages the floury flavour, and when properly made proves long so there are many large holes. Its great success means many commercialized types are imposters, of right shape but ordinary texture. Often flavoured with such trendy additions as sun-dried tomatoes, herbs, olives or olive pastes, arcane cheeses and the like.

Chapati: an unleavened, Indian flat bread which should be made of wholemeal flour.

Cheesecakes: true cheesecakes have a recognizably cake-like texture, in which cream or curd cheese is simply a flavouring. In the traditional small English cheesecakes, baked in a pastry shell, there is usually no cheese at all now; but curd cakes, cheesecakes or curd tarts were always popular, and once flavoured with rose water, nutmeg, orange, lemon, sherry or dried fruits.

It is unlikely you will be able to buy this style of cheesecake unless you can find a predominantly Polish, Russian or Jewish area or a shop run for these people. Austrians and Germans also make these, perhaps the richest versions of all.

What I call the 'wet ones' are baked cheesecakes in which cheese is the major ingredient and flour and eggs are there simply to bind it (home made ones would include cream or soured cream or often yoghurt too). These are the most common commercial cheesecakes, and usually have a biscuit base and a topping of fruit in a thick syrup or sauce. Provided they are slightly chilled they make a satisfying and attractive snack or pudding.

The third type of cheesecake is often found in small delicatessens where food is made on the premises. These are the unbaked types, often set with gelatine, which is no bad thing as long as they also contain a measure of whipped cream or yoghurt to give a fluffy, light texture. Those without gelatine often use only flavoured cream cheese and are thin and miserable, scarcely thicker than the biscuit base, a swizz and a disappointment.

Whatever your delicatessen does, you should always store cheesecake in a refrigerator, for even if made with the finest ingredients it will go sour in warmth, or it will dry out, or both.

If you can buy some quite plain cheesecake it can be made rather special as the accompaniment to a purée of sharp fruit – blackcurrants, gooseberries, red currants with orange, or rhubarb with orange and a touch of green root ginger would all be good.

Thin slices of chilled cheesecake on beautiful plates are the best way to extend small amounts of exquisite fruits. A slice of lemony cheesecake with just half an exquisite peach, or some passion fruit pulp, with perhaps a slice of mango or with some lime splashed kiwi fruit slices would leave guests wishing for nothing more – unless of course they knew you had some chilled, well-matured elderflower wine, which goes with all cheesecakes.

Chelsea buns: to be authentic these buns should be made from a slightly sweetened, white, yeasted dough and must incorporate both lemon zest and some mixed spice. The flavoured dough is rolled flat, covered with a mixture of butter, currants and brown sugar, rolled up and then sliced – to make spirals of dough. They must be laid flat and arranged so that when they prove and swell they just touch one another, giving the authentic slightly square shape. When cooked, Chelsea buns must be glazed with boiled milk and sugar syrup, then sprinkled with castor sugar.

Chollah: essentially a large loaf of yeasted white flour with milk and a little egg, often slightly sweetened too. The usual shape is a plait, sprinkled with poppyseed. Particularly associated with Jewish food and festivals but not that much different from the small English milk loaves.

Cob/coburg loaf: the name for any round loaf of leavened white, brown or wholemeal bread. They are sometimes slashed or pricked or topped with whole grains but are never baked in a tin.

Corn breads: because no type of corn contains gluten it cannot make leavened breads by itself. Thus cornmeal, a relation of sweet corn, is used to flavour leavened breads or, much more commonly, is made into chemically raised breads. They are fairly soft and cake-like and thus spoon breads, which are served in the baking dish and spooned out as you eat. Pone, Johnny Cakes and a dozen other funny names all mean the same thing. A commercially available sourdough corn bread mix is terribly good.

Cottage loaf: bread loaf of any type made of two rounds of unequal size, the smaller sitting on top of the bigger. Not often made commercially now.

Crisp bread: an unleavened, thin bread from Scandinavia. Made domestically only with rye flour but commercial manufacturing often dictates the addition of wheat and other ingredients.

Croissants: one of the heights of yeast baking, croissants are made by rolling up a rich yeasted dough with layers of a great deal of butter – in fact they are really a yeasted puff pastry. Although now far more easily available, even in supermarkets, many of the mass-produced croissants have a metallic taste induced by the use of fats other than butter and are not worth the money. Croissants are found throughout Europe, varying mainly in their sweetness – Polish and Austrian are the sweetest. Several places claim the invention of these crescents of cholesterol – I plump for the Viennese baker who is said first to have fashioned them on the morning the crescents of the invading Turkish army were finally repelled from his city gates.

If not too sweet themselves, croissants go surprisingly well with some of the sweeter meats, especially ham; such combinations make a change in a picnic basket. If you make your own croissants, roll the dough around slices of ham and make the croissants bigger than usual for a more substantial breakfast; these are good hot or cold with herby, chive or garlic butter or with flavoured cream cheese.

Crown loaf: a specialty loaf made by baking a circle of rolls of white dough in a tin – they should only just touch. To make it more crown-like, some bakers use two circles, the top one smaller and joined to the bottom in the same way cottage loaves would be.

Danish loaf: a long, oval, crusty loaf of white bread with a central slash, lightly floured. Not baked in a tin.

Danish pastries: these are made with a rich, yeasted dough similar to that of croissants but the butter is usually incorporated all in one layer and the dough turned and rolled without further additions. The pastry is then cut into decorative shapes, filled, iced or flavoured in dozens of ways and the finished products are served hot or cold at almost any time of the day. The secret of the fascinating but fugitive flavour of the better ones is ground cardamom. Probably invented in Vienna but particularly associated with Scandinavia (the Danes call Danish pastries Wienerbrod!).

Diet breads: other than so-called slimming breads, diet breads are usually either salt-free or gluten-free. The former helps in some heart conditions but is fairly unappetizing; the latter is almost impossible to buy but gluten-free flour, something of a contradiction, is available on prescription for sufferers from coeliac disease which is caused by an inability to digest the gliadin in gluten. Some health food shops sell a gluten-free, bran bread mixture.

Doughnuts: chunks of leavened white flour dough, sometimes filled with jam or fruit, then fried in fat or oil and smothered in sugar or a thin icing. Extremely widespread. It is mainly Arabs and Americans who make the ones with holes in the middle and these are often chemically leavened. Poles and Russians are addicted to their jam-filled *ponshki*. The Greeks make them smaller then soak them in warm honey and call them *loukoumades*. The Dutch, who normally make boring food, make wonderful doughnuts, stuffed with grated apple and fruit and spices and then give them the delightful name *olliebollen*.

Enriched breads: the additives which enrich the flavour, vitamin or mineral content of breads often improve keeping qualities, too. Milk, eggs, butter and cooking fats or oils are the most common enrichers, but soy flour, bran, wheatgerm, molasses, honey, and sugar are all found in commercial loaves. Most such additives are unnecessary if you regularly eat proper wholemeal bread. In any case the milk or egg was probably added to commercial loaves in powder form.

Essene bread/Manna bread: made from sprouted grains and without yeast or flour of any kind. Fruits and seeds give sweetness and flavour.

Farmhouse loaf: a white bread loaf baked in a tin both wider and more shallow than the usual tin loaf. The word farmhouse is imprinted on the side of the loaf, which is sometimes slashed lengthwise and floured.

Focaccia: a thick, light, flat, round Italian bread that is dimpled on the top and drizzled with olive oil and herbs. Sometimes it also has herbs, tomatoes and the like in the dough. It is thus a sort of thick and semi-naked pizza and with its minimal but strong flavouring much more like the original peasant sustenance.

French bread: the name generally given to any yeasted bread baked in long rolls, even though French flour or techniques may not have been incorporated. Usually called French sticks, but there are correct names for most types. *Baguettes* are the crisp, golden, medium-sized sticks that bulge in the middle. The very long thin ones are properly called *ficelles*. Large, hand-shaped, cylindrical or round loaves are usually *pain de campagne* or *pain de ménage*. If French breads are baked in roll pans, which gives them straight, even sides, they are called *longuets*.

It has long been said that French stick breads get their delicious taste merely by the use of low-gluten soft flour. Far more important is that they are proved very much longer than our breads, something you can check by the number of large holes in each loaf, which British bakers think is a sign of badly made bread. Additionally, they are baked in specialized ovens which shoot steam onto the loaves from time to time, and thus were never and can never be a domestic product. For years supermarkets tried to foist us off with dense, quickly-made breads in long roll shapes; now they have taken the trouble to install proper ovens and to let the bread prove properly before baking it. French breads are now British.

Granary loaf: a commercial brown loaf to which is added a measure of malted wheat grains for flavour and texture.

Grissini: these are the thin, well-baked breadsticks so beloved of Italian restaurants. There is no secret to making them yourself other than rolling your dough evenly and thinly.

Gugelhopf: this egg-rich, yeasted cake, also called _kugelhopf_ and related to babke and brioche, contains chopped peel and other dried fruit. Dozens of recipes. It may be eaten plain but the very high yeast content means it stales too quickly for the taste of those not from Central Europe. But butter, jam or syrup will put that right. Like babke, gugelhopf may also be covered with chocolate and nuts.

Lardy cake: sometimes available in small, independent baker's shops, this is bread dough rolled and folded like a simple puff pastry, except that instead of butter, pure lard, brown sugar and sultanas or mixed fruit are used. The dough should be scored with a sharp knife and the baked lardy cake broken on these marks rather than sliced. It is better warm than cold but either way is wonderful.

Milk loaf: a generic term for white bread mixed with milk or milk and water which gives a sweeter flavour, softer texture and longer life. Often made in small sizes and usually glazed.

Muffin, American: like a large cup cake and rarely seen plain. Its most common manifestation once was studded with blueberries, but we eventually latched on – unless they are very fresh and wild, cooked blueberries have virtually no flavour. Now we have cranberry muffins (excellent), banana muffins, courgette (zucchini), chocolate, double chocolate and everything else muffins which have gone well beyond their appearance at American breakfasts. Some will argue there is a special muffin mixture, and there probably is, but frankly you can bake any cake mixture in suitable tins and call them muffins. The absolute best I ever had were served warm as a lunch time dessert on the terrace of the Hotel Martinez in Cannes; they were almost black with bitter chocolate and just under the top crust were a couple of rum-soaked cherries in syrup. For the days I find myself anywhere but Cannes I have always relied on the comfort of Betty Crocker muffin mixes.

Muffin, English: only found in the United States and Australia. Chewy, yeasted and flat, and when split rather like crumpets. Related to the sort of muffin which used to be hawked through British city streets, sort of…

Nan: a yeasted Indian bread traditionally cooked on the inside surface of a tandoori oven and thus they should properly be rather tear-shaped, a result of gravity and the force with which they must be thrown onto the inside of the oven. Available fresh and frozen, often as mere rounds, and an invaluable way to jazz up any meal, for even from frozen they are crisp outside, chewy and sweet inside, after just a few minutes under the grill; but you must follow the instructions first to sprinkle or quickly rinse them with water. I use them as a type of pizza base; spread with from-age frais or soured cream and topped with smoked salmon drizzled with truffle oil and scattered with rocket, for instance. The Sloane Hotel in Chelsea bases much of its room service menu on this wheeze and does a roaring trade in hot nan topped with yoghurt, chicken tikka and mango chutney.

Panettone: a rather dry, yeasted cake from Italy which includes lots of dried fruit and is traditionally found at Christmas time.

Petits pains au chocolat: the ultimate sin in breakfast fare – or at any other time. They are usually made of brioche or croissant dough in which is embedded a chunk of rich dark chocolate, rather like a sweet sausage roll. Such is the sweetness and richness of these delights that those made with a simpler white bread are actu-ally more enjoyable than those made with richer doughs.

Pitta: a flat oval of white or wholemeal bread recently popularized by the growth of interest in Greek and Arabic food. Usually served heated and torn into small squ-ares and used as a scoop. Otherwise it is cut in half and the space inside encouraged to become a pocket which is then filled with salad and sliced hot meats or kebabs. The flourishing of Middle-Eastern shops means we are now seeing many variations, some thinner, some thicker and many scattered with unusual herb mixtures. *Man-koush* is a common name found associated with such breads, but seems to be all things to Middle-Eastern bakers.

Pizza: originally a Neapolitan way to fill hungry stomachs cheaply – now an easy way for restaurateurs to fill bank accounts. True Neapolitan pizza (and the better American ones) is a thick slab of yeasted white or wholemeal flour dough mixed with milk to give lightness and more sustenance. It should be very crisp under-neath and around the edges thanks to the generous application of olive oil to the baking tray. Originally toppings were simple and yet rich and chosen to blend into the dough rather than curl and crisp on top in the way modern pizza ingredients do. Cheese has become a common ingredient, especially the chewy Mozzarella or grated Cheddar – but neither is authentic. Although now essential, tomato as a topping would originally have been unknown. For a long time after they were introduced to Europe, tomatoes cooked to a pulp were merely one of the optional sauces you poured over your chunks of hot white dough in Naples. Elizabeth David says the absolutely original pizza-type dish is from Armenia and the topping was of minced lamb. The French *pissaladière* covers dough (or thick slices of bread fried on one side only) with a mush of onion cooked in olive oil and decorated with black olives and anchovy fillets – a tomato-less pizza, in effect. Arguments rage that thin, crisp bases are the original but the Neapolitan woman who taught me to make pizza scoffs at that, saying that bread was what her poor ancestors could afford, not topp-ings. But who really cares? You want thin crusts, you have them.

Pumpernickel: the many packaged varieties of unleavened German, wholegrain breads are essentially the same, with slightly different emphasis given to one or the other whole grain. Thus pumpernickel and *vollkornbrot* are much the same and versions from Westphalia and Osnabruck differ on purpose, as both these German areas claim to have created the original as far back as 1400. There is just as much controversy over the origin of the word pumpernickel. Some say it is onomatopoeic for the flatulent effect on the eater. Try saying it with a German accent, and you'll hear what I mean.

It is not easy to make at home; the commercial pumpernickels are often baked for 24 hours at a very low temperature in a closed container. This makes a moist, dense, dark, flat loaf which is now usually bought ready sliced. It should be refrigerated when opened. Pumpernickel and similar unleavened loaves, which might include grains other than rye, are excellent bases for open sandwiches; but as they dry and split easily I find it is better to cut each slice into squares or fingers before they are covered. A thin layer of butter keeps pumpernickel slices and pieces supple and prevents them either drying out or becoming soggy when on a buffet.

Rum babas: are part of the classic French repertoire. They are made of a savarin dough, that is a sweet, very highly yeasted dough, and are baked in small ring moulds. They should be saturated with rum-flavoured syrup, which dissuades the growth of mould but which does not always disguise the taste of staleness which is precipitated by the high yeast content. If they are nice and fresh they can be decorated with chilled fresh fruit and whipped cream to make a super pudding.

Rye bread: a generic term for any bread which contains a proportion of rye flour. The actual content varies from as low as 15 per cent, which gives a light-coloured, light-textured loaf, to 100 per cent, which gives a dark, dense loaf. Most often baked in a bloomer shape in this country, with or without caraway seeds. Some delicatessens sell sourdough rye breads, which, surprisingly, are rather sweet. These should be cut in very thin slices.

Sally Lunn: this light, sweet bread was either originally sold in the streets of Bath by a woman of the same name or the name is a corruption of the French *sol et lune*, for these delicacies are supposed to look like the sun and the moon – a rich shining golden top over a pale delicate base. Put more simply, a Sally Lunn loaf is a white flour, yeasted dough bread mixed with full milk or milk and cream, slightly sweetened, perhaps slightly spiced and thus a sort of lesser brioche. It should be glazed with beaten egg yolk and scattered with crushed cube sugar whilst still hot. In Australia and New Zealand they replace the crushed sugar with white icing and dessicated coconut. They would.

Sandwich loaf: white, brown or wholemeal bread baked in an enclosed tin to give a rectangular shape. Usually made only with modern fast-rising 'bread' and then sliced and wrapped.

Slimming breads: also called starch-reduced or high protein breads as they are generally made with flour to which extra gluten has been added. This creates a bulkier, more aerated loaf. Slice for slice these breads have more air and less starch – but ounce for ounce they are exactly the same as other breads. They only assist dieting if you eat the same number of (or fewer) slices than you would normally eat of 'heavier' bread. Some would say bread wasn't the problem anyway, but what we put upon it.

Soda breads: any breads leavened with baking soda and an acidic milk or with baking powder and a sweet milk. Normally a cob shape, sometimes deeply slashed with a cross.

Sourdough breads: breads leavened by the addition to the dough of some old, soured dough (the souring creates a gas which gives the rise). Usually the action of wild yeasts which feed on the flour assists, and this creates unique flavours. Because there is relatively little yeast content, sourdough breads tend to last well. The best way to make sourdough breads is to fly to San Francisco and stock up on their sourdough mixes.

Split-tin loaf: a tin loaf with a long slash down the middle. It can also be made by placing two long rolls of dough side by side in the tin. Almost always made with white dough.

Sweet/savoury breads: not often sold commercially now, although lardy cake is an example. But once small amounts of dough were always kept back from the batch and used to make fruit breads, cheese breads, herb breads and so on.

Tin loaf: generic term for all loaves baked in metal tins, but especially applied to loaves which are long, rectangular and have a markedly high rise.

Unleavened breads: the unleavened breads of India, Asia and America are used as plates, forks and spoons. *Chapatis*, the Indian staple, are well known to devotees of red flock wallpaper throughout Europe and although made just of wholemeal flour and water, are quite tricky to get right. Indian cookbooks will give instructions and introduce you to more adventurous chapatis, including the vegetable-stuffed *parathas* and the deep-fried *pooris*.

Other easily available unleavened breads are the Jewish *matzoh*, which is crisp, and the Mexican *tortilla*, which is not, unless it is a *taco* which is a fried tortilla.

The Swedish crispbreads and the dense German *pumpernickel* and *vollkornbrot* (which simply means whole grain bread) are further examples – strange to think these relative exotica are related to the damper, that flour and water paste wrapped around green sticks, baked over fires and called bread by followers of Baden-Powell.

Vienna loaf: this is a style of bread rather than a shape of loaf and the difference is in the technique used. It is not often made commercially but is essentially a milk dough baked in a bloomer shape. The shape has become so associated with the vienna loaf that ordinary bloomers are sold as 'viennas'.

Wholemeal bread: the extraordinary difference between domestic and commercial wholemeal loaves is due to ignorance as much as anything else. Dough made with only 100 per cent wholemeal flour should be handled as little as possible or it will not rise – yes, kneading the dough of wholemeal flour gives worse not better results. If you like to knead, mix a high proportion of strong white flour with wholemeal flour. Commercial or domestic bread makers who turn out a bad loaf that is flat and heavy either have kneaded it too long or have not let it rise long enough.

Zwieback: this means 'twice-baked' and these are rusks or slices of bread that have been baked dry, but which are usually thicker than commercial French or melba toast, which are made the same way.

Storing: there are two great fallacies about bread storage: one concerns refrigeration and the other concerns air. Although refrigeration will certainly slow down the appearance and growth of mould, it also hastens the drying process, particularly when the bread is in a plastic bag. It also affects granulation of the starch, giving a hard crumb.

The reason why refrigerated bread feels moist is simply that it is refrigerated, and therefore attracts condensation from the warmer atmosphere into which it is introduced. By heating refrigerated bread in a hot oven for ten minutes you can return the starch to a softer state and so render the bread more palatable.

Surprisingly enough, bread keeps better if there is circulation of air. The reason is simple. In a space without an air flow there will be a build-up of the moisture given off by the bread. A moist atmosphere is a basic requirement for the growth of mould: the more tightly the bread is sealed, the better the chances of it going mouldy.

Any container that can easily be washed and cleaned and that is not porous is suitable for bread storage. If you have a bread bin that does not allow circulation of air, prop the lid open with a few pieces of cork.

Simply wrapping bread in a clean tea-towel and storing it on a cool, airy shelf is just as effective.

Deep-freezing is the perfect way to maintain the moisture content of bread, provided each item is absolutely fresh. Each must be well sealed, and any type can be used, although crusty French loaves tend to crack and must be refreshed in the oven before use.

The dimensions of most domestic freezers dictate that square-sided loaves are most suitable for storing. They stack more easily, with almost no wasted space. Bread can be thawed either slowly at room temperature, or finished in the oven, or thawed entirely in the oven.

At room temperature a fairly large loaf will take anything up to four hours to thaw completely. Condensation will form inside the freezer bag and settle on the bread, which will affect the crust. The softened crust will shorten the life of the bread. To obtain a better crust, open the bag and take the bread out as soon as you can. Ten minutes in a moderate oven will finish the job and ensure that you avoid serving a loaf with an icy core.

When you need bread immediately and have no time to start defrosting it at room temperature, transfer the bread directly from the freezer to the oven, unwrapped. Half an hour at a moderate temperature is usually enough, but use a metal skewer to check for a heart of icy crumb.

If you wish, take this opportunity to glaze or re-glaze your loaf by brushing it over quickly with some milk or cream.

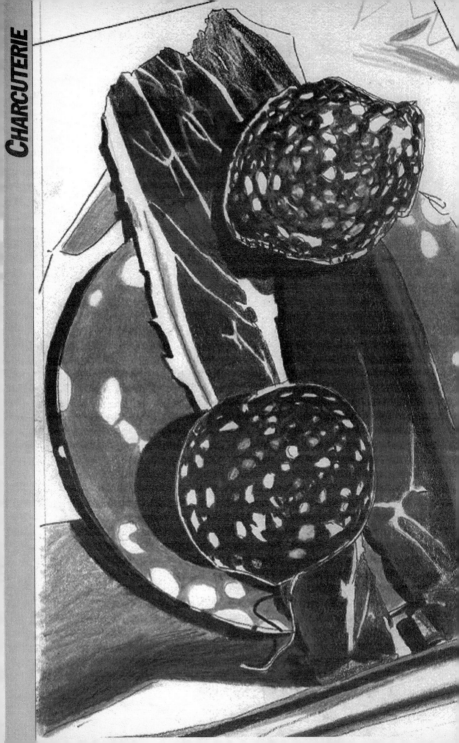

F or thousands of years the pig furnished virtually all of the meat of the European peasant and was prized both for its ability to prosper where other animals starved and for being almost totally edible.

For city dwellers, too, the pig was a mainstay. The urban poor scavenged the pigs who scavenged the litter of the filthy streets. Street pigs, which were usually ownerless, were common in New York well into the 19th century and in Naples until even more recently – they were the only street cleaning service this notoriously grubby city could maintain.

It's just as well that the pig is the most prolific animal after the rabbit (one sow is supposed to be able to accumulate almost 6.5 million descendants in a mere 12 years). For it is still *the* meat of much of the world, especially about the Pacific and south east Asia.

Almost every fact about the pig is superlative. For every 45kg/100lb of feed, a pig will produce 10kg/20lb of flesh whereas cattle would struggle to covert the same amount to 3kg/7lb. Pigs are also the animal world's most efficient converters of carbohydrates into protein and fat.

Neither is any animal easier to preserve. Once the pigs had been fattened on the last of the summer's fruits and vegetables each cottager would in turn hire the slaughterman, and neighbours would come to help quickly preserve the pigs' flesh. The fine rear legs were made into hams, salted then smoked or air dried. Other joints were put into brine cures until needed – salt pork. Some bits and pieces were minced and flavoured and cooked and put under protective coatings of the pig's fat – the pâtés and terrines. The same minced flesh and back fat might also have been forced into cleansed intestines to make the sausages, saucissons and salami to be slung from rafters. The belly and loin were salted, dried and smoked to make bacon and if your pig was the type that had a long jaw, its cheeks were similarly treated (these would be called chaps). The head was made into brawn. The small intestines were chopped and used as stuffing for sausages, chitterlings or andouilletes, or they were dried for later use as sausage casings. Even the blood was made into black puddings, thickened with barley or oatmeal and textured with glistening blobs of back fat. Only a few choice pieces, like the liver and the trotters, were enjoyed fresh with the neighbourly helpers – if there was a real abundance, for the liver could also be used in faggots and pâtés, and the trotters could be boiled and stuffed and kept for ages in their own jelly or under fat.

Even then the dead pig kept working for you for its dung is one of the best manures of all and throughout winter the rain would wash the nutrients back into the soil, there to feed new growth in spring. When Mao decreed he wanted there to be one pig per person throughout China, he was more practical than the king who merely wished there to be a chicken in the pot of each peasant.

Modern husbandry, refrigeration and transport give us fresh pig meat and offal throughout the year, and thus many cured pork products are increasingly difficult to obtain. Those that are marketed often cut corners and are certainly far less salty or smoked than the originals, for once given the chance, modern palates decided to avoid the flavour of well-preserved meats. Indeed, today's processing methods have so changed the flavour of today's pig and its products that the general public is tending neither to recognize nor like, say, a genuine ham, which is relatively dry and dense. Instead they prefer the moistness and bright colour of products which have artificially high water contents, and have been battered and re-shaped into a false and often slimy tenderness. Sad.

Even to the uninitiated it must be obvious that the avalanche of pork products that tumble through our shops and supermarkets are largely variations on a very few themes. As with cheese, it is more important to be able to recognize the basic groups, to understand the manufacturing process and the ultimate aims. After that it is really up to you to get out and taste, and decide what you like.

In France you would go only to a *charcuterie*, for they specialize in pork produce. Charcuterie is also the word widely used to describe the products that follow.

UNCOOKED, AIR-DRIED MEATS

Salami and saucisson secs are the same thing, so for simplicity I will use mainly the former name.

The best-known products in this category are the salamis of Italy, the *saucissons secs* of France and the 'raw' hams such as the Parma, Bayonne and Westphalian. Most are meant to be eaten raw, but English air-dried hams are usually cooked.

SALAMI AND SAUCISSONS

It is a dreadful shock for many to learn that a salami is actually raw pig meat; even more are mortified to the point of nausea to learn the origin of some salami casings. And almost no one believes that the white powder on these skins is not flour or 'preservative' but an artificially encouraged bacterial mould.

Salami are made from raw pork minced with back fat and, sometimes, beef. In France a variety of spices and herbs plus salt and pepper will be added. Italians use fewer spices and herbs but are more likely than the French to incorporate beef.

The flavour of salami is first determined by the proportion of meat to fat and then by the texture to which each ingredient is minced. In my experience the larger the pieces of meat and the lower the proportion of fat, the sweeter the salami; look for the plump *Jesus de Lyon* if you like this style. If you like strongly flavoured salami, go for those with a fine texture and/or high fat content, both of which can be judged by sight of the cut edge; the Italian Milano or the Hungarian are popular examples.

Further effects on eventual flavour can be expected from the casing into which the basic preparation is forced. Ideally they should be the cleansed intestine of the pig. As each part of an intestine harbours or attracts different types of bacteria and accompanying enzymes, so will each part donate a different flavour to a salami. A long thin salame will dry at a different speed from a thicker or shorter one and this will affect the outcome, too. Some of the casings are quite extraordinary; in the instance of the large saucisson called *Rose de Lyon*, the last few feet of the pig's large intestine are used, including the sphincter. Thus the saucisson's name has nothing whatsoever to do with its rosy colour.

Once the prepared mixture is encased it might then be tied overall with string in a traditional manner or simply tied both ends so it may be suspended. With minimum attention in a constant temperature, the salame should lose about 35 per cent of its weight through evaporation of its water content. The time taken may vary from a few weeks to many months depending on the size and the degree of dryness required. Some Italian salami are cured not in air but by being pressed between boards. The boards, which absorb the liquid expressed, are changed at regular intervals and these products, immediately recognizable by their flatness, thus cure faster than those left to evaporate in the air.

During the air curing process some salami will regularly be wiped free of exudate, some will not; some may be dusted with talcum to seal any holes in the casings, others will be dipped into herbs or black pepper. In Hungary and Italy a fine white ambient white bacteria is encouraged to grow on the skins, because the enzymic action of its by-products further tenderizes and flavours the meat.

Of course modern techniques have been applied to salami, too. Many have artificial casings and may even contain preservatives. The startling pink of *Danish* salami is due to the meat being pre-salted, a process that incorporates saltpetre, which gives rise to the hue. I understand that the meat is sometimes slightly cooked, too.

The theory behind the preservation and long life of all air dried products is that all bacteria dangerous to humans require water to flourish. Salame's combination of high fat content and low water level means a properly made and stored salame is impervious to the attention of putrefactive influences. But manufacturing techniques which do not allow proper drying can make a salame very dangerous indeed to eat. When the French government tested salami samples from throughout the country they found that only the largest and oldest manufacturers could be relied upon consistently to be absolutely safe. I will never eat a salame that is soft or spongy in the centre or that smells sharply; it may simply be too young but it could also have unpleasant digestive effects.

An Italian salami made only of pork will bear a metal tag stamped with an 'S', if beef is included it says 'SB'. It is a commonly held fallacy that most Italian salami include garlic. Some do, but it is rare, for it is likely to go rancid. There are salami with a garlic-like flavour, but this is rarely induced by garlic itself.

Finely textured *Milano* salami contain garlic and must mature three or four months; *Napoli* is a coarse, lightly smoked type which matures in a couple of months and is rather aromatic; *Felino* is flavoured with white wine and is notably slim, lean and delicate; *Varzi* salami, made between the Po and the Appenines, are coarse meat with fine fat, garlic and red wine and after four months have a soft texture and sweet taste.

Both Hungary and Switzerland make salami flavoured with paprika, well worth seeking out, but some are really very hot. Much more easily available is Spanish *Chorizo*, but be certain you are buying a slicing sausage, for the same name is given to scalded sausages flavoured with paprika which must be cooked before eating.

HAMS

Such sweet, air-dried hams as Parma, thin slices of which are constantly assassin-ated by luke-warm hunks of dreadful melon, differ from salami in two ways: (a) they are always brined before drying and (b) they are left whole. True hams are made only from the detached rear legs of the pig; if perchance the leg is cured still attached to the side of the animal it should actually be called a gammon, but this is how Wiltshire hams are cured.

The traditional way to get fine flavour and texture from an air-dried, uncooked ham is to begin with dry-salting. The raw meat is rubbed with dry salt at regular intervals. This slowly draws the fluids from the flesh, which in turn dissolve the salt which is absorbed back. The high salt content preserves the flesh, as bacteria cannot flourish in such conditions. There is always the risk that the brine will not penetrate right to the bone and the unsalted meat there will go off, causing a very nasty taste and potential danger known as bone taint.

It is by the addition of sugar and spices to the salt that different styles of cure and flavours are encouraged, and naturally the food given to the pig will also have some influence. The famous Virginia hams should be made from pigs fed on pea-nuts and peaches; the Smithfield (which is in Virginia, not London) pig should dine on acorns and other wild nuts before being fattened on corn and peanuts. I suspect few of the animals responsible for furnishing the 'Virginia' hams sold in the United Kingdom have ever seen a peanut, let alone a peach.

A faster method of salting is simply to soak the meat in a brine bath, but this always leads to a tougher end product. The newest technology of all automatically weighs each raw ham and then injects it with a predetermined proportion of brine, using a major artery as the point of entry. By using the animal's natural channels of communication the brine travels quickly and evenly throughout the flesh. Results seem better than the brine bath, but experts say they can easily detect a certain toughness.

Once salting is completed the ham must be dried. This can be done green (un-smoked) or after being smoked and once again the time and type of wood used will influence the flavour. In Ireland peat smoke is used, in Virginia apple and hickory wood are popular and here oak is common.

Smoking and drying, which allow the final development of flavour, can take as much as 24 months and this is why real hams are so expensive; the cooked pressed hams, hams for slicing and those sold sliced will have been salt-cured but not dried, indeed they have extra water added to them. Sometimes air-dried hams are boned before curing, some are boned after curing. Beware of boned hams that have too ob-viously been pressed into an even shape. This is often done after curing but before drying and so some of the liquor is expressed which is not conducive to great devel-opment of flavour. Given the choice, it is better to choose a ham which has been cured whole then de-boned.

It would be pointless to even attempt to estimate the different types of air-dried hams produced, even in Britain, for those who make them on a farm will do it differently each time, and even the well-known ones will vary a little. But if you have the inclination, luck (and money) here is the guide to what you may find in stores.

BRITAIN: all up and down the country small producers make an ever-increasing range of air-dried hams, both for cooking and for eating raw. In Romsey one company has created a new breed, with blood from the wild pig, and is apparently having success converting this lean flesh into very tasty charcuterie of all kinds. Another producer in Ripon offers air-cured, oak-smoked haunches of farmed wild boar. In Cumberland, Ashdown makes very large numbers (comparatively) of both ham types from conventional pigs and to considerable acclaim (and are also fighting the battle to re-establish macon hams, made from sheep). Yet, when I wrote in *The Sunday Telegraph* about real ham and gave addresses of suppliers it generated more complaints than anything else. As far as I can see the produce was probably good, but expectations were for something different – few appreciated the firm texture and saltiness of real ham. Or was it that they did not know how to cook it? I have had ham from the same suppliers which was almost too good to eat......

Still, it is an industry well worth supporting, and whenever you are out and about in the country, do look out for local ham makers and give them a try, as many sell in small portions and sliced packs, too. Apart from Ashdown there are a couple of other names you might expect to find nationally.

Bradenham: smaller than most hams, the Bradenham cure includes molasses, thus making it also one of the most expensive hams. It has a very black skin and a highly individual flavour, drawn both from the molasses and spices such as juniper. It has been made in Chippenham for just over two centuries and needs to be soaked for a good 72 hours before being baked, but like York ham is now made by one of the big conglomerate companies.

Suffolk: this is also quite sweet and is smoked before being allowed to develop its 'blue bloom'. I rather like this one for it is a rich colour and has a good full flavour.

York: well-known even in Europe where anonymous ham will also be sold as *Jambon d'York*. A real York should be mild and pink and might have been smoked to varying degrees. A dry salt cure is used, so any sweetness is due to careful tending during the maturation, which takes three months and should be accompanied by the growth of a green mould. A York needs only to be soaked 12-24 hours before cooking.

FRANCE: it is said the pigs of Corsica are closest to those of the Ancient Romans, and they are still matured on forest-foraged chestnuts and acorns until their haunches give the correct hollow ring when thumped: find Corsican hams, salami and the like on the island or from countless stalls in markets in the south of France for a genuine taste across the ages.

Jambon de Bayonne: the best known. This is eaten raw and differs from the hams of Spain and Italy by being lightly smoked.

Jambons de Campagnes: local variations of the Bayonne and depending on their excellence will be recommended for use as they are or for cooking.

GERMANY: one of my favourite hams of all is the **Westphalian**. It is a darker colour than many and quite smoky. I know some experts, such as the late food writer Tom Stobart OBE, believe its smoky taste is better without accompaniments but I think the more assertive flavour is a fine complement to a really succulent pear or syrupy fig, which sometimes overwhelm the delicate Bayonne or Parma.

Black Forest: is more highly smoked than Westphalian, and thus useful as a foil in mixed sandwiches or salads when a subtle product might be overwhelmed. But as well as these two, there are many regional smoked hams, often simply called Lachsshinken or country hams – you can tell at a glance if they are air-dried or one of the equally populous cooked hams, some smoked, some not.

ITALY: prosciutto is Italian for ham; if you want one of her excellent air-dried hams you must ask for *prosciutto crudo*. But which?

Carpegna: the smallest production and most expensive, produced in a small area between San Marino and Urbino. They are not covered in fat for maturation.

San Daniele: the hams are flattened and always keep the trotter. The small production area is in the far north east. They are branded with an SD.

Parma: properly *Prosciutto di Parma*. Around eight million hams are produced from pigs bred and grown all over Italy, but to the same standards. The specially sweet flavour, moistness and light skin colour are a result of their two-step curing: during the second stage the skin is covered in peppered fat, slowing moisture loss and preventing discolouration. Look for the branded ducal crown and the word PARMA.

Venetian: only 400,000 are made in the hills between the provinces of Padova and Vicenza. They are branded VENETO and display the winged lion of Venice.

Speck: you will find this rather like German air-dried hams, for it comes from the alpine valleys of Bolzano, in other words the South Tyrol. The smoking gives away the connection. Although *speck* is the German word for bacon, this isn't – and see page 37 for other produce with the same name which is not.

SPAIN: Spain claims to be the biggest producer of hams in the world.

Jamon Serrano: the basic air-dried product, which is guaranteed up to very high standards if stamped with the elaborate 'S' of its consortium and has taken at least nine months to produce. This includes the *calado,* when it is poked in three places by a sharpened horse bone to test for maturity and sweetness by smell.

Grander by far are the **Pata Negra** hams. Produced exclusively from the small black-footed Iberian pigs raised in the west of the country as...

Jamon de Guijuelo: small hams with pink to purple flesh likely to be a little salty and made only from the blackfooted Iberian pig or agreed others with 50 per cent of that blood. Class 1 is fattened only on acorns, class 2 starts with acorns and finishes with fodder, class 3 is fed on fodder only. These hams are guaranteed under Spain's Denominacion de Origen system.

Jamons de Teruel: also protected but made with bigger pigs. The meat is sweeter and more delicate, and made with Landrace and related breeds.

Once you start looking, you will find that most European countries have air-dried hams that are worth exploring. The Dutch have the smoked **Guelder ham** and the **Coburger**, which is only the top part of the ham. The Swiss make an excellent **Röhschinken**. The Belgians are justly proud of their **Jambon d'Ardennes** and the **Prague** ham, from what was called Czechoslovakia, of course, is considered the best ham of all to be served hot. Of all the rare and wonderful treats I have enjoyed I specially remember homemade hams on the Isle of Elba, encrusted with peppers and herbs in a way I've seen nowhere else. Almost mahogany in colour, the flesh resisted the teeth but then released a flavour that hung on the tongue for hours. With a glass of chilled Elban wine and a sun-warmed peach direct from the bough, I had lunched enough, and hardly ever better.

OTHER AIR-DRIED MEATS

Although some countries go to great lengths to dry mutton and lamb, these end up being rather too special in flavour for any but the initiated or the starving. But there are several beef products that are worth exploring. They are **Bresaola** from northern Italy and **Bundnerfleisch** from the Grisons in Switzerland. Fatless and very hard, they were originally fillet or some other lean cut and are never chopped or minced. To serve, they must be sliced very thinly indeed, and although I was constantly served these translucent, scarlet slithers with smart apres-ski drinks in Gstäad, I always thought they tasted of soap. Even when served on a plate and moistened with excellent olive oil and a little lemon juice, I find air-dried beef over-rated. I far prefer **Coppa Cruda**, from Italy. This is a piece of air-dried pork mainly from the neck, pressed into a skin. It has often some

> ### PANCETTA
> *This is a unique Italian bridge between air-dried hams to be eaten raw and bacon to be cooked, and is unaccountably neglected in Britain. It is made from the piece of belly which gives us streaky bacon but the brine is flavoured with herbs, nutmeg, fennel seeds, pepper and garlic and the meat subsequently air-dried for up to four months. It was traditionally air-cured between boards, pancetta tesa, which gives an old-time shape to the slices, but these days this is increasingly unusual. It is more likely to be rolled, pancetta arrotolata; there is also a magretta version, almost totally fat free.*
>
> *I generally come across pancetta in American recipes where it is almost universally specified instead of bacon by smarter cooks; but it is really only worth paying the extra money if you are using enough to appreciate the flavour. A few slices in a large stew is pretentious: quite a lot in a simple pasta dish is ambrosial.*
>
> *However, once I discovered you can and should also eat pancetta raw, this opened a spectacular new world, for here you really appreciate its subtle extra flavouring. I know it sounds worrying, but when I served it as part of a buffet choice with smoked salmon, many people found the combination wondrous, and quite without the slightest prompting from me.*

quite noticeable runs of fat throughout; coppa cruda is essential in antipasto, sweet and satisfying and acceptable to those who do not usually like salami. Swiss

Rospeck is air-dried belly of pork or streaky bacon.

Lachsshinken, too, is a great but rarer treat. This is the lightly-salted, slightly dried, lightly-smoked loin of pork, wrapped in fine fat. It is soft, meltingly so, and its name means 'salmon ham'. It should be served just below room temperature in quite thin but not too thin slices, and never cooked.

I suppose *Biltong* from South Africa should be included here too. It can be almost any kind of meat but the source makes little difference – it is all pretty filthy except for ostrich biltong. That is absolutely filthy. *Pemmican,* by the way, was air-dried buffalo meat, somehow combined with cranberries. As well as being a staple of the American Indian, it was popular with early Arctic explorers. The modern equivalent in the United States is something called *jerked beef* or *jerky*; it is strips of sun-dried beef, and last time I was in Los Angeles everyone carried some around as a low calorie way to assuage hunger. Now I understand they eat nothing but strawberries, unless it is Wednesday when they eat nothing but pineapple, and jerky is only available where people hunt and shoot and fish.

Serving: salami and saucissons are made to be eaten simply, with bread, and perhaps some cheese and a few unobtrusive pickles. The Scandinavians, Dutch and Germans tend to serve them for breakfast.

In general I don't think salamis should be cooked, but a leftover end piece of salami might be cut into chunks to finish a spaghetti sauce or for inclusion in a salad. Or you can roll slices around a flavoured cream cheese as a snack. Oh, it should *always* be skinned, unless it has been coated with herbs or peppers. If you have a piece which you are to slice yourself, peel it first.

There is a proper way to go about slicing an air-dried ham on the bone, as you might expect. It is based on what will desiccate soonest. Thus, you should begin with the flesh of the narrow shank and then move on to the shank half, that is the narrower of the portions on either side of the bone, essentially the upper front when the leg was alive. Only then should you move on to the thicker juicier butt half, as it is the longest lasting portion. Do it the other way round and by the time you get to the shank it will have dried so much it will be inedible. A serrated knife should never be used and the fat must only be cut away as you go, for it helps protect the uneaten flesh and keep it moist. Each slice should be cut towards the shank, with your left hand behind the knife. Once sliced, or if you have bought slices, I think refrigeration is recommended, but let them warm slightly, still covered, before serving or you will not enjoy the essential sweetness.

I grant that melon is a good accompaniment if it is a fine specimen but fresh figs or a juicy pear, again not too cold, are infinitely better. It is also good to serve such a ham sliced onto a plate and scattered with an excellent dressing made with olive oil and lemon juice or a mildly flavoured wine vinegar. As a wrapping of flavour and excellence for special vegetables, whole truffles, even fillets of fish, translucent slices of uncooked ham cannot be bettered. But the more robust flavour of the smoked Westphalian ham is usually more appreciated than the rather fragile unsmoked or lightly smoked varieties.

The end of knuckle pieces are delicious diced and thrown into a sauce or pasta dish, or when finely minced as the basis of a stuffing; but do check for rancidity.

The raw beef products are eaten sliced extremely thinly, sometimes also sitting in a little first class olive oil spiked with a little lemon juice, or less wine vinegar.

Storing: whilst they are still whole, air-dried products are better kept out of the refrigerator and simply hung in a cool, well-ventilated place. But once they have been cut they must be treated with care. They may not go mouldy, but will easily go rancid, particularly if they are already sliced. Even the flavours of the more robust salamis are actually rather delicate and likely to be swamped by something powerful in a refrigerator, so always wrap these products well in cling film, but let them warm a little before eating, otherwise the essential sweetness will be lost to your palate.

An unfluctuating room temperature is generally thought more conducive for air-dried hams than bringing them in and out of a refrigerator once cut. The tradition is for them to be loosely covered with a light, open-textured cloth which allows 'breathing'.

FRESH SAUSAGES

These are the sausages made for immediate use and thus are as often made from fresh meat as from slightly salt-cured meat, which gives a little more flavour and colour because of the use of saltpetre. This type is known as **Röhwurst** in Germany.

This section specifically deals with sausages that have not been treated after they have been put into their skins and which must be cooked before eating.

In England the fresh sausage is the famed 'banger'. Although we seem always to have included bread or cereal in many of our sausages, it is thought to have been the Industrial Revolution that increased the content to its now high but accepted level. The need for cheap, filling food for the thousands of labourers who had left the country for the city meant that traditional sausages were extended with a variety of cereals or farinacea. Don't be persuaded by phrases such as 'all-pure pork' or even 'beef' sausages. The rules about naming sausages refer to that proportion that may not be other than meat, ie if a certain type of sausage is allowed to have 30 per cent filling and the rest is all pork it will be sold as all-pork.

For a premium and with some individual effort it is easier to buy chunky chewy sausages, and ones with real herbs rather than that infuriating range of nature identical oils, which are neither natural nor identical. With modern electrical machinery there is no reason for every butcher not to make proper sausages; those who do are always famed far afield even when selling trash. Entrepreneurs sometimes offer ranges which go as far as including champagne, barbecue sauce – almost anything you can conceive. I welcome them, in the hope that greater choice will drag up the standards of the basics. Well, that's what I hope......

Beef sausages have become slightly easier to buy in Britain, because they are popular with the many new Muslim inhabitants of the country, who can't eat the pig. Yet again, don't be misled. Most 'beef' sausages also contain a proportion of pork. Look carefully at the label if you want to avoid a Holy War.

There are few truly fresh sausages sold; most having been treated in some way or another.

... WITH CASINGS

American breakfast sausages: generally smaller and slimmer than British sausages. They contain considerably less cereal and are also more coarsely cut and generally rather peppery or with a distinct herb flavour. Some are smoked and these are my favourite, especially with buckwheat cakes and maple syrup. These are always a pleasant surprise, and infinitely more interesting than the English kind.

Actually, you are as likely to find sausage mixture sold without casing, and cooked as patties, which makes much more fat in the pan, the basis for delicious milk gravy, made by stirring in flour to create a simple brown roux, and then milk.

SAUSAGES IN BEER

You can use any style of beer for this, from a light ale or lager up to something as rich as Guinness. I reckon the hopped flavour of beers and ales works better than the unhopped lager.

Serves 2 or 3

4-6 skinless sausages
At least 15g/½oz butter
1 onion, thinly sliced
1 or 2 bay leaves
Black pepper, coarsely ground
At least 575ml/1pt beer

First you must stiffen the sausages by covering them with boiling water for two minutes. Drain and dry them, then put into a pan with the butter, onion and bay leaves. Brown and seal the sausages, flavour well with the pepper and pour in half the beer. Turn the heat up high and let the beer reduce by at least half its volume. Then add the remaining beer, or as much as is needed just to cover the sausages. Bring back to the boil, put a lid on the pan, then simmer slowly for 15 minutes.

Serve the sausages and thin sauce onto a bed of mashed potatoes, or thicken the sauce with

Bratwurst: this famous German sausage is increasingly available in the United Kingdom. It can look like a rather longer, straighter, thicker frankfurter or a thicker, uncooked English sausage. Either way the filling will be chunky and there will be nothing but pork, fat and flavouring inside the skin. Bratwurst are used in many ways: they can just be boiled in water and served with sauerkraut or, more simply, with masses of hot buttered green cabbage and mashed potatoes. I think they are better if, having been boiled for about five minutes until cooked through, they are then gently browned in butter. They are sometimes sold 'scalded' in commercial packs, meaning they have been slightly cooked to give a longer life. Either way they make a welcoming and satisfying winter dish.

Chipolata: essentially a smaller English sausage, very popular with children and those with barbecues. The name is derived from *cibolla,* Italian for chives, for they should contain some of this member of the onion family. I'd be surprised if you ever found one that did. Cook as you would the English banger.

about 1 tablespoon of potato flour, cornflour or
arrowroot.

SAUSAGES WITH SOURED CREAM
Serves 2 or 3
4-6 large skinless sausages
15g/½oz butter
1 onion, thinly sliced
142ml/5fl oz soured cream
at least 1 tsp mustard
salt and pepper to taste

Fry the sausages with the butter and sliced onion
until nicely browned then remove from the pan
and slice thickly. If they tend to fall apart, leave
as they are.

Take a small carton of soured cream (if the
contents are a little different from the amounts
mentioned above it won't matter) and turn it into
the pan together with mustard. Stir well then add
salt and pepper according to your taste and that
of the sausages. Return the sausage slices to the
pan and heat through gently in the sauce. Serve
sprinkled with parsley and a little hot or sweet
paprika accompanied, inevitably but deliciously,
by mashed or boiled potatoes.

Cotechino: this might well be described
as the Italian bratwurst, but it is considerably bigger, usually weighing about
½kg/1lb. It should be pricked slightly
and then cooked in simmering water for
several hours. Again, I also like to finish
it off by browning it in a little butter or
fat. It will have been air-cured for a while, up to a month, and thus is properly
thought of as one of the rare salami
designed to be cooked.

Cumberland: one of the few traditional
British sausages that remains and tastes something like it should. Essentially
a pork sausage with a minimum of bread or cereal, coarsely cut and peppery.
You can buy it readily in Cumberland,
and each good butcher has his own recipe. It comes in coils and should be baked
slowly in the oven until golden brown
and swimming in its own fat. Its pepperiness and the fat combine marvellously
with excellently mashed potatoes and a
simple green vegetable like cabbage,
which has an affinity with virtually
every hot sausage of merit.

English beef: generally a paste of beef
and pork with permitted fillers and
perhaps a little herby and peppery. Not very common other than in the north of
England and in Marks and Spencer's (but most of their's have pork as well).

English pork: there are as many of these as there are manufacturers. Generally
made from a paste of pork and other ingredients to enhance flavour, extend and
preserve life. Here and there you do find a butcher who will go to some trouble to
achieve a degree of authenticity, ie to include detectable amounts of sage and a few
pieces of meat to chew upon, even if they are gristly.

I'm afraid we put up with bland sausages simply because we put up with them
and that's that. The cost of increasing the texture and enhancing the flavour by including some decent herbs would seem to be negligible. Up north tomato-flavoured
sausages are made, and they can be quite good, especially in Carlisle's market.

Undoubtedly there is only one way to cook sausages if you have the time and
that is slowly, unpricked, in a very low oven. It may take 45 minutes, but the skin
turns a wonderful colour, the flavour is nutty and the smell they make whilst they
are gently roasting makes even the least good one taste better on the plate, expecta-

tion being the greatest stimulus to enjoyment.

Salsiccia: this is the generic Italian term for all sausages, fresh and cured. Few are available here, and those that are are usually like bratwurst, which is a suitable substitute.

Saucisses: French sausages. Saucissons are air-dried salami.

Toulouse: this is the most famous French fresh sausage and available in fairly good versions in this country at specialist butchers – certainly in Soho. It has a high meat content and is further flavoured with quatre-épices. The French have a variety of fresh sausages, none of which contains anything but pork and flavouring. They are usually thinner and longer than ours. The best I ever tasted were offered to me by a four year old French girl on a beach by the walled city of Aigues-les-Mortes in the Camargue. They were crammed with chunks of chewy pork, with tiny slices of garlic, leaves of fresh thyme and coarsely ground pepper. The meat had obviously been lightly cured for it was bright red. The sausages had been cooked by the little girl's family over an open fire and they were quite simply superb. When I asked what name they had, the answer was, 'Oh, no special name – they're just the saucisses that our local charcutier makes.'

Zampone: this Italian sausage is stuffed into the skin of a pig's trotter and is probably rather rare in its uncooked

SMOKED FOODS

The phenomenal growth in smoked foods available is an encouraging indicator of the growing number of small specialty food producers striving to give us wider choice and new flavours.

Originally smoking was a preservative measure, usually after salt-curing of some sort – the flavour was either bane or bonus depending on your palate. In countries where smoked food was essential to winter survival, Scandinavia for instance, you generally also find very bland or sweet cheeses, made as a welcome foil.

But today we have the luxury of using smoke as a flavour enhancer, a savoury adjunct to the essential flavour of the food. Or we should. In competition after competition I have judged there has been universal agreement that most manufacturers grossly over-smoke, completely negating any flavour difference that might once have existed between, say turkey, venison or mussels. This is particularly sad when the produce smoked has been farmed venison or seafood, both intrinsically delicate and expensive. Even the recommended technique of allowing vacuum-packed smoked foods to breathe out of their packs for ten minutes or more does not help that much.

Extraordinarily there are also sensationally good smoked products made and sold. My personal favourite is smoked queenies, tiny scallops lightly smoked on the half shell. Certainly you can taste and see the smoke, but you can also detect a slight saltiness and all the sweetness of the shellfish too. Unfortunately the smoker's competitors seem not to have noticed how wonderful these queenies are.

state in this country; if you find it at all it has probably been scalded to lengthen its life. Cook in the same way as cotechino, perhaps slightly longer, to ensure the skin is deliciously gelatinous. It is especially good with hot pulses and potatoes.

... WITHOUT CASINGS

Some sausage mixtures are sold without the usual skins. In England this is simply

Another producer I like always wins the smoked cheese class at competitions with cheeses made from ewes' or goats' milk, which are specially suited to smoking; but none of the other entrants seems to have bought or tasted his cheeses to find out why they are so successful, instead they constantly present cracked cheeses seemingly painted with boot polish and tasting as though stored in cinders.

Quails and quails' eggs, venison and prawns, mussels, sturgeon and Cheshire cheese are just part of the smoked food choice; buckling and bloaters seem to have disappeared, Arbroath smokies are threatened by the EC and we still must endure the insult of artificially flavoured and painted 'smoked' fish. I can only hope that once again experience and the innate good sense of the public will win. Eventually we will be offered food which is both smoked and tastes of itself. What a treat that will be.

In broad terms, cold-smoking is best when the food has a distinct and tasty fat content – hams and eels, mackerel and herring, wild duck and pork sausages. Well-known exceptions to the fat rule are trout and such white fish as cod.

Hot-smoking is much less used and combines cooking with smoking. It is exceptionally good with fish and if the food is eaten when still hot the smoke has not had time to penetrate and ambush the flavour. Hot-smoked salmon seems to work best of all and when lightly reheated (the microwave will be best), it is a wonderful thing to confront, needing only potatoes, a little creamy horseradish and a sweetish ale or perhaps a brisk cup of tea.

called sausage meat and is much used, although I wish it were not, as the base for stuffings. If you buy some, mix it with fresh herbs, breadcrumbs, grated lemon rind, some mace, nutmeg and black pepper, perhaps a little wine or vermouth, and then bake it in pastry. It makes delicious picnic fare.

Crepinettes: are usually made from minced pork, but sometimes other meats, seasoned and spiced and wrapped in a piece of caul fat; thus they are similar to our faggots which usually include some degree of offal as well. Whilst researching my book *Edible France*, I discovered that faggots are known as *gayettes* in one of the dialects of northern Provence. Honest.

Keftethes: perhaps the best known of other uncased sausages are these Greek sausages which are really meat patties, I suppose. Beef or veal are the usual bases and there is always a proportion of breadcrumbs, onion and the obligatory oregano and mint. They are not the same if they are not cooked in very hot olive oil.

SMOKED DRIED SAUSAGES

Cervelat: this finely-minced salami-like sausage, usually a mixture of beef and pork, is packed into a long gut and smoked a golden brown. The texture and mild flavour are popular with those who are not normally keen on charcuterie.

Landjaeger: a popular snack with skiers, these robustly-flavoured small sausages usually have a flattened look as they are pressed between boards for smoking. They should be quite hard and dry and consist mainly of spiced beef. Red wine is incorporated into the mixture, too. Excellent with hot wine or cold beer.

Katenrauch(wurst): a coarse, heavily smoked sausage usually cut on the diagonal to give oval slices.

Mett(wurst): this can be many things and each area will have its own, ie ***Brauns-***

chweiger Mettwurst, **Berliner Mettwurst**, etc. Made from pork and beef, it is air-dried then cold-smoked. It has a very smoky flavour and this one can be heated to eat with, say, cabbage. Sometimes made as a spread, too.

Tee(wurst): spicy and salmon pink and smooth but available in many variations. **Ruegenwalder Teewurst:** is considered the best and is made only of pork and spare rib bacon. Usually sold in small sizes and is also available as a spread.

Schinken(wurst)/or ham sausage: a Westphalian specialty of coarsely chopped or flaked ham, mild and tender. **Schinkenplockwurst** has large pieces of fat but is easy to cut. If the colour is dark this indicates a high beef content, otherwise the meat used for this one is pickled pork.

SCALDED SAUSAGES, SMOKED AND UNSMOKED

These are what the Germans would call **Brühwurst**. They are usually rather finely minced and sometimes smoked, but always lightly cooked to prolong their life and preserve their texture. This is by far the largest group of sausages, and many are for slicing.

Bierwurst: a large, German slicing sausage which does not contain beer, but which is excellent with it. It is always eaten cold and has a peppery flavour.

Bierschinkenwurst: is the same thing with small chunks of ham included.

Bockwurst: this is really a subsection all of its own. The name is used generically for most sausages that are extremely finely ground, like **frankfurters** and **wieners** and **knackwurst**.

Boiling ring: this Polish sausage, which is usually tied into a horseshoe shape and weighs about ½kg/1lb is chunky, garlicky pork lightly smoked. Basically cooked like the frankfurter, it is invaluable for adding to things in slices, especially cassoulet, bean casseroles, and rugged poultry dishes. Also eaten cold.

Bologna: many things to many people. Known in America as **baloney**, and in Australasia as **Devon** or **luncheon sausage**. It is finely minced pork with a peppery taste, sometimes smoked and usually made in a fattish shape. Quite good sliced and fried but usually eaten in bread rolls or as part of a mixed hors d'ouevre.

Cervelas: not to be confused with **cervelat**, which is German and a type of salami, this French saucisse is not unlike a shorter, thicker frankfurter, but might contain garlic and is often slightly dried. Cooked like the frankfurter and its family. In Switzerland it is also called a **Chlöpfer** and served grilled.

Cheerios: always referred to as 'little boys' by my mother. These are 'cocktail-length' saveloys or frankfurters, useful for parties. Usually red-skinned, they are often called 'weenies', which also takes us back to mother, I suppose.

Chorizo: although Spanish by name, this paprika-flavoured sausage is made by a number of countries and is not always scalded, eg the Hungarian paprika-flavoured salami. There are hot and sweet versions made in France and in Spain. They may be cooked whole or in slices and make an excellent addition either way to dishes of beans, cassoulets and that sort of thing. Genuine Hungarian paprika sausages are much harder to find nowadays but worth the money; they are called **Gyulai** –

COLD MEAT AND POULTRY SALADS

When faced with wanting to do something interesting with a cold chicken, turkey, ham and so on, rather than arrange bits and pieces around a plate, mix them all together and bind with mayonnaise.

Almost anything that would appear together on a plate can be combined in such salads. By substituting some of the mayonnaise binding for whipped cream or good, plain yoghurt, you can add even more individuality.

Whether ham, chicken, turkey, tongue or smoked sausage, the basis for making any salad bound with mayonnaise is the same. The flesh must be in big pieces, so ask your delicatessen to slice ham, for instance, at least 1¼cm/½in thick. Thicker slices are even better, then you can make generous chunks. A proportion of 450-675g/1-1½lb meat to 300-425ml/½-¾pt mayonnaise is a good basis for planning your shopping list.

Choose ingredients on the basis of a contrast of texture and flavour. Nuts always finish such a salad marvellously in my opinion, especially if they have been lightly toasted.

Neither should you be shy about including a little alcohol in the mayonnaise. If you were to make a salad from cold pork, mixed with a little apple, celery and chopped walnut, dash in some calvados. A salad of prawns, cucumber, chicken and avocado would only be improved by brandy, doubly so if there were some cream in the dressing.

Fruit juice can also be used. Some unsweetened pineapple juice would certainly help a salad of cubed ham, pineapple pieces, some kernel corn and a small amount of green or red pepper.

Tongue is very good with orange; a refreshing and unusual salad is made by mixing cubes of tongue with some ham or chicken, some peeled and seeded very ripe tomato, and some segments of orange. Add a little grated orange rind to the mayonnaise and just enough chili sauce to add a bite rather than to reflavour.

similar products are now being made in London.

Fleischwurst/Extrawurst: This is a slicing sausage, one of the nicest of the finely ground types. It is pale, firm but moist, and variations contain garlic, pistachio nuts or pieces of red pepper. Their decorative appearance makes them perfect for *aufchnitz*, which means a selection of sliced meats – what the Americans call cold cuts. I know the Swiss make excellent sausages of this type.

Frankfurters: these should be made from a paste of fine pork and salted bacon fat and be cold-smoked, which gives a yellowish colour to the skin. Often they are made with whatever is to hand and even in Germany such sausages can have lots of fat or none at all. Frankfurter is now a name for any long thin sausages and in the United States you can buy chicken, turkey, ham or beef frankfurters. Once they get around to making one with fish, that really *will* be a fish finger. To heat these and other similar sausages, put into cold water and bring slowly to the boil – they will burst if you plunge them into hot water. Sliced frankfurter is delicious in hot or cold potato salad or a salad of cold French beans. A frankfurter is what you usually find in a hot dog – except when you find a weiner.

Garlic sausage: one of the best-known slicing sausages and made by most European countries. The French ones are usually fairly fat and in an artificial casing; sometimes they include chunks of ham and thus are simply a ham sausage containing garlic. There are some thinner Polish types which have a wrinkly brown skin and are only a few inches in diameter. I think they are better than most; ask for **krakowska**.

Ham sausage: together with garlic sausages, the big two of the slicing sausage trade. Chunks of ham in a paste of ground up ham, stablizers etc. Again the Polish variety is usually a better choice.

Jagerwurst: finely minced veal and pork with a very peppery taste, sometimes with green peppercorns.

Kabanos/kabanossi: piquant, highly-smoked chewy pork sausages that are very thin and long. There are two types, the soft and the dried – one is simply older than the other. The soft one makes an excellent snack or, cut into thick slices, a good addition to salads. The hard one is popular for chewing but better sliced and cooked, especially in a dish that has lots of either garlic, tomato or beans, or all three.

Knackwurst: short fat frankfurters, really, usually tied together in strings.

Krajana: another Polish one of roasted ham and pork, but without garlic.

Krakowska: an excellent Polish mixture of ham, pork, beef and garlic with a flavouring of nutmeg – you should be able to see big pieces of flesh. The darker, wrinkled, older and drier version is quite different from the fresher one, but both may be enjoyed sliced and cold or cooked in any way you can conceive.

Mazurska: not a dance but music to anyone who is a Polish sausage lover. Like a slightly larger 'banger' in size but filled with chewy pork, garlic and pepper, and smoked. Simply heat in water and serve with buttered cabbage or spiced red cabbage and some good relishes. Perfectly indispensable for cooking in winter dishes but equally wonderful sliced and served cold in summer. One per person is usually more than enough.

Merguez: thin, very spicy sausages brought to us from Algeria via France. Nice barbecued or cut up into casseroles.

Mortadella: the big fat one for slicing. There are many, many, many types and some horrid stories – this is the one that really was once made with donkey meat, I think. The best types should include green pistachios but all have cubes of fat, thus it can be disagreeable if warm. Chilled enough to keep the fat solid, it is nice on fresh crusty bread or in mixed platters, but not memorable.

Strangely, true mortadella is considered a cooked salame, for cured meats are used; bologna is said to have been invented as a simpler and, in American eyes, safer substitute.

Mysliewska: a dry short sausage of pork that is heated in water like a frankfurter. Coarse and chewy and quite peppery, but I prefer the mazurska.

Saucisson: confusingly, the Swiss name for a delicious smoked sausage containing ham, brandy, leeks and paprika. Served hot.

Saveloys: a corruption of the French *cervelas* as far as etymology goes, and a corruption of most other things as far as the product generally goes. It should be made from finely minced pork and, like a fat frankfurter, should also be smoked. But they often have a scarlet coating, perhaps with some artificial smoke flavour added, and this colour should be a warning if you are looking for something of quality.

Schüblig: a lightly smoked, fine Swiss sausage with a thick skin. Served hot.

Tuchowska: another slender Polish sausage of pork plus beef and a little garlic, coarse but solid and smoked. Excellent cold but can be sliced into casseroles. Slightly wetter and fatter than wieska.

Weinerwurst: first cousin, if not brother, to the frankfurter, but often shorter in length. The *real* 'little boys' – *(see CHEERIOS)*.

Weisswurst: varying in size but always very white and firm. Strangely, I have seen them sold as white bratwurst. They should be made of veal, perhaps with some chicken, and often include parsley. Like bratwurst they are especially good if they are first heated in water and then browned in fat or butter. A little mustard is all they need as an accompaniment.

Wieska: one of the basic Polish sausages, and one which can be eaten sliced and cold, boiled, grilled or stewed or as an ingredient in stews and casseroles. It has a full flavour and coarse-textured mix of pork and beef with a touch of garlic.

COOKED OR BOILED SAUSAGES

Nearly always based on offal or blood or some such combination, these products (the German ***Kochwurst***) are steam-cooked in their casings.

Black pudding/Blutwurst/Boudin noir: based on blood thickened with cereals like barley or oatmeal and often with cubes of back fat and onion flavouring. This is made in many qualities and sizes and is usually sliced and fried to serve hot, especially for breakfast. Some skin it first, some don't (I don't). The French boudins are often more delicate, containing cream and spices. The Polish ***kashanka*** available in this country is rather firm and is usually made in a natural casing. ***Rotwurst*** *is* a variation, spicier and coarser.

Brawn: made properly, with lots of pepper and *big* pieces of meat, brawn can be the most delicious of charcuterie treats. It should be made from the many contrasting meats of a well-boiled head set in an aspic from its own cooking. The English brawn stops there but continental ones tend put the whole lot into a gut, or even a stomach (the Poles do). This is much better if served slightly chilled with a sharpish accompaniment, like a vinaigrette sauce, pickled cucumber, gherkins and olives. If you make your own, defy tradition and add herbs and spices. Orange and lemon peel, finely chopped garlic, horseradish, chives, mint, thyme, mace, and whole peppercorns – white, black or green – make this normally bland dish into something quite marvellous. It is doubly good, if you have well-flavoured the cooking stock, with vermouth, bay and citrus in particular. Germans call this ***Sulzwurst*** and the French ***Fromage de Tête***, which is why the Americans call it ***head cheese***.

Haslet: this is particularly English, a sort of meat loaf made only from offal and which should be cooked in a lace of caul fat... not often available and not often worth eating. But it could be. Eaten cold or hot in slices.

Leberkäs: a speciality of Bavaria, but not often special, for it is a baked meat loaf with a high liver content – and meat loaf is nearly always awful unless you make it yourself. Thinly sliced and grilled or fried it can be fine in Bavaria, but those we find here are usually too crammed with filler and preservative. The Swiss *Fleischkaise* is also a meat loaf, but contains little liver. It is served sliced, hot or cold.

Liver sausage/leberwurst: The price and quality depends both on the amount of liver actually included and the type of liver used. Generally such sausages are made with pork liver and pork meat. Some are firm enough to slice and are wrapped in fine fat, others are meant to be spread and these are often richer in flavour. There are variations also in the texture of the mixture and the inclusion of spices, onion and so on. The most expensive are made only from calves' liver, *Kalbsleberwurst,* or from goose liver. None is usually heated before use, but if they are rich and full-flavoured some of the slicing liver sausages could be fried or grilled or heated on toast, perhaps as an accompaniment to game. Mix some good sausage with a little brandy and crushed green peppercorns to make good stuffings for *petites bouchées* or to slide under the skin of a roasting fowl.

Tongue sausage: one of the best-looking sausages for making arrangements of *aufschnitz* or cold cuts. The German tongue sausage *Zungenwurst* is usually a superior blood sausage in which whole pieces of tongue are suspended. Generally it looks better than it tastes.

COOKED HAMS

Cooked hams, boneless and meant for slicing, are the charcuterie counter's equivalent of sliced white bread. Now there are some exceptions, usually from the continent, but this is generally what happens, and it is important that you begin this voyage of discovery at the end rather than the beginning. First, most ham is not ham (that is, from the rear leg of the animal), not even that in a ham shape, and what you are buying is as much water as anything else.

Pork for such products can come from all parts of the animal, and is always cured in a salt brine; those sold as Virginia hams probably have some sweeteners added to the cure. Once this is completed the meat is shredded and tumbled to make it even in texture. Then it is pressed into moulds, either square, 'd' or ham shaped, and steamed to prevent weight or moisture loss. Oh yes, and the animal has been treated so that the flesh retains far more moisture than normal.

All this is done to bring a cheaper product to the market, you understand, and there must be some merit in that. But how sad to see people preferring this literal dilution of one of our oldest foods, thinking real ham too dry or too strongly flavoured. You do get what you pay for with ham, and the bottom end of the scale in cooked hams is tasteless, and barely worth eating nutritionally.

OTHER PRODUCTS

Bacon: not usually thought of as being from a delicatessen (although *see PANCETTA*). Yet sometimes these are the only shops where the rare, dry-salted traditional British bacons might be obtained. It is worth looking for **Speck**, German bacon, of which there are many varieties. The most useful is probably the type which is simply salted back fat: sometimes this is smoked and **Ziguener Speck**, coated in paprika. Thinly sliced or cubed, it can be used to add richness to cooking, for rendering or to make crisp lardons. The paprika speck is eaten as is, very thinly sliced, an interesting experience.

Bozcek: is Polish and is lean belly of pork, salted, smoked or unsmoked, cooked or uncooked. The cooked smoked bozcek is delicious sliced and eaten with mustard and can also be fried or grilled. The raw bozceks are the best way I know to get a smoky bacon flavour into any dish, from pâté to casseroles.

Kassler: is made by various countries. This is the eye of the loin, salted, smoked and mashed. Cut thin or thick it is succulent and delicious in sandwiches, salads or *aufschnitz*. It makes the most superior and attractive looking ham for ham and eggs. The outstanding Polish version is called **Sopocka**, but this is generally smaller and leaner and gives a more elegant oval-shaped slice.

Pastrami: common enough in the United States but only now beginning to appear in the United Kingdom. Pastrami is, or should be, salted, spiced and smoked brisket of beef. Firm of texture and covered with black pepper and other spices, it should be sliced extremely thinly and served cold or hot, especially in sandwiches – who hasn't heard of pastrami on rye? When you are planning a cold buffet, the bite of pastrami can be a welcome relief amidst the sweetness of ham, chicken and turkey.

SIMPLE SPICED SALT BEEF

Here is an interesting way to enjoy spiced beef, which was long traditional at Christmas time, without first having to brine the meat yourself. Allow about four days before you can cook it, and a couple more before you eat it if you can.

To serve 6 generously

85g/3oz brown sugar
2 tsp black peppercorns
1 tsp ground mace
1 tsp ground nutmeg
1 tsp mustard powder
1 tsp ground coriander
1-2 ground cloves
6 dried bay leaves
3-6 garlic cloves
2kg/4½lb lean salt beef

Pound the sugar with the black peppercorns then mix in the spices. Crumble in the bay leaves then crush and mix in the garlic if you are using it.

Stand the meat on a substantial plate or dish and press the spice mixture firmly into as much of the surface as possible. Then cover the plate tightly with aluminium foil – perhaps using two layers to ensure the garlic and other scents do escape to invade other goodies. Refrigerate for 4-6 days.

Put the meat into a saucepan and cover it with cold water. To the water add whatever you like in the way of flavourings – onion, juniper berries, carrots, parsnips, turnips, etc – or cook just as it is. Simmer gently for 4 hours or longer if it needs to be really tender, but don't boil it ragged.

It may be served hot but is perfectly marvellous if left to cool in the liquid and served the next day. The vegetables used in the cooking will unfortunately be useless.

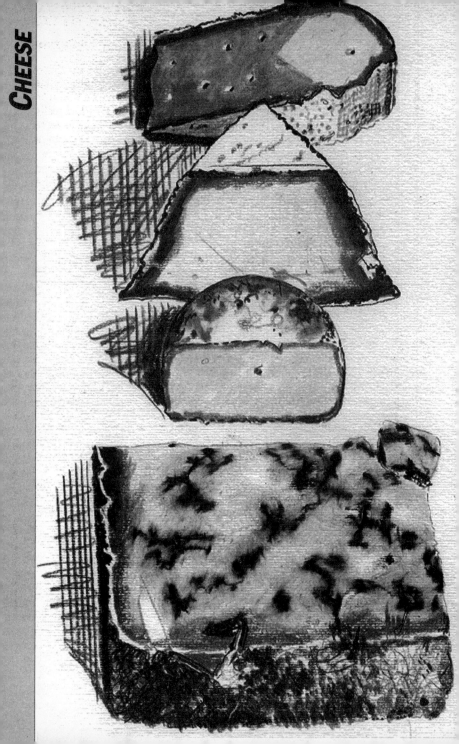

'**D**on't touch the Stilton, it's refrigerated,' hissed the photographer to his editor over a crowded banqueting table. To make it worse he said it in French, '*Pas le Stilton, cherie, etc...*' What a stupid poser. If he had really known about cheese he would have welcomed the sense of a banqueting manager to keep the cheese protected from heat, smoke, insects and airborne bacteria. After a few minutes in the hot room the small portions were at a perfect temperature to enjoy and, more importantly, safe to eat. Nothing is worse for cheese than heat and air, for these encourage rotting rather than ripening and although to the novice they might look and taste somewhat the same, the difference can be deadly.

If cheese didn't exist, you probably couldn't imagine it. Who would believe it possible? Hundreds of different foods spanning every imaginable taste from savoury to sweet and all made simply by forming solid curds from the casein in milk with rennet or acid. If only it were that simple. The slightest difference in temperature, of fat content, of pressure on the curds – even the time of year – will give you an utterly different result. And that's just with cows' milk. Cheeses are also made from goats' milk, sheep's milk, buffalo, camel and mares' milk.

But amongst all that there are basic threads of commonality which, once understood, can help even the inexperienced to appreciate the potential offered. Each cheese offers visual clues to judge how it might taste well before you put it in your mouth, and there are simple ways to know if an unfamiliar cheese is in good condition or not when it is smelly, runny or sharp tasting. Most facts are obvious once you have a rudimentary understanding of cheesemaking, which in spite of the huge number of cheeses actually falls into a surprisingly small number of categories. Each of these creates a recognizable family of cheeses, with flavours and appearances which are broadly related.

All casein-based cheese begins with a curd, that is the solidified protein content of milk, and this can be obtained two ways. An acid curd is the original way, simply allowing milk to sour (also called ripening) naturally after which the lactic acid formed will solidify the milk; this effect is achieved instantly by adding vinegar or lemon juice to fresh milk. Such cheeses will always have an acidic bite, refreshing when balanced and new, but quickly turning harsh and sour.

Rennet, obtained from the stomachs of young ruminants, allows heated fresh milk to be made into curds which are sweet tasting, and that discovery, probably on the Steppes, is really where cheesemaking began. Absolutely fresh milk or cream is rarely used, for as it sits and ripens it develops a fuller flavour. Getting a balance of sweet and sharp is the secret of many great cheeses; traditional Lancashire cheese was always made from a mixture of morning milk which had been stored to become riper and sharper, plus fresh sweeter evening milk.

These days much cheesemaking milk is pasteurized, which kills both the potentially bad bacteria and the good ones which actually create the flavour and texture of matured cheeses. You cannot make worthwhile cheese with this sterile milk and so a carefully cultivated mixture of the best bacterial cultures, known as a starter, is put back into the milk and allowed to develop flavour before it is then renneted. Even unpasteurized milk will have a starter added to ensure the proper development of acidity. So-called vegetarian cheeses use a curdling agent based on vegetable products; they should not be confused with curd made from soymilk which is thus all vegetable.

Understanding the fat content of cheese is a complicated subject, but very important for those who wish to control their calorie intake yet include cheese in their diet. Any fat content stated is not a percentage of the cheese bulk you see or buy, but is expressed as a percentage of the cheese's solid matter only.

A pressed cheese like Cheddar with 48 per cent fat content or Parmesan at 32 per cent will have very little moisture content so this means that what you eat will be close to the nominal fat content percentage. Yet a creamy tasting but wetter Brie (up to 60 per cent) or Camembert (up to 50 per cent) will actually be much lower in fat weight for weight, as each mouthful contains rather a lot of moisture and that is not where the fat resides. Portion for portion, soft cheeses, other than enriched triple-cream cheeses, will generally have less fat and calories per mouthful than pressed cheeses. This explains why a 28g/1oz portion of Parmesan made with semi-skimmed milk may contain up to 140 calories, but a full-milk Cheddar be about 116 calories and the same weight of Camembert an average of 85 calories.

Skimmed milk can be used to make most cheeses but will generally give a meaner, harder and coarser cheese than a full fat milk. The cream (fat) content of goat and sheep milk cannot be separated and so these are always relatively high in fat, especially those made from ewes' milk, which is particularly rich.

FRESH CHEESES
Fresh cheeses deteriorate and sour exceptionally easily and must be kept chilled at all times. They are the exception to the rule that cheese tastes better when at room temperature – these taste better when below room temperature, lightly chilled rather than deeply refrigerated.

Curd cheese: although all soft cheese is basically curd, this term is usually used for those not made with full fat milk. Even the lowest fat versions should smell clean, fresh and milky with no sourness, but they may have a chalky graininess. Quark, fromage frais, fromage blanc, *qv*, are essentially all the same thing, varying in consistency through the amount of renneting, the commercial addition of stabilizers and emulsifiers or homogenization.

Cream cheese: this causes much confusion. You can make a cheese by curdling cream alone, but it is very rich and you would have to be to buy or make it. Italian Mascarpone is one of the few. A commercial cream cheese is so called because it is rich and creamy, made with full milk. Homogenization of curds and whey – *(see FROMAGE FRAIS)* means lower fat cheeses can now ape their betters.

Cottage cheese/farmers or pot cheese in United States: curd cheese which has been drained and washed so there is no whey remaining, which although fat free does contain lactose, the milk sugar. Its richness and calorie content will depend on the fat content of the milk used, but it is most likely to be made with skimmed or semi-skimmed milk, hence its blandness and thin flavour which easily sours.

Fromage frais/fromage blanc: these French fresh cheeses are suddenly everywhere. They are only soft curd cheeses but generally have a deceptively rich texture and velvety mouthfeel, even those which are absolutely fat free. This is because once made, the curds and whey are forced through fine nozzles to homogenize the mixture, and that gets rid of any grittiness.

RIPENED CHEESES

The following broad guide to ripened cheeses is based on how much is done to the curds of the cheese by way of heating, cutting, draining, milling, moulding, pressing, flavouring and so on, including treatment of the surface. These are the things you can identify from the appearance of the cheese, your start to guessing how they should look and taste when in good condition, and your guide to assessing if they are or not. Beyond this you need a cheese guide, of which there are several excellent examples available.

Soft-paste, with bloomy unwashed rinds, eg Brie, Camembert: the curds are sliced into molds and drain naturally with no pressing. They mature in about a month, developing a characteristic white furry mould on the outside – *penicillium candidum*. These are mild, buttery cheeses in flavour and appearance, and the rinds should have a mushroomy smell. They ripen from the outside – a chalky centre means immaturity. Cheeses made with unpasteurized milk have a deliciously distinctive lactic farminess and only these types (Brie de Meaux, for instance) should have any appreciable brown or red markings on the rind. The rinds may be eaten, but it is eccentric and dangerous to eat these cheeses when runny and ammoniacal.

Soft-paste, washed or brushed rind, eg Pont l'Evêque, Maroilles, St Paulin: the curd is broken up as it is put into molds but rarely pressed. During the one or two month ripening period the rinds are washed with brine or other liquids which encourages a straw or red coloured bacterial growth on the rind. These are the 'smelly feet' cheeses, but universally have a sweeter and more delicious flavour than you expect. The surface should not be overly sticky, the body is usually buttery and perhaps a little rubbery. The rinds are rarely eaten.

Scalded cheeses/also called pressed, uncooked cheeses, the biggest range by far:

a) Lightly pressed, eg Caerphilly, Cheshire: the curd is obtained from hotter milk than for bloomy or washed rind cheeses and the curd is cut and drained at a higher temperature again, the scalding. It is lightly pressed in molds and retained whey shortens the cheese's life. They have no appreciable rind. Expect a clean, slightly lactic flavour, sometimes salty but with underlying creaminess. They sour very easily and should have no moulds on the outside or discolouring on cut surfaces.

b) Hard pressed, eg Cheddar, Gouda: the curds are pressed harder and longer, giving a firmer cheese which takes longer to mature. Curds for Cheddar are milled to evenness, the actual cheddaring process. These cheeses usually have a noticeable rind; Gouda is brined, commercial Cheddar is sprayed with hot water and cheesecloth is also used. Avoid any which are cracked, mouldy or 'oiling' on the cut surface. Acidity on the palate is a good thing but bitterness indicates something has gone wrong, often with the starter culture.

Cooked cheese, *eg Swiss Emmental and Gruyère:* the curd is cooked at a high temperature, to give dry and tough curds which are pressed very hard indeed. They take a long time to ripen during which they soften and sweeten and then last well. Swiss Gruyère also has a washed rind and thus a slight stickiness and rich nose is to be expected. Its nutty tasting body should show small eyes, often with a drop of liquid; Swiss Emmental is the one which has the big holes.

Plastic curd cheese, *eg Provolone, Caciotta, Mozzarella:* made mostly in Italy. Usually strangely shaped like tops and skittles. The curd is soaked in hot whey which makes it putty-like, thence it is kneaded and teased into shape. True Mozzarella is made with the milk of the buffalo, the most common milking animal of southern Italy, and is always stored in whey or light brine: compared to the plastic-like slabs of commercially made cows' milk Mozzarella, the light, sweet buffalo cheese is like eating milky clouds. Provolone is typically aged, when it is piquant and firm enough to be grated as a flavouring.

Whey cheeses, *eg Ricotta, Mizithra, Gjetost:* not strictly cheeses because they are not made from casein. Heating whey makes the available albumen collect in cloudy flakes, a process known rather wonderfully as flocculating: they contain much of the vitamins and sugars of original milk. Today milk is often added to the hot whey to increase the yield. They are moist and relatively low fat cheeses but the sweetness indicates the presence of lactose, milk sugar. Must be refrigerated or they quickly sour. I find decent Ricotta one of the most useful of all cooking cheeses, lighter and more biddable than curd or cream cheese for everything from stuffings to cheesecakes, cooked or otherwise. Try lightening it with cream then firming it to cutting texture with ground almonds and flavouring that with orange flower water and orange zest; serve as is or in pastry. The same basic mixture can be made savoury too, say with chicken flakes, fresh tarragon and toasted almonds. These cheeses are sometimes dried and grated as a condiment.

In Scandinavia the process of boiling is continued long enough to caramelize the lactose (sugar) and turn the cheese golden brown. Albumen cheeses, made by heating whole milk until it coagulates are very rare, but include Swiss Schabzeiger.

Blue cheeses, *eg Stilton, Blue Cheshire, Fourme d'Ambert, Roquefort:* these are invariably made with a scalded, lightly pressed curd which leaves spaces for the moulds to grow. In French the effect is called *persillé,* as the blue veining looks like parsley; it is incorrect, as some text books say, that blue veining was once encouraged by mixing parsley into the curds, although mouldy breadcrumbs were certainly used. Today the curds are usually injected with *penicillium roquefortii* or something similar; the softer body of Italian Gorgonzola is due to the related *penicillium glaucum.*

In general, the warning signs of a blue which is past its best are browning, sourness on the nose rather than the expected acidity, oiliness or excessively moist crust (especially with foil-wrapped Dolcelatte, Roquefort and the like). The crusts should never be eaten: making soup with Stilton crust is brainless pursuit of novelty at its most ludicrous.

Goat and sheep milk cheeses: most traditional British cheeses would once have been made with ewes' milk and goats' milk, for cows were too expensive to feed. The cream cannot be separated from either milk as it is in much smaller globules than that of cows' milk, and hence the easier digestibility of these milks.

Goats' milk cheeses are often surface ripened by candidums; they are not generally pressed but some excellent Cheddar types are now being marketed. Goat cheeses are likely to retain the musky, sometimes rank smell of the animals themselves; the body is always very white unless they are pressed, when they will be a pale yellow.

Sheep's milk has the highest fat content of all milks and gives the greatest yield of curd per quantity of milk, hence its appeal to peasants and to Britain's small producers who make many outstanding cheeses. Pecorinos from Italy should be made with ewes' milk but are often cows' milk with a special starter culture added to give acidity and punch; the same is true of Feta, which should properly be ewes' milk but is as likely to be bleached cows' milk. Sheep cheeses have less 'animal' taste and are usually sharper and saltier; the high yield of curd means they are more likely to be pressed cheeses, although some fresh ones are available.

Multi-media cheeses: recent marketing successes have been based on combining several techniques, most notably soft Gorgonzola-type blue cheeses with the white outer mould of Brie. Some are more successful than others, as may be imagined, but all are probably preferable to processed cheese, a triumph of science over conscience – except that such bland products have enormous appeal to children and to unsophisticated palates and so are both an important protein source and an introduction to cheese eating anyway.

Flavoured cheeses: many well known cheeses also exist in other forms, flavoured with spices or herbs, smoked or marinated in this or that after maturity. Cumin seeds are very common additives, found in Holland and Alsace for instance. Recently Britain in particular has seen the rise of flavoured cheeses with combinations bordering on the ridiculous: White Stilton with stem ginger, pineapple or apricot, Cheddar with asparagus and leek, Cheddar and Red Leicester with Marmite, Cheddar with garlic or smoked garlic. I trust you as the aspiring connoisseur, will leave these alone. Good cheese doesn't need such fancy dress.

In Burgundy washed cheeses are regularly marinated in alcohol and throughout France many an *affineur* will have his own flavoured version of a local product. Smoking generally ruins a cheese unless it is intrinsically brightly flavoured and savoury, ideally ewe or goat milk. The use of ash will help dry a cheese and encourage the controlled growth of moulds which will affect the texture and flavour of the body, commonly done with goat cheeses and on the few cheeses made in Champagne, where it makes something rather dry and chewy. We should be grateful though, for once they used to mature the same cheese under the bed, yes, in the contents of the chamber pot – it was called *fromage de cul*. Served as a nice wee cheese, I suppose? Not all progress is bad, clearly.

Serving: you could once guarantee cheese was served after the meal in Britain, whereas in Europe, France particularly, it was more likely to appear before the pudding. This is a reflection of ancient eating habits. The main British meal of dinner was once served as early as 10am, and in the evening a light supper was followed by cheese, believed to seal the stomach while you slept. The unemployed upper classes and emerging middle and merchant classes gradually moved dinner later and later in the day, dining at 3 or 4pm in the 18th century until it eventually became an evening event, when it was neatly joined on to supper, still completed with cheese. Wine was rarely drunk with meals but between them. But the French did drink wine as they ate and served cheese after the main course to accompany the last of the red wines served, before moving on to sweeter things.

When there is just one or two eating it is probably wasteful and pretentious to serve more than one perfect cheese. For more than that number there should be a maximum of one cheese for every couple of guests – three cheeses for a table of six. On a buffet table the proportion should be less, with a maximum of six for 30 people. This way you will always be displaying large inviting pieces of cheese, rather than small mean pieces which will quickly crumble and become untidy as they are cut by your guests; even so, it is horrific beyond contemplation to discover cheese pre-cut into pieces or portions on a buffet.

Take care to eat cheese only in prime condition and a phenomenal world of excitement is guaranteed. A perfect piece of cheese has taken extraordinary care and skill to make. It seems only fair to give it equal respect when it is in your care.

Storing: this is where most fine cheese is ruined, often by the adherence to old and new wives' tales and a misunderstanding of the basic cheesemaking process. The body of cheese ripens anaerobically, that is without direct contact with air. Once cheeses have been cut they should be stored at a cool temperature with the exposed edges protected from the air until the last minute before eating, and yes that does mean cling film and a refrigerator. For the best flavour, cheese should be at cool room temperature when eaten, but letting cheese 'breathe' unwrapped or storing it in a cheese bell at room temperature – or both – are the worst and most dangerous things imaginable, for both encourage the growth of unwelcome bacteria and this is especially threatening to the very young and the very old. Cheese is the most perfect medium for bacterial culture, but makes no distinction between good and bad.

Those who mock the advantages of cling film as a safe, convenient and airtight storage medium do not understand cheese or cling film. Neither do those who say a refrigerator destroys cheese. Why should it? There is many an old fashioned larder and safe which would have been very much colder in winter than a domestic refrigerator... the widely available cling film designed for fatty foods and the warmest part of a refrigerator are possibly the best friends cheese has ever had.

You will only see cheese sweating in cling film if the cling film is not tight or the temperature is too warm, which would happen whatever the wrapping medium. Greaseproof paper does cheese badly for two reasons: it slowly absorbs the fat content and, being porous, lets air in and out, whilst also keeping a layer of slow moving air trapped against the surface, exactly right for the growth of moulds. Foil is as impervious as cling film, although I have seen one 'expert' quoted as saying it will allow cheese to breathe! In extremis, foil might replace cling film, but it can react with acidity and is thus best used only briefly, unless it has been specially coated.

However, except where it is part of the manufacturing process, storing _whole_ cheeses wrapped in film or foil would do terrible things to them, as the crusts and skins must breathe; it is through them that moisture and excess gas made by the processes of maturation must leave, otherwise off-flavours, unbalanced moisture and trapped gas cause awful problems, including 'blowing'. I suspect most of the mistrust of cling film comes from confusion about the plastic wrapping of factory-produced block cheeses. These are a problem, for the crust, skin or outer surface of whole cheese must be open to the air to mature properly; moisture seen on the surface of such cheeses is indeed a sort of sweating as part of maturation, which would never normally be apparent on natural skins and crusts, and which clearly affect proper flavour development.

Therefore whole cheeses should never be sealed from the air. But _cut_ cheese must be properly protected from the air and kept wrapped as it comes back to eating temperature. Let no one tell you otherwise.

The worst posturing of all is a restaurant cheeseboard with lots of cut cheeses, virtually a guarantee they will universally be too warm, rotting, oxidized and generally absorbing smoke and smells. Far better to have two or three cheeses in superb condition, kept cool and protected until wanted by the customer. Of course, in your own home, you can have as many as you like at once, provided they have been kept in good condition and you wrap them closely the moment you are satisfied.

CHEESES OF THE WORLD

AUSTRALASIA

Once there were only **Cheddars**, mild or tasty, and exceptionally good they were and are, especially from New Zealand. But when the apron strings were cut by Britain joining the EC, Australia and New Zealand looked inward and discovered ingredients and expertise without peer in almost every aspect of food and drink. Their wine has changed expectations of flavour and value all round the world, and although you may not taste them unless you are there, their cheesemaking is improving by huge leaps. Australia's **King Island Brie**, **Gippsland Blue** (indeed almost any cheese from this district of Victoria) and washed rind **Mungabeera** have their fan clubs, but tops for me are **Kervella** goats' cheese, sheep's milk **Meredith Blue** and **Heide Gruyère** from Tasmania, available made with pasteurized or unpasteurized milk.

New Zealand's range has suddenly expanded tremendously. She has long made an excellent blue vein cheese in the Danish Blue/Roquefort style and equivalents of British territorials but now makes outstanding bloomy rind cheeses and ewes' milk styles too, all of which must by law only be made with pasteurized milk. Currently, New Zealand suffers a proliferation of ever-more arcane flavoured cheeses, sad to see when there is so much scope for making a greater basic variety from its high quality milk, thus complementing some of the world's best natural produce and most worthwhile restaurant cooking; veteran international travellers and eaters regularly tell me their best eating experiences anywhere have been in Auckland or Wellington.

BRITISH ISLES & IRELAND

There is probably more potential for exciting discoveries amidst British and Irish cheeses than anywhere in the world. Here are just a few that you will find in delicatessens, cheesemongers and supermarkets.

Caerphilly: a lightly pressed cheese made from pasteurized full cows' milk and matured for two or more weeks. White, granular texture, slightly crumbly; clean, sharp smell; sourish, buttermilk flavour. White-grey mould acceptable on farmhouse cheeses. Suitable ingredient, but an acquired taste in cooking. Creamery Caerphilly is more sour and turns quickly; excess moisture or yellowing is bad.

Cheddar: England gave the world Cheddar and in the process relinquished control over the standards of one of the best and best known cheeses in the world. There are now fewer than 20 farmhouse Cheddar makers producing in the traditional way and only a handful of those use the traditional unpasteurized milk.

Cheddar consumption in this country represents over 60 per cent of the total but most of this is immature, over-refrigerated, plastic-wrapped mediocrity. I hate being so negative but there is a desparate need to save Cheddar – mainly from itself. If you have never done so, make the effort to buy a true Cheddar that is at least ten months old and which was made on a farm in Somerset, Devon or Dorset. You will be astounded at its full complex flavour and join me in wondering how the other stuff can possibly be allowed to masquerade under the same name.

Cheddar is a hard pressed cheese made from full milk. Mild creamery-made cheeses are released after three to five months: mature should be over five months, up to nine and perhaps more. Don't expect to get full value from properly made farmhouse Cheddars unless they are at least nine months old – these days some are not released for two years, the so-called vintage or extra mature cheeses. It should have a smooth, yellowish, waxy texture, a full, sweet nose, and rich nutty flavour. The slight aftertaste bite increases with greater maturity – as does crumbliness of texture. Useful in all cooking. Creamery or foreign Cheddars often have bite but no flavour because the milk has been treated with a type of starter which develops quick acidity, to give the effect of maturity with none of the accompanying gains in flavour.

Traditionally, farmhouse cheeses were round and cloth-wrapped and you could tell creamery cheeses because they were oblong; today both sorts of establishment make both types. Cheddar, more than any other cheese, requires the buyer to beware.

Cheshire: a lightly pressed cheese made from full milk, invariably pasteurized, and which takes from six to eight weeks to mature. Crumbly, moister and less compact than Cheddar.

Red: this is the best known version, the salmony-pink one. It has a haunting mellow, sweet flavour with salty overtones and a light, clean smell. It is a very good cheese for cooking, and melts well on toast.

White: this faster ripening variation, uncoloured, acidifies easily. Not much to recommend it, but sometimes used as substitute for Feta.

Blue: one of the world's greatest cheeses. Look for opulent marigold colour and buttery texture. Brown discolouring is only acceptable when close to the rind. Quite unique flavour, very rich, full, nutty and tangy. You may like to temper it with butter. Surprisingly, many women prefer its robust flavour to that of Stilton.

Derby: not very well known but a hard-pressed cows' milk cheese maturing in only four weeks. Flakier and moister than Cheddar, paler and more delicate in flavour, too. 'Lesser Cheddar' is an apt but sadly damning description of this subtle and overlooked cheese. The first English cheese to be made in a creamery, in 1870.

Sage: marbled, artificially coloured and flavoured with sage oil. Highly individual, rather perfumed flavour; best appreciated in rather small amounts. Interesting when lightly grated over tomato salad. The growing interest in good cheese means that sometimes you see sage cheese made the old way, with rolled sage; Sage Lancashire cheeses are the best I have tasted.

Dunlop: very much like Derby, this popular hard pressed Scottish cheese is similar to Cheddar and to Double Gloucester. It is paler, blander and moister. Naturally enough it is best with Scottish accompaniments, oatcakes in particular.

Gloucester, Double and Single: two relatively hard pressed cheeses. The Double is commonly found and the Single is making a well-deserved comeback. The Double is orange rather than yellow, and has a smooth mellow flavour even when mature. It must never bite back in the mouth and has a particular affinity with fruit and salad. Double Gloucester claims two reasons for its name, first that it is bigger than the Single, and second, that it was always made from a mixture of the whole morning milk plus the cream of the evening's milking, thus making it a double cream cheese.

Single Gloucester – also called Berkeley – is a faster maturing cheese of the same diameter but half the depth. Originally made from a blend of the skimmed evening milk plus whole morning milk.

Lancashire: a hard pressed cheese which is ready to eat in two months or so. There are two distinct styles, essentially mild or mature, both the result of a unique technique based on mixing fresh and matured curds. Both styles should be white, crumbly but have a butter-soft texture. This mild but richly flavoured cheese is the one for cooking and melting, the proper cheese for rarebits. Mature Lancashire has a wonderfully full flavour and developed sharpness, but must not leave any trace of bitterness on the tongue.

Leicester: hard pressed and mature enough to eat in six months. Rich russet-red colour, granular looking but actually a moist, elastic texture. Clean buttery flavour. Often marketed too young, as the flavour develops before the texture, so avoid dry, crumbly-looking cheeses.

Orkney and Islay: small, hard cheeses with an ancient provenance but such a similarity to better-known English cheeses as Cheddar that their purchase is on impulse rather than cultivated demand. They are delicious, nonetheless, so do buy if you see them, if only for something to talk about.

Shropshire Blue: invented only a few years ago in association with Paxton and Whitfield of Jermyn Street, London, one of the world's oldest cheese shops. It fits neatly between Stilton and Blue Cheshire in texture and flavour, with a touch more bite than Stilton but not the aggression of Cheshire. Its colour is somewhat more golden than the Cheshire, too. Very good indeed and perhaps the first new proper cheese to come onto the market for over 100 years. I'm not sure why they called it Blue Shropshire, as it is not made there.

Stilton, Blue: none of this most famed cheese is now made with unpasteurized milk, but it once was and should be again. The slight risk associated with unpasteurized milk is wildly exaggerated, generally based on a misunderstanding of the listeria scare, which turns out to have been caused by cheese made with pasteurized milk, because the infection invariably happens after the cheese has been made.

Stilton should have a soft buttery texture, and blue-green veins radiating from centre to crust. The wrinkled brown-grey skin should be dry, not slimy. Some brown discolouration close to the skin is acceptable, but anywhere else it is a sign of inferior milk or bad manufacturing. Neither flavour nor smell should be sharp or strong. Do not accept white and chalky (unfortunately not a rare commodity) or yellow and oily Stilton. One is too young, the other too old. Can, but should not, be used in cooking. Port is an accompaniment, not an ingredient.

White: a crumbly, very white cheese with strong nose but deceptively milder, slightly sour flavour. Ideal substitute for Feta in Greek salads – but that's about all.

Wensleydale: a lightly pressed cheese that has had a mixed history of late but which is now well on its way back to stardom, as a small number of farmhouse and traditional makers have found ways to distribute nationally.

White: a rapidly maturing cheese that has a definite character of its own, but appreciation of its subtle, mellow, honey-like flavour requires the possession of a fairly tuned palate. Sourness and yellowness indicate excess age. It has no rival as an accompaniment to apple pie, a classic English combination of flavours well worth discovering.

Blue: though smoother, whiter, smaller and less veined, it is undeniably similar to Stilton but has a grey, corrugated crust. Wensleydale curd is never soured, giving it potential for a richer, rounder flavour. A perfect example could well rival Stilton.

*... **and others:*** there has been an extraordinary renaissance of small cheesemaking and a tremendous return to goats' and ewes' milk in Britain and Ireland. Makers of classic farmhouse regional cheeses now tend to shy away from using unpasteurized milk, even though they are permitted to do so, in case of bacterial problems; yet some remain faithful and their products are worth seeking. But small cheesemakers do it the old way. Some make new cheeses, like the ewes' milk ***Beenleigh Blue,*** admired for its minimal saltiness, or use hops and nettle leaves mixing old and new techniques; others recreate old cheeses like soft ***Cambridge***, pressed ***Exmoor*** or Welsh ***Llanboidy***, made with the milk of rare Red Poll cattle. Jersey milk is the basis of Wales' ***Llangloffen*** and Scotland's most famous Brie-type, ***Bonchester***.

The Specialist Cheesemakers Association has done a sterling job encouraging and maintaining standards of artisan cheesemaking throughout Britain, and thoroughly deserves every bit of your support. A similar organization exists in Ireland and is chaired by the maker of ***Chetwynd Blue***, one of the country's new artisan blues. ***Cashel Blue*** is perhaps more famous and widely distributed; the Irish enjoy eating this fine cheese in sandwiches. Lovers of washed rind cheese should seek out ***Croghan, Milleens***, ***Gubbeen*** and ***Ardrahan***.

FRANCE

Although revered as a cheesemaking haven, France's claims are really based on making the world's broadest range, and not even the greatest franco-fromophile would claim that all are wonderful. Most were originally made to be eaten fairly soon after they were made, and close too. Thus to eat them elsewhere, even in France, often means their natural maturation period has been inhibited or extended or techniques have been changed to make them more robust. As well, modern demands mean many are made at times when the milk is simply not its best, fine if you are experienced and know what not to expect season to season, but a great disappointment if you are not up on such minutiae.

The great French specialties are Brie and Camembert types, and only France makes anything approaching the wonderment of those which begin with unpasteurized milk. The rare Fougères, thicker than Camembert and cured in ferns, are worth any trouble to hunt out. The next most famed types are the smelly washed rind cheeses, and once you understand their bark is not as bad as the bite you are likely to eat them rather more regularly than you imagined.

Eating French cheese in Britain or abroad can be rewarding but nowhere near the thrills found in France, where most towns will have at least one famed *affineur* who ripens cheeses on the premises so they may be bought and enjoyed on the precise day, even hour, that they are perfection.

The Appellation d'Origine Contrôllée (AOC) extends to cover 32 of the country's most highly prized cheeses. Many are not readily available outside France and others that are will often vary in quality simply because they were not originally designed to travel. The complete list can be found on page 346, but the following is a selection of AOC cheeses you should be able to find in specialist shops and, increasingly, in one or two supermarket chains, although cheeses from these may suffer unduly from the very low temperatures required by multiple retailers.

Bleu d'Auvergne: a cows' milk Roquefort, sharp, salty and rich. A foil-wrapped cylinder with a thin pinkish skin which is at its best after six weeks. Avoid any stickiness or over-blueing which looks grey-green as this is an over-aged cheese which has been poorly matured. At its best it is light and melting on the tongue.

Bleu des Causses: very like the previous cheese, but matured in caves. Another economical Roquefort substitute, but tends to be rather variable.

Brie de Meaux: the most commonly available of the farmhouse *(fermier)* Bries and made exclusively with unpasteurized milk, these cheeses are bigger than creamery made examples and have a much browner and spottier surface even when immature. The smell and flavour are tangier, but still clean, lactic, and with no trace of ammonia. Enjoyable even when slightly young and with a chalky centre. This was voted King of Cheeses in 1814 by the Congress of Vienna. Expect to pay quite a lot, up to 50 per cent more, if and when you can find it, although in recent years even supermarkets have come alive to its existence.

Brie de Melun: the strongest tasting of all unpasteurized milk Brie cheeses, it was probably the original. A Meaux may weigh up to 3kg, but the Melun never exceeds 2kg. When ripe its rind will be more red and brown than white but not sticky or horrid.

Camembert de Normandie: this is what to look for on a true AOC Camembert made from unpasteurized milk. Late spring, summer and autumn are when to find the real thing, which will also bear the inscription *lait cru* on the chipboard container. Increasingly available, often made with milk from unsprayed grass, like the Brie *fermier*, it is browner and tangier, delicious when slightly young, expensive but worth every penny. Expect a rather stronger flavour than, say, a Brie de Meaux but nevertheless avoid any suggestion of ammonia or a cheese which is running all over the place – runny means rotting.

Cabichou/Chabichou du Poitou: small truncated cones of goats' cheese with a strong animal smell and very full flavour. The texture should be firm but not hard and white rather than grey or blackened.

Chaource: a wonderful thing, surface ripened like Brie and Camembert cheeses but a drum shape rather than a disc. Its bulk makes it difficult to mature evenly, but even when a little chalky it will still have a fragrant, sometimes floral flavour overlying the richness – it has a high fat content. This in turn is balanced by saltiness, making it an excellent accompaniment to other foods.

Crottins de Chavignol: you know what the name means, don't you? Droppings, that's what, for old ones are dark and sharp and surprising things for anyone to put in their mouth. But the AOC was given to younger versions of these small goats' milk cheeses which are lighter and more approachable: they will have a golden or blue mould surface.

Fourme d'Ambert: a tall slim cylinder of blued cows' milk, often thought of as a French Stilton. Pinkish-grey rind and with a salty full flavour that leaves an intriguing aftertaste. Some bitterness is acceptable, and so is a light musty smell, but neither must be pronounced. Avoid sticky, cracked rind, over-blueing or grey/brown appearance.

Maroilles: small, square and with much presence. The washed rind is typically reddish and has an assertive smell, the pale, shiny, homogenous body is vigourous and strong without being sharp. Ammonia should not be detectable, neither should dryness nor runniness.

Munster: a famed washed rind cheese with a heritage said to date from the settling of seventh-century Irish monks – *(see SWISS APPENZELL)*. Round, flat, orange-red rind and rich yellow body. The typical washed rind cheese smell is penetrating and the flavour equally strong. Locally eaten rather young, often accompanied with cumin seeds.

Neufchatel: the snowy-white, downy coat of these small cheeeses may show a little red pigmentation without being thought too old to enjoy. The body is soft and creamy, like its big brother the Brie, but these will be saltier and quite lactic. Most are creamery made, but if you stop on your way to Dieppe, a visit to the market will reveal artisan examples. The heart-shaped version, *Coeur de Neufchatel* is most commonly seen in the UK, but there are also barrels, loafs and squares.

Pont l'Eveque: the real one is only about 10cms/4in square. These washed rind cheeses should have a smooth gold-yellow rind, sometimes with straw indentations, a tangy sweet flavour and a moderately strong smell. Many variations include the larger Pavé, from which better shops will cut a portion; even bigger – 30cms/12in square or more – is the Tour Gris. These are equally expensive as the small ones but you can buy smaller amounts. Take the same care you would with any washed rind cheese.

Reblochon: a flattened disc of lightly pressed curd, but which also sports a surface mould. Traditionally made with the richer second half of a milking, the cheese will have a creamy, sweet but throaty flavour which is not as pronounced as might be expected. It will weigh up to 500g/1lb and be fairly expensive, especially if made with unpasteurized milk, but this really is worth the expense, if only to experience one of the few *gouts verités*.

Roquefort: the world's most famous sheep's milk cheese, and perhaps the most famous blue, too, but don't tell that to the Brits. Sadly, we struggle to get Roquefort the way it should be, for there is a tendency to over-salt the ones which are exported. The milk should all come from the Lacaune breed of sheep, and although milk used to be imported from other areas, Roquefort currently supplies all it needs. Expect a clean sharp smell and a pronounced sheepy flavour with a rich, salty aftertaste. The blueing should be even but more green than blue. The rest of the body is a subtle ivory-like white, rather like some unsalted butters, and that gives a clue to the ideal eating quality; the texture should be buttery, but if you ask for a small portion to be cut from a block expect some crumbling from the edge.

This remains one of the few cheeses matured the way it always was: mechanization within the maturing caves of the Combalou mountain is impossible – every cheese is still wrapped and turned by hand. I have just learned that each of the caves is best suited to or harbours a slightly different strain of *penicillium roquefortii*, and thus that true experts know which cave they prefer. Many labels actually state the cave in which the cheese has been matured: some to look for are Caves de l'Abeille, Cave Baragnaudes, Cave Arnals, Cave Le Saul, Cave Rodat. The first is the most common and thought a light style suited for everyday eating, the second is considered an exceptional cheese and for great occasions, the third – no, you do it.

Whilst showing off such information you may as well add in that the fissures which ventilate the caves are called *fleurines* and that the draughts are fiercer the deeper you go.

Saint Nectaire: another ancient cheese, pressed for only 24 hours and then ripened on straw for two to four months. It has a dry violet-to-pink thin rind with a slightly mouldy smell. There will be a firm texture and fruity flavour with a slight bite. For such an aristocratic cheese it cooks very well; it melts nicely on toast and in the Auvergne, where it is made, they will stir it into soup.

GREECE

Yes, there is something more than ***Feta***, which should properly be made from ewes' milk and stored in brine; a delicious cheese for adding savoury bite to stuffings and firm enough to crumble into salad dressings. In Greece it is used very much like a condiment, even if it has been made from imported powdered cows' milk. ***Halloumi***, most often made in Cyprus if seen abroad, is almost a plastic curd cheese. It should be rinsed clear of any brine before use and may be sliced and lightly fried. ***Kasseri*** is a kneaded pressed cheese which melts well; ***Kefalotiri*** is a piquant ewes' milk cheese used in cooking – a little goes a long way.

ITALY

Very underrated cheeses, with a range running from rich dessert cheeses through challenging blues to the complex piquancy of Pecorinos, Granas and Parmesans. The north tends towards cows, the south towards goats and sheep, but also favours the water buffalo for the original Mozzarella.

Bel Paese: a firm, pearly-white textured cheese with a full, fruity nose and a clean creamy taste that leaves a sweetish finish. A mild washed rind cheese perfected by Galbani this century and the basis for their international fame and fortune. Keeps very well but beware an excess suggestion of paraffin under the foil, a fault easily detected by your nose.

Dolcelatte: a milder, creamier, commercial version of Gorgonzola, using richer milk. Dolceverde is the same thing made by a different manufacturer – (_see_ GORGONZOLA).

Fontina/Fontal: ripened for three months and sold according to the season in which it was made: that made on alpine pastures during summer is always the best, of course. Fontal is the commercialized version made with pasteurized milk. It is a pale yellow cheese with a sweet aroma and delicate, nutty flavour and can be made up to 18kg in size. A few small round eyes in the body are acceptable. It is a good melting and cooking cheese, especially when matured.

Gorgonzola: Italy's best known blue cheese, a world and flavour of its own, for it is one of the few blue cheeses which does not rely on _penicillium roquefortii_, but _penicillium glaucum_. It has a thousand year history and was once made only with so called _stracchino_, the 'tired' milk of winter. The body is a yellow colour and the veins are green rather than blue. Avoid a brown appearance, bitterness or sourness, but expect a pungent, rich flavour with a definite bite – sometimes the difference is hard to spot, and only a great deal of eating will teach you.

Grana: in fact, the proper name for the type of cheese we call Parmesan. Parmesan is unrecognized in Italy, and Parmigiano, or more properly Parmigiano Reggiano, is a type of Grana.

All are hard pressed cooked cheeses made from semi-skimmed milk and are the salt and pepper of Italian cuisine. Grana Padano is made all over Lombardy from cows fed on grass and hay, but only south of the Po. Parmigiano Reggiano is made north of the Po in the province of Mantua, where cows are fed clover and lucerne.

Grana Padano cheeses will generally be lighter in colour, faster to mature and flakier. Parmigiano Reggiano cheeses take longer to mature but are also much underrated as a table cheese when young. In Italy, at least, you can buy them as giovane, tipico, stravecchio and vecchio, progressively older – and more expensive of course. Italians believe it to be one of the great aids to digestion, long life – and almost everything else I bet.

Mascarpone: purists would say this isn't a cheese at all, but for all that it appears in every list of Italian cheeses. They would be right, for it is essentially an Italian cremé fraîche, that is, cream which has been thickened by the action of a lactic fermentation. Thoroughly and wickedly delicious, it is suddenly everywhere, usually in tiramisu, the pudding which layers it with sponge fingers, coffee, chocolate and alcohol and masquerades as a traditional pick-me-up (which is what the name means) but was actually only invented a few decades ago – hence the hideously huge variations, and why there are tiramisu shops in Tokyo which sell it flavoured with any and everything, except seaweed, so far.

Mozzarella: a plastic curd cheese *qv* originally made to be eaten within hours – a farmer's wife would make it in the morning for their lunch. Thus it will, or should, have very little smell and flavour. The very best of all is made from buffalo milk, and modern transportation systems mean it is in our supermarkets, an extraordinary thought. Not even the factory-made cows' milk versions should be the slightest bit sour to smell or taste. An excellent foil to stronger flavours, from sun-ripened tomatoes to pesto and balsamic vinegars. Bocconcini, little mouthfuls, are small balls of Mozzarella

Pecorino: a unique family of piquant ewes' milk cheeses associated with the south of Italy. Although the name can be used for any cheese made with this milk, it is specially applied to hard pressed types, usually made in small drums or wheels with convex rims. The most famous types are Pecorino Romano, traditionally made in Lazio, but much is now made in Sardinia as Pecorino Sardo; frankly, you are just as likely to be buying something made in a factory from cows' milk with a usefully sharp starter added. If you can buy it young it makes a superb table cheese, and there is a version of Pecorino Siciliano which contains black peppercorns. Otherwise it is an oustanding cooking cheese, a sort of sheepish Parmesan.

Provolone: more complicated than most of us think, this plastic curd cheese can be anything from sweet and mild to piquant, partly because it has been curded with lamb or kid's rennet. They are molded by hand, usually into something curved and remotely phallic. Some are tiny, some are known to weigh 200kg, and each area will call the same cheese a different local name or pack it differently, with raffia for instance, so even Italians do not claim to know everything about them, which is really saying something. For all the effort, the cheeses are mild and buttery when three months old, but after six months they strengthen to a full, slightly salty taste that intensifies with further age. Old ones can be sharp enough to grate and use as a condiment, but there is always the risk of an undercurrent of soapiness. Smoked Provolone are common and will thus be easily confused with Scamorza, which seems to be the same thing to me anyway.

Ricotta: one of the most useful of all dairy products, although not a true cheese in its original form, the collected albumen from whey. These days it is as likely to be made from milk, but retains the sweetness of whey. It has all the clean fresh flavour of milk without the fattiness and when bought from a wicker-impressed cake which is still drooling with excess moisture makes the best cooking cheese of all, perfect for everything from savoury stuffings to sweet cheesecakes. How some supermarkets dare sell tubs of fine-textured, solid white cheese as Ricotta beats me, or have I been spoilt by the real thing?

Scamorza: the pear-shaped one which has the typical soft and springy texture of all plastic curd cheeses. It is often smoked, when the rind takes a golden brown turn. Once only rarely found in truly ethnic shops, the smoked version, particularly, is available from many good cheese shops and supermarket chillers.

Taleggio: this was created either early this century or a thousand years ago, depending on your reference book. It is a slab of creamy full fat cheese with a thin rind which should be pinkish-grey, but which is more often seen looking distinctly blue or grey in the United Kingdom – yet this does not seem to matter. Essentially mild, it should have a distinct fruitiness but often develops a bitterness which should be firmly rejected if encountered. Excellent examples in perfect condition can be aged twice as long as the recommended six weeks, when it will deepen in colour and develop greater aroma and attraction. Taleggio deserves to be far better known.

Torta: these layered cheeses look as though they are the modern invention of a mad marketing man, but they are actually a tradition of the Trieste area. All should be served slightly chilled and the best version layers Gorgonzola with Mascarpone, which is outstandingly good with a ripe pear.

NETHERLANDS & GERMANY

The early establishment of international trading centres in Holland and Germany ensured both countries were guaranteed constant exposure to advances in cheese-making techniques which, in some ways, makes it harder to understand why most cheeses from both countries tend to be bland but sweet. The exceptions are a few ripened German cheeses that are so strong they frighten most foreigners. Perhaps it is in direct contrast to the smoked, pickled and salted foods so beloved by both countries, but if you care to look hard enough there are a few treasures to be found.

The average German eats more cheese than most and cheese production all over Germany is prolific although much ends up in prepared foods. In recent years the Germans have given us some interesting smoked cheeses, although too many are highly processed, and increasingly they have developed a number of very sweet, fruity cheese confections which arguably should not even be described as cheese.

Cambazola: often erroneously called Blue Brie but actually a soft cheese with a white Camembert mould on the rind and a blue Gorgonzola (not Roquefort) mould inside. Usually cut from the disc, it should be creamy in texture and flavour, the bite coming from the blue rather than the rind. Inevitably, its success has spawned many 'me-too' cheeses, some better than others.

Edam: is a full flavoured cheese despite its lower fat content, but the shame of it is that most is sold and eaten long before its true flavour has had the chance to develop, which is why it is frequently called the cheese for people who hate cheese. It is a medium pressed cheese with a distinctive rind that is the result of immersion in whey and brine baths, and salting after it has been pressed. Any sourness tells you it is too immature but a good one is quite useful in cooking with its most notable attribute being its relative cheapness. When you are there, remember the red coat which makes Edam so easily recognized throughout the world is for export and never seen in the Netherlands.

Gouda: is richer, larger and yellower than Edam and has more flavour. Salt rubbed on the rind helps develop the flavour, which continues to develop for well over a year. At a food exhibition in Birmingham in 1992, we offered tastings of a two year old Gouda with a close texture and rich, golden colour that took everyone by surprise with its tangy, full flavour and spicy nose. An excellent cooker whatever the age. When in Holland, look out for the farmhouse versions, **Boeren**, made with unpasteurized milk and often flavoured with nettles, cumin and other spices or herbs.

Limburger: is oblong and loaf-shaped and bigger than most washed rind cheeses, therefore there is more of the brick-red rind to assail your nostrils. Usually foil wrapped. The rind should be smooth and only just moist; the yellow, smooth-textured body has a full flavour much less assertive than the farmhouse odour might suggest. Beware of any hint of ammonia, sliminess on the rind or runny paste, which is a sure sign the cheese is tired and way past its best.

Mainzerkäse/Handkäse: a group of cheeses that also includes **Sauermilchkäse**, all made from naturally curdled sour milk and hand-shaped into opaque yellow or buff coloured bars, discs, rolls or just about any design the maker can conjure up. Those found in the UK tend to be small, indented logs wrapped in cellophane but some variations are covered in mould smears and nearly all of them have a penetrating smell and close textured body that ranges from piquant to overpowering.

Münster: these cheeses also come in several sizes which means different maturing times of five to 13 weeks depending on size. All are flattish discs with a white to yellow body with the occasional hint of red, thin skin rather than rind, a strong smell and a slightly sharp sweetness of flavour. Avoid dryness, cracking or very moist, slimy skins.

NORTH AMERICA

It's hard, but you can find decent cheese in North America, especially now the rules on the use of unpasteurized milk have been slightly relaxed. Farmers' markets are a good bet and it's increasingly worth asking about cheesemakers in places suitable; there is an unsuspected Camembert-type made just outside San Francisco, for instance. A sensation at the London International Cheese Show in 1993 was **Dry Jack**; this is an aged **Monterey Jack**, essentially a type of Cheddar molded informally, and this one featured a rind coloured by cocoa, pepper and oil. It produces a robust, full cheese somewhere between a matured Cheddar and a Parmesan and thus good both to eat or to grate and use in cooking. In Vermont, traditional sage cheese can be found, with the rubbed herb rather than horrid oils and colours.

Ewe and goat milk cheeses are on the increase, and this, it will be no surprise, is especially true in Canada, where there has never been much interest in anything between those and Cheddar, which they make well, of course. Washed rind **Brick**, **Armenian String** cheese, **Treasure Cave Blue** and **Maytag Blue**, named after the washing machine company which paid for it to be invented (!) are probably easiest to find on a quick foray to the supermarket, gourmet or specialty food shop: there a delicatessen is a fancy sandwich shop.

SCANDINAVIA

A bewildering variety of bland, slightly chewy cheeses which look and taste pretty much the same makes standing at a cheese counter in Sweden or Denmark a nightmare of yellowness. It is perhaps as well they are unassuming for in these countries cheese is eaten at breakfast, not as noisy as cornflakes but substantially more of a challenge. The most extraordinary exceptions are whey cheeses, the Gjetost and Mesost which are brown because the sugar in the whey is caramelized in the process. There are spiced cheeses, tasty cheeses and supposedly a smoked cheese made from reindeer milk which must be dunked into coffee to make it palatable. I would be surprised to learn it was worth the trouble.

Danablue/Danish Blue: a twentieth century invention designed as a substitute for Roquefort, but whilst the young pretender to the crown has been an enormous commercial success, any similarity to Roquefort in its eating characteristics has eluded me. Its sharp saltiness belies its richness which is due to the use of homogenized milk in the making. Should be white rather than creamy, with blue rather than green veining, and crumbliness is perfectly acceptable if there is plenty of moisture. Much used in cheese mousses, blue cheese dressings and other Americanisms but mixed with butter it makes an excellent savoury spread.

Gjetost: the cheese that looks like caramel fudge. Made with goats' milk whey or a mixture of cows' and goats' milk whey. When pure goats' milk is used, it is called Ekte ('real') Gjetost and is even more of an acquired taste than the more commonly found Ski-Queen Gjetost. Sliced very thinly, this nutty-flavoured cheese is a great complement to herring and other fish dishes.

Havarti: comes in two types, one with a dry rind and one with a washed rind. The dry rind version was once called *Danish Tilsit* and although it is mildly aromatic it is basically a bland tasting cheese. The washed rind Havarti is fairly full flavoured at three months and develops a more pungent taste as it matures further. Made in loaves weighing 4.5kg.

Jarlsberg: was extinct until the 1950s when this old Norwegian recipe was spruced up and given a new lease of life. Now it is widely marketed, particularly in the United States. It has some similarity in texture to Gouda with a paste that is soft, smooth and mildly aromatic.

Munajusto: this Finnish cheese is literally translated as 'egg cheese' and indeed contains one or two eggs for every six litres of milk. The yolks give the cheese a wonderful colour. Good for melting and grilling.

Mycella: the Danish Gorgonzola, with a full but unaggressive flavour, a yellowish, supple body and green, not blue, veins. Steer clear of any brownness or overblueing, sharp smell or bitter flavour. *Castello* is Mycella with a surface, Camembert-type mould as well, which is intentional.

Samso: probably the head of Denmark's most important cheese family. All those ending in 'o' of this type are related with the first part of the name indicating the cheese's origin. Samso is firm, yellow and nutty with cherry-sized holes and a flavour which varies from mild sweetness to distinctive strength. Made in a cartwheel shape. Flavour preference is highly personal and rather arbitrary; varying fat content may have some bearing. Useful in cooking. Types include *Danbo*, square-shaped and sometimes flavoured with caraway; *Elbo*, which is firm, loaf-shaped and with holes; and **Tybo**, brick-shaped, very firm and red-rinded.

Ridder: a modern cheese from Norway. Similar to Saint Paulin, it has an orange, lightly washed rind and a buttery paste.

SPAIN

Her inclusion in the EC has meant Spain's cheeses are slowly becoming better known but a visit to the country is very rewarding as much cheesemaking remains artisanal with localized distribution. Ewes' milk cheese is the most common, of which the **Manchego** of La Mancha is the most famous, sold either young or ripened at least a year in olive oil. **Cabrales** is the best known blue cheese, often made with mixed milks; Spaniards are said by Sandy Carr to like it almost totally blue and alive with mites and maggots. Why?

Both Manchego and Cabrales are protected under Spain's Denominación de Origen (DO) system which supervises and guarantees the standards of the country's most esteemed foods. Other DO cheeses are: **Liebana** cheeses from the eastern Picos de Europa, which includes mixed milk **Picon**, juniper-smoked cheeses and fresh or matured baby cheeses; **Cantabria**, relatively fresh and made only with Friesian milk; **Idiazabal** made only with Laxta and Carranzana breeds of ewes' milk in north west Spain; **Roncal** made only with Lasa and Rasa ewes' milk in just seven towns of the Roncal valley of Navarre; and **Mahon** made in Minorca from Friesian milk. **Iberico** is a comparatively new mixed milk cheese matured from 15 days to six months. The matured versions have a distinctive dark rind.

THE CHEESEBOARD

The classic cheeseboard goes for contrast. A savoury blue cheese (Stilton), a full-flavoured pressed cheese (Cheddar) and a creamy soft cheese (Brie) gives an ideal foundation. Within each of those flavour styles there is much opportunity for originality. The savoury cheese might be a goats' cheese rather than a blue one, then the pressed cheese could be a lighter sweeter Wensleydale or Swiss Emmental, and the soft cheese made with unpasteurized milk. This is what might be called a vertical cheeseboard, offering a choice of flavours from top to bottom of the spectrum. But a horizontal board offers wonderful eating too, especially if it is to complement a wine you know well.

A horizontal board presents only cheese of similar style, either made by the same technique or from, say, goat or sheep milk. Such a board might offer both soft fresh and aged goat cheeses for a rugged dry rosé, a choice of flowery Swiss Gruyère and other surface ripened cheeses with a decent Meursault, English territorial cheeses with elegant Australian Cabernet Shiraz, or a trio of unusual French Blue cheeses with a chilled sweet, late-picked botrytis Riesling from New Zealand.

Forget the decoration and garnish, throw away the straw mats and the vine leaves and all that. Offering perfect cheese at optimum temperature gives much more pleasure. Fruit and nuts and celery and stuff? In my view they only accompany cheese when it is served directly after a main course and there is nothing else to follow, ie if you are combining cheese and dessert. Otherwise, bread and crackers will do. Oh yes, and butter too if that's what you like.

SWITZERLAND

Swiss cheesemaking has a pedigree you can trace directly to Roman heritage and traditions. Some like Sbrinz were actually known and appreciated by the Romans, but others have a relationship linked through monastic Ireland. Let me explain.

It was Romans and their roads which took civilized eating and sophisticated agriculture westwards, including cheesemaking. But when the Vandals and Goths took the same route and pulled down the curtains on civilizations, repositories of that knowledge retreated ever westwards, until only the monasteries of western Ireland kept and upheld Roman tradition. When the Dark Ages left, barefoot Irish monks took civilization back to Europe and reintroduced cheesemaking technology to the country which we know as Switzerland. Today the Swiss have still not heard any convincing argument to change the way they make their renowned cheeses, some of which are amongst the very few truly useful to the cook. Indeed Swiss cheese cooking traditions are well worth anyone's interest.

Appenzeller: some 700 years ago a cheese from the Appenzell region was recorded as a tithe payment to the Saint Gall monastery but how much it resembled the cheese of today is not known. Its yellowish brown rind is the result of regular washing with a brine marinade of herbs, spices and frequently wine or cider. At its best after three to four months maturation, this semi-hard cheese should have a tangy, quite strong flavour. Whole cheeses weigh between six and eight kilos with a diameter of 30cm. When explorer Tim Severin sailed across the Atlantic in a leather boat to recreate the supposed sixth century discovery of America by Irish monk St Brendan, I supplied him with food of the period. When they used modern foods on the first half of the voyage they were sick and weak, but with the Appenzeller, grains and smoked, salted meats of the sixth century they thrived. A lesson for us all.

Emmental: although cheesemaking in Emmental can be traced back to 1293 the earliest mention of this cheese by name is in a register of donations handed out to the inhabitants of Langenthal whose houses were burnt down in 1542. Since then it has been copied all round the world but in Switzerland, it is made only from unpasteurized milk, of which it takes 1,000lt to make each 80kg cheese. Although such a big cheese, it requires minutely detailed care to get right, which explains the despair of its imitators. The eyes should be fairly evenly distributed, the body a light yellow, the rind smooth and free from mould (which may, nonetheless, easily be wiped off, and causes no ill effect). The smell and taste should be sweet and clean, not bitter and assertive in any way. The milk is usually only from the mottled Emmental cows of the Emme valley and hills

Useful in cooking but will draw threads if heated too highly. Real Emmental always has 'Switzerland' stamped on the rind in red. A drop of moisture or 'tear' in the eyes is a very good sign of a perfectly mature and well-developed cheese. Cheese book author Sandy Carr quotes the makers as saying: 'Anyone can make the holes, only the Swiss can make the cheese.'

Fribourgeois: – (see VACHERIN FRIBOURGEOIS).

Gruyère: another cheese with a long tradition dating back to the twelfth century

and today there are around 60 alpine farms making Gruyère during the summer at heights mostly over 1,000m/3282ft, close to Lake Geneva with milk from black and white cows bred exclusively in the region. Over 400lt of milk are needed for a cheese weighing 35kg and during the maturing process the rind is wiped with salt water to encourage a briny dry sharpness. Smaller and firmer than Emmental, only half the size, the development of the rind flora gives a fuller, fruitier flavour which is sweeter and has a hint of nuttiness. The texture is supple with very few holes, no larger than a cherry. Check for the 'Switzerland' stamp on the surface. Some sliminess on the rind can be dealt with and ignored, as long as the cheese has not become bitter or sharp. One of the world's great cooking cheeses as it rarely strings, a combination of Gruyère and Emmental makes the only true cheese fondue. Gruyère is quite the best cheese for topping gratins, flavouring pastry and sauces and for cheese soufflés, perhaps pointed with grated Sbrinz.

Raclette: the name literally means *scraper*, a semi-hard cheese made from either raw or pasteurized milk, which has a typically fruity flavour from a paste that is almost gold in colour and very buttery. Its name comes from its individuality to a dish called Raclette. The cut surface of a halved Raclette cheese is exposed to an open fire, and as it melts is scraped onto a plate and eaten at once with potatoes boiled in their skins, gherkins and pickles.

SWISS SOUFFLÉ

It may come as a surprise, but you should always ensure your eggs for soufflé are not too fresh. They should be two or three days old at least as this will give you a better, stronger froth. In this recipe you could also use four egg yolks and five egg whites.

Serves 4

300g/10oz Swiss Gruyère, coarsely grated
60g/2oz butter
45g/1½ oz plain flour
300ml/½pt milk
1 tsp salt
5 eggs, separated
60g/2oz Sbrinz, grated
fine breadcrumbs

Prepare soufflé dish by greasing with butter and dusting with breadcrumbs.

Melt butter in a saucepan, stir in the flour and cook for two minutes, being careful not to let the roux brown. Add milk and stir until you have a thick, white sauce. Remove from heat and add salt, egg yolks and Gruyère.

Whip the egg whites until soft (not stiff) peaks form. Stir a quarter of the egg whites into the cheese mixture to lighten it, then fold in the rest slowly and gently. It does not matter if the whites do not mix in evenly.

Ladle the mixture into the prepared soufflé dish. Bake at 170°C/350°F/Gas Mark 4 for 50-60 minutes. Ten minutes before the end of cooking, carefully open the oven door and sprinkle the soufflé with grated Sbrinz. Return to oven, finish cooking and serve immediately.

A perfect soufflé will not be solid but *baveuse,* or slightly runny, in the middle.

Sbrinz: probably the country's most ancient cheese, and related to Italian Granas, this extra hard cheese has for the last 400 years been made in the Lucerne valley from its distinctive brown cows. Immersed in salt baths after pressing, the young

SWISS FONDUE

It's well worth giving you a proper recipe for Swiss fondue, if only to prove how sad anything else will be. But rather than merely dipping into the melted cheese and wine with the traditional cubes of bread, I now offer guests lightly cooked green vegetables, boiled small potatoes, hard-boiled quail eggs or very small hen eggs, cherry tomatoes, baby corn cobs, cubes of grilled polenta, oil-soft sun-dried tomatoes – in fact anything which goes with this delicious mixture of cheeses and wine. The presentation looks terrific, offers a balanced meal, and is even more fun.

Serves four

200g/7oz Swiss Emmental, coarsely grated
400g/14oz Swiss Gruyère, coarsely grated
1 clove garlic
300mls/½pt dry white wine
1 tsp fresh lemon juice
1 heaped tsp cornflour
small glass kirsch or other eau-de-vie
nutmeg, pepper
cubed bread, raw or blanched vegetables, sliced pears, apples, grapes

Mix the Emmental and Gruyère evenly. Rub a fondue dish or thick saucepan with the cut clove of garlic and then add the wine. Heat until just simmering, and then add the lemon juice which helps amalgamate the wine and cheese. Stir the cheese into the wine and once this is melted and the mixture is creamy, mix the kirsch into the cornflour and quickly stir this in. Reduce the temperature and let cook a few minutes then season with freshly grated nutmeg and pepper – white pepper looks better than flecks of black pepper.

Put the completed fondue on the burner, reminding everyone that each time they dip, they should give the fondue a stir, helping to keep it creamy right to the end.

There are all sorts of stories about what should happen to those whose food drops into the fondue. Generally if the accident happens to a woman she is expected to kiss a man at the table; a man making the same mistake is expected to buy more wine.

Sbrinz is allowed to sweat out fat and water in heated maturing rooms. Throughout maturation, the cheese is regularly wiped dry and over a period of at least eighteen months, it develops its aromatic, full flavour and becomes a very easily digestible cheese. In fact one old recipe recommends taking a small piece of Sbrinz daily to help with stomach disorders. Serve broken or shaved into thin slices. A favourite of mine is simply to slice it thinly and immerse in a little balsamic vinegar. Serve before the meal as an appetizer – it's irresistable. Try grating finely in sauces, on rice in soup – in fact, it never strings, which makes it very easy to use.

Tête de Moine: made in the Swiss Jura, this 800 year old cheese comes in tall cylindrical shapes and is made from milk drawn from spring through to autumn. Because it is uncooked but pressed, the body is soft and supple but what singles it out is the way the Swiss say it must be served to appreciate the cheese. It must not be sliced but shaved in a circular motion using a tool called a 'Girolle'. This creates thin shavings of Tête de Moine that are traditionally served as rosettes which release the spicy, aromatic flavour of the cheese. Served this way, I have always found it essential not to leave the rossettes too long before eating as they can quickly dry. Often eaten with pepper and ground cumin.

Tilsiter: used to be known in this country as Royalp and is made in eastern Switzerland in the canton of Thurgau. It is enormously popular in Switzerland itself, a semi-hard cheese with a reddish-brown rind and a pale yellow paste that at four months develops a mild but creamy flavour. Those with red labels are made from unpasteurized milk, the green labels are pasteurized.

Vacherin Fribourgeois: quite frequently confused with Vacherin Mont d'Or, which is a very different cheese and this is probably why the Swiss have increasingly dropped the Vacherin and tend now to call it simply Fribourgeois.

Yet another Swiss mountain cheese with a pedigree dating back to the 15th century, it is still made in the canton of Fribourg in small dairies. A semi-hard cheese with an ivory to yellow paste, it has a mild, delicate flavour and after three months it starts to develop a distinctive aroma. Those exported are washed at three months then covered with a yellowish brown coat. Good in mixed cheese fondue or in a pure Fondue Fribourgeois, but if you are offered it on a cheeseboard, do try it.

Vacherin Mont d'Or: unusual for being a winter cheese. Moulded in a strip of pine which gives a light resinous flavour, the cheese can be anything from 200g to 3kg in size but all have top skins which crumple when the cheese is ready to eat. It is very rich tasting, a true dessert cheese for a dinner party, when it is correct to remove the upper crust and then spoon out the body. If it is cut into wedges, the paste must be held back with a piece of glass or wood to prevent it flowing away.

U ntil I was 14 I had never tasted coffee, and I was 18 before I could be persuaded to try tea. Cocoa was the hot drink that fortified me through the rigours of cub camps, bible class socials and school examinations. It would not have if it had been like the first chocolate drinks Europe enjoyed, which were bitter, fatty, thickened and scummy. Clearly, fashion was as much part of its popularity as pleasure, and the entire history of chocolate is equally redolent of the unexpected. It involves Columbus and Montezuma, a disgusted Pope, an Italian entrepreneur, Jewish exiles, a Dutch invention, crusading Quakers – and that's just cocoa and drinking chocolate. Solid chocolate in bars was an English invention that only emerged, with some nicety of timing, in the middle of Victoria's reign. Thence, their backbones further fortified by Mr Fry's novelty, Englishmen more readily went out to conquer; and still no mountaineer or explorer feels right unless there is a bar of chocolate about his or her person. But how many pause in mid-traverse to ponder the vital part cocoa beans played in the fertility and puberty rites of the Mayans? or that Madame du Barry employed hot chocolate as an aphrodisiac? or that Casanova found it more invigorating than champagne? or that only English speakers say cocoa rather than the correct cacao? Apparently it was decided we couldn't pronounce the latter, so we didn't.

The cacao tree probably originated in the Amazon Basin, being taken to the Yucatan by Mayans about 600 AD. Colombus carried some beans back to the Catholic kings, but they showed little interest. Later, when Cortes was greeted by Montezuma, gorgeous in gold and shimmering feathers, he was presented with a placatory drink of frothy, bitter chocolate, for he was thought to be the saviour promised to the Aztecs. Cortes was to take rather than give life, yet throughout the slaughter and greed that followed, he recognised the restorative and energy-giving qualities (it contains caffeine) of the drink, and Spain monopolized the product for the next century. Once Spanish grandees learned to mellow the drink with vanilla and sugar it became quite the thing. It seems to have been nuns who discovered it was infinitely better hot, and by 1569 hot chocolate had been brought to the attention of Pope Pius V. He didn't ban it during Lent, as he could not conceive anyone would ever care willingly to drink something he found disgusting.

Spain's monopoly was broken in 1606 by Antonio Carletti who managed to take the secrets of the fragrant drink back to Italy and by 1700 the famed coffee houses of Venice and Florence were equally acclaimed for their chocolate. The French were introduced to it by Jewish exiles from Spain and Switzerland, now Master Chocolatier to the world, learned of it in 1697 from one Heinrich Fischer on his return from Brussels. 1657 seems to be the first time it was mentioned in England, and by 1662 Henry Stubbs, a doctor returned from Jamaica, wrote a whole book about chocolate, *The Indian Nectar*.

London's coffee houses quickly learned to serve chocolate to those who could afford it, and Pepys used it to settle his stomach after the debauches that marked the coronation of Charles I. Yet it was not until 1828 that Coenraad J van Houten invented a press that extracted two-thirds of the fat from the chocolate, leaving a dry powder we would recognize as cocoa, thus making possible a simpler and more reliable form of chocolate drink. Only 20 years later Joseph Fry of Bristol discovered how to combine that extracted fat – cocoa butter – with other parts of the cocoa bean plus sugar to make eating chocolate.

The new drink of cocoa was cheap enough to be useful to the poor and was seized upon vigorously by the Temperance Societies of the 19th century. Both the Cadburys and the Rowntrees were Quaker families and dedicated to the movement. They combined the manufacture and marketing of cocoa with a drive for social reform here and abroad and much of the profit they made went to practical, socially-responsible projects – they even organized boycotts in Europe as protest against the conditions of slaves in Portuguese Africa.

Cocoa (and chocolate as a drink) are now far less important. It is to solid chocolate that most of the world looks for the voluptuous thrill of the cacao tree's products. Indeed, chocolate is perhaps one of the world's most enduring and universal treats, as much appreciated in sweets on remote Pacific Islands as in the lavish presentation boxes of hand-dipped confections without which many sophisticated urban celebrations would be incomplete. But what is it and how is it made?

Pictures of cacao trees always make me smile, and my first view of a real one, on St Lucia, actually made me laugh outright. They don't look real. The tree has large glossy leaves and white or pink blossoms which appear all year round and become ridged pods up to 28cm/10in long. These slowly turn from green to yellow through purples and reds to a russet brown – and that is the attraction. At any one time scarcely two of the pods are the same colour, giving the tree a perfectly ridiculous musical-comedy look.

Despite the tree's constant readiness, possibly why it was so worshipped in South America, it is harvested only twice a year. The pods are taken from the tree and split and the beans, or seeds, are left out on the ground for two to nine days to ferment, which diminishes some bitterness and develops the fat content. Then the beans are shipped to a factory, at home or abroad.

Processing continues with a roasting which dries the outer skin of the beans. This is removed together with the germ, leaving what are known as nibs. Once these have been ground into a paste with some application of heat, the cocoa butter can be removed under pressure, leaving a paste called chocolate liquor. This sets on cooling, and is the basic, unsweetened chocolate. The liquor might be further pressed, which results in cocoa powder. Or it can be blended with more cocoa butter, sugar and flavouring, including dried milk powder for milk chocolate, before the final process, conching. This is really a slow whipping which ensures even texture and a good gloss. Of course every part of the process, from roasting to flavouring and beating, can be varied to produce different tastes and textures.

As with coffee there have traditionally been two major types of cacao beans, the *forastero* and the *criollo*. Today these have been joined by a slowly increasing number of hybrids and crosses, the most important of which is the *trinitario*.

And as with both coffee and tea, the precise flavour a bean gives is a combination of its essential characteristics plus the effect of the climate it is grown in, whether it is harvested late or early and the method of fermentation and drying – to say nothing of the care with which it is processed. The expert blending of different styles of the same bean and of other varieties of beans give particular chocolates their special appeal – or otherwise.

Forastero: this represents 95 per cent of all cacao trees, and is thus somewhat the equivalent of robusta coffee – it is a high yielding tree and the beans give an immediate mouth flavour and sensation which is generally rather coarse and undistinguished. West African beans tend to be spicy and acidic, Indian Ocean beans fruitier and often actually bitter; but the same bean grown in Ecuador gives a soft, floral and clear chocolate flavour with overtones of orange blossom. Like poor quality coffee, it tends to be roasted very high to disguise the shortcomings and it is often this you will taste rather than real chocolate.

Criollo: this is the aristocrat, appropriately compared with the chardonnay grape which gives us champagne and chablis. It now grows particularly well around the Indian Ocean, giving beans which donate spicy floral notes with welcome acidity and a long-lasting aftertaste, their particular and important contribution to fine chocolate.

Trinitario: this is a remarkable cross

THE CHOCOLATE TRUFFLE

If you do not like your chocolate to snap back at you, you are probably a truffle lover. Or you may want to bite through snappy chocolate to a velvety truffle mixture. Here is a classic recipe from London's Sara Jayne, who reckons to have made and dipped over a million, and subsequently developed truffle dipper's elbow.

Bring 600ml/1pt of double (heavy) cream just to boiling point then remove from the heat and tip in 900g/2lbs of broken chocolate of at least 50 per cent cocoa solid content, but higher is better. A white chocolate truffle mixture will need an extra 150ml/½pt of cream. Stir until melted, at which point you might also whisk a few seconds for added lightness. Now add flavouring if you like. Rough brandy works better than decent cognac, young harsh Calvados better than an aged one, eau-de-vies better than sweet liqueurs, but suit yourself. When cool, shape by hand and roll in cocoa, chopped nuts or crushed amaretti biscuits; or dip into chocolate.

The problem with dipping is that the chocolate is likely to resume its dull appearance if it is not retempered, but this is usually avoided by using a very high cocoa solid chocolate, melting it exceptionally slowly and not heating it too much. If you have the patience to do this, almost anything can be dipped in chocolate, which will set again to a shiny snappiness – truffles of course but also preserved ginger, shortbread and other biscuits, dried fruits, strawberries and, when no one else is around, your fingers...

---

between the previous two varieties, which produces particularly good beans in the Caribbean. It rather combines the best of the forastero and the criollo, with the concentrated syrupy fruitiness of dried fruits balanced by a flowery woodiness and good acidity which together many think reminiscent of very fresh tobacco. Most importantly, it also gives a distinct lingering aftertaste thus multiplying the pleasures of the criollo.

Few chocolate makers tell you which beans they use but the Valrhona Company of France erupted onto the scene by doing precisely that, selling chocolate by variety or specified blend and with a choice of cocoa solid content.

When The Chocolate Society did a blind tasting of chocolates with over 50 per cent cocoa solid content flavoured only with natural vanilla, Valrhona styles took the first three places. Their range includes Manjari, made with a single estate pure criollo, and Pur Caraibe, based on the trinitario.

The basic types of chocolate are few, variations being the result of both content and manufacturing technique.

Baker's/baking chocolate: the former is a trade name in the United States and thus means little. But *baking* chocolate is the general term for chocolate substitutes, made from vegetable fats and chocolate flavourings, and thus should not really use the name at all. Be careful never to confuse this stuff with the next two.

Cooking chocolate: doesn't really mean anything for the term can be applied to anything with which you decide to cook. In older cookery books, and to those with unsophisticated palates, cooking chocolate is likely to mean any bitter, high cocoa solid, low sugar chocolate, the sort which has now become so popular to eat. It is best not to use this term, for it denigrates and confuses. If you need dark chocolate for a recipe and it is unobtainable, substitute a mixture of 20g/¾oz/3tbsp cocoa powder plus 15g/½oz unsalted butter for 25g/1oz of dark chocolate.

Couverture: a type of chocolate with a very high cocoa fat content, specially liked in the catering trade because it melts and covers easily. It can vary in cocoa solid content, but it is generally good and high. All those vegetable fat chocolate 'flavour' products on the market – *(see BAKING CHOCOLATE)* – are attempting to do the same thing cheaply for the consumer market, but shouldn't. Couverture is often confused with the following:

Eating chocolate: all chocolate can be eaten, and this description is a hangover from the days when sweetened chocolate bars and elaborately filled chocolates were considered the thing, and plain, bitter chocolate was 'cooking' chocolate. Like cooking chocolate, it is a term which should be dropped.

Milk chocolate: chocolate to which condensed milk has been added, which thus means extra sugar and an unavoidable caramelized flavour, which you love or hate. Difficult to use successfully in cookery because its flavour is already diluted, but this doesn't stop many serving pallid, sticky and bland objects, yet describing them as chocolate.

White chocolate: some purists say white chocolate is not chocolate at all because it doesn't contain cocoa solids. It is however made from cocoa butter, plus sugar and milk, and has a similar texture. Whatever it should be called, it is delicious and increasingly popular. Be sure when using white chocolate in cooking that you buy one of good quality. Cheaper, mass market white chocolate gives very disappointing results.

Savouring chocolate

The first thing to check, of course, is the label. The higher the cocoa solid content, the richer the flavour and the less sugar will have been used. Sugar or milk products are the cheapest ingredients and, as contents must be listed in descending order of volume, you will not want to see these preceding cocoa bean solids. Vanilla is the most expensive constituent, followed by cocoa butter, generally four times costlier than cocoa solids. Lecithin, a natural emulsifier, is widely used to enhance shelf life.

The best chocolate will have only those ingredients and use real vanilla rather than vanillin for flavouring: vanillin and high sugar content are usually indicators of low-grade cocoa solids, depressing ways to reduce cost at the expense of quality.

The colour should be deep, and any veering towards ruddiness rather than black is a sign of high quality. There should be a conspicuous gloss, almost a mirror finish. When you break or bite into it there must be a decisive crack and snap, revealing a texture like that of tree bark: the characteristic snap of quality chocolate is a major basis for judgment before tasting. The chocolate should also crack when you bite it in the mouth, and then begin to melt.

The unique (as far as I know) claim

COCOA POWDER

The ultimate result of experiments to reduce the excessive (and unpleasant) amount of fat in cacao beans and thus in true drinking chocolate. Cocoa powder is about 20 per cent fat by weight, which is negligible in the amounts used. There are two types, straightforward cocoa powder which has no further processing and is the most common in Britain, and 'dutch' or 'dutched' cocoa.

In 1848 Conrad van Houten further processed the fat-reduced chocolate solids he had produced by treatment with alkali. This darkens the colour of the powder, and by reducing its natural acidity gives a blander but more mellow flavour. In fact, the fats have been saponified, that is turned into a sort of soap!

'Dutched' cocoa is especially good for baking and for milk-based products or drinks as it dissolves in milk and blends with cake or biscuit mixes more easily. On the other hand, untreated cocoa will give richer flavours to baking and bigger, broader flavour in drinks. Chocolate makers in Britain usually use ordinary cocoa but some highly commercial snack products, especially in the United States, use the alternative. As a drink, I find dutched cocoa a comforting, less aggressive choice from time to time, and thus usually keep both types around. In the United States dutched cocoa is commonly referred to as European-style.

of chocolate is that it's the only food which melts at precisely the same temperature as human body temperature, hence the way it so easily coats the mouth: cocoa butter is solid at 33°C but molten at 34°C and thus it should also melt quite quickly in just a few seconds if held in the palm. Slow melting chocolate tells you it has low cocoa butter content or cocoa butter substitutes included (five per cent may be added in the United Kingdom without being mentioned on the label).

This is the stage when a 'bitter' – high cocoa, low sugar – chocolate is at its most naked. In those first full moments of melted flavour you will learn to detect overroasting, inferior materials or poor manufacturing. A well made chocolate of finely balanced beans enhanced with a little sugar and genuine vanilla should create flavours of berry fruits and almonds, of balsam and of the forest.

Once you have chewed, allowed the chocolate to melt on your tongue and then swallowed, think about where the flavour lingers. If it is on the front or middle of the mouth, none or few finer beans have been used. If it lingers at the back of the mouth and down the tongue into the throat you have been well treated and got your money's worth.

Cooking: whether you choose ordinary cocoa powder or dutched cocoa for baking, the best tip I ever received was always to use cocoa powder rather than flour for dusting the baking tins or trays of chocolate cakes, biscuits, brownies and so on. It prevents unsightly white dusting or nasty combinations of unflavoured flour and butter on your baking, and adds extra chocolate depth, too. Speaking of which, if you feel a recipe is not going to have enough chocolate flavour for you, possibly because you have not been able to buy one of the fantastic high cocoa solid chocolates, it is always best to add cocoa powder rather than more chocolate, for its added fat and sugar may unbalance your recipe.

In Australasia, chocolate is often combined with orange to make a flavour they call jaffa. It is quite wonderful: try grated orange rind or an orange liqueur on (or in) some chocolate ice cream, or make a butter icing for a plain cake with orange juice and cocoa. Fresh lime too makes an interesting but more demanding combination.

Rose water mixes with chocolate to great advantage and a chocolate cake is the best way to prove how well it combines with red soft fruits such as raspberries,

DRINKING CHOCOLATE

Modern eating chocolate makes a much better drink that the original, usually described as floury and gritty. But the ingredients and method for hot chocolate remain pretty much the same. Increasing the amount of chocolate or replacing some of the milk with single or double cream are all ways to add individuality.

Chocolate is traditionally served in small, narrow, straight-sided cups, which help conserve the heat. The liquid must be whisked vigorously just before serving; in Mexico they use a special wooden whisk, the *molinillo*, but a wire whisk does just as nicely.

HOT CHOCOLATE
4-6 servings, according to cup size
50g/2oz dark rich chocolate
8 tbsp water
750ml/1¼pt milk
vanilla bean or 1 tsp vanilla essence
sugar to taste
cinnamon sticks
whipped cream at room temperature

First prepare the cups, by pouring hot water into them and letting them stand whilst you make the chocolate. Gently melt the chocolate and water together, ideally in a double boiler. Put the vanilla bean into the cold milk and heat until scalding hot; remove the bean. Flavour the milk with essence if you do not use a bean. Sweeten the milk to taste, with a teaspoon or sugar or so per serving. Pour the hot milk onto the melted chocolate, whisking as you do.

Quickly empty and dry the cups, and put a cinnamon stick into each. Whisk the hot chocolate again and serve. Top each cup with a dollop of whipped cream. If you have no cinnamon sticks, the cream may be sprinkled with very fresh ground cinnamon.

This may also be served cold, over crushed ice.

BRAZILIAN MOCHA

This is less rich than plain hot chocolate, but more stimulating.

4 servings
35g/1½oz dark rich chocolate
2 tbsp sugar
300ml/½pt boiling water
150ml/¼pt hot milk or single cream
150ml/½pt hot double cream
450ml/¾pt hot strong coffee
1 tsp vanilla essence

Soften the chocolate with the sugar in a double boiler and then stir in the boiling water. Bring to a simmer, then add the hot milk, cream and coffee, which should only just have been made. Taste for sweetness, add vanilla, whisk and serve, perhaps sprinkled with cinnamon.

SPANISH DRINKING CHOCOLATE

The egg yolk gives this simple drink an added comforting richness

4 servings
60g/2½oz dark rich chocolate
pinch cinnamon
600ml/1pt milk
1 egg yolk

Melt chocolate in milk over gentle heat. Add a generous pinch of cinnamon. Beat egg yolk thoroughly and stir into chocolate mixture. Serve warm.

strawberries, currants and cherries. Mint is really the only herb I can think of that works with chocolate but most of the sweet spices have a natural affinity, especially as additions to hot chocolate drinks or in icings for cakes and biscuits.

Perhaps the most astonishing use of chocolate is as the perfect finisher of any rich, spicy game sauce. Try it the next time you make a casserole of hare, pigeon or venison. Just add a square of dark chocolate per person to the sauce, but taste as you go – it should only just be noticeable, and only if you know. A final point: when you are melting chocolate, it is better to do it over a low heat and a small amount of water. Too much heat, or steam, makes it go solid.

Forget all that stuff about you are what you eat. You are actually what you drink. When you consider we are all essentially rather a lot of water held together in a greater or lesser state of appeal, it is amazing how little care we take with our liquid intake. Alcohol? Yes, of course, it is pleasurable, but actually dehydrates rather than quenches thirst. A bit of a blow that, but it has to be faced. Yet water is commonly thought dicey, pricey or ignored altogether. That leaves us with coffee, tea, tisanes and cocoa.

Potentially, these offer more pleasure and reward than any aspect of the speciality food spectrum. All day and all night. But for too many, their experience will only be slurps of tepid instant coffee or of water clouded by a double-dipped tea bag. Oh yes, plus memories for some of cocoa sipped in a sleeping bag.

What a world of pleasurable discovery lies ahead of them, shadowed only by possible clashes with tea freaks and cappuccino clowns, those who need written introductions and complete genealogical and geographical backgrounds to individual leaf or bean before they buy. You know the type, I'm sure. By the time they have chosen the blend, admired the equipment, explained the process and timed the extraction you've had to reach for a Diet Coke.

Somewhere between the two lies the norm. A world of genuine interest in good tea and coffee of all types and at all levels. Sure, enjoy your First-Flush Darjeeling, or Monsooned Malabar. But know how to get the best from a tea bag too. And make your cocoa a talking point. You owe it to your body.

COFFEE

It is extraordinary to think the watery instant beverage millions drink is known by the same name as a drink which, for centuries after its discovery, was considered a gift from God, and which properly made smells and tastes quite as though mixed by that divine hand.

Coffee has been forbidden in Mecca, by a governor who was later put to death, blessed by a pope, accused of making men unfruitful, banned by Frederick the Great, and written about by Bach in a temporal cantata. English coffee houses were temporarily closed by Charles II, but nonetheless changed the city of London forever.

Coffee, national drink of the Americas and of the Middle East, had its origins in the latter. Legend or tradition suggests it was first recognized in Ethiopia, by a shepherd who noticed a distinct spriteliness in his sheep after they had eaten a certain red berry. Even he, the shepherd Rhaldi, felt invigorated after trying some, and passed the knowledge on to local Sufi mystics. Deciding such pleasure could only be associated with the devil, the monks threw the berries onto the fire; the heavenly aroma that ensued convinced them of an opposite provenance. They raked out the remaining charred seeds, threw them into water... and so on.

The stimulus given by this new drink sharpened men's ability to worship God, and so monks kept coffee secret for years. But no one keeps secrets from followers of Islam, who adopted the drink with fervour, for it helped them through long and repeated religious services. The first public coffee house opened in Mecca about 1511 and thence the habit of combining the stimulus of society and caffeine spread north via Constantinople into Europe. By 1645, anyone who was anyone, or hoped to be, had taken coffee with Signor Floriano in Venice, as noted for his prodigious propensity to gossip as for the excellence of the coffee he served on the Piazza di San Marco. The first coffee houses in Paris were lavish and oriental, captivating bored society by having the drink served on bended knee by Turkish slaves, which would recommend most things to Parisians. In England, coffee houses became centres for democratic discussion, where for a penny a cup one could be assured of commerce and conversation. There was one in Oxford in 1650 and two years later London had its first, in Cornhill.

They were restless, exciting places where you could hear uncensored news but they soon had their day. Although remaining a vital part of much European life, the coffee house in this country disappeared, the few that survived altered out of all recognition into clubs or institutions. The Commercial Union, Baltic Exchange and Lloyds all have their roots in coffee houses.

The Americans began by drinking tea, turning to coffee in protest at taxes on tea that went to England rather than to their benefit. Once they turned the East India Company's tea out of chests and into Boston harbour, coffee became a demonstration of independent thinking. It is interesting to note that the American's modern tea blends are far paler and more fragrant than those of England, a clear memory of the style of China tea their forefathers would have known, before India had been made into a tea-growing phenomenon.

But is it just colonial interests that have made the English so addicted to tea? In coffee's heyday it was often flavoured with mustard, boiled unconscionably, mixed with oatmeal, ale, wine, butter or spices. I think the English prefer simpler food, and tea had to triumph. More coffee is being drunk again, one is told, but witness the rise and fall of the fifties' coffee bars. It was a chance to become a coffee nation again, but was refused. I suspect this is largely because there is so much mystique about coffee making, and it is much easier to ruin coffee than any other beverage. Many who have persevered for years as makers of 'real' coffee have still to taste a good cupful. It is far easier to make tea, much easier to appreciate its differing blends and styles; or you can drink instant coffee, the worst of which at least have the merit of being simple to make and consistent. It is tradition rather than ceremony the English like with familiar food and drink; the care and ceremony concerned with coffee is just too foreign and unrewarding. At least that is how it seems to me, and the more I know about coffee the more I know that getting value and flavour is never easy and cannot be cheap. Yet little else can be so rewarding if you succeed. The path from coffee tree to you is no less fraught with danger, mystery and failure.

The coffee bean is the seed of an evergreen shrub with glossy green, lance-like leaves and a white flower with the heady scent of jasmine which grows in volcanic soil between the Tropics of Cancer and Capricorn; the best quality is produced over

1,600m above sea level. The costs involved in coffee production become starkly obvious when you learn the very best trees only produce 3kg dried weight of coffee beans in a year: Brazilian bushes each produce only 500g of coffee a year. Its fruit is known as cherries, for this is what they resemble as they ripen from green to purple. A major complication is that everything from blossoms to green, ripe cherries and over-ripe ones may be on the same branch at the same time. Thus, harvesting should be done berry by berry as they ripen to the precise degree, for green or over-ripe berries will add inferior flavour to the finished drink.

But, most modern foods are grown and processed with speed and economy in mind, and coffee is no exception. It is increasingly rare for it to be picked by hand or with any real care. Instead whole branches are pulled mechanically away with an mixture of beans in many states, the hope being that processing will separate the good from the bad.

Each cherry has a skin, a pulp, a tough parchment, a thin silver skin and the seeds or beans, in that order. Normally there are two seeds, facing each other with their flatter sides together, but sometimes only one bean will develop, and this rounder seed is sometimes separated out and sold as peaberry coffee. Theoretically it should be more flavourful. In fact such berries usually come from stunted or old trees and the liquor made from them is no different, but they look nice. Kenyan Peaberries are the exception.

The pulp and skins can be removed from the beans in two ways – the wet or the dry. The wet method is far preferable but requires great amounts of water, not necessarily available where coffee is grown.

Washed coffees: a pulper removes most of the outside skin and flesh. Next the beans are fermented, softening the remaining mucilage which may then be washed off. This fermentation must be most carefully timed for it affects both appearance and flavour. The special advantage of the washed coffee process is that under-ripe berries, which will give a distinct peanut flavour, float to the top and can be removed, radically improving the overall quality. Unfortunately over-ripe berries, known in the trade as 'stinkers' and which give a flavour rather like silage, will remain and can disastrously effect the flavour of the ultimate brew – well, it would to most Europeans, whereas oddballs in the Middle East pursue and encourage such eccentricity. Some French fancy the flavour too, actually calling such coffee *le nectaire*, which is a bit of a worry really when they are supposed to know about food. Washed green coffee looks better than unwashed, but the process is no guarantee of higher quality. The beans are now known as parchment beans, and the parchment and silver skin are removed by a machine similar to the roller mill. Washed beans are often given a polish in another machine which makes both colour and quality more durable. The treatment undeniably gives finer looking coffee beans, but often the crop will be so big that available machinery cannot cope and the older, dry (unwashed) method will be used.

Unwashed coffee: the coffee cherries are dried in the sun until crisp. They need constant attention so that they dry evenly. Rain or dew means the cherries must be

Coffee as a drink is judged on its body, acidity and fragrance. Just as soil, climate and altitude will make the same grape give wildly different flavours, wine language is relevant to assessing coffee.

The range of effects is created by roasting, essentially caramelizing the sugars present in the bean. Slow maturing, high-grown beans have bigger quantities of sugar and other aromatics and it follows that the process will thus create richer and more complex flavours. It is a sin to highly roast the best beans and a blessing that the cheaper ones should be.

The *body* of coffee means its overall effect in the mouth; a full-bodied coffee fills the mouth with a velvety softness, stimulating taste buds over the entire palate to thus give a so-called 'long' finish, flavour and sensation which lingers in the mouth and down the back of the throat. Lesser coffees, robustas in particular, are flatter and less sensual and are usually 'short' or 'middle' finishers – that is they only affect taste buds in part of the palate, often boldly but just in the front, and do not do that for very long.

Acidity in coffee is what you would call dryness in wine: it is what makes the liquid feel clean in the mouth, giving satisfying balance to the initial sweetness. It must not be confused with bitterness, found in coffee which has been over-roasted or over-brewed.

Just as in wine, a good coffee will tell you most of what there is to say by its nose. Like wine, it should not be sniffed in namby-pamby little whiffs but with a big, single breath which is held so it can permeate and stimulate and tell you what you want to know.

covered, and as soon as the sun comes out they must be spread again or they will mould.

Once the drying is thoroughly done, often with mechanical help today, the pulp and parchment can easily be removed. The drawback with the dry method is that there is no guarantee of consistency of colour or quality, and often lesser beans and other debris are included in the final product in spite of careful grading.

The green coffee beans will last well – indeed some, such as the Java, are said to improve for up to twenty years – but the flavour we appreciate so much comes only after the bean is (usually) blended with others and then roasted, which releases the oils and aromas present and adds others.

Coffea arabica: is indisputably the finest coffee variety. Originally from Ethiopia, or somewhere close anyway, it will grow higher above sea level than other varieties and, like high-grown tea bushes, these slower growing and maturing beans thus have the time to produce greater amounts of integral sugar and a better, more refined flavour. The bean shape is an elongated oval and they are usually quite flat.

Coffea robusta: is native to Zaire but can grow more easily and prolifically over a wider geographical area than arabicas. It is far more disease resistant too. The faster-grown flavour is muddier and less refined than arabicas but when well-produced adds attractive and useful up-front boldness to blends. It also contains up to two and a half times more caffeine than arabicas and, as it is also cheaper, is bound to be the dominant content of cheap bean mixtures. The special appeal of robusta in the past was its suitability to the instant coffee process but, now this has been improved beyond conception, more and more arabica is being used in instants. However not even experts guarantee to tell arabicas from robustas once they are roasted. The green robusta bean is smaller, irregular, convex, and browner than arabicas.

Coffea liberica: is a very bad third rate and can, or should, generally be ignored.

CHOOSING A COFFEE

Knowing your way around coffee is a lifetime study, and much more exciting because of that. Just when you think you know it all, something changes. Some years ago frosts in Brazil destroyed their crops and world prices quadrupled: it seemed dreadful, but actually encouraged drinkers to look further afield and discover new coffee pleasures. The frost effect is unlikely to be repeated for Brazil has now moved much coffee production further north to areas where frost is only what happens on beer glasses.

Now there is world over-production by some 25 per cent, so prices and competition are getting greater which should mean your choice is better. Here are some broad outlines, which you will enjoy filling with your own colours.

AFRICA

West Africa is the home of robusta coffee, East Africa is probably the origin of arabicas and produces some of the finest available in bulk, and most countries produce a quantity of both.

WESTERN COUNTRIES: West African coffee, largely from Angola, Cameroon and Zaire is virtually all robusta, strongly flavoured, reliable croppers but lacking character, subtlety or variety. You are most unlikely to find any sold by name.

EASTERN COUNTRIES: *Ethiopia:* civil war has made these rare for many years but the market is moving again. At up to 2,600m above sea level, the Highlands produce some of the world's highest grown coffees, exceptionally fragrant, almost perfumed and usually described as winey or gamey: at a comparative tasting offered journalists by Douwe Egbert in Utrecht, an Ethiopian Mocha Djimma was almost universally thought the best on offer, and there was sensational competition. Most Ethiopian coffee is unwashed and Harar Longberry is considered very superior, sweet and subtle rather than having the punch and acidity of a Kenyan. Harrods usually stock it. Look also for Limu and Sidamoo.

Kenya: almost universally good quality and the top ones are everything coffee should be. Kenya Peaberry really does offer small beans which have all the flavour and body that would have been packed into two normal beans. High-grown Kenyan coffee has superb natural sweetness and thus can give a really full flavour when only lightly roasted; a medium (after dinner) roast develops extra acidity which balances the accompanying increase in flavour. Kenya has developed a system which will remove over-ripe berries from washed coffee using ultra-violet light.

Tanzania: similar to Kenyan but perhaps a little thinner.

Uganda: outstanding arabicas, with all the quality of Kenyan coffees.

AMERICA

Brazil: this country produces a quarter of the world's 60 million kg of coffee beans each year. It's an awful lot of coffee and a lot of it is awful. Unusually, Brazilian coffee trees have a main crop season from April to June, which means most beans are harvested then and subsequently hang around a while. A top Santos will have wonderful body, elegant acidity and excellent colour and flavour. Even more extraordinary is the rare true Santos Bourbon, an aristocratic traditional variety which few grow any more; I am happy to tell you the entire crop of the major grower comes to a single distributor in Britain.

Colombia: the world's second biggest producer, and the best is truly great coffee. Colombian beans actually produce more liquor per bean than anything from Brazil and have a full sweet flavour that is rarely marred by excess acidity. Unlike Brazil, its trees produce all year and thus continuously send fresh beans to the market. Of all coffees Colombian most deserves to be described as winey, for it fills the mouth with the typical velvety smoothness of a well-matured red wine. It is thus depressing to hear it sometimes described as bland, but that is probably because it is the favourite coffee of the United States. Most Europeans find American coffee pointless or undrinkable. Don't blame the bean. Americans roast coffee much more lightly and brew it much weaker than Europeans, sometimes only a quarter the strength; they have been fooled by the appearance of strength given by the fast and full colour of the high liquor production into using less beans. If American coffee is not so much pointless but plain undrinkable it was probably made in the unspeakable percolator or kept hot for longer than 30 minutes, which is almost as bad. Doing both deserves death.

Colombians you might find and enjoy are Medellins, Excelso, Manizales, Armenicas, Libanos, Bogatoas and Buccaramangos – doesn't the last one even sound great?

Costa Rica: the connoisseur's secret. Well-perfumed, mild and with quite a tangy acidity, rather like aristocratic clarets, delicious full sweetness supported on a firm tannic platform.

Ecuador: thin sharp coffee which thus appears anonymously but usefully in blends.

Guatemala: they have a rather heavy full body and good acidity, but high-grown Guatemalans are essentially mild and mellow with a particularly fragrant bouquet. Look specially for Coban and Antiquas.

Mexico: mellow and mild coffees of excellent quality, but the coffee they drink themselves has often been roasted with a sugar coating that gives a strong caramel flavour at best, but which quickly slips into horrid bitterness.

Hawaii: stretching a geographical point, I know, but worth it. Kona coffee is grown on the volcanic soil of the Kona district of Hawaii, the Big Island. It is sweet and mellow but with a unique extra flavour, best described as nutty. Even if it does not come from that precise district, all Hawaiian coffee is sold as Kona, except in Portugal where that is a fearfully rude word. I suppose it must be in Brazil too, but it's unlikely Brazilians would give you the opportunity to discuss other coffees.

Peru: tangy and with well-bred body.

Venezuela: as elegant and delicious as Colombian coffees but more delicate and lighter and thus too easily misunderstood or dismissed. The most aromatic are the Meridas, described as peculiarly delicate and neither acid nor bitter. Caracas coffees are equally distinctive but lighter and especially popular in France and Spain.

ARABIA

The Yemen is the home of what is thought to be the original Mocha, which can be so full-flavoured it is sometimes said to taste as though mixed with chocolate, often also called a gamey flavour. Most Mocha sold is a blend if you look carefully. It is the proper high-roasted coffee/blend to be pulverized for making Turkish/Greek/Arabic coffee. But beware – Mocha, or any other variety from this part of the world, may include over-ripe beans or stinkers, and then gamey becomes farmyard.

CARIBBEAN

The cost – up to £20/lb – would have you believe Jamaican Blue Mountain is the world's best coffee. It is certainly rich, sweet and mellow but the cost is more properly a market led reflection of the small quantity produced, and proof that the quality-intoxicated Japanese pay almost anything to buy almost all of it each year. Like Mocha, any Blue Mountain coffee you might see at a reasonable price will be a blend and most of us will only guess at its accuracy.

Generally, all Caribbean coffees will have mellow, sweet and mild characteristics. Cuban coffees can be just as good as Jamaican and Haiti produces very top-shelf stuff. The Dominican Republic and Puerto Rico also produce respectable coffees.

INDIA

Mysore is the one you are most likely to meet. It is mellow and quite light but to me can be muddy. It is commonly used in Mocha blends or blended with Mochas.

Monsooned Malabar is recognizable in green form because the beans have turned yellow, if you follow me. When roasted they give a dark chocolate flavour with a bitterness which in this case is attractive. The effect was originally the result of the humidity and time involved in sailing ship deliveries. Now the beans are monsooned by being exposed for several days during monsoon season temperatures.

INDONESIA

Java: rich, heavy and almost spiced, these are amongst the hallowed names of coffee. Old Colonial is the most common name these days for what used to be known as Old Java or Old Government Java, once guaranteed to have had a minimum ten years tropical storage. In fact the slightly musty flavour and dark brown colour was a greater degree of the effects of the slow humid shipping which once created Monsoon Malabar. Any you find are likely be delicious, but younger and paler.

Sumatra: when these are good they are now considered amongst the world's best. Like Javanese coffees they are notably heavy and full in the mouth, but syrupy and flavoury and thus refreshing and stimulating. Madheling and Lingtong are worth pursuing.

The Celebes: Bali and Timor produce pretty good coffee too.

PAPUA NEW GUINEA

Coffee's home is in the Highlands and these wildest ones of all now produce coffee quite as good as Kenya's, from whence came the original stock. A constantly rising star, and a definite talking point at a sticky dinner party, which can acceptably go on to such related subjects as birds of paradise, uncontacted tribes, nose-piercing, penis sheaths and all that. Very useful.

DECAFFEINATED COFFEE

Caffeine, the substance in coffee that gives you the lift, is also found in tea and chocolate. It upsets many a stomach when too strong (Swedish coffee is a real killer in the mornings) and is universally blamed for many sleepless nights. Caffeine is an odourless, slightly bitter alkaline with the following improbable formula: $C_8H_{10}N_4O_2$. The content in coffee can range from just over 0.5 per cent to about 2.8 per cent but the average is usually around 1.2 per cent, which means 0.1g per strong cup of coffee.

There are three basic decaffeinating methods, all applied to the green coffee bean. Liquid carbon dioxide, water, and organic solvent – ethyl-acetate or methylene chloride. Liquid carbon under pressure removes caffeine and then evaporates, leaving no residue. In the water method, the cycle begins when green beans are brewed in water, which is then drawn off: the caffeine is removed from this liquid which is used for the new brew and as it is then saturated with everything but caffeine, will only remove caffeine from the beans. The organic solvents which are specific to caffeine have been criticized of late, but as with most food scares, the facts barely warrant attention. They do indeed leave some trace deposits, about one in a million; when coffee is subsequently brewed the traces are not measurable. You would need to drink oceans before any major effect might remotely be caused, by which time you would be dead through over-hydration.

Each method removes 97-98 per cent of the caffeine and there is a move to produce 'light' coffee with about 50 per cent of the usual caffeine levels.

Any criticism of taste changes detected in decaffeinated coffee is more accurately aimed at the quality of coffee used or the instant coffee process than decaffeinating itself. If caffeine is a real problem, remember robusta beans contain twice as much as arabica and that instant coffees are generally robusta based.

INSTANT COFFEE

The range of instant coffees is fast approaching the complication of fresh coffee and the best instants are better than inferior real ones. This is because improved techniques mean more arabica beans are now used; on the other hand this will mean instant coffees are measurably less stimulating (because arabica beans have less than half the caffeine content of robusta).

First, the coffee must be brewed, usually by a carefully controlled percolating system for maximum extraction, and then the brew is concentrated; it is this prolonged exposure to heat as much as the quality of beans used which result in the difference between instant and fresh coffees.

The original technique then made a powder from the concentrated coffee by spraying that onto a hot drum. The heat involved lost even more of the valuable aromas and oils, so you always knew you weren't drinking the real thing, even though it was 100 per cent coffee. Freeze-drying changed all that. Freshly brewed coffee is frozen then ground and when these are passed through a vacuum tunnel the solid water content is turned to water vapour which is exhausted without first having changed to a liquid. The particles are left dry and containing most of what the original coffee began with.

Instant espresso coffees are an innovation which has been particularly successful and they are very good for cooking, too.

You get the best flavour from instant coffee by using water which is under boiling point, and pouring it from rather an exaggerated height both helps guarantee that and aerates the brew, which also helps.

COFFEE ADDITIVES
The best known additive to coffee is chicory, which is toasted and ground, and added for the sake of its bitterness and for economy. Understandable in times of war or famine, during which extraordinary foods have been used to eke out our coffee, and chicory has always had its adherents and its enemies. Its popularity is slightly on the decline in this country, where it has never had a really large following, but it is still popular in parts of France. What is becoming more popular here is so-called Viennese coffee, which includes ground dried figs. The added flavour is fascinating, but I can't really see the point.

Spices are perhaps the best known additions to coffee – cardamom, clove or cinnamon being the most usual. The first two might be added in a pinch, ground, or as a seed or two put into the coffee pot. A simple way to use cinnamon is to stir the coffee with a cinnamon stick until the desired flavour is reached. Otherwise sprinkle some ground cinnamon on top of whipped cream on each cup.

The mixtures of coffee and liquor are legion and very few alcohols are actually awful with hot coffee. It is certainly the most warming and stimulating drink imaginable when you are very cold or unhappy. But don't do it by half measures in small cups or you will not be able to use a practical amount of alcohol without making the coffee cold. At dinner parties it is no longer fashionable to serve liqueurs in coffee, but if you decide it would complement your meal or your clients, then use cups rather bigger than the demi-tasse or hold back on the alcohol. Far better to enjoy coffee and liqueur from their individual containers. But if you are doing something rugged outdoors, and if you use rougher *eau de vie* like calvados, a mixture is obligatory and practical.

Irish coffee, which originated at Irishman's Wharf, San Francisco, is a good example of an ordinary thing becoming popular when generosity with the liqueurs is possible; is it the only thing Irish about which no one has made a joke?

The newest wheeze is to impregnate coffee beans with such flavourings as amaretto, raspberry, royal mint and almost anything else. They remove the hassle of serving liqueurs at a stroke, and keep everyone sober. But is this anyway to treat the stuff? You may be assured it is not done to high quality beans. Plain or otherwise, coffee beans are now available coated in chocolate, a delicious snack and pretty useful for adding every possible type of stimulant to otherwise benign cakes, puddings and ice creams.

Buying coffee: most coffee we drink is blended, that is coffees from different countries, or of different types from a country, are mixed to obtain this sort of flavour, that sort of mellowness, another type of strength. The variety at the hand of the blender is extraordinary, as varied as the thousands of styles of wines, and within each country and type of bean from that country, there are grades, based on quality of bean.

PERFECT ESPRESSO

For the true caffeine maniac, there is no such thing as a simple espresso. These definitions are from *Esprit d'Espresso*. In spite of the clash of languages in its title, this is an excellent concentrated treatise on the subject by Cornell and Sullivan (Dastro).

Espresso: a demi-tasse of no more than four tablespoons (about 60 or so ml) of coffee produced under pressure from water at a temperature below boiling point. Technically, the temperature should be 93-96°C, the pressure should be 9bar and the dark-roasted, finely ground coffee should be a tightly packed wad of 6-7g per serving: brewing time is 20-25 seconds. Originally, the method was invented by a Frenchman, Louis Rabaut in 1822, but it was the Italians who perfected the technique and sped it up, thus the meaning of espresso. It was only in 1902 that the Italian company Bezzera patented the first successful commercial system. Essentially it works by letting hot water build up a head of steam in a tank: when a valve is opened beneath the water level, the steam pressure forces the water out, and thus through the compacted coffee.

Because the amount of liquid is small, and the coffee grounds have retained much of its heat, espresso should always be made directly into hot cups: even espresso made in pots, as many domestic systems do, should be poured into cups which are at least warm, for many believe the flavour deteriorates if it is poured onto something cool or cold. Even if this is untrue, the coffee quickly cools anyway, another reason for the convention of drinking a single espresso in one gulp. Sipping is cissy.

Arabica coffees are thought most suited to producing the correct honey-like dribble of flavour, but robusta adds a brightness of acidity and some extra effervescence to the essential bubbly froth that a good espresso displays: but add too much robusta and the froth has gone before you can drink. The precise grind is very important, and like cars, both commercial and domestic machines differ one from another, even when produced on the same day, and infinite variations of blend, grind, pressure and compactness of coffee keep espresso nuts out of our hair for hours at a time.

Most blenders would agree that, whatever they wish to achieve, they should blend within the same or similar grades and with some reference to how the coffee bean is to be roasted. This latter point is an important consideration for those who like to blend their own flavour of ready-roasted bean.

The flavour of coffee is achieved by what I call 'the two Bs' – the bean and the

Home espresso coffee makers are the current fashion and frightfully modern many of them look too. Coffee producers tell me that unless you have spent a good £200 you are unlikely to get the pressure required properly to force the steam through the fine grounds and extract the full payload of oils and flavour. Stove top espresso pots can make a decent approximation, but require the same minute adjustments to get it right; some think those made from aluminium risk over-heating the finished coffee.

Promptness of serving is just as important as any other part of the espresso ritual.

Caffe Latte: espresso coffee with (usually) three times its volume of hot steam-heated frothy milk. The correct form is to pour coffee and milk in at the same time from either side of the cup. At breakfast time?

Cappuccino: ideally ⅓ espresso, ⅓ hot steamed milk and ⅓ foamed milk. Italians think of it mainly as a breakfast drink and rarely garnish the top: a sprinkle of cinnamon, grated chocolate or cocoa is thought a Middle European thing, for they prefer it as an accompaniment to snacks and sweet things later in the day.

Con panna: espresso with a little blob of whipped cream.

Doppio: a double espresso, for those who either know their stomach or don't care.

Latte Macchiato: a tumbler of foamed milk, about half full, with a single measure of espresso poured into it, slowly creating a cloud of differing colour and flavour.

Macchiato: espresso marked with not much more than a smear of foamed milk – 'coffee with a dash'.

Mocha: a mug of equal portions of espresso, unsweetened hot chocolate and of frothed milk.

Ristretto: the water flow is halved, giving just two tablespoons of very strong coffee. A 'phlegm cutter' is just one of its less vulgar names. If the coffee used has a large robusta content, the relative caffeine measure is phenomenal.

Romano: an espresso served with a curl of lemon peel or thin slice of lemon.

burn. The less roasting given a bean, the more it must rely on its intrinsic quality, rather than the flavour of caramel. It follows that if a bean is to be very highly roasted it need only be a lesser quality, for the drink will savour of the burn rather than of the bean.

So, just as it is wrong to blend fine beans with those from the other end of the scale before roasting, it is wrong to blend highly roasted beans with lightly roasted beans, even if it does look pretty. It is the equivalent of stretching a fine, vintage claret with some Corsican plonk you brought home in the back of the car. Those who blend dark and lightly roasted coffee will find that good Kenyan or Brazilian blends will usually give the mixture of flavour and bite they wish.

There are other points to consider when buying roasted coffee in the bean. Expensive coffee blends should have a uniform appearance, in colour and size. Blended or unblended, the best quality beans retain a noticeable amount of the silver skin remaining in the seam down the middle of their flat side, and flecks of this can be clearly seen when these are ground: this is also an indication that this is washed coffee. Blends of arabica and robusta beans are generally spotted by the range of size seen, yet should not contain misshapen or broken beans if the price is towards the top of the range, but you would be wise to expect a little more of this if you travel down the price scale. There was once an exceptionally big Brazilian bean from a single estate called the Margogype, which commanded a premium; today this is more likely to be large beans which have been graded out of any sort of coffee, and the term is not a sign of particular origin, quality or flavour although many are indeed of high quality.

The most expensive coffee in your shop should be very even in appearance and lightly roasted. Never pay as much for a dark roast as a medium or light roast unless you have chosen the beans from green yourself and know what you are doing. The smell of a whole roasted coffee bean is mean and tantalizing nasal short-hand for what can be expected. Each bean has been grossly swollen by the gases created. Indeed they should not be put into a sealed container for 24 hours after roasting as there is some seepage of gas which will 'blow' plastic bags and find the weak point of other containers: it is to cope with this phenomenon that some packs have one-way pressure valves in them. Even after resting, each roasted bean is a miniature bomb, with its contents under a pressure of five to seven atmospheres. Only when it is broken or crushed will the full aroma be released and this is how best to make your judgments, at the same time checking that the colour of the roast is even throughout the bean, greatly important.

Once ground, the beans revert to their original volume, so a spoonful of beans may give only half that volume after grinding.

If you can, also smell the container of beans, checking for any hint of rancidity for this is quickly picked up by beans; the higher the roast, the more the problem, as some 'Continental' roasts are finished by polishing the beans with a little butter.

Apart from the sight and smell tests, it is terribly difficult to give advice on coffee based on names alone, for the finest Blue Mountain coffee from Jamaica might look well, but actually be suffering from inadequate or too prolonged storage and only a highly trained nose would be able to tell without actually brewing a cupful. And then, the way you make coffee can destroy the finesse; so can the type of water that comes from your tap, the condition of your milk or cream.

Making coffee: here is where it can all go wrong, and easily. The rules are essentially simple. Scrupulously clean everything. Freshly drawn water which is either only just boiling or just off the boil. And made and drunk when you want it.

The fabulous proliferation of machines which do everything but drink it for you are not the good idea they seem. Get the coffee grind wrong and it will be over or under brewed because the water is flowing through too slowly or too fast: after that it will stew and lose goodness. None of that is necessary when making good coffee is so simple.

Best of all is to make it like tea. Use a medium ground coffee and put one dessertspoon or so per cup into a warmed jug. Pour in water just below boiling point, stir a couple of times and leave for three to five minutes. Strain as you serve. This has the very distinct advantage of letting you taste as you brew. If jug coffee seems too strong or too bitter you have used grounds which are too fine, should change to a lighter roast or higher quality. If it is too light you have under-brewed (possibly because the grounds are too coarse) or should choose a darker roast. The medical view is that something in coffee made this way (not the caffeine) can cause cholesterol to rise, but you need to be drinking more than five big cups a day.

Filter coffee is the next best system, provided you are certain the water is in contact with the grounds for the correct amount of time to extract what you have paid for. It is essential to encourage this by first lightly wetting the coffee and waiting 30 seconds or so for it to swell before pouring in the rest of the water, which should be just under boiling point. Filter coffee should be ground medium fine and if you are unhappy with the results the observations about jug coffee are just as relevant.

Hot milk rather than cold certainly seems to add a silkiness and warm cups keep coffee hotter longer. Raw sugars sound like a good idea for sweetening but their distinct flavour will get in the way of really good coffee, as will honey. If coffee is too bitter for you, drink a higher quality and get what you have paid for – natural sweetness and fragrance.

The continuing mystery for me is why people will wrap their palms around cups of coffee. Is the coffee somehow too heavy? Have they just come in from blizzards and decided actively to encourage chilblains? Or merely been watching too many advertisements? Mugs are worse. Especially in Hampstead.

Iced coffee can be made with leftover brewed coffee, but it should then be served without ice cubes as it is unlikely to be strong enough. Best brew a double strength batch, to make your own essence with lots of instant coffee and a little water, or to use a liquid coffee essence.

You may serve iced black coffee but most people seem to prefer it with some dairy addition or another. Mix with chilled milk, cream or half melted ice cream, in which case be creative, using, say, chocolate ice cream to make a mocha iced coffee... whipped cream would be a welcome topping and so I suppose you might as well add nuts, grated orange zest, crushed coffee beans.

Cooking: strong coffee is used to marinate lamb in Sweden, but is more usually found in sweet dishes, iced desserts and baking. High quality coffee is wasted and so strong instant coffee or liquid coffee essence is used. But if you are flavouring a custard, sorry *crème anglaise*, for a coffee trifle or pudding, a mousse, ice cream or icing, it might be more rewarding to use a coffee-based liqueur, Tia Maria or Kahlua; these are very good melted with chocolate to make mocha flavouring, which echoes the elusive coffee-chocolate savour of such coffee.

Rather more interesting is to use freshly crushed coffee beans. They must be very fresh so they make a real crunch or some diners will be uncomfortable. Scatter them over anything coffee or chocolate flavoured, including cakes and biscuits, hot or cold puddings, ice creams and such. They are very good on sliced mango or peaches, particularly white or rarer red-fleshed ones. Those beans flavoured with everything else under the sun offer broader horizons of affinity and use; use flavoured coffee beans with chocolate coating and there will be no limits to what you might do with them, or what the rewards might be.

Storing: the moment beans are roasted – light, medium or dark – the essential oils released, which give the flavour, begin to evaporate. Once the beans are ground, these evaporate even faster. Those that remain turn rancid. For value for money, coffee should be made from freshly roasted and freshly ground beans and the time between roasting and grinding should be short.

Roasted coffee beans can be stored for up to two weeks if they are kept relatively cool, but after that the loss of flavour will be noticeable. Ground coffee kept in an airtight tin will last no more than a week.

Very dark roasted coffee can oxidize very quickly and so bulk-produced varieties might be coated with vegetable oil, gum arabic or glucose after roasting. This encourages much longer life but adds alien flavours and effects.

There is much discussion about storing coffee in the refrigerator but I don't keep coffee long enough to know if this works to any noticeable degree; it is possibly more important that the coffee grounds are kept closely wrapped in foil. Very finely ground coffee, packed tight, lasts longer than coarsely ground coffee, through which air can pass more easily.

Coffee beans can be frozen but after a month the oils go temperamental. If you really have to store coffee for a long time, buy it in vacuum sealed bags or tins. Many shops now buy their bulk roasted coffee for grinding like this, a great advantage to the customer, especially of the slower moving coffees.

SLIMMER'S TIRAMISU

Tiramisu is the dessert that's sweeping the world and you'll find recipes for it and ready made versions everywhere – so you don't need to hear anything more about it from me.

What I can offer you however is a delicious low calorie version for slimmers which replaces the Mascarpone with creamy rice, but retains the coffee, cocoa and rum for flavour. Present the tiramisu in ramekins. You can use the microwave after the tiramisu is assembled to drive off the alcohol and its calories – but this is optional!

Serves 6-8

50g/2oz short grain pudding rice	600ml/1pt skimmed milk
liquid or powdered sweetener to taste	4 tbsp dark rum or a few drops rum essence
6 thin slices ripe banana per serving	6-8 tsp instant espresso coffee powder
6-8 tsp cocoa powder	

Cook the rice in the milk over a very low heat, stirring occasionally until it is soft and creamy. This can take up to an hour. Let it cool and add the sweetener. Add rum or essence. Place a layer of sliced banana at the bottom of each ramekin. Sprinkle with ½ tsp espresso powder and ½ tsp cocoa. Divide rice between ramekins and top with the same amount of coffee and cocoa. To drive off the alcohol, pop each ramekin into the microwave for 20-30 seconds, according to size. Chill before serving.

TEA

What must we do to make tea as fashionable as coffee? It is infinitely more variable in flavour, much harder to ruin in the making, and so naturally flexible in caffeine content that it is kid's play to match your tea to your mood – an Assam to startle the senses, an Oolong to refresh, a Rose Pouchong to soothe. If only we could be asked which tea we would like, rather than being offered whatever is to hand.

Britain introduced tea drinking to the world, and yet with few exceptions it remains a very difficult country in which to get a decent cup of tea. You would think there are only low-grade blends, chosen for instant colour and quick harsh flavours which must be mollified with milk and sugar to be remotely palatable. How sad, when our better merchants and blenders offer a remarkable range of quality teas, and amongst the nationally known brands there are truly outstanding products at bargain prices – if they are made and served properly.

Tea is a liquor made by steeping in boiling water the dried, top leaf-shoots of a type of camellia. The habit of drinking it began in China, where tea was certainly used as a beverage by the sixth century. By the eighth century it was popular enough to have been taxed; about the same time the Japanese adopted it and began their amazing ritualizing of tea making and drinking.

It was not until the mid-17th century that tea began to be seen in England, first imported via Holland. There wasn't much of it, even though Charles II's Portuguese queen, Catherine, had popularized it in court and aristocratic circles. But by 1689 the East India Company had begun direct importation and in 1721 was given a monopoly in the trade by Parliament. By the mid-18th century tea was so popular it was the principle drink of all classes. It was perhaps the first hot drink the poor had ever had and, as with white bread they were determined to keep up with the nobs, even though 450g/1lb of the very cheapest tea probably cost a third of a man's weekly wage. There was plenty of it, however, because England had the ships to bring it from China. Russia became a tea drinking nation early in the 17th century because their tea could go overland by caravan, which was considered a better way to transport tea than by exposing it to salt air.

The taxes on tea imported into this country were exorbitant and led to an enormous trade in smuggled tea. Anxious for the lost revenue, Prime Minister Pitt compelled the East India Company to import enough tea to supply all needs without raising prices and smuggling ceased. Some would say that the drinking of tea is also what finally ended London's gin era when there were twice as many burials as baptisms.

The suspiciously close liaison between Parliament and the East India Company was an important contributor to the loss of the American Empire. In 1765 Parliament decided to tax the colonies and their imports. When they refused to pay the tax on tea, the colonists quickly generated a smuggling trade from Holland. The East India Company forced Parliament, who acted like a subsidiary company, to give them absolute rights to the tea trade with the American colonies – they were to take tea direct, cutting out the European exporters and the American importers.

Resentment and self-interest erupted and the colonists decided to forgo tea. In December 1773 the first East India Company ships arrived in Boston. On the night of the 16th a group of colonists dressed as Red Indians threw the tea into the water. Tea parties at other ports were quickly organized. Parliament closed Boston's port... and it was war.

Fifty years later the great Indian tea plantations were established, but the huge, growing market of America was not interested.

The tea bush *camellia sinensis* is native to a fan-shaped area that starts in Vietnam and expands westwards to Assam and eastwards into China. It has a fragrant white flower and if not kept plucked would grow into a 40ft tree. In the last 20 years, more and more tea has been grown in East Africa, so much so that these countries are now major exporters. The plant is remarkably free with its affections and, like humans, almost every new bush can be quite different. Like coffee the height above sea level at which tea is grown is a major influence on its body and flavour. Low-grown and 'mid-country' teas grow furiously in the lush, damp and humid foothills, giving large volumes of leaves with plenty of colour and body and straightforward, robust flavour without finesse. High-grown teas produce more slowly in the cooler days and cold nights at 4,000 to 6,000ft; the crop is very much smaller but has greatly superior flavour, fragrance and delicacy – high-grown Darjeelings from such single estates as Castleton have fetched over £60/lb at auction in India. As the flavour of tea is also affected by soil, temperature and weather, like grapes, some way had to be found to control consistency, at least within small areas. Today cloning of specially suitable plants seems to have curbed tea's propensity to individuality.

Only the top two, very new leaves and the emerging leaf bud between them are plucked to make tea, something that has never been successfully mechanized. In some areas the gathering can continue year round, in others there are dormant periods. But there are always better and worse times for picking. The best are called the flushes; the first flush is early in Spring, the second a little later, and the third flush, after summer, gives the autumnal teas. In between is when the standard teas are collected.

There are three types of curing process, each of which gives a distinctive and easily recognizable type of leaf and flavour. The essential processes are first withering, to reduce the moisture content of the leaf, crushing or tearing to release internal juices, fermenting or oxidizing those juices to develop colour and flavour and finally firing, to dry the leaves: as with wine or cheesemaking the slightest difference in technique makes more or less of the particular characteristics given by the soil or climate.

Green tea: the original tea. Most teas that first came to this country would have been this style. Once the leaves are gathered they are withered and dried immediately. This preserves colour and means the tea will have a definite taste of vegetation. Originally this drying or firing was done by hand in very large woks, and some

TEA GRADES

Let's put the world's greatest misconception about tea absolutely right. Broken Orange Pekoe has nothing to do with quality or flavour. It is merely an indication of leaf size and thus a BOP tea can be everything from low-grown undrinkable to high-grown nectar.

Once dried, the leaves are mechanically sorted according to size of leaf and whether they are broken or not. There is generally a premium for the larger sizes, and starting with them, the most common grades are: Orange Pekoe, Broken Orange Pekoe, Broken Pekoe, Fannings, Dust. The last category is absolutely not the sweepings from the floor, as I am sure you have heard, but an old and proper term for the smallest tea leaf particles.

Sometimes these grades will have other prefixes which are an indication of style and thus an FBOP would be a Flowery Broken Orange Pekoe and so TBOP would mean Tippy Broken Orange Pekoe.

Amongst China teas other words you will see are Pouchong, Souchong and Congou which simply mean large leaved teas of one sort or another.

The importance of knowing the size of the tea leaf in your pack is paramount, for this determines how long it should be brewed – the larger the leaf the longer – (see MAKING TEA). Interestingly, a brown leaf of any size generally gives a darker brew than black leaves.

of the highest grades are still finished like this: they are known as pan-fired teas and the process can also shine the leaf giving it a metallic taste (hence Gunpowder). They are graded according to the size and shape of the fired leaf; the highest grades of the rolled leaves (sometimes helped into shape by steaming) are the smallest and called pin head. Country green teas are generally the brightest and freshest tasting green teas.

Green teas have relatively less caffeine and tannin content than semi-fermented or fermented (black) teas and are thus ideal for later in the day and to soothe rather than stimulate; this is also why the Chinese can put tea leaves directly into a covered mug, to which they add water again and again. You could not do that to black teas for the tannin extraction would be unpalatable.

Semi-fermented tea: the most common are Formosa and China Oolongs. After the initial withering, leaves for oolong tea are slightly crushed, and the exposure of the interior juices begins the fermentation or oxidation of the leaf. This chemical change is what develops the character and flavour of the tea, creating tannins and so on, and is accompanied by an obvious change from green to brown. Oolong teas are allowed only to part-ferment, so the leaves are fired whilst still part-green, part-brown. First flush Darjeeling teas are generally made this style too, but retain a fresh greenness which are uniquely their own.

Oolongs and Darjeelings are too good to drink with milk or lemon, but the lesser grades of China Oolong may benefit from a little sugar.

Black Tea: the withered leaf is crushed and fermented fully then it is fired; the Chinese often call this Red tea.

Once, all tea was larged leafed, or orthodox; quality, unblended or green teas will still be like this. Now we also have something called CTC tea. This is a process invented in 1928 which cuts, tears and curls the leaf into smaller pieces, which gives a faster, stronger brew in the cup.

As well, we have tea bags, invented earlier this century by an American who started taking his samples about in silk envelopes. It is theoretically possible to get respectable tea from the modern bags, or it would be if there was not such insistence upon speed. Read on and you will find out why.

CHOOSING YOUR TEA

It is a very broad view but if you start in China and move westwards you have an overview of tea styles and tannin/caffeine content. Chinese green teas are the mildest, next come Oolongs and the black Chinese teas. Now go to Sri Lanka for liquory teas with exceptional fragrance and background body, and up through India until you find Assam, the strongest of all. The exceptions are the fruity Darjeelings of Northern India and the world class teas now coming from Kenya, which are closer to Sri Lanka than anything else. Within the picture there are thousands of variations.

CHINA

The greatest tea gardens are in the east. Fuzhou (Fuchow) in the south east was

OOLONG TEAS

Oolongs are a world unto themselves with their own grading system. Basically they divide into Formosa (from Taiwan/Formosa) and (Mainland) China Oolongs, which are usually from the Fukien province. Formosas are generally much finer and more delicious: the very highest qualities have a distinct fruitiness and a beguiling sweetness, sometimes reminiscent of peaches. China Oolong teas are noticeably coarser with a distinct earthiness, but are just as refreshing, yet a rather expensive one I bought in Hong Kong was thought by a food-wise MP of my acquaintance to smell of fish-paste. I wish he had not said so, for on reflection it was undoubtedly true. The difference in leaf picked in spring and in autumn is greater than with any other type of tea but the early summer teas picked from late May to mid-August are generally thought the tops. Freak conditions producing one-off results and complicated intermediary gradings make these a lifetime study, so it is really worth taking advice – and spending good money.

the great port from which the clippers sailed. Together with Japan and Taiwan she is one of the world's few producers of green teas and Fukien province is the only area producing Oolongs other than Taiwan. Her black teas are divided between north China blacks and south China blacks (sometimes reds); these teas never have the astringency or bite of Indians. The Chinese have a well-organized and carefully observed system of numbered quality standards, and thus if you find a tea you like a lot, try to find its number so you can get it again.

Bohea: an old broad term for China black teas in Britain.

Brick Tea: finely powdered tea leaves compacted under great pressure. Can be green or black and you grate or chip a little into a mug or tea pot. Its only claims are that you can carry it in your pocket and the drink it makes is hot. The Tibetans whisk rancid yak butter into it, which will give you some idea of its appeal.

Ching Wo: a South China Black (or Red Congou), and considered amongst the very best. Gives a reddish liquor, as the type suggests, which is very aristocratic and even the look of the tightly rolled leaves is high class. Like Gunpowder green teas it has the gift of giving its flavour to lesser teas in blends.

Chrysanthemum: the only infusion or tisane commonly encountered in China, made from chrysanthemum petals but rather less acrid than you might expect. Sometimes mixed with Pu-erh tea.

Dragon's Well or Longjing: one of the best branded green teas, fired flat and with a rich green colour and flavour. It should be made only with the top shoot, hand picked with no accompanying leaf, no matter how small. Made near Hangzhou.

English Breakfast Teas: once another name for North China black teas, which are fragrant, full-bodied and naturally sweet when of high quality, and include Keemuns. A few companies still make such blends, but rarely – *(see BLENDS, page 95)*.

Gunpowder: is the best known of the green teas and instantly recognizable because the leaves are always rolled into balls. The smallest and highest grades are known as pinhead. This is the base of mint teas in Morocco, and by itself is especially good after a spicy meal: a sprinkle of it encourages greatness in Ceylon tea particularly and the combination of Gunpowder with China black

Oolongs are always orthodox teas and show rather a large leaf which requires a good long brew – up to seven or eight minutes. In Chiu Chow restaurants, China Oolongs are often brewed by the Gung Fu method, in which small pots are stuffed with the leaves and a quick, very strong brew indeed is made from them; it is usually a type of tea called Iron Goddess of Mercy, served in mercifully small cups for it is bitter and metallic in the extreme.

It is generally only the top few of the eight main categories we see in Britain. They rise from Fine grades to Finest (sometimes called Poppy or Peony Oolongs) to Fancy (Peach Blossom) and Top Fancy – the latter are sold as Silver Tip Oolong. Peach Blossom and Silver Tip Oolongs are the ones with the fruitiest nose and flavour, a wonderful way to finish a special meal whether heavy or light for they manage to assail and astonish the senses whatever has preceded. China Oolongs are graded differently, taste earthier and are much more of an acquired taste: Kwai Flower is one you may enjoy.

was the most common result, when hostesses always mixed tea for guests from the containers in their prized tea caddy.

Chun Mee: a common green tea made from young, medium sized leaves which roll neatly and thinly; because they curve to look like pencilled brows it is known colloquially as eyebrow tea. It is the best grade of a style called Young Hyson, all rather sharper tasting than Gunpowder teas.

Hyson: an old generic name for all green teas in Britain, but actually a style made from bigger leaves than the previous tea and thus rather coarser.

Keemun: from Anhui province and generally thought the best of North China black teas although they were always made as greens until the 1880s. The best have a naturally sweet, mouth-filling flavour which has variously been described as orchidaceous, winey or like chocolate. I think it is all those things. Twinings' Prince of Wales blend is a very fine example of a Keemun based tea, but only available outside Britain whilst we have a living Prince of Wales. Worth travelling for.

Pai Ma Tan: very large leafed green tea which is also very slightly fermented and thus looks like the aftermath of weeding the herbaceous border. A very acquired taste, but some do. This is often sold as white tea, but is not.

Panyong: one of the best known of the South China black teas, traditionally also called Red Leaf teas. These teas from Fukien province are less immediate than Keemuns, more clarets than Burgundies – *(see CHING WO)*.

Pu-erh: this is a warning rather than a description. Pu-erh, from Yunnan, has a challenging earthy flavour that can seem mouldy; indeed it is purposely kept a long time and can be so. Cantonese like it enormously and describe old ones as having a velvety feel on the tongue. It is the most common tea served with dimsum in Hong Kong, but it can be so strongly flavoured I find it nauseating even to have on the table. Ask for Jasmine, Keemun, Oolong or a Coke – anything…

Souchong: like Congou and Pouchong, descriptive of a style of large leaf in China teas.

White tea: rare and expensive, this is a green tea made only from the smallest and newest leaf tip, which is covered with a silvery fur. It is too young to offer any depth of colour or real flavour, but its rarity and cost mean the Chinese imbue it with every kind of medical magic, especially for bronchial disorders. A status symbol rather than a culinary treat, rather like eating raw fish, which if good enough and fresh enough won't taste of fish.

Yunnan: these teas from a western province are generally of a very high grade and often glowing with leaf tips. They have a bold earthiness and to some have overtones of lapsangs: a single leaf of lapsang in a potful or Yunnan will magically enhance this.

INDIA

The country has three main styles, South Indian which are similar to Sri Lankans, North Indian which are amongst the world's strongest, and Darjeeling, also northerly but producing a light and fragrant style found nowhere else in the world.

Assam: the most important tea producing area of India, in the Brahmaputra valley in the north east. Strong, heavy-liquoring, malty teas which cream massively, a daunting phrase which means simply that the tannin extraction is so high the teas go creamy and cloudy as they cool. Assams are generally used in blends as the solid base for all the breakfast blends you have ever drunk, good or bad.

Assams do have excellent flavour if you brew them properly – subsequently dilute with more water if you like, but it's not an Assam if you have merely dunked a bag or brewed for a few seconds. The finest grades show a lot of golden tips and may even contain stalk, a characteristic of the teas produced late in the season. Any tea sold as an Assam will mean it has the character of Assam and will contain Assam teas, but has been extended and tempered by teas from other areas and countries. Constantly improved standards and processing techniques now mean it is also possible to buy unblended teas from this area.

Darjeeling: the only Indian teas which are universally self-drinkers, that is fine enough not to require blending. They grow in the Himalayan foothills of Bengal at up to 6,500ft and have long been the highest priced teas sold in quantity. There are three main seasons, first flush, second and autumnal.

Most first flushes are semi-fermented, but the tea gardens would rather say they are lightly fermented; whatever you call it the leaf has not been fully fermented and shows quite green yet gives a liquor that is darker and richer than you would expect, combining body with a unique astringent, grassy freshness and fragrance. The leaf is not as big as either of the oolongs but will still require up to five minutes to brew perfectly.

Darjeeling tea is specially famous for having a muscatel flavour, but few drunk in Britain have this character, most commonly found in second flush and mid-season.teas (July to September). Virtually all these go to Germany, where they are prepared to pay the premium prices. I have drunk one just once and it was indeed like sipping a bunch of grapes.

Autumnal teas are delicious, floral, syrupy and with a heavier liquoring: unfortunately they lose their character very quickly and must be cared for with great skill. Although self-drinkers, Darjeelings have a famed ability to add to other teas and if you are blending at home this is a good place to begin. I was secretly given a canister of tea said to be HM the Queen's private blend. It was clearly Assam based, strong, rich and immediate, but Darjeelings added a syrupy fragrance and sweetness and it was excellent without milk and sugar or with both. Darjeelings offer tremendous opportunities to taste individual estates: Castleton and Margaret's Hope are famous and expensive.

Nilgiris: this is the best-known of many teas grown in southern India, possibly because it grows at up to 6,000ft and thus is a generally higher quality than, say, teas from the Madras district. It is quite like Ceylon teas and can sometimes taste pleasantly citric.

INDONESIA

Generally found only in blends, but highly thought of in the tea trade, and could throw up some individual stars, in the same way coffee does in this region. Sumatran teas are very similar to Assams, but cheaper, and most find their way to Ost Friesland where they like their tea even darker and stronger than the Irish.

JAPAN

There is much more to tea in Japan than the ritualized tea ceremony, as much about porcelain and frocks as the drink itself. Pan-fired teas have been polished in an iron drum giving a whitish sheen; basket-fired tea is a more careful process and gives better taste.

Ban-cha: the least of teas, the prunings from shaping bushes at the end of the plucking season. Particularly low in caffeine. You use boiling water and drink directly. Ban-cha Hougicha or Hoji-cha includes fragrant stems and has been toasted to turn it brown, giving a coffee-coloured drink which is light in every other way.

Genmai-cha: an extraordinary mixture of green tea with brown and puffed rice, rather like tipping allyour breakfast into a pot, and thus thought very gratifying.

Gyokuro: the best. Specially selected leaves from shade-grown bushes make a naturally sweet and fragrant green tea. Terribly expensive too, £75/kg wholesale in Britain in 1993. It should be brewed for 90 seconds to two minutes with freshly boiled water that has been allowed to cool in a bowl for 90 seconds and is thus 60-65°C.

Matt-cha: powdered Ten-cha for the tea ceremony; the water should be only 60-65°C, you use about 2g per teacup and there's a lot of whisking involved to encourage a froth on top – the longer that lasts the better your chance of remaining in top kimono circles. Modern Japanese without a Tea House in their minuscule apartments also make Matt-cha with hot or cold milk and with iced water. It is an excellent base for unusual sweet and savoury sauces (pheasant is a common victim), sorbets and ice creams. Hiki-cha is a high grade of ceremonial powdered tea.

Sen-cha: basic green tea. Three teaspoons will make enough tea for three people and it should be brewed for 30 seconds with water that is just below boiling.

Ten-cha: a lesser Gyokuro but dried as flat leaves rather than rolled. Usually powdered to make Matt-cha.

KENYA

Now one of the most important of all tea producers. Most of the production is CTC tea for blending and the characteristics are very similar to high-grown Sri Lankan tea – brisk, clean, red-liquoring and very refreshing. Blends of Kenyan tea alone are now sold and are generally very good indeed; the best tea is now so good some of the highland gardens are producing orthodox-leaf self-drinkers. Individual estates worth seeking are Marinyn and Subukia.

SRI LANKA

The country has changed its name but the teas are still commonly called Ceylon teas. Many British judge a good cup of tea by the look of the brew and generally think a thick dark brew a promise of decent tea – until they are presented with a good Sri Lankan or Ceylon tea. For even though the liquor remains clear and brilliant they offer wonderfully brisk and fully flavoured teas with none of the harshness or aggressive punch of Assams. The best pluckings are February and March and then in August and September, but other months produce greater quantities, except January which is disappointing from every aspect. Unusually, some of the coarsest looking leaves produce some of the finest drinking teas.

There are four major growing regions in Sri Lanka and all produce teas which may be drunk unblended.

Kandy: the lowest-grown teas generally used in blends to give recognizable Ceylon character without great finesse. Commonly thought to be a better all-round drink than many mid-level teas.

Uva and Dimbula: these similar mid-level regions give a stronger, bitier liquor which is typically reddish and fragrant. They offer good looking leaves for orthodox teas which make long elegant twists. Single estates with good reputations are Rosita and Kenilworth, but there are dozens worth noting.

Nuwara Eliya: wonderfully fragrant high-grown teas with a light liquor, great sweet fragrance and a clean, refreshing and very long finish. Lover's Leap and Tommagong are highly rated.

BLENDS

Once, most people blended their own, often combining black and green teas; when commerce took over they went to the trouble of blending for the water of individual districts. There are still merchants who will do this, even for individual stores. As with coffee, when you see a country or area name on a tea blend, it is most likely to be indicative of a style rather than origin.

Breakfast blends: usually based on Assam teas to give a kick start to the system. Irish Breakfast is probably the strongest, English Breakfast used to be largely China Blacks and gentler but this is less usual these days.

Caravan: sometimes called Russian Caravan. Usually a blend of orthodox China black teas, imitating the style of tea which went overland to Russia rather than by sea, and which was thus thought less likely to have been affected by tropical heat or salt sea air.

China black: can be almost anything, and as it is fairly easy to get identified tea and blends, I should avoid this catch-all style.

FLAVOURED TEAS

Earl Grey: if this tea flavoured with oil of bergamot (the citrus, not the flower) was once a secret recipe given to an earlier Earl Grey in China, it follows it should be made only with China teas. There is only one company I know which bases theirs on Keemuns and it is so marvellously superior I cannot imagine why everyone does not follow suit. As it is, each company has a different idea of how Earl Grey tea should taste and most are based on black teas from other parts of the world. It is sacreligious ignorance to choose such a perfumed tea and then to add lemon or milk, whatever the label says, but a little sugar will enhance the citric fruitiness. If it is too aggressive for you, Earl Grey may be mixed with other decent black teas; I have heard this mixture called 'staff tea', but that's rather rude, isn't it?

Jasmine: traditionally made in the green tea gardens of eastern China. When jasmine is in bloom it is harvested early each morning and strewn onto great piles of tea leaves, which are turned with pitchforks as they absorb the flowers' oils and scents. Every 24 hours the flowers are sifted out and replaced by more; the number of times depends on the quality of the flowers. The amount of labour involved makes the low cost of these teas remarkable. F9301 is the usual standard sold in the United Kingdom, but if you can find it, FS904 is very much better – it is sometimes known as Chun Feng. Some gardens used to use a much faster steaming process, but this is said to be on the wane. Very good digestive, indeed, and if made strong enough also the basis for sensational ice creams and sorbets – (see COOKING WITH TEA).

Lapsang souchong: large leaf tea which is smoked over a type of pine after firing. It is one of the few teas which is better under-brewed. It may be mixed with plain black teas, and a small percentage in Earl Grey teas tastes rather good when drunk in the open air, where sturdier flavours are appreciated. There are two basic styles, Mainland or China Lapsang and Formosa Souchongs. In direct contrast to Oolongs, it is the China Lapsangs which are of higher quality. The ragged leaf and size of the Formosa Lapsangs absorb so much smoke they would be undrinkable in a sane world: yet it is the latter which are most popular. The best China Lapsangs are found in Germany. Funny old world.

Lichee couchong: flavoured with lichee fruit. Rather less known than jasmine and rose teas and rather more delicate of flavour. A delicious and haunting change.

Rose pouchong or congou: a large leaf China black tea made the same way as jasmine tea and thus imbued with the natural scent and oils of fresh roses. Extraordinarily delicious, soothing and calming. The rose flavour is specially good with the best afternoon tea baking, especially cream scones and strawberry or raspberry jam. The alternate names given merely indicate minor techinical differences in leaf appearance. Available loose or in tea bags, and both must be transferred to an air tight container immediately or the virtue of the rose goes within days. Wonderful in ice creams and sorbets, of course.

Spiced: seen rather more in the United States, but increasingly popular in Britain during winter: some are called Christmas teas. Wonderfully stimulating and warming, but you can easily make your own flavour by adding a cinnamon stick, a clove and lightly bruised cardamom pods to the pot. Fresh or dried orange peel is good too, and so when I am in the United States I stock up on a tea blend with spices and orange which is outstandingly calming and delicious.

Others: but are these teas? And they are not always cheap. A German blender has created La Composition du Ciel, very high-grade Keemun tea with rose petals, orange blossom and natural peach oil which in 1993 was wholesaling for about £15/lb; the importers swear that if a cheaper black tea had been used the combination would have failed, and that thus this definitely is a tea...

All these flavoured teas are very good for making super-strong as a flavouring for sauces, creams, ices, cakes and so on and very much appreciated when made into iced tea the proper, cold-water way.

There are also Fruit teas: see next section.

TISANES

A brew-up of leaves or flowers, often herbal, and generally with some medical properties or claims.

Camomile: a natural tranquillizer, but if you don't like the bitter flavour it adds sparkle to blonde hair as a rinse-conditioner. Related to fever-few which is supposedly an aid in avoiding and treating migraine. Honey is a better sweetener than sugar.

Fruit teas and blends: tannin- and caffeine-free blends of dried fruit pieces, rosehips, hibiscus blossoms and flavouring oils, and thus not really teas. The best I ever made, quite by accident, was made by pouring boiling water over glacé pineapple pieces. There is a tremendous vogue for fruit-flavoured teas and new ones on the market every month – pineapple and coconut, passion-fruit with vanilla, mango, wild strawberry. I know they give a lot of pleasure but honestly feel they should be called something rather than tea.

Hibiscus: not the exotic bloom of the South Pacific but a related mallow flower, much appreciated in Egypt and some Caribbean islands (as roselle) and used as the bright base for many commercial brews and blends of exotic 'natural' things with every possible type of health, wealth and wisdom claim: sort of sweet and roseate and very red. The *mauve* found in Corsican and Provencal markets is a mallow.

Lemon balm/melisse: (but sometimes, *citronelle*, confusingly) also good as a relaxing sleep inducer and calmer of migraines.

Lemon grass/citronelle: used extensively in some parts of the Caribbean and as a way of life in Mauritius. Everything is claimed for it, but none of that matters as much as how delicious and refreshing it is.

Lime blossom/tilleul: the flowers of the linden tree – muscle relaxer and inducer of sweating.

Mate/yerba mate: the leaves of a South American shrub which are dried and roasted and then brewed like tea to produce a caffeine-rich drink that tastes like wet haystacks.

Mint: dried or fresh mint of all kinds makes a very calming and refreshing hot drink and is especially good as a digestive. All Arab mint teas are not the same; in Morocco the pot will always include Gunpowder green tea too, but as you move eastwards towards Egypt this disappears and only fresh mint is used.

Raspberry leaf: is said to aid giving birth.

Rose hip/gratte-cul: an important aid for those who retain water for it is a reliable diuretic.

Rosemary/romarin: reduces summery headaches and is good for the liver. May be fresh or dried and is generally combined with black tea.

Rose petal: immensely calming – when you are in Hong Kong or China buy masses of unsprayed dried pink rose buds and brew them for five or more minutes in covered cups or bowls to retain their fragile scent. Quite the most sensuous way to finish a meal imaginable. In public, anyway.

Verbena/verveine: a slightly citric digestive and nerve soother. Often macerated in eau-de-vie as a digestive with kick.

Making Tea: you draw it, mash it, stand it or brew it. In Australasia you might boil it in a billy can over an open fire, and you certainly boil it in Turkey and such places. But, apart from *not* boiling it, European tea making is simple:

■ Boil water that is as freshly drawn as possible. It must never be taken from the hot water supply, especially if that is from a tank for it will have lost much of its edge. As we rarely have teas blended for individual water supplies, it is well worth exploring filter jugs or systems, which are specially good for removing the hideous scum on pots and cups which over-loaded hard waters will leave.

■ Shortly before the water boils, pour some into a tea pot, let it warm thoroughly, pour it out.

■ Add the tea, using rather less than one teaspoon per person and forget the one for the pot, a marketing ploy if ever I heard one.

■ Take the pot to the kettle – never the other way around – and pour the boiling water into the pot.

■ Let the tea infuse. Most people do not leave tea long enough, confusing colour with strength. Orthodox leaves require five to seven minutes to develop flavour and colour, and the CTC blends need at least two or three. Naturally this gives stronger colour and flavour than when you only brew for one minute, so you need less tea and get a finer flavour. That is real economy and true value for money, and that includes tea bags, which are rarely allowed to give of their best.

The colour that comes quickly from most modern teas, and especially from tea bags, is from teas called Bright Colouring Africans, included simply because they colour water so quickly. To dip tea bags in and out of hot water a few times is to retrieve only a small percentage of the flavour and colour that is inside. One tea bag will make two or three delicious flavourful cups of tea if allowed to brew for two or three minutes – either do it in a tea pot, or brew in one cup or mug, divide the brew between the others, then top up with more water. When I gave this advice on BBC TV's Pebble Mill at One, a woman wrote to say I had all but saved her marriage as until she allowed tea bags to brew, she was constantly insulted by her husband about her tea.

■ Almost the most important thing to do is to take the brewed tea off the leaves. It was once common to make tea in two pots, one for the brewing and one for the drinking but if you cannot do this you should consider changing to tea bags, which can be fished out as soon as done. A rather worse way to treat tea is the tea cosy. Tea brews best in cooling water: if you pop on a cosy the higher temperature will extract bitter tannins at the expense of the more delicate flavourings. If that is the flavour you like, go for Assams, and only use a tea cosy after the tea leaves or tea bags have been taken from the brew.

I can't stand milk in tea, but I know it can divide man from man. The Royal Geographical Society abounds with tales of expeditions which found themselves noting who was MBT and who TBM – milk before tea or tea before milk – and socializing accordingly. Scientifically, tea added to milk distributes the fat globules of the milk more efficiently, giving a richer, milkier flavour.

Sugar is unnecessary with fine teas but essential with most of the wicked blends sold in this country. Russians drink tea with strawberry or raspberry jam, Tibetans mix theirs with rancid yaks' butter, and the people who work on Indian plantations mix their tea with sweetened condensed milk; the latter have an excuse, for much of the tea grown in India is far too assertive to be drunk unless blended, and these people are probably drinking unblended tea. Lemon may be used in strong Indian or Ceylon teas,

TEA SMOKING

The most extraordinary use of tea leaves is to smoke food in a wok. You need only basic tea leaves, nothing scented or special, some sugar and rice or barley. Because the food is sealed in the wok, this is a 'hot' smoking process, which can cook as well as smoke. Thus you can use it to add smoke to food which is already cooked, anything from duck, the usual Chinese target, to chicken, sausages or shelled hard-boiled eggs. You can cook and smoke at the same time, and fish is the best possible choice, particularly the oily ones, mackerel, salmon and so on. Large ducks or lamb joints may be smoked for ten minutes before roasting.

Mix together 125g/4oz rice, barley, wheat or rye grains and 50g/2oz black tea leaves. Line a wok and its cover with aluminium foil, and put the smoking mixture in the base. Add a rack, and put onto that the food, leaving plenty of space for the smoke to circulate. Jam on the lid, and seal with wet tea towels. The smoke smells delicious but is incredibly permeating and will make everything smell for days if it escapes. Some would add 50g/2oz of sugar to the mixture, but this only makes a more acrid smoke more quickly. I no longer bother.

Put over maximum heat for ten minutes, for large amounts of food then reduce the heat and continue smoking for up to five minutes; for small and thin foods, remove from the heat. Leave at least ten minutes before removing the lid. The seal keeps food warm and very moist for ages, up to an hour. The only thing you might do wrong is over-smoking at first, but you soon learn and it is one of the most impressive of techniques for entertaining. I have been doing it since 1980 and it has never palled.

but it is thoughtless to use it in China or scented teas, as they should be enjoyed simply for what they are.

Cooking: tea is exceptionally fragile when heated in cooking and so the ploy of soaking dried fruit in cold tea is quite pointless; water will do as well but doesn't sound as good. I expect the habit began when tea was very expensive and none could be thrown away. If you really want tea flavour in fruit loaves or other baking the brew must be really strong, at least 25g/1oz of tea leaves or tea bags to 600ml/1pt of boiling water, milk or orange juice. Such strong fruit juice teas may be highly sweetened and used as a hot or cold sauce for ice creams and puddings.

Storing: natural black, Oolong and green teas have quite a long life if protected

TEA SORBET

Wonderfully refreshing, tea sorbets can be made with dozens of different flavours, although they will all be the same colour. Rose Pouchong, Earl Grey and jasmine tea make the most elegant versions; you can also experiment with a mixture of half tea and half fruit juice – Ceylon tea and pineapple juice, for instance. Choose a quality tea with large leaves if you make it without extra flavouring. If you add fruit juice, a lesser quality tea with smaller leaves can be used. Tea sorbets seem especially suited for serving with tropical fruits.

Serves 4-6
60g/2oz tea leaves or tea bags, dry weight
600ml/1pt boiling water or fruit juice
150g/5oz white sugar (optional)
lemon juice (optional)
1 or 2 egg whites

Pour the boiling water onto the tea leaves and brew, 7 minutes for large whole leaves and 5 minutes for medium leaves. Quality tea bags are suitable and need only brew for a few minutes. Do not over-brew or too much tannin will be released.

Strain the tea through a coffee filter paper if using leaves and make the liquid up to the original 600ml/1pt with more water or juice. Add most of the sugar but finish sweetening when the liquid is cool (it will taste less sweet when it is cold and much less sweet when it is frozen). Only add the lemon juice if the tea you are using is an ordinary blend; it is sinful to put lemon into perfumed teas such as Earl Grey, rose or jasmine.

Freeze in a covered container until mushy, beat back to a consistent texture quickly and fold in 1-2 beaten egg whites. Return to the tray and freeze without further interference.

For ice creams, make the tea with boiling milk, brew it very well, strain through muslin and then make up to the original quantity of liquid again. Tea-flavoured ice cream is especially wonderful when you use jasmine or Rose Pouchong.

from too much heat and light – they do not contain oils which will oxidize, the way coffee does. But the oils and fragrances of flavoured teas are fairly fugitive and so it is always best to keep these and any tisanes in air-tight containers in a cool place. This also means a container not very much bigger than the tea or tea bags themselves. I try never to let them become less than half full, then add a new pack and shake it all about, whether tea bags or leaf tea.

WATER

The profit to be made on bottled waters is greater than almost anything else you put into your mouth, but little of that profit will be to your account. Indeed, it can be quite the reverse. It depends on knowing the difference between mineral waters and spring waters.

Mineral waters have been commercial products a long time, but as medicines. Very few of us read labels, but if we did we'd find this mineral water was touted as good for that, that for this, and if you believe them, for most ailments and then some. Before we knew that much about medicine they were usually considered efficacious in direct proportion to the filthiness of their taste. Even when this improved they were useful for assuaging thirst in foreign countries when nothing else was available, but too much of a mineral water with a high salt content would make any problems of dehydration rather worse. And not long ago it was found that the majority of bottled mineral waters in a major Mediterranean country had higher levels of dangerous contamination than most tap waters one was paying to avoid. A few had other practical uses: Vichy water for example is so high in salt you can use it to cook vegetables, carrots in particular.

Spring waters make no claim to health other than being pure and safe to drink. Modern confusion and fantasy about what comes from our very own taps, let alone those of foreign countries, have led to a dramatic explosion in the sale of such water and no American now seems able to leave home without a plastic bottle of water to suck on.

Don't imagine that these waters are all bottled just as they come from the well, wherever they do. They will have been tested, filtered, and probably had their gas level changed up or down: they may be naturally gaseous but few come to the surface with anything near the bubbling force you find in a bottle and will have been force-fed with more, albeit of the same kind and, even, from the same source.

For general drinking and especially for making tea and coffee, an effective domestic filter jug is a much better and cheaper plan, if only because they help keep kettles unfurred and stop that hideous scum on cups of tea and coffee. I can't wait for a restaurant to offer me filtered tap water instead of overpriced bottled water, if only to see how much they dare charge. Sparkling waters have little more to offer than an excess of carbon dioxide, so you can make your own version of these, too. We used to call it soda water, didn't we?

Like wines, teas and coffees, all bottled waters, including so-called pure spring and mountain waters, have distinct flavours which are only noticeable if you are invited to a comparative tasting. It is remarkable in these situations how often the most attractively packed or massively marketed never come anywhere near the top of the preference leagues, indeed they are often far from it. And whilst we drink water from bottles from far away places so we remain healthy and natural and all that, might it not be worth sparing a thought for what it is doing to natural water tables and local resources? Already a rather famous French brand has had to stop exporting as the source is drying up.

M ilk must be the world's most important food, even though it is still largely ignored in China and miscellaneous easterly places. It is fashionably railed against as being the source of much cholesterol-related disease but I think the benefits it can bestow generally outweigh the disadvantages.

The modern reliance on products made from milk, or containing milk derivatives, is extraordinary and it makes it difficult to imagine that the entire American continent and all the great South Pacific had no knowledge of milk as a human food before the arrival of the European. It is even more astonishing to remember that for all its health-giving potential, milk was until a century ago one of the most dangerous of all foods, contaminated with tuberculosis, adulterated with water and worse, dirty through lack of hygiene and a dearth of sealed containers – and usually sour. And that was just the stuff in the country. The few people trying to improve soured milk and rancid cheese used such things as borax and formaldehyde. The herds and their maids were respectively dirty and slatternly, equally contributing to one another's painful demise. Yet it is these same maids who are so romantically sung and portrayed. The reason is quite simply a continuous publicity stunt of the first degree. The job had to be made to appear to be romantic, for no girl in her right senses would otherwise choose such back-breaking work at such unsociable hours. When Marie-Antoinette toiled for minutes at a time in the rustic dairy farm she had built in the purlieus of Versailles, it was merely *pour encourager les autres*. The French queen had real dairymaids to do the real work. Perhaps it was the dairymaids' requisite brawniness that gained them such universal admiration; but the flush of their cheeks was more likely to be tubercular than virginal. Milkmaids needed to be as strong as a bull (the more personal domestic duties of which she might also have had to supervise) and needed a stomach quite as strong as the forearms which heaved pails of milk and wheels of cheese.

I've never been able to drink fresh cow's milk and at times in my life have been forbidden all kinds of products even remotely associated with it, including tranquillizers, which like most drugs are sweetened with milk sugar, lactose. I often found it simpler to stick to a Jewish pareve (milk-free) diet and wish I had had the nerve to present my charge card at Selfridges Kosher Counter. Yet I look with pride at today's huge milk-fed children (have you been to Japan recently?) for it was an ancestor that prodded the whole operation into being, by first applying scientific methods to raise cattle exclusively for dairying.

John Christian of Cumberland was first cousin to Fletcher Christian of *Bounty* and head of the family. After his first wife died he married Isabella Curwen, last representative of one of England's ten oldest families. By combining the names, estates and fortunes of the Christians and Curwens with his extraordinary gift for advanced agricultural thinking, John Christian Curwen made himself into a one-man vanguard of experiment both on the farm and in mines. His achievements are many and include organizing the first agricultural shows. Early in the 19th century he noted that the Cumberland town of Kendal had more milk carts and fewer child deaths than other parts of England. Deciding this was evidence that milk was vital for health and growth, he consulted the few other people who had come to the same conclusions (notably in Scotland) and then set out to do something about it. By 1813 he had eschewed the traditional longhorn for shorthorn cattle and was getting an average daily milking yield of 11½lt/10 quarts per animal.

He achieved these unheard of results by unheard of methods: he actually planted grasses and clovers in his fields instead of letting nature take its course; he stall-fed the animals and made much use of oil cake, and thus established the country's first true dairying herd. And what did he do with these vast quantities of milk? He distributed them free to the poor of Workington, much to the amusement and derision of other landowners; it was the world's first organized free milk service and later John Christian Curwen introduced legislation into Westminster that is now acknowledged to be the first step anywhere in the world towards the Welfare State. This remarkable man and his achievements are almost unknown, perhaps because he refused a peerage twice.

It wasn't until the 1860s and 1870s that anyone else began seriously to establish specialized milking herds. Not only did they get on to a profitable band wagon, they also utilized the wagons of the new railway system, which allowed transportation of country milk to the towns for the first time. By 1900 the Great Western Railway alone carried 25 million gallons in one year, the produce of 50,000 cows. Remember, the unpasteurized, unchilled milk of the time would have soured and curdled terribly quickly as it was carted over the rutted roads of the time. Indeed, rail-transported milk still did as often as not, so country milk was not much better than that from the horrible town herds, which were tethered or wandered wherever there was room, and milked and fed and calved there, too. In 1865 and '66 there were widespread epidemics of cattle plague which decimated the town herds to a state from which they never recovered.

Cooling and refrigeration were gradually introduced through the 1880s and 1890s. About the same time the first milk purity laws were passed and by 1900, with the invention of milking machines and the establishment of wholesale dairies, there was a distinct improvement in hygiene and a decline in milk-linked disease. But milk was still transported and sold in bulk, often by horse-drawn cart and did not begin to be pre-packed until the 1920s. Even at the end of the 1940s I remember running barefoot in the morning down the garden to collect the billycan from under the letterbox after it had been filled by our milkman – this was in Auckland.

In 1923, Britain officially recognized the benefit of pasteurization – the process in which milk is heated to 71°C for 15 seconds and then cooled quickly. Since then the strictest safeguards have been rigidly enforced to protect us from contaminated milk or diseased animals and our average consumption of 137½lt/242pts per annum is four times what it was a century ago.

MILK

The vitamins and minerals and proteins and so on of milk, and its abilities as a cure-all, are far too complicated for this book. In any case the structure changes according to the animal and its food, as well as the time of the year. It's more important to know how and when to use milk. For instance, hot boiled milk takes far longer to digest than cold milk, as all milk clots very quickly when it hits the stomach and hot milk clots even faster into an even harder curd and this can put a strain on a delicate stomach. Hot milk should be drunk as slowly as possible to allow the stomach to cope with it properly. Whole milk and skimmed milk take exactly the same time to digest and the soured or fermented milks, including yoghurt, take the least time of all.

There is direct medical evidence to support the belief that warm milk helps you sleep. Apparently milk's calcium has a slight hypnotic effect on nerves, genuinely aiding a temporary relaxation of the body; anything else containing available calcium would be as effective. A word of advice to the elderly: a diet heavily balanced in favour of milk, acceptable to infants, who are thoughtfully born with a special store of iron, can lead to anaemia or at least an iron deficiency in the adult.

I once went to a lecture on food hygiene in a catering establishment and the bacteriologist speaking said that with all his knowledge of the horrors of food poisoning there was only one thing he would categorically not do, and that was to drink unpasteurized milk. He said that many disease-free attested herds in this country still manage to include animals with notifiable disease, including, in his opinion, tuberculosis. If you are in the position of only having raw milk to drink, you should boil it, or failing that, leave it to ripen until it has a definite sourness; the gradual increase of lactic acid in souring milk acts as a germicide of sorts and makes it marginally safer. If undisturbed the acid-producing ripening process continues until the lactic acid level solidifies the milk protein, making sour curds. Although goats and sheep are tuberculosis-free, they can have other nasty diseases, but less commonly, so their unpasteurized milk is generally safer.

Fresh cows' milk

The widespread introduction of the tetra-pack for milk in the United Kingdom has made it easier to know what sort of milk you are drinking – you can read the words rather than have to translate the colour coded foil tops. In the past few years the styles of milk available have dramatically increased, largely as a result of the push towards reducing fat in the diet. Skimmed and semi-skimmed milks are very much the fashion, and thus likely to become unfashionable given time. And now, just in case you still need to translate foil tops:

Pasteurized milk: the basic silver-top milk. Made with milk other than that of Jersey, Guernsey or South Devon cows, so is white rather than creamy, and has only thin cream on top.

Channel Islands and South Devon milk: the gold-top milk, made only from Jersey, Guernsey and South Devon cows (who may of course live anywhere in the British Isles). It is a richer colour because of a higher carotene content and has more, thicker cream on top.

Untreated milk: is raw milk and hard to find but will have a green foil top if from most cows or a striped green and gold top if it is unpasteurized gold-top milk.

Homogenized milk: this is red-top milk. By forcing full milk through a tiny valve under pressure the fat (cream) globules are reduced in size and then do not separate from the milk and rise to the top. This results in a milk with a richer, creamier texture and taste, which is also more easily digested as it forms a much softer curd during digestion. Homogenized milk is not often suitable for making cheese.

Sterilized milk: usually sold in what look like French wine bottles and capped like beer. This was the first type of preserved milk marketed, about the turn of the century, and tasted pretty rotten I understand. Homogenization changed that. Sterilization destroys bacteria and other micro-organisms more completely than pasteurization. Generally the milk is heated, homogenized, bottled and hermetically sealed. Then they are heated to about 110°C for 30-40 minutes. This high temperature causes slight caramelization of the milk sugar giving a definite 'cooked' flavour. It will last for two or three months without refrigeration as long as the container is unopened. Personally I wouldn't bother, now that we have......

UHT or Long-Life milk: this milk is heated to 132°C for one second then packed under sterile conditions into aluminium foil-lined containers. It lasts unopened for months (it's usually date-stamped) but is just like ordinary milk once opened. The advantage is that its flavour is exactly the same as pasteurized homogenized milk; those who say they don't like it are usually comparing it to ordinary silver-top milk, from which it is certainly different. It is apparently quite the best of all for making yoghurt.

... and in other countries: in America plain milk is as difficult to find as sweet cream is in France. There is enormous emphasis on low-fat (partly-skimmed) milk and milks which are also fortified in some way, and although good to drink can do strange things to cooking. Flavoured milks are very popular and easy to buy, and fermented kefir comes in an extraordinary range of natural flavours.

In Australasia, milk drinking is as much a religion as Vegemite and rugby. Milk bars, which are sort of like dairies here, but more like echoes of the soda shops of the United States in the 30s, 40s and 50s, still make fabulous milk shakes containing real ice cream – the flavour range is exceptional – and often use real fruit bases. The well known Sanitarium shops, which are terribly old and well established health food shops, also sell lots of healthy drinks and have a special meal-in-a-glass which includes milk, ice cream, wheat germ, lecithin and other goodies. Ice cream sundaes are still made and in many dairies you can have a take-away fruit salad of tropical fruits put into a carton and topped with cream and ice cream – a fabulous lunch to enjoy in Sydney's Hyde Park on a hot day; there's more than enough flesh about, both rare and roasted, to balance its fruitarianism!

Much of Australia's milk is now low fat, thanks to a long term nationwide campaign to reduce heart disease. Brands like Shape and LiteWhite are household staples and more recently a mixture of milk and canola oil ironically called Farmer's Best, has been popular. The idea was to replace the saturated fat in milk with the mono-unsaturated fat of canola oil (which is lighter than that of the olive). The taste and mouthfeel have a definite hint of oiliness, but backed by the persuasive powers of national hero and former tennis champion John Newcombe, its success was almost guaranteed.

Soured, cultured and fermented milks

The fact that a high acid content makes milk safer is behind the popularity of so-called fermented milk drinks which are also easier to digest. Interestingly, they are found in both cold and hot countries – whereas I thought only the latter had need of preservative methods. Fermented milk drinks are made with the addition of a specialized culture of lactic-acid-producing bacillus; they give the milk a pleasant tang and thicken it slightly but do not let the process continue to form a curd unless left a very long time. In general these products are less sour than yoghurt and although usually used as a drink, have their uses as bases for summer soups and in cooking.

In Sweden you can buy all types of fermented milk and throughout the Middle East, including Israel, they are very popular, as they are in Middle Europe and the Balkans – indeed the only such product available in Britain is smetana, which is of Balkan origin. You can get something similar by adding water and sugar to plain yoghurt, another common Eastern practice. Other fermented milk drinks include leben and kumiss.

Buttermilk: is possibly the best milk-derived but non-fermented drink and is what is left after you churn cream (milk fat) to make butter. If made from unripened cream it is quite sweet; ripened cream gives buttermilk with a slight sourness.

Cultured buttermilk: has a bacterial culture added to it, a culture of bacteria similar to those that naturally curdle milk to make cheese but which are killed by pasteurization. Thus, cultured buttermilk ripens and thickens slightly, becoming slightly acidic as the lactose (milk sugar) is turned into lactic acid. If you want to use buttermilk in a cooking recipe it must either be cultured or made from unpasteurized ripened cream or it will not have the acidity necessary to interact with baking soda and so form a leavening gas. If you use sweet buttermilk in cooking you have to exchange the baking soda for twice as much baking powder or add a squirt of lemon juice.

Most buttermilk here and in the United States is made from skimmed milk, so is not buttermilk but fermented skimmed milk; the real stuff is often sold as 'churned' buttermilk.

Soured pasteurized milk: is not safer from germs than soured raw milk. Quite the reverse. All manner of bacteria can make milk sour and thicken and most of those that settle and grow in pasteurized milk are downright dangerous. You should dissuade friends and children from drinking soured pasteurized milk.

Condensed and evaporated milk

Invented for the easy transportation and storage of milk's goodness, all of these products have inbuilt problems of nutrition. But today's better methods of milk preservation have led to less dependence on condensed milks, especially in the poorer countries and they cause very few dietary problems now.

Condensed milk: diluted according to directions is easier to digest than ordinary milk but its basic imbalance in favour of sugar and against fat is inherently bad and it should never be used in the diet for extensive periods. Nevertheless, a couple of generations of the inhabitants of hot countries are hooked, and every beverage, including tea, is served with condensed milk, a habit I recently noticed sweet-toothed Englishmen quickly adopting in Bangkok. Usually the milk has been reduced by two thirds.

Evaporated milk: a term usually used for unsweetened condensed full milk whereas condensed milk usually indicates sweetened full milk or sweetened skimmed milk.

Milk powders

Milk powder is quite simply milk with most of its water content evaporated to produce solids with a moisture content of five per cent or less. It can be fine powder or freeze dried in granules and is made in quite a lot of different degrees of fat content, from full milk down to skimmed milk; all except the latter are homogenized before treatment.

There are two main ways of preparing this invaluable powder. The first spreads milk thinly on hot revolving rollers. The water evaporates leaving a film of solids which is then scraped off. This gives a powder which does not reconstitute readily and usually gives very lumpy results when mixed with water. The alternative method pumps milk as a fine spray into a chamber of hot air. As the water quickly evaporates the powder falls to the floor. This reconstitutes very easily and may therefore be considered preferable.

Wholemilk powder contains all the nutrients of milk except vitamin C, thiamin and B_{12}, which are affected by the heat of the process. Skimmed milk powder contains almost no fat and the other varieties of powder vary according to their original constituents. Provided the storage temperature is moderate-to-cool, milk powders keep a very long time. Those containing fat are liable to rancidity on exposure to air. There is also available a range of dried milk powders that include non-dairy or vegetable fats, the advantage of which as far as I can tell is purely that of price. This mixture or total use of non-dairy fat is what gives us the 'whitener', a milk or cream substitute sprinkled into hot drinks in place of the real thing. Palm oil is the usual source of such fat, although manufacturers are not required to state the exact fat used.

Storing: heat and light are the two worst enemies of milk, both of which destroy or affect flavour and vitamin content. So you must take it inside as early as you can and keep it cool and dark. If you don't have a refrigerator, keep it in a draught – the floor is always cooler than a table top. Cupboards should only be used if they are well ventilated.

The old fashioned method of keeping milk cool works very well: you put the bottle or jug in a basin half filled with cold water and cover it with butter muslin saturated in cold water. You can also leave milk wrapped in a wet towel in a relatively warm place and it will become quite chilled – an interesting point to remember when on picnics.

Everything that comes into contact with milk should always be rinsed in cold water before going into hot; this avoids the formation of a film which is almost impossible to remove.

Pasteurized milk should keep in a refrigerator an average of six days.

Commercially-frozen milk is pasteurized and homogenized and frozen extremely quickly by using a special brine solution. Domestically frozen milk can be problematical – it is better to freeze only cartons of homogenized milk.

CREAM

Cream is the lighter, fatty portion of full milk and contains all the major components of milk but in a different balance. It is largely water but also contains most of the butterfat; in single cream this is up to 20 per cent of the volume but in double cream it is about 48 per cent and is then the biggest component.

Cream may be separated from milk in two ways. You can let full milk rest for 12-24 hours during which time the cream will float to the top, and is then skimmed off by hand. But you always include some of the milk and the composition of your cream is thus constantly varying. Mechanical separators first heat the full milk and then pipe it to a stainless steel bowl, fitted with conical plates, which revolves at about 6,000rpm. The heavier milk is thrown to the outer edges of the bowl whilst the cream flows towards the centre and each is collected through different outlet pipes. The skim milk is usually then heat-treated to clear it of bacteria and used for making milk products or for feeding to animals.

Different types of cream are obtained not by subsequent dilution, as I once thought, but by different degrees of separation, so that single cream for instance has more of the original milk in it and double cream has less. To make single cream from double cream or to make double cream go further when you are whipping it, dilute with full or skimmed milk.

Most cream for sale is pasteurized to improve its keeping quality without affecting its flavour. You can buy untreated cream from accredited herds quite readily and if it is from Jersey cows it is altogether thicker, richer, yellower and tastier, and has a slight extra acidity which makes it a particularly good accompaniment to soft fruits. And chocolate cake.

It is not true, as I have seen put about in the United States, that French cream has more lactic acid in it – it has been allowed to *develop* lactic acid, as any cream would do. To get fresh sweet cream you must ask for *crème fleurette* and if you get it you'll be lucky. In America, cream is pretty much the same as here but with different names: our double is called heavy, our single is their light and coffee cream is Half and Half. *But* our whipping cream is not theirs. American whipping cream usually has the lowest possible fat content to comply with its definition – about 30 per cent – and gets its texture from added vegetable fats and oils that behave in the same way as cream. You can also buy it in aerosol packs.

Crème fraiche: peculiarly French, but actually only a cultured soured cream. Because the cream might have 40 per cent fat content or more, almost that of double cream, it will be altogether richer, sweeter and creamier than sour soured creams based on single cream. The gorgeously ivory-cream coloured *crème fraiche d'Isigny* from France actually has an Appellation d'Origine Contrôlée and is rather like eating smooth clotted cream with a touch of acidity. That slight bite is very similar to the flavour of unpasteurized cream which has been allowed to age a little and is thus a much more traditional flavour to enjoy with strawberries than ordinary whipped or clotted cream. Crème fraiche is particularly good for finishing or making savoury sauces but can be used anywhere you would a clotted cream.

Double cream: this has the blue-and-silver top and has a minimum butterfat content of 48 per cent. It does everything, and can be diluted with milk to extend it. Reduced to half its volume by gentle simmering and then flavoured with herbs or a vegetable purée, double cream gives the simplest rich sauce of all.

Extra-thick cream: double cream which has been homogenized in the same way as many *fromage blancs*, so that it spoons from the carton as thickly as whipped cream.

Whipping cream: with its green top is now more readily available since the price of milk and its derivatives began to climb. It has a minimum butterfat content of 35 per cent, which is the ideal for getting maximum whipped cream from your liquid cream. Because you have to whip it longer than double cream you incorporate more air, giving more ultimate bulk. Perhaps this is of interest to caterers, but I prefer the taste and texture of whipped double cream to such mouthfuls of air.

Single cream: this must have 18 per cent butterfat and is used as a pouring cream. It can be whipped if you incorporate egg white into it. It has the red foil label and is always homogenized to prevent separation of the cream and milk.

Half cream: not widely available, this has a butterfat content of no less than 12 per cent. It's what is usually called coffee cream in Europe and Half and Half in America. Really a sort of super-rich homogenized milk, it is perhaps too rich for day-to-day drinking but excellent for cooking, for the higher fat content would help cakes and biscuits to keep longer.

Clotted cream: this is the richest and most heavenly cream of all and still mainly produced in Devon and Cornwall. It has a minimum fat content of 55 per cent and is traditionally made by putting full milk in shallow pans which are left until the cream has risen. Then you slowly heat this to a temperature of 82°C and allow it to cool overnight. In the morning the coagulated, lumpy cream can simply be skimmed off. Commercially, the same effect is obtained by scalding separated cream in shallow pans and then transferring it into tins or bottles. I don't think it tastes as good, but this may be because it is subsequently sterilized.

A continuous controversy rages over the proper use of clotted cream in a traditional cream tea. Do you put your cream onto the scone and then add jam or do you do it the other way round? Those who argue for the former say that as the cream is replacing butter it must go on first; but then you can't spread jam over the cream and so you miss out the combination of flavours for most mouthfuls. Those who spread the jam first and then dollop on the cream are assured of the best possible tastes with every mouthful and that's the way I prefer it, perhaps because that way you can have butter on the scone as well.

Frozen cream: one of the best new products available. Double cream is frozen in single portions and sold in free-flow packs, so you never need go without cream or have to throw away any which has gone off. Thoroughly recommended.

Sterilized cream: made exactly the same way as sterilized milk but packed in smaller containers. It usually has a butterfat content of about 23 per cent (between single and whipping cream) but can also be made from half cream (12 per cent). It is homogenized and the treatment gives it a unique flavour that does not compensate for its ability to keep virtually indefinitely until opened.

Bottled cream/long-keeping cream: this is now tending to disappear from the shops but a lot of old people like it for nostalgic reasons. It fits neatly in all respects between pasteurized cream and sterilized cream, both in keeping ability and flavour, and this applies to single, double or clotted cream, all of which are treated this way.

UHT or long life cream: treated exactly the same way as UHT milk to give a very long life with no refrigeration. It should mean that the individual portions of liquid used in trains, hotels and planes for your tea or coffee *are* milk or cream, for there is no wastage problem with UHT treated items. But if you look carefully, those little pyramids of liquid are nearly all totally artificial.

Soured cream: note the name – it is *soured* not *sour*. This is single cream which has had a culture of bacteria added to it after homogenization and pasteurization. The culture forms acid as a by-product, giving the subsequent thickening and acidic flavour. It keeps very well under refrigeration and is perfectly indispensable once you know about it. If you can't buy it you can appreciate the flavour and texture by reducing double cream over heat, cooling, and adding lemon juice; a better bet is to whip or sieve cottage cheese and then add a little milk or cream – cheaper too.

Cooking: to boil or not to boil is a very vexed question and there is a great deal of disagreement both within each country and between countries. Some of the hysteria is probably because cream is often added in association with egg to thicken and enrich – this will naturally curdle if heated too much. In my experience cream can be boiled and it can be simmered in sauces, and so can soured cream. There will be sauces or cooking liquids that have such high acidity that the cream will curdle when added but often curdling is a matter of bad technique, ie you must add potentially troublesome liquids in a certain way – you should always pour the thicker into the thinner (do it the other way and curdling is almost certain). If your sauce has a flour base, curdling is less likely. Reduction of cream or a cream sauce is basic to fine food and when making a cream sauce I always reduce the double cream by a third or a half before adding it. The flavouring liquid is reduced even more drastically, if possible, for curdling seems more a problem when you have large amounts of liquid. Reduction is essential for nothing is worse than a so-called cream sauce that has no coating consistency or body. You do not get globules of butterfat and any other fat that rises in can be beaten in; indeed the beating in of butter is again basic to the proper finishing of sauces. English soured cream does not curdle in sauces in my experience, but perhaps I have been lucky for there are others who swear it always happens to them. I use soured cream more and more to finish wine-based sauces, partly because it is cheaper and partly because it gives extra dimension of flavour. You must never use cream which has turned sour, just as you must never drink pasteurized milk which has soured; neither is the result of the natural lactic souring of raw milk, but is the result of the sterile liquid being infected by whatever was passing. At best it will be bitter or unpleasant to eat and at worst be dangerous, especially to children and the elderly.

Storing: pasteurized cream should keep in a refrigerator for an average of six days. Frozen single cream tends to separate, but double cream freezes very well giving best results if it is slightly sweetened. It should always be well stirred or whipped after defrosting.

BUTTER

Without mountains of glorious, glistening butter, there would have been no *haute cuisine* – and there would probably be fewer heart disease problems, too. But for me to attempt to live without butter because of possible future health problems would be the same as cutting off a leg in case I might stub a toe. I was brought up eating masses of butter with everything, and that's that. I comfort myself with the knowledge that Australasians don't have a heart disease incidence anywhere near as

APPELLATION D'ORIGINE CONTRÔLLÉE

The Appellation d'Origine Contrôllée or AOC system of France currently recognizes and strictly controls the following dairy products. For other AOC products and the DO foods of Spain see page 346.

Butters: beurre Charente Poitou , beurre de Charentes, beurre des Deux-sevres, beurre d'Isigny (note the unpasteurized beurre d'Isigny does not have an AOC as the regulations require that AOC beurre d'Isigny should be made from pasteurized milk).

Cream: cremé d'Isigny.

Cheeses: Abondance (usually Tomme d'Abondance), Beaufort, Bleu d'Auvergne, Bleu de Causses, Bleu du Haut-Jura (also known as Bleu de Gex, Bleu de Septmoncel), Brie de Meaux, Brie de Melun, Camembert de Normandie, Cantal (or Fourme du Cantal, and Salers) Chabichou du Poîtu, Chaource, Comté, Crottin de Chavignol or Chavignol, Fourme d'Ambert, Laguiole, Livarot, Maroilles or Marolles, Mont d'Or or Vacherin du Haut Doubs, Munster or Munster Géromé, Neufchâtel, Ossau-Iraty-Brebis Pyrénées, Picodon de l'Ardèche or Picodon de la Drôme, Pouligny-Saint-Pierre, Pont l'Evêque, Reblochon or Petit Reblochon, Roquefort, Saint Nectaire, Sainte-Maure de Touraine, Selles-sur-Cher, Broccio Corse or Brucciu.

high as their butter intake might suggest. We're built differently.

Butter making is a specialized art, involving far more than churning cream for longer than required to make whipped cream. Even today there is no such thing as totally automated butter making. The great stainless steel churns which hold from 4,500-6,800lt/1,000-1,500 gallons of cream all have windows through which watch expert butter makers, who must stop the churning at a precise moment or risk losing the whole batch.

Basically what happens is this: the rotation of a churn half-full of cream cracks the envelope of non-fat solids that encase each of the fat globules of the cream. When this happens – it is called 'breaking' – the butterfat globules begin to coalesce into pieces about the size of a wheat grain and the other solids are dispersed into the liquid content of the cream, becoming buttermilk. This buttermilk is drawn off and the butter grains are washed with cold water to rinse out any remains of buttermilk which would reduce the butter's quality and keeping ability. Once the water has drained enough to reduce the liquid content to within legally enforced limits, salt may be added. This is a very delicate operation, requiring a balance between market tastes and marketing requirements; the former is purely nationalistic, the latter depends on how long the butter is to be stored or how far it is to travel. As might be expected, the more salt, the longer the butter will last.

The salted or unsalted grains are then churned a further 10-15 minutes, which is called 'working' and blends the grains into a solid mass. It is then packed into small packets or in large cartons for commercial use; in the latter process it is usually slightly compressed, which helps avoid problems of shortened life which can be caused by trapped pockets of air.

The wide variety of flavours offered by butters comes as a surprise to most peo-

GHEE

Ghee is a sort of clarified butter, which may be bought or made at home: concentrated butter gives very much the same flavour. The point is to make a butter-based fat or oil with no solid content for that is what makes butter burn. It will cook at a far higher temperature than butter.

The proper way is to melt a good quantity of butter over very gentle heat and then let it simmer gently until those white particles of milk solids have stopped forming; only then has all the water gone and that might take as long as 45 minutes. Either scoop away or strain through muslin. It lasts as long as butter when kept refrigerated.

ple. These variations are achieved in three basic ways, starting with the characteristics of the cream used. This relies on the type of cow and the feed it is given. As these vary during the year, so will the resultant butter, but usually the changes are more likely to be in the balance of minerals contained, and flavour differences would be beyond the detection of most of us. Perhaps the most widely used method of flavour manipulation is treatment of the cream.

Provided there has been a preliminary 'holding' of the cream to ensure uniform hardness of the fat globules, you can make butter from sweet cream to which you have done nothing else. But if you then leave it longer to ripen, the naturally occurring bacteria will multiply and their enzymic actions and side effects will increase the flavour, by raising the acid content in particular. Such a flavour enhancement or a flavour change can be aided by the addition of a cultured 'starter' as with the making of cheese. All the cream used to make Danish and Dutch butter is culture-treated, thus giving the distinctive and consistent but differing flavours of these countries' products. Confusingly they are sold as unsalted butters, as though they are merely cream converted into butter, but as I have just explained their flavour has been manipulated and they are more properly known as lactic butters.

Salt is the last and final way of affecting butter's flavour. The combination of basic dairying technique, treatment of the cream and salting gives an enormously wide potential of flavours. Colouring is sometimes added also, but you shouldn't take it for granted that all brilliant butter has such additives. If the cream used is from Jersey or Guernsey cows it will naturally have a brighter glow.

Butter which is made with unpasteurized milk or milk which has not been subjected to the action of a lactic culture is known as sweet butter even though it may have a salt content. It is exceptionally difficult to find in Britain but common-place in the United States. In cooking it gives a flavour of rich creaminess, rather like clotted cream, and this explains the vast superiority of the flavour of much American baking. The closest British bakers can get are the unpasteurized butters of France and I especially recommend *beurre d'Isigny*. Lightly salted Normandy butters also give outstanding flavour in pastry and baking but are so much cheaper.

There are three main types of butter generally found in the United Kingdom: salted, slightly salted and unsalted (lactic). You can generally judge how much salt there is by ascertaining how far the butter has had to travel; hence butter from New Zealand is likely to have a higher salt content than butter from, say, Wiltshire.

So-called farmhouse butter, usually from the western counties, is usually slightly less salty than most, which is one of the contributing factors to its notoriously short life. In my experience it has a special predilection for rancidity, which may be due to inefficient churning and washing or because it is often made close to cheese dairies and picks up foreign flavours. Either way, farmhouse butter should always be given a discreet sniff to ensure it is sweet and wholesome. You should also check for streakiness: this indicates the combination of different batches and possible problems with rancidity. Salted Welsh butter is possibly the saltiest regional butter of all, especially when cut from great blocks by farmers' wives in Swansea market.

Slightly salted butter gives a blander flavour which suits much continental cooking and many palates.

Unsalted butter is usually the most expensive and potentially the most troublesome kind, for without the preservative advantage that salt gives it is prone to all manner of afflictions. Again, a trained and perspicacious nose is a definite aid.

Cooking: if you have problems with butter burning when you are frying or slowly cooking vegetables, the simplest technique is to lower the heat. Or you can add up to an equal quantity of oil, which allows you to use a much higher heat without the butter burning. Otherwise you have to buy or make clarified butter, which is quite a good thing to keep in your refrigerator – *(see GHEE)*.

Storing: all butter is affected not only by heat but also by light, so it should be kept both cool and dark.

ICE CREAM

In the days when Saturday matinée movies were preceded by a stirring serial and Walt Disney cartoons, it used to cost 6d to sit downstairs and 9d to lord it in the superiority of the balcony. I used to be given 9d, which meant an invidious choice. Did I sit upstairs and command considerable social envy? or did I sit downstairs, enjoying the status of a 2d ice cream, save 1d, and have two ice creams next week? The ice cream plan usually won. If I'd studied social history in my first ten years I could have saved myself the trouble of choosing, for ices have always had a greater social cachet than mere position. The Romans and almost every other ruling power spent fortunes having snow and ice rushed over great distances so they could freeze food and so astound *hoi polloi*. In England and America, lesser fortunes relied on the building of underground ice houses in which to store winter's ice, so providing them with the means to make cooling ices and sorbets, a special need in the humid summers of the southern states of North America.

It was the society-levelling Americans who popularized ice cream and it's very much part of everyday life for millions and millions of children and adults. Huge containers of ice cream are stored in the family freezer, to be scooped into as a snack from breakfast to bedtime. But, like so many convenience foods now in the public domain, much of it has very little in common with the real thing, other than temperature. In fact, true dairy-based ice cream simply doesn't exist as far as most major producers are concerned: their product contains no cream and any milk is probably added in the form of powder. The fat, so essential to the texture and enjoyment of real ice cream, is nearly always from the oil palm, at least it is in the United Kingdom. Thus, if the EC continues on its legislative way, it will soon prohibit such products being called ice cream, which would be a very good thing. This isn't necessary in Australasia and in some of the stronger dairying states of the United States, where the real thing is protected as a birthright.

Ice cream in its simplest form was once just flavoured and frozen cream and even this probably didn't appear until the 18th century. Ices had been closer to what we would call sorbets; it's thought the Chinese invented these concoctions of fruit and that the Italians took up the idea and then introduced it to the rest of Europe. Charles I, who first fell for them in this country, protected the recipe with a sentence of death for anyone who divulged it. The classic form nowadays is a flavoured egg custard made with milk or cream. The best I ever ate was made in an old-fashioned ice cream churn or dasher, in which the mixture is turned over and over again surrounded by salted ice. It takes a long time and a lot of patience but gives such a wonderful silken result. Other recipes give smooth results too and you can also buy small electrically-operated machines which will churn ice cream in the freezer or the ice-box of your refrigerator. But, although rather satisfying to do, it may not be necessary. In the last several years there has been a distinct move back towards the commercial making of true ice cream in the United Kingdom.

You are quite right when you say bought ice cream isn't the same as Mum makes. That's because it is made from different ingredients by quite different techniques. At first these differences were invented to make commercial ice cream taste and look like the homemade thing, basically frozen creams or custards, but slowly its popularity generated the creation of absolutely new products, containing no cream, but priced so their pleasure was available to all.

Today's ice creams are based on milk but, as that is icy when frozen, fats are added for taste and texture. The first process required by law is pasteurization to kill all possibly harmful bacteria. Next, to give the velvety mouthfeel of frozen cream, the mix is homogenized, which reduces the size of the fat globules, keeping them suspended in the milk rather than rising to the top. The homogenized mixture is then frozen, and air is whisked in, which bulks and lightens the texture. The more air, the fluffier and easier it is to eat, and this 'stretching' of the ingredients means it can be sold more cheaply. Sugar, flavours, nuts and the like may be added at the start or the end of the process.

The commercial advantage of homogenizing is that the fats added to the milk may be of cheaper non-dairy or of vegetable origin. It will be no surprise that so-called standard ice creams also contain other ingredients to help emulsification, slow down melting and so on, but all are approved to high Government standards. Modern technology now means that by adding such emulsifying and stabilizing agents, even milk can be frozen to look and behave like ice cream, but in the United States this must be called iced milk.

The days of only vanilla or chocolate ice creams and perhaps strawberry on a Saturday have gone thank goodness. The move mainly came from America, where ice cream is eaten by the gallon all year round. Dayville and Baskin-Robbins suddenly opened shops selling dozens of flavours with such fantastic names as Rocky Road, Blue Lagoon and Fudge Nut Cookies. They came and often went just as quickly but a taste for something bigger and better had begun. Super-premium ice cream has become a permanent high street star. They are very high in dairy fat content and use unusual, high-quality ingredients, often in challenging combinations.

Isn't this talk of non-dairy-fat and additions a bit worrying? Not at all. Provided you know how to read labels all the information you need is there. After that it is up to you, for the success of modern retailing is based on choice. And pleasure in eating comes from eating the widest variety of foods available.

ICE CREAM TYPES

Once you can understand what the labels mean and promise you should be able to put any ice cream into one of the following categories, and then decide if you are being overcharged _before_ you spend the money:

Standard ice creams: the names you recognize, made to the basic standards and competitively priced. Always milk plus non-dairy or vegetable fat and containing the maximum amount of air permitted. Often sold in bulk packs. The type of fat should be clearly identifiable on the label, as should the flavourings.

Premium ice creams: can contain dairy or superior non-dairy fats. Will contain less air, cost a little more and will generally be packed in 1 litre packs, maximum.

Super-premium or luxury: dairy ice creams exclusively, with high fat content and low air additions. More likely to be in smaller packs of 500g, 750g or individual portions. Egg and egg yolks sometimes also included.

Air: the content not mentioned on packets is air, and it is not until you eat ice cream that you can tell how much has been whisked into it. In general the cheaper the ice cream and the larger the pack the more air is likely to have been included; the premium and luxury ice creams have progressively less air content and are generally packed in smaller containers, but as they are richer and more solid the amount in them is likely to be just as satisfying as larger amounts of lighter products.

Dairy ice cream: when you see this on a label it guarantees the fats included are all dairy fats.

Emulsifiers: these are essentially a chemical way of achieving what homogenization does mechanically, mixing water and fats. But these emulsifiers are more certain to keep them mixed and thus the product may be treated a little more ruggedly.

Flavour/flavouring: if you find either word included in the name or description of the frozen product, it means precisely what it says, a flavouring has been used rather than the real thing, and that could also mean colouring too. Thus chocolate 'flavouring' means it is not the real thing; 'strawberries with strawberry flavour' would mean a mixture of strawberries and a flavouring to make them go further.

Ice cream: if the label only says this, the contents will be made from milk and other fats and the label must also say 'contains non-milk fat' or 'contains vegetable fat'.

Stabilizers: these act like sponges to soak up excess water. This achieves two things. First, ice crystals are prevented from forming when frozen product fluctuates in temperature and second, the product's ability to be whipped and thus to trap air is dramatically increased. This is no bad thing as long as you are not paying premium prices; premium products are unlikely to use stabilizers.

Sweeteners: sugar is essential to ice cream, especially for flavour but also for bulk and texture. Government regulations declare artificial sweeteners are not allowed in any standard or dairy ice cream; but the demand for lower calorie ice cream products means that sugar-reduced, calorie-reduced products are increasingly seen. Provided they are labelled as such, they may include fructose (fruit sugar) or alternative sweeteners.

Sorbets and sherberts: sorbets are water ices, basically a mixture of water, sugar and fruit juice or pulp plus other ingredients and frozen with the addition of air; without air they are the popular iced lolly. A sherbert has some dairy content, often milk or ice cream, and is always frozen with an air content. Those who believe they are saving on calories by ordering a sorbet rather than ice cream will never get thin.

YOGHURT

So many claims, so much claptrap. Yoghurt is simply pre-digested milk and when eaten its components are available to our system up to three times faster than would be the case with milk itself.

The predigestion is usually the work of two bacilli, *lactobacillus bulgaricus* and *streptococcus thermophilis*. They are not natural components of milk and thus yoghurt cannot occur naturally. As the bacilli digest the milk to fuel their lives, they create acidity which thickens the milk and kills much intrinsic bacteria and, so, even if not pasteurized or boiled, the milk becomes safer and longer lasting. Those qualities alone imbued yoghurt with seemingly magical health-giving properties. But in the west we gave it a reputation it did not deserve, for we thought the bacilli were the same as those in our digestive systems.

The theorists taught yoghurt would thus purify our bowels, making us healthier and less mortal. They reasoned this had to be fact because Bulgarians ate a lot of yoghurt and lived a long time. Quite apart from ignoring genetic contributions, yoghurt's proselytizers chose to ignore that Bulgarians also lived a basically healthier life on a more balanced diet than most in the west – but yoghurt alone was given the credit. An echo of this belief is still heard in claims that yoghurt will replace digestive flora lost by taking antibiotics. This simply is not so, for although yoghurt bacillus are similar to some in our guts, they are quite different and do not survive. Anyway, for many sick people eating milk products quickly and reliably makes them worse if their digestive system is upset, for milk is simply a ready supply of food upon which bad as well as good organisms thrive. However, contemporary research shows that a much rarer yoghurt bacillus, *lactobacillus acidophilus* might have some part to play internally – even if it doesn't, it gives yoghurts a sweeter, smoother flavour which is very attractive, and as it is now widely available I should choose that anyway.

Although seeming rather foreign and funny to a lot of Europeans, yoghurt is another of the world's oldest processed foods. Pharaohs and Israelites enjoyed it in Egypt, Greeks and Romans employed it medically and the Arab world has long respected it, a Damascene extolling its virtues in a book written in 633. Even these are *un peu arriviste* as it is thousands of years older than that. Some go as far as saying it could have been accidentally discovered at the dawn of the Neolithic age, some 10,000 years BC; this is unlikely as domestication of animals didn't start until 4,000 years later.

Persian invaders took yoghurt to India, where bare yogis mixed it with honey as part of their strict diets 2,000 years ago. When the nomadic Bulgars of Asia settled in the Balkans in the 7th century they too brought yoghurt and,

---

FROZEN YOGHURT

This is a new star but most of it doesn't taste of yoghurt and seriously runs the risk of being labelled a cynical marketing ploy, unkindly aimed at anyone who still believes yoghurt is automatically slimming, healthy, or both. Tofu (soy bean curd) frozen desserts however, have some claim to help those with cholesterol problems or vegetarians who eat no animal products of any kind.

The problems of frozen yoghurts all stem from there currently being no laws and regulations about yoghurt itself other than an Industry Code of Practice. There are three basic methods of manufacture all of which must start with a dairy or a dairy and vegetable-fat base.

■ Yoghurt is bought-in, sometimes in concentrated form, and mixed into the base with flavourings.
■ A dairy base is made into which yoghurt bacteria are introduced and the entire mass is allowed to ferment before freezing.
■ The richest result begins with a low-fat ice cream base and a separate yoghurt made with lactose-reduced skimmed milk, both produced by the same manufacturer, thus giving absolute quality control. Häagen-Dazs, who make the only frozen yoghurt which I can identify with my eyes closed, use this method and also include cream and egg yolks as they do in their ice cream.

---

like the Mongol hoards of Ghengis Khan, had used it as absolutely basic subsistence for they made it from the milk of the mares upon which they rode.

Yoghurt was probably first seen in Europe some time in the 16th century, but apart from pockets of fanaticism and monasteries it remained virtually unknown until the early part of this century when Metchnikoff, leading light of the Pasteur Institute, succeeded in isolating the two bacilli responsible for turning milk into yoghurt. Now it was possible to make yoghurt commercially and save western man, or so it seemed. It wasn't until 1925, nine years after Metchnikoff's death, that a Spaniard called Carasso opened the first yoghurt factory, in Barcelona. This was the Danone company, still a major producer. It was many years before propaganda, sweetening and flavouring made yoghurt into the widely available and generally abused food it has become.

And now the burning question – is your yoghurt live or not? The answer is invariably yes, whatever the package says or does not say. But some are less live than others. The addition of growth inhibitors to lengthen shelf life make them distinctly enfeebled, fighting for their own existence rather than winning bacterial battles on your behalf.

In the interest of high sales, long life and profit, this cheaper yoghurt is first extended by dilution with some liquid then emulsified and restored to something like its original viscosity with a chemical stabilizer, which works like gelatine. A natural yoghurt has a certain graininess but altered types are detectable by being jelly-like and smooth on the tongue. This treatment combined with low temperature storage means the further growth of the bacilli is inhibited, extending the yoghurt's life and emasculating the preservative quality of its acidic content. But even these yoghurts will eventually bubble and fizz and go over the top if left long enough. Higher quality yoghurts which have not been extended or stabilized artificially are likely to produce a thicker texture and a whey-like liquid, which can be stirred back gently. Vigorous stirring or beating causes yoghurt to thin considerably and in this state it is often used as a refreshing drink throughout the Middle East; in Turkey it is mixed with soda water, which is even nicer. If you want a really thick yoghurt, like that used in India, the simplest way is to hang yoghurt in muslin as though it were cheese curd and let this drain.

The connections with good health mean yoghurt is often thought good for dieters, and it can be, provided you think clearly and read the labels.

Low-fat yoghurts: will have been made from skimmed or part skimmed milk and are usually sweetened with artificial substances. But not always.

Fruit and flavoured yoghurts: may be made from any kind of milk, but are generally sweetened with sugar and thus offer far more calories than you imagined.

Strained yoghurts: often called Greek yoghurts, for these were the types first marketed. By compacting the solids through straining off the whey, the fat content is also concentrated and fat is calories. Yoghurts made with sheep's milk are particularly high in calories as its fat cannot be separated from the milk which is very rich anyway: a strained sheep's milk yoghurt is thus a nightmare for dieters. Goats' milk always keeps its fat too. Note that this high calorie count exists in unflavoured yoghurts, before any sugar or fruit is added...

Everyone I know who makes yoghurt swears that UHT/long life milk gives the best and creamiest result, possibly because it is homogenized. But you can use any milk, including that made from powder.

Bulgarian yoghurt was traditionally made with goats' milk which gave rise to the widely held belief that only this is proper yoghurt. Although that is untrue, goats' milk yoghurt is especially delicious and is becoming more widely known. The availability of powdered or frozen goats' milk means making your own is easy.

Cooking: unlike cream, yoghurt will infallibly curdle if added to hot liquid which is subsequently boiled. You should let the yoghurt come to room temperature then whisk it in the hot liquid just before serving. Otherwise you can stabilize plain yoghurt by heating gently and thickening with cornflour.

The traveller in eastern Mediterranean countries will constantly be surprised where they find yoghurt. In Izmir I watched a chef make stuffed pasta which was then cooked in broth, exactly the way you would ravioli or tortelloni. The hot pasta was drained into a serving dish then dolloped with thick cold plain yoghurt over which was poured hot butter flavoured with paprika and chilli. It sounds and looks like the bland leading the bland, but turns out to be extraordinarily complementary and contrasted.

Scandaweigans bake layered fish and potatoes with yoghurt as a topping and yoghurt finishes many an American cheesecake. Strained yoghurt is essential to many Indian marinades – and if you can't be bothered cooking, few things are more refreshing than yoghurt diluted with soda water and a dash of rose water.

YOGHURT, APPLE AND MARMALADE TART

This is based on a prize-winning recipe by a Nottingham (then) teenager Andrew Foss. The marmalade suggested by Andrew was grapefruit, but you can use any thick cut marmalade as long as it is sharp-tasting rather than sweet.

Serves 6
315g/10oz wholemeal or shortcrust pastry
1 egg, separated
375g/12oz Bramley apples, peeled, cored and thickly sliced
2 generous tbsp marmalade
300ml/½pt plain yoghurt, drained
30g/1oz walnut pieces

Roll out the pastry to line an 18cm/7in flan dish and bake blind at 200°C/400°F/Gas Mark 6 for 10-12 minutes. Brush the bottom of the flan with the egg white and return it to the oven for 3-4 minutes to make sure it is set. Reduce the oven heat to 180°C/350°F/Gas Mark 4.

Mix the apples with the marmalade and the egg yolk and pile into the baked case. Return to oven and cook for 30 minutes. While the tart is cooking, strain the yoghurt through a fine sieve or a sieve lined with muslin.

Let the tart cool for 10-15 minutes, then spread the yoghurt on top and sprinkle with walnuts. Serve at once.

OPTIONS: the apples make a delicious syrup as they cook, and a little of this should be put on each plate as the tart is served. If you prefer, you can top the tart with whipped cream or soured cream, but the tart should be only just warm.

It is only in delicatessen shops that you are likely to have a *choice* of eggs, a possibility that may not have occurred. But there are several distinct types of hen eggs, as well as eggs from other birds, that are worth including in your repertoire. The classification system for hen eggs is as follows:

Free range: the birds must have continuous daytime access to open-air runs mainly covered with vegetation. Maximum 1,000 hens per hectare and housing as for deep litter.

Deep litter: seven birds per square metre of floor space, but kept in a hen house with a litter of straw, wood shavings, sand or turf in which the birds can peck and scratch and which is deep enough to ensure the top surface is never constantly damp, which would increase the risk of parasite infestation and other disease.

Perchery/barn: sold as barn eggs. A variation of the previous standard. Perches and feeders at different levels give a stocking level of 25 hens per square metre and birds each must have 15cm/6in of perch space.

Battery: this production method does not have to be mentioned on small egg packs. Three to five birds are kept in a cage which must be well ventilated and give free access to food and water and kept free of manure. All eggs, other than those sold by a producer at a farm gate, from a market stall or on a delivery round must be tested for quality by candling, that is, inspected against a light source for any contamination, cracks or spots. The quality classes are:

Class A: naturally clean eggs with an air cell not exceeding 6mm in depth; the yolk should not move perceptibly when the egg is rotated. Must not have been cleaned, refrigerated below 8°C or preserved.

Class B: will have an air cell between 6mm and 9mm and may have been cleaned, refrigerated below 8°C or preserved. They must be stamped individually to state which of those three has occurred.

Class C: eggs fit for human consumption but which do not fall into the previous classes – used for manufacturing.

Extra: this indicates Class A eggs with maximum 4mm air cells and which have been collected by packing stations at least twice a week. The band classing them as Extra must be removed from packs unsold after seven days.

Other Grades: As well as all the above, eggs are graded according to size, which means weight; 1: 70g and over; 2: 65g but under 70g; 3: 60g but under 65g; 4: 55g but under 60g; 5: 50g but under 55g; 6: 45g but under 50g; 7: under 45g.

Duck eggs: rich and flavourful, these are popular with children because of their pretty green-blue shell. Let them be eaten, by all means, but never serve soft-boiled duck eggs. Because the shells are so thin, and because they are laid in wet and dirty places, duck eggs contain much higher levels of bacteria than any others you are likely to eat. They must be thoroughly cooked. The better use for duck eggs is for cake making, especially whisked sponges. They can be used in combination with hen eggs or alone to give improved colour and flavour. I remember sitting on a high stool in the kitchen as a child, whisking duck eggs for my mother; then she would make a sponge and win a prize at the local church. I can still smell the rich creaminess of those eggs now, and taste the sponge.

Quails' eggs: much smaller and now available fresh most of the year – if you know where to shop. Quails' eggs are served the same way as gulls' eggs, but, being cheaper, they can be eaten more often. If you can buy them fresh, boil for just one minute. The tinned ones from China, shelled, are very good indeed. Either way, serve them as is, or include them in a special salad, or in mayonnaise with lobster, prawns or other shellfish. They look very nice served with cold asparagus mayonnaise, and are very special with hot asparagus and a sauce maltese (hollandaise flavoured with blood orange). The Connaught Hotel serves them soft-boiled on pastry bateaux with a bed of much reduced mushroom purée, coated with hollandaise, and they or gulls' eggs on a nest of mayonnaise sauce are the perfect accompaniment to cold salmon, smoked salmon or gravad lax, especially if you chop plenty of fresh dill into the mayonnaise, and/or mix a portion of whipped cream in, too.

Other eggs: some enterprizing farm shops and specialty shops in the country will often offer other eggs; I have bought in London guinea fowl eggs, pheasant eggs and bantam eggs. All these and others are good, interesting for their size rather than their flavour, although pheasant eggs seem to have something extra.

I've never eaten plovers' eggs, because now they may no longer be gathered, but they are supposed to be the best of the small eggs. Generally you can buy gulls' eggs in the summer, which are considered a good substitute. These greeny-blue eggs, dappled with brown, slightly more pointed than hen's eggs and 2½-5cm/1-2in long, taste excactly like hens' eggs, with none of the fishy taste that many expect. If anything they are rather more mellow than the usual breakfast egg. Although they look very pretty in their shells, I deplore the habit of serving gulls' eggs unshelled at buffets and cocktail parties. How do you peel an egg and balance a glass? Even if you manage, what do you do with the shell? Serve them shelled, slightly chilled, with bowls of mayonnaise, celery salt, sweet paprika and slices of brown bread. You can always display the shells around the dish or bowl or basket, to show the eggs are not from some frightful extruding machine (which, incidentally, are responsible for most of the sliced eggs you find in or on catering food these days – yes they actually make a sausage of egg and slice that!)

Cooking: the freshest eggs taste best, but eggs for baking are better for being several days old. Test them for freshness by putting into water, the flatter an egg lies the fresher it is. It is alright but a bit old if it stands up, but once it starts to float in the water, crack open to check it has not gone off. If it floats *on* the water, throw it away.

Fresh eggs should display three distinct textures when broken: the yolk, supported by a thick cushion of white, itself surrounded by less viscous liquid. As the eggs get older the white becomes more watery and eventually the yolk also flattens out. These may still taste alright but don't look too good poached or fried – use them for baking.

When baking, always bring eggs back to room temperature first. You will get more volume and lighter results; it is particularly important to have the whites at room temperature when making meringue.

Storing: remember that eggs are not designed as human food, but as the nursery and cradle of a bird. The shells are porous and thus can collect flavours, smells and germs. If shells are dirty and wet, eat these eggs quickly, and always eat right away any eggs you have had to wash.

Kept cool and away from other strong smelling foods, eggs actually last much longer than is usually thought, but buy in small quantities.

BACON AND EGG PIE

Strictly speaking this isn't delicatessen food as all the ingredients can be bought from a supermarket. But it is something so simple that it soon becomes a standby of anyone who makes it and far more popular than 'quiche'. In New Zealand no picnic or beach trip is complete without a couple.

Serves 6-8

350-400g/12-14oz puff pastry
225g/8oz streaky bacon
Diced green peppers, slices of fried onion, or potato, green peas, sweet corn kernels (all optional)
6 large eggs
black pepper, be generous

Line a shallow 20-22.5cm/8-9in pie dish with 175g/6oz of the pastry. Coarsely dice the bacon and fry until the fat starts to run. Spread the bacon evenly over the pastry and some of the interesting extras if you have them; never mind if you don't.

Break the eggs over the bacon, encouraging the whites to join together by gently tilting the dish. Best plan is to have five eggs around the edge and one in the middle. Try not to break the yolks.

Pepper the egg yolks generously, cover with the remaining pastry, crimp the edges and decorate with any leftover bits and pieces. Glaze if you have an extra egg about.

Bake for 25 minutes and a pre-heated 200°C/400°F/Gas 6 oven, then a further 15 minutes at 160°C/325°F/Gas 3. Serve warm or cold in slices.

Fish was once a mainstay of British life. Every big house and most villages raised carp in ponds, the rivers were fished and salt cod or red herrings kept them going through the long hard winters. Fresh fish was probably more easily available than it is in many areas today, at least it was during the summer when dirt roads were passable. There were laws to ensure such produce was edible: mackerel for instance could be sold in the streets of London on a Sunday for their high fat content meant they never lasted overnight once landed. Other sorts of fresh fish were kept alive in huge tanks in the holds of fishing vessels as they waited to land the catch.

Salting and smoking as ways of preserving fish are increasingly unfashionable. We want food to taste of itself, and even smoked salmon rarely tastes of anything but fish. Nonetheless, our choice of fresh and preserved has never been better and, with frozen goodies as well, the fish lover has not had it so good for centuries.

Abalone: meat from the univalve mollusc, sold cooked, in cans. The best kind is from Japan or the Shandong province of China. Can be eaten directly from the can, if cooked again best done quickly to avoid toughening. In New Zealand there is an equivalent, the *paua*; the irridescent and inner shell makes spectacular jewellery, often confused with that made from butterfly wing.

Anchovy: once you've been introduced to anchovies you either love them to distraction or hate them with a passion engendered by no other finny thing I know. They belong to the herring family and although inferior to them when fresh are much superior when preserved. Basically, the anchovy should be thought of as a flavouring agent rather than a major ingredient of a dish.

Native to the Mediterranean and the English Channel, the anchovy is nevertheless caught as far away as the Black Sea and Scandinavia. The best are said to come from the area between Nice and the Spanish province of Catalonia, as do many of the best recipes for their use. The simple method of salting and preserving whole anchovies originated with the Greeks and Romans, who also used them as the basis for their fermented fish sauce, *garum*. Like herrings, they are often preserved in fillets, flat or curled, which are considered easier for packing and selling these days. They are sold in many forms, whole or filleted, in brine, in oil or in vinegar, although whole anchovies in salt are difficult to buy these days. The Russians preserve them in a spiced vinegar, the Norwegians in a spiced brine.

In western Australia a new industry cans anchovies as Ozchovies, a beaut name if ever there were one, and Australian TV chef Iain Hewitson says they are good enough to eat.

You can sometimes buy fresh anchovies and they are easily distinguishable. A maximum of 10-12cm/4-5in long, they have an extraordinarily big mouth which stretches back almost as far as their gills. I have soused them and also served them freshly grilled, but they were not very good.

Anchovy essence, which comes in all manner of mixtures and strengths, is perfectly magical, with the special ability to pull together flavours which aren't blend-

Anchovies are usually used as a flavouring rather than as a main ingredient, but not so when it comes to appetisers or savouries at the end of a formal meal – then their piquancy is most fully appreciated. Here are some ideas.

■ To make anchovy butter, mix 15-25g/½-1oz butter with each pounded anchovy fillet. Only you will know how strong you like it.

■ Soak about 20 big Pruneaux d'Agen or Californian prunes in cold water overnight, dry them and carefully stone them by opening down one side. Then, pound the hard-boiled yolk of two eggs with 25g/1oz of butter and some anchovy paste or essence. Pass this through a sieve then pipe it into the prunes, making a nice swirl. Decorate with one anchovy fillet cut into thin strips. Spread the remaining stuffing on small pieces of toast and put a stuffed prune on each. Decorate overall with a little watercress.

■ Anchovy-stuffed mushrooms are a very simple and very good idea. Mix some pounded anchovy fillets, some anchovy paste or some essence with cream cheese, fromage frais or ricotta then beat in one egg to each 100g/4oz of cheese. Put this into peeled mushroom caps (they don't have to be too big) and bake in a dish until the cheese has started to set and the mushrooms are well heated through.

■ If you can get your hands on some smoked salmon pieces, mix these into egg and soft cheese as above and then sharpen the flavour with anchovy. Very glamorous as long as you don't use too much anchovy and have the smoked salmon chopped very small, almost to a paste. This might be finished in pastry or on toast fingers.

ing and to make something new and wonderful. Naturally good in fish dishes, it can be used to advantage if employed with discretion in many meat dishes. It can add intriguing life to rice dishes, to mayonnaise and, perhaps best of all, to vegetables. Broccoli or spinach take very well to a little anchovy essence mixed with butter. Used secretly and in small amounts, anchovy essence or pounded anchovy can be used as a marinade for lamb and mutton before roasting, but better not tell your guests, even if they implore you for the secret. I once saw someone vomit on receipt of such information.

Serving: anchovies packed in brine or oil are interchangeable, although the former should be rinsed with water or milk and the latter are less highly flavoured. The most common uses for flat fillets or curls of anchovy are on pizza, in salads (such as Salade Niçoise) and for assertive canapés.

The unexpected ability of anchovy fillets to dissolve into an unctuous paste when heated with olive oil, or merely to disappear into other liquids, is what makes them a standby of those who like savoury flavours. Merely stirring a couple into the oil or butter, or both, to go onto pasta opens new vistas of flavour. Naturally, you would add lots of sliced garlic from the start (chopped would be too mimsy here), and chunky fresh herbs to finish would do no harm; parsley is one of the best, provided you have not ruined it by chopping it finely. If you want to add life to, say, some tomato passata, make such a mixture first, to ensure the anchovy is well emulsified.

Along the edge of the Mediterranean and on some of her islands they make an extraordinary type of sauce-cum-dip, usually known as *anchoiade* or by some similar name. Often composed of an anchovy paste (usually made from salted whole ones), parsley, oil and garlic, spread on oil-soaked bread and baked until brown, it is really a peasant version of the anchovy toast served as a savoury in London's men's clubs. The Piedmontese of Italy make something called *bagna cauda*, which is used as a sauce for pasta, or as a hot dip for bread or raw vegetables, and always regarded as being perfectly indigestible unless you've been brought up to it from birth. You simply heat 75g/3oz each of butter and olive oil then add 75g/3oz of anchovies in pieces and 75g/3oz (that's right) of finely sliced garlic. Simmer for ten minutes then keep hot over a spirit lamp. As Elizabeth David points out in her *Italian Food*, it requires great quantities of coarse red wine and the constitution of an ox. I think I prefer the French olive-caper-and-anchovy paste called *tapénade*, or the civility of Patum Pepperium, the Gentleman's Relish, which is anchovy-based and bliss when spread on hot toast with decent tea in front of a drawing-room fire.

Caviare: those languid heroines of Russian sagas who existed on but a spoonful of caviare and a sip of champagne knew a thing or two. The hard roe of the female sturgeon has twice the nutriment of most meat and is equal to the finest pork flesh. But its powers of sustainment are not why caviare is so esteemed. It is worshipped both because of its scarcity and its superlative flavour. The latter is often hotly debated, usually by those who have never tasted it, with hissed platitudes about 'acquired taste' and 'just because it costs so much'. That's as may be, but I've adored it ever since I breakfasted upon a pot of Beluga aboard a luxurious American cruise liner on January 1 1961, my nineteenth birthday.

Genuine caviare comes only from the sturgeon, a fish once so common in Europe that its roe was used as bait. It was eaten occasionally in Britain but did not became popular until the l9th century.

The sturgeon is one of the world's most ancient and fascinating creatures. There is a variety in every one of the earth's oceans, making it the most widespread species of fish. This is because, like the crocodile, it is an unchanged survivor from prehistoric times. For all commercial purposes most caviare sturgeon are caught in the Caspian Sea, by the Russians in the north and the Iranians in the south, and all fishing is in government hands. There are other minor sources, and as well as the twelve or so types of caviare sturgeon in those waters there is one in the waters of France's Gironde river. The biggest sturgeon, the Beluga, can weigh anything up to 25cwt and as much as 158kg/350lb of roe has been taken from a single fish; the usual haul is between 4-15kg/8-35lbs, depending on the species. Caviare can vary in colour from a yellow or brown to light grey and black and varies tremendously in size. The colour and size has little bearing on flavour, for the most important factors are the time of year, age of the fish and method of preservation; the Beluga for instance must be eighteen to twenty years old before its roe is considered suitable. It is generally considered that the earlier in the season and the lighter the salting, the better the flavour.

Sturgeons are usually caught in the deltas of the rivers which flow into the Black and Caspian seas. Although the fish and waters are exactly the same, 'Russian' and

Iranian caviare can be quite different. In Iran, on the southern shores, this is still an artisan's business, often family run and working on just one fish at a time. Thus they are able to judge the amount of salt and watch the process more carefully, giving a more consistent and, some would say, more elegant product which will vary only to reflect the individuality of each sturgeon's age and eggs. The more commercialized operation on the north of the seas (what one called Soviet Russia but is now many things) must perforce work on averages and in greater bulk and thus will vary in a less sensitive way. But I shouldn't worry, unless you have won the Pools and intend to eat caviare every day, such variations are unlikely to strike you.

Sturgeons are bled before gutting to avoid contamination of the roe, which is sieved several times to remove the connecting tissues of the eggs, and then lightly salted. All caviare so treated will be labelled *malassol*, which actually means little salt, and this is considered the greatest delicacy of all.

Virtually all the caviare exported to the West is eaten by people with their feet off the ground – no, not that! – by people in aircraft. And in spite of the salting it has usually also been lightly pasteurized; the rare experience of eating unpasteurized and thus raw caviare was likened by writer and artist Adrian Gill as 'not only having the brass section, but the woodwind and strings, too'. He had been drinking of course. On the other hand explorer Robin Hanbury Tenison recently lived on nothing but salmon and fresh caviare for weeks on end in the remote Kamchatka Peninsula but yearned for tea, toast and Radio 4.

As the summer gets hotter the caviare needs more salt to preserve it and the 'hot season' caviare is packed in small wooden tubs and labelled 'fresh salted'; this is very rarely seen in Europe. Towards the end of the season the inferior roe of this time is salted and pressed and usually sold in tubes for relatively little – it makes pretty canapés and offers lots of decorative possibilities.

Of all the types of sturgeon from which we get caviare the most productive is the monster **Beluga**, the white sturgeon. It provides the largest and many think the best, but Beluga caviare is also the most fragile and does not keep well. The next most important source is the **Sevruga** which never exceeds 1¼m/4ft in length and usually never gives more than about 4kg/8lb of very small-grained roe. Many hold that this fineness gives a better flavour than the coarser Beluga, but this is a subjective argument that can never be solved. The third most important source and generally the cheapest is **Oscietre** which provides masses of eggs that vary from grey to black and are medium in size. It is these three that provide the majority of caviare sold in the United Kingdom and United States. The best place to compare each type and thus to decide your preference is a caviare bar and restaurant. They have long existed in Paris and open and close in London with diverting regularity. The world's newest is at the top of the Mandarin Oriental hotel in Hong Kong, which provides a view as priceless as your fare.

The Oscietre produces so many sizes and colours of caviare it is not unknown for wicked packers to pass off the larger ones as much more expensive Beluga. There is an infallible test. If you crush a Beluga egg on the ball of your thumb (or anywhere else for that matter) the resultant smear will be grey-black; Oscietre will always leave a brown-yellow smear. And speaking of testing, the traditional test for freshness and flavour is to smear a small helping onto the ball of your thumb (nowhere else in this case), sniff deeply and then to lick it off. The slightest whiff or taste of fishiness means something is wrong. You do not employ such technique after you have washed in something scented, or have not washed for some time.

The fabled golden caviare is obtained two ways. In the days of the great Russian Empire, patriotic and hardy Cossacks would hack holes through the late winter/early spring ice, through which they would spear sturgeons. Their immature roe was golden yellow, with a rich flavour that made the senses reel, so it is said.

A lesser golden caviare is sometimes sold these days, which comes from young Oscietre. But I was once allowed to taste a few grains of a very golden caviare: the occasion was conducted with much secrecy and ceremony and I quickly inferred I was not to ask questions about its origins. The appearance was extraordinary, tiny translucent balls of sparkling gold, like sunlit dew on a black horn spoon. No lemon juice, or bread, or anything, of course. The first impression was of lightly salted cream and then... of egg, good old hard-boiled egg yolk! Oh the disappointment. I hope this was the fabled Shah's golden caviare, which supposedly comes only from exceptionally rare albino Oscietre sturgeon and was eaten only by those deposed potentates. No wonder they kept the secret, a sort of Persian Curate's egg.

Keluga or **Mandarin** caviare is produced in Manchuria from a sturgeon very like the Beluga, but with eggs which have the greeney-golden caste more associated with Oscietre. It is cheaper, often saltier and very variable, but worth watching. Once the Chinese get it right it will be a useful addition to the shelves.

Caviare was once so commonly made in the United States that New York bars gave it away, expecting its saltiness would encourage a greater sale of beer. Pollution and world wars decreased both the fish and the knowledge. Today someone has done some urgin' and sturgeons are increasingly seen in the rivers of the north west States again. In Seattle you find sturgeon on menus and locally made caviare. They are different sturgeons from those found in the Caspian and Black Sea, but sturgeons none the less.

You might also come across tins labelled **Ketovia** or **Keta.** This is the hard roe of the dog salmon, common in both Canada and Russia. This 'lesser-caviare' is pink and large and much cheaper. But in candlelight and with overawed friends I have known it presented as the legendary golden caviare with total success.

American salmon caviare is almost certainly from the same or similar species of salmon. But the golden eggs are as big as tapioca and quite salty and fishy – would you eat fishy tapioca?

Considerably more delicious and attractive is small-grained, luminously golden **Löjrom**, which Swedes make from the roe of the bleak. It is regularly touted as the new craze in this or that restaurant column but so far has valiantly resisted the dead hand of trendiness; The Savoy Grill uses it a lot though, so that's all right.

The Danes, bless them, have given us a black and red 'caviare-type' product at a most reasonable price and not too bad a flavour. Used to accompany smoked salmon or on canapés of thin, buttered toast, it is pretty and expensive looking. Once, desperate for a new idea for a dip for crudites, I mixed a pot of the black version with a little mayonnaise, lemon juice and cream cheese. It was an absolute sensation. Not for the flavour, but for the colour. It turned a bright blue and both children and adults ate it with mixed gusto, and horror. Blue food tends to do that.

These caviare substitutes are made from the roe of something called lumpfish, and have brought a new meaning to the phrase 'like it or lump it'. You can like caviare but serve lumpfish roe instead.

Serving: caviare has two natural enemies and hundreds of thousands of unnatural ones. The first two are air and metal. Caviare deteriorates rapidly when exposed to the air and the finer the caviare the faster the deterioration. It might last for an hour but if it has not been treated properly before opening it will oxidize and sour sooner – much sooner. You should open caviare to the air for no more than the moments it takes to transport it to the table. Those carved extravaganzas of ice into which you are invited to dip at buffets are a pretentious guarantee that the caviare they contain will be awful. Hours of exposure to hot, probably smoky air mean it will first oxidize and then freeze. Next, you should avoid touching it with metal; bone, horn, wood or semi-precious stones are best. You might remember that one of the star exhibits at London's Victoria & Albert Museum's Fabergé exhibition was a caviare scoop of amber. Its exquisite simplicity and delicacy was perfectly in harmony with its intended use.

Now for those hundreds of thousands of enemies. These are the people who perpetuate the malpractices of our Victorian and Edwardian forebears who could not conceive of food being served simply. Their presentation of caviare with chopped eggs, pickles and, worst of all, raw onion, is sacrilege of the first degree. But it may not have been their fault. When caviare first became fashionable, transportation was slow and refrigeration non-existent. Or, as happened during the First World War, it had simply been stored badly and for well past its best. But serve it with onion to blind the nostrils to the smell, and egg to coat the palate so you can't taste the fishiness and *voila!* – you had your profit and your victims had their conspicuous consumption. Those who so eat caviare only reinforce the opinion of others that they do it not because they like the taste, but because it costs so much. You cannot appreciate the flavour of caviare (or much else) with the harsh, acidic bite of onion in your mouth. Raw onion masks every other flavour even after it has been swallowed and anyone who argues to the contrary is a fool, or has no palate. Either way they should be forbidden caviare.

So, caviare should be lightly chilled in its container then, just before serving, turned into a delicate dish of the finest, whitest porcelain and taken to the table over ice, with a scoop of something non-metallic per person. If you don't have implements of horn or lapis or malachite, then dip into the caviare with your blinis or toast. And make sure you finish every scrap.

Robert Carrier taught me to eat caviare on toast with thickly smeared Isigny *beurre cru*, and, as usual, he was absolutely right. Soured cream is also an excellent accompaniment, and at Christmas time I usually begin the main meal with hot saffron-flavoured brioches, a bowl of chilled soured cream and as much Oscietre as I can manage. The colour, temperature and texture contrasts forbid anything but festivity. Soured cream is the right thing to have on hand if you are being Russian and serving caviare with small blinis, pancakes of wheat flour or buckwheat. And lemon juice?… well, only if you use the absolute minimum, and even then…

All types of caviare are increasingly used in cooking. Jurg Munch at the Mandarin Oriental began it ten years ago, serving fresh Chinese noodles with warm vodka and caviare grains. Now it is seen in French sauces; the best of those is served with warm sea bass, freshly smoked in the kitchens of the Michelin-starred Oak Room at London's Le Meridien Hotel – (see *TEA SMOKING*). If you have the will or the bank account to cook with caviare, ensure it is added at the very last second, or read the next section.

Storing: optimum storage for malassol caviare is -2°C/30°F but this does not mean deep-freezing. A deep-freeze is fatal to caviare, reducing it to a sorry sort of soup. Unopened tins and jars keep well for several weeks in a domestic refrigerator. As this is usually the way the biggest and smallest stores keep them it is always a bit risky to buy from anywhere that does not have a fast turnover – even then I could tell you a story or two! However you will usually find the bigger caviare agents will deal direct with you, and in return you will pay retail rather than wholesale prices. Once you have your caviare it is vital the container is turned upside down every day or so, to keep the oil evenly distributed. Anyone who does not know this and do this should not be allowed to sell caviare. If you are not prepared to go to that trouble, you had better gobble it up.

Clams: Baltimore is one of the blackest cities in the United States and, being considerably smaller and much whiter than virtually everybody on the streets, I wasn't really having a good time. But there were things that had to be done, which included visiting the famous Lexington Market. It didn't seem American at all, with its noise and untidiness and hundreds of small garish stalls selling everything edible and a few items that, although once falling into that category, were right over the top. It was nice to see Americans being unhygienic about food for a change.

Right at the back of the market was an oyster bar and as we were on Chesapeake Bay which is famed for all manner of seafood, we had to make our way there. Far more than an oyster bar, it sold all manner of extraordinary fish, sea urchins, a variety of hard and soft shelled crabs plus some skinned animals that I'm sure were possums and others that I think were squirrels, and others… But I digress. Around a circular bar, men and women were slurping great raw oysters accompanied by special sauces and ice-cold beer. As well, they were eating clams, *raw* clams. I'd never heard of such a thing, and when I saw the size of them I still couldn't believe it. You had to cut each in two, at least I would have, but the experts here managed to slip the lot into their mouth, chew a couple of times and swallow slowly with bliss beaming on their faces.

Enquiries and many clam meals later proved that eating clams raw was indeed very common and uncommonly good. Not at all like the tiny things in Italian spaghetti or Japanese tins. In the British Isles you are only likely to be able to buy tinned clams or clam juice.

Tinned clams or baby clams: these are essential in any store cupboard once you know them, and can be either Japanese or Spanish. There are far more in each can than you would imagine and almost any brand is alright as long as they are in brine or a light soup of their own juices. They are cooked, of course, and can be used straight from the tin with the least preparation, just some lemon juice, perhaps some oil and garlic or a special mayonnaise. But they help all other seafood dishes too. Mix them with prawns to make the usual boring cocktail more interesting, or use them instead of prawns in fish sauces, stuffings and so on. Chop them roughly into batter and make fritters for lunch or serve as an extraordinary accompaniment to roast chicken or turkey, which were once regularly stuffed with oysters. Put them at the bottom of fish soufflés in lots of garlicky butter or stir them into pilaffs of saffron rice. Like all shellfish they toughen if cooked too long, so don't.

Clam juice: you constantly come across this in American cookbooks and occasionally on the shelves of better stores here. It is the liquor left after clams have been steamed open and is certainly the best stock for fish sauces or fishy flavouring. It makes a fish pie, and finishes a soup or can be the basis of one, cream or otherwise. It is also a rather interesting mixer with alcoholic drinks and is becoming so popular as an ingredient in Bloody Marys that you can now buy it ready mixed with tomato – it is called Clamato, wouldn't you believe?

Crab: America is a marvellous place for crab lovers to be. Either their crabs are more numerous or Americans like the meat more, but you can certainly buy and enjoy crab easily. One of the greatest American treats is soft-shelled crabs. If you see them on a menu, and ensure they have been cooked very simply indeed, order them. They are smallish, 10-15cm/4-5in crabs that have just shed one shell and are waiting for the next to grow. You eat all of them. I sat rigid with disbelief for quite some time in the august New York Yacht Club when told this, for the fact had not been vouchsafed until the creatures were placed in front of me. Once I was able physically to put a fork with a couple of claws and half a shell into my mouth (and that took some doing) I found the effort very worthwhile.

Further south, around Chesapeake Bay, you are very much in crab country and can hardly drive more than a few minutes without being exhorted by billboard and neon to try the 'only authentic' Baltimore or Maryland crabcake. I never tasted one worth the fuss. Frankly, I found them all over-peppered and under-crabbed. Perhaps I just didn't get to where the *authentic* ones are.

If you love the idea of crab but can't face the expense, use it as a flavouring rather than an ingredient. In a subtle cream or tomato sauce with some fine white fish fillets or even in a mayonnaise over a seafood salad, a little goes a long way. For the ultimate cheat, use it in a sauce over pieces of gently poached monkfish, which has the same texture and flavour as lobster. Make sure you have a dollop of brandy in the sauce, which is one of the most important ingredients of all in any fish sauce, hot or cold. It makes an extraordinary difference. Crab is excellent with avocado, pineapple, mango and other tropical fruit; a small amount added to a stir-fried mixture of vegetables or of vegetables and chicken will be a triumph. Otherwise it seems almost anything can be a flavouring for crab; in Singapore's restaurants their famed chili crab relies on masses of tomato ketchup to be authentic.

The problem with buying much of the imported crabmeat on the delicatessen shelf is working out exactly what is inside the pack, frozen or canned.

Dressed crab: this usually means that inferior brown meat (from inside the shell) plus other impertinences have been mixed with a small proportion of white meat, often into a khaki-coloured paste. Full details are usually revealed by perusal of the list of ingredients on the pack, and those who do not do this may regret their inattention to detail. Even where white and brown meat is included but kept apart in products sold as dressed crab, the proportion of white may be distressingly low in the interest of marketability. Buy warily, or do your own dressing.

Crabmeat: frozen or canned, this is usually better value for money as there is unlikely to be any adulteration. Indeed, you may be buying just white meat. Russian and Alaskan crabmeat is considered superlatively good and interchangeable as they come from the same geographical area. Any Russian crab from the Kamchatka Peninsula is sold under that name and this generally signifies that the crab was processed within hours of being caught and the can will contain only the leg and claw meat of male crabs, plus natural juices. This is usually what the Americans would sell as Alaskan King Crab.

Eel: no one knows a lot about the private life of the eel, except that it lives in the sea and spawns in the rivers; where it lives precisely has never been discovered but it is thought the Sargasso Sea is one of the likeliest spots.

The Romans liked eel so much they used to farm it, but we seem slowly to have lost our interest in eating it in Great Britain. True there are still places where jellied eel is available, but where are the shops that used to sell nothing else? Now the English catch their own eels and send them to Dutchmen to smoke, who send them back to us, expensively.

Serving: it is in smoked or tinned form that you will find eel on sale in your delicatessen. You can find smoked eels in two forms. First is the whole thing, head, tail and fins included. Chunks are cut off and you take it home to skin it and serve it quite plainly. Otherwise you will find long, thin, smoked fillets, which are often frozen. These taste not unlike raw kipper; with a sharp knife and equivalent turn of phrase you can make substitution of one for the other at considerable benefit to your pocket. Eel fillets go very well with other smoked fish as a starter – they like hot or cold scrambled eggs, and their shape is terrific for decorating such creations as a seafood mousse. I have been served them with chilled melon and I'm still trying to make my mind up about it years later. Probably not a good idea, I suspect.

The Spanish like very baby eel, elvers, which they call *anguillas*. They are white and matchstick-like, and available here in small tins. Being pre-cooked they are soft and delicate, with a nutty rather than fishy taste. Drain them gently and serve with a little oil, lemon juice and garlic. Or put them into a light frying batter to make fritters, which is how I like them best.

In New Zealand, these elvers are what we call whitebait, and whitebait fritters are part of the standard diet. The crunch of the bones and stare of the eyes of European whitebait (which is the fry of herrings and sprats) have turned many a colonial's thoughts to home faster than snow and ice ever did. New Zealand's eels are quite the most hideous things you can imagine and thus they are not eaten much there other than by the Maoris who are delighted to have this delicacy to themselves. Or almost. Eel lovers increasingly agree smoked New Zealand eel is possibly the best in the world and it can often be seen at Billingsgate, usually frozen. Thicker, fattier and more succulent than small European eels, it is wondrous cold but unctuous enough to survive grilling or other heat. It makes a sensational pâté, mashed and seasoned with lemon or lime juice and cognac, mixed with half its weight of melted but cooled unsalted butter and then folded with lightly whipped cream in the proportion of 300ml/½pt per 450g/1lb of mixture; the lemon juice and cognac will firm up the cream and the butter set it.

Herrings: herrings are one of man's oldest foods from the sea; remains have been identified in prehistoric settlements in Denmark, France and Portugal. Native to the north Atlantic, herrings migrate in huge numbers from the polar seas to the English Channel and thereabouts, starting in March.

Considering that each female herring lays some 50 million eggs a year it is little wonder shortages were rare until recently. They remain one of the cheapest fresh fish, yet are surprisingly unpopular in the British Isles, perhaps because of their association with poverty in the past.

Herring flesh is equal in nutrition to that of salmon, and a damned sight moister and more interesting much of the time. There is the problem of the bones, of course, but a little practice licks that. Start at the tail end and pull the flesh towards it, the way the bones point. Anyway, you can eat the bones, they are very good for you.

Most of the herrings eaten in Scandinavia and Europe are preserved, usually by salting. Today the catch is deep-chilled at sea and mixed with coarse salt in great concrete vats on return. There is a great art to the salting: to be right, the salt should have combined with the liquid straight from the fish and fully dissolved to form a strong brine in ten days. This is your basic salted herring. It is distinctly inedible, but will last for ages.

Smoked herrings must also be salted to some degree, and depending on the exact cure, or the habits of an area, the fish will either be smoked close to the smoke source, which is called hot-smoking and slightly cooks the flesh, or they will be smoked where they are not heated at all, and that is cold smoking.

Distinctions between types of salted and smoked herring are easily blurred, but I think the following list will explain most of what you are likely to come across.

BRITISH HERRINGS

Essentially the most famous styles of processed herrings are all smoked to a greater or lesser degree.

Bloaters: in spite of today's excellent cold storage and transport systems, these have virtually disappeared because they 'don't keep'. Bloaters are whole herrings salted for a very short time (in brine rather than dry salt) then cold-smoked. The very best are supposed to have come from Yarmouth during October and November and were eaten almost as soon as they had come from the smokehouse. 'The epicure will eat them before he goes to bed rather than wait for breakfast,' said the Wine and Food Society in 1944, when you could still get them. They were grilled or lightly fried and a very few shops in Norfolk are said to make them still. Harrods have them.

Buckling: these are lightly brined after having been beheaded and gutted, but they are unsplit and the roe or milt will be left in place. They are hot-smoked and so keep quite well. Increasingly more difficult to buy, they may be eaten cold or grilled and make an excellent paste. Bucklings are made in other countries (they were originally German), but the Dutch *Bokking* is still the entire fish, cold-smoked, and must be cleaned before consumption.

Kippers: relatively new on the scene, and probably introduced no more than a century ago. Kippering is a way of treating fish, salmon in particular, by splitting, brining, then smoking it. What we call smoked salmon was once called kippered salmon. If either salmon or herring is cooked before smoking it may not be called kippered.

A KIPPER PRIMER

Discussion on how to prepare kippers can lead to blows. I'll play safe and detail all those I know and you can choose your own.

Grilling: this gets rid of some of the excess oil, but must be done gently or you will also dry out the flesh and further toughen the outer layer. Open all the windows. Serve with a pat of butter.

Slow roasting: if you have an Aga or some other slow-combustion kitchen range with a permanently luke-warm compartment, place your kippers in a covered container with some butter and perhaps a little milk and leave overnight.

Steeping: boil some water, pour it over the kippers until they are just covered and leave for a few minutes, until they are warmed through. Jugged kippers are done like this too, except they are plunged vertically into a jug, but you do risk the tail coming off when you remove the fish. Steeping gives very moist results and the water also dissolves some of the salt. I think it is the best way.

Flaming: it is said Irish enthusiasts pour heated whiskey over their kippers, set it alight, then set-to when the flames die. Can you imagine an Irishman (or anyone else, for that matter) burning his whiskey?

Other cooking: kippers make excellent pâtés but you may as well buy the boned fillets for this. Uncooked kippers, skinned and divided into long strips, are a successful substitute for smoked eel, but good enough to serve without subterfuge. A little cold, creamy scrambled egg, some dill-pickled cucumber, a slice of lemon and some black olives would all make good accompaniments.

Only the Isle of Man and a few places in Scotland still make proper kippers smoked over oak chips. Most of those you buy have been cooked in some way to prolong their life, and the colour and flavour of smoking has been painted on so they are not really kippers. You only have to see one real kipper to be able to detect fakes; real ones have a glorious pale golden glow rather then a dark, treacle-like coating. The best time for kippers from the Isle of Man is July and August.

Red herrings: you can rarely buy these nowadays, but they used to be the most important of standbys before refrigeration. Red herrings were highly salted and highly smoked and thus almost indestructible. If you find some, soak them for many hours in milk or water before grilling or poaching. A soft-poached egg, cooked without salt, is a perfect foil, as with so many smoked fish.

CONTINENTAL HERRINGS

European processing styles are based on salt or vinegar rather than smoking.

Bismark: these are fresh herring fillets marinated in vinegar with onion, so are fairly rugged.

Fillets: in bulk or in jars, this is the way tons of herring are eaten. The fillets have usually been salted, then soaked and treated in a number of ways. Some go into a red wine sauce, some into a tomato sauce, some are in oil. There are dozens of varieties commercially available and hundreds more are made in the home. The Danish range, bought in jars, keep excellently in the refrigerator; use the fillets as part of an hors d'oeuvre, or slice them small for use in potato salads. They can be mashed into a paste with stewed, or chopped, raw apple and with egg yolk as a simple pâté. Most fillets are called *matjesfillet* (but they may not be, so see below).

Matjesherring: used very generally for all herring fillets or salted herrings but properly means a herring gathered in early summer when the roe is still developing. They may be treated two ways – either lightly brined with some sugar content or heavily brined in the usual way of salt herring. If you are buying them 'straight', ie direct from the brine, I think it likely that *matjesfillets* have been lightly salted and whole *matjesherrings* are more heavily treated. In either case, soak them in water or milk to remove the salt you do not want. If preserved other than in brine, you will not need to soak them.

They may be eaten just like that, especially the fillets, or perhaps with onion – and in Holland green beans are usual. Or you can then make a marinade, warm or cold, and flavour them according to taste.

Rollmops: these are totally eviscerated fresh herrings, the two fillets joined together only by skin. No bone or fins should remain. The double fillets are rolled around pickled cucumber, sometimes with carrot and onion, and kept in an acidic-brine liquid, usually made with a white vinegar. It is easy to play with this idea at home, using spices and apple with cider vinegar for instance. Soured cream, dill and more pickled cucumbers are by far the best accompaniments. Oh, and ice-cold vodka or aquavit. It is said rollmops are a great cure for hangovers but I suspect the accompanying liquor is far more useful.

Salt herring: the basic preserved herring, which must be soaked for at least 24 hours before it can be used. Fillet this and serve it with soured cream, pickled beetroot and cucumber, onion rings, potatoes, hard-boiled eggs, gherkins and decent wholemeal or rye bread. Once soaked the whole or filleted herrings can be vinegar-pickled or put into any number of mustard, tomato, onion or sour cream sauces.

Strömming: this is a _sort_ of herring, the Baltic herring, which is smaller and leaner than the Atlantic variety. It is less likely to be highly salted and once soaked is usually put into _mild_ pickles, with mustard and dill sauces or in sour cream and dill – using small amounts of raw onion rather than vinegar to provide any acidity. The Swedes use an acid they call Attika, which I think is acetic acid and has a pleasant sweetness. All in all I think I prefer the serving style of the Baltic herring to the more fierce German and Dutch herring types. If you are ever offered something called _surströmming_, think very carefully before agreeing. These are Baltic herrings which have been packed with only half the normal amount of salt then sealed in barrels which are left in the sun. Alan Davidson's _North Atlantic Seafood_ says that birds drop dead from the sky when the barrels are opened. It is acceptable to find tinned surströmming bulging, a sign of proper fermentation. Open these tins in the open air, standing up wind, and have on hand some water for rinsing and some ready-chopped red onion which allows you to get the fillets to your mouth before your nose realizes what is happening. Thank you – but no thank you...

Mackerel: although its cheapness means it is often ignored, the mackerel is quite one of the most fascinating – and delicious – fish there is. Even the reason for its name is bizarre. Mackerel is simply the English version of the French nickname for the fish, _maquereau_. _Maquereau_ means 'pimp' or 'procurer', and the name was given because the female makes a point of escorting inexperienced female shad to ripe males; for this, American gourmets, Eartha Kitt and Nöel Coward are grateful. When waiters bring shad roe to discerning diners, they bring what is arguably the most delicious of all roes to table – only caviare excepted. When in the United States, and on the Atlantic coast during winter, it's certainly worth singing for. But, back to mackerel.

The mackerel has a furious temper when in schools, which it usually is, and so brave it attacks fish far larger than itself. Indeed, in Norway there is a story of a sailor being dragged underwater by mackerel while swimming and released ten minutes later bereft of most of his flesh. It is also a stupid fish, and frightfully easy to catch. It has the highest proportion of fatty matter of any fish and this deteriorates very quickly.

Like so many fish, they spawn in August and September and fresh or smoked mackerel should be avoided then. In October they start putting on condition, and by December are quite perfect. I tend not to rate tinned mackerel of any kind or provenance, especially the ghastly smoked mackerel pâtés, which are overburdened with farinacea (as, in my opinion, are most English-produced seafood soups, but perhaps you have better luck). Many mackerel products come from abroad and are thus a slightly different and always inferior species, by common consent.

But smoked English mackerel is something else, and when good surpasses any trout I have ever eaten. The boned, smoked mackerel fillets – flat and torpedo shaped – that are the staples of many a wine bar, are overcooked and then artificially coloured and smoke-flavoured, a process that often reduces the flesh to a gummy paste. But, when you find mackerel whole, with only the head and gut missing, their skins a pale, iridescent gold rather than lurid copper, well then you've found the real thing – almost certainly from Cornwall and quite superb. When buying them, avoid a slimy skin (which will actually be poisonous) and go for something firm but not rigid.

Interestingly, mackerel may be sexed at sight; those with wavy lines on their bodies are females, those with straight lines are male, and much tastier.

Serving: smoked mackerel is best served quite simply and it is cheap enough to allow ventures into pâté making or mousses, something I don't normally hold with in something of this quality.

Whether serving a whole or a half smoked mackerel, you should take the spine out. This is simply achieved by first extending the slit in the gut right back to the tail. Then with the point of a sharp knife gently fold the top half of the fish back, having a pair of poultry scissors on hand to cut any intransigent bones. You can now lift out the whole backbone and it remains only to remove the finer ones that remain around the stomach cavity.

For basic serving I like them slightly chilled, served with lemon wedges and a good, creamy horseradish sauce, which is indispensable when presenting mackerel in any form.

Cubed beetroot also goes exceptionally well with smoked mackerel. For a stunning but simple buffet presentation, arrange boned halves of smoked mackerel like the spokes of a wheel, with the pointed tail ends in the middle. Pile cubed beetroot in the centre. Pipe horseradish cream down the centre of each mackerel half and sprinkle this with a little sweet paprika. Fill the space between each fish half with trimmed, thin lemon wedges and large sprigs of parsley. This is especially popular with men, who fall upon its hearty flavour with relief.

You can lightly grill smoked mackerel, which then need something quite sharp to accompany them. I would suggest spiced red cabbage and a purée of celeriac, into which you have stirred a lot of finely chopped parsley and garlic. Great on a cold, boring winter's day for lunch or supper.

The most common use of smoked mackerel is for making a pâté, more a fish paste really, but whoever decided it should be combined with cream cheese? For years I made such a mixture for my delicatessen customers, and felt sick every time I did – a horrid idea with a nasty colour and, often, a disconcerting texture too. Eventually I found the alternative, canned kidney beans. Whizz together a couple of large, skinned and boned fillets with two or three small cooked beetroot. Then add 125g/4oz of drained cooked red kidney beans until you have a good rough look: pulse in a teaspoon of horseradish to taste, then spoon out and fold in a small carton of soured cream, or the equivalent of fromage blanc. Dribble on some olive oil when you serve it with lots of roughly torn parsley.

Mussels: in New Zealand, mussels are huge, so huge that after de-bearding and de-tonguing they must be cut in half, at least. They have a certain rugged appeal, I remember, but cannot ever equal the sweeter delights of the smaller European mussels.

Now, somewhere between those types we have the Kiwi green-lipped mussel. It is the shell which has jewel-like iridescence and thus these mussels arrive on the half shell. They are farmed, processed within minutes of being harvested, and deep-frozen. Some are smoked and very good indeed. You will see there are two colours, a rich buff cream and bright orange; these are not different varieties, but sexual difference. The pale ones are male and the orange are female. Sexual confusion has no place in that country. Increasingly available, green-lipped mussels are good just as they are in salad and seafood platters. If used in hot dishes they must only be warmed through as they are already cooked and will shrink and toughen if heated further. Often marketed in European sauces and styles (marinière for instance) but perhaps best served as they come. Provided Europeans can face their larger size.

Although available packed with flavours ranging from tomato to onion and pickles, or with vinegar, I find mussels packed in tins or bottles with brine and their own juices by far the best. They are usually from Scandinavia, Norway's Limfjord being perhaps the best source. They are exceptionally useful, not least of all because they have enough size and colour to make a contribution to the eye as well as the tongue.

Serving: Pasta salads seem particularly good receptacles for ready-prepared mussels. Seafood sauces to put into pastry cases or to complement poached fish fillets are much more interesting with mussels than with prawns.

If you follow my instructions for cooking rice, add some saffron and use the juices from a tin or bottle to make up the cooking liquid. When the water level reduces to that of the rice, lay the mussels on top of the rice, then cover the saucepan and proceed as usual. They will be steamed to a succulent softness, any juices they lose being transferred to the rice. When it is ready, stir gently with a fork and you have a supper or lunch dish that is attractive, filling and satisfying.

Deep fried in a decent batter, heated in hot butter, garlic and parsley, tossed in a dressing with orange segments and Mozzarella cheese or served in a hot white wine sauce on rice, mussels are worth your attention if they have so far escaped it.

Oysters: it would be possible to write an entire book on oysters, and I suppose someone has. In this country they were once a staple of the grateful poor, as was salmon, and not so very long ago, either. Now like many simple local foods they have become rare and expensive and likely to be served fancifully and badly.

The oysters of most European and American sources have been transplanted, cross-bred and artficially brought-on to a degree that has eroded some of the ancient clear-cut distinctions of flavour. Most fishmongers who still sell oysters on the shell couldn't tell you what type they are. A far cry from France, where in the tiniest inland markets the fish stalls will offer a choice of eight or nine varieties for prices that start at only £1 for ten. The one really to go for there is the *verte de Marenne*, which is a bright, curious green – my hat goes off to the man who was first brave enough to put one in his mouth.

The original European oyster, the native *ostrea edulis* is immediately recognisable for having a flat and only lightly ridged shell. But this is rare for it has been decimated more than once by disease. It was first replaced by the *portugaise*, which isn't a true oyster but *gryphea angulata*, and, when that too succumbed to disease, by a Japanese variety, *crassostrea gigas*, often called a *creuse* by the French.

America has a wide variety of interesting oysters, some of them bordering on the monster-sized and needing to be cut up before ingestion. The coastal towns and cities make much of their local seafoods and you can usually get good advice and buy specifically. In Australasia the choice is more limited but those who know rate the rock oyster of the eastern Australian coast as amongst the most succulent in the world. They have the added advantage of being equally suited to cooking.

In ancient Greece, where paper was short, you voted to ostracize someone by marking an oyster shell.

Serving: smoked oysters, which usually come in tins from Japan and are eaten by old bachelors with as much relish as spinsters eat soft roes, are delicious. But they are often ruined by being served in the filthy cotton seed oil in which they are preserved. They should be be fully drained and then sprinkled with the smallest amount of lemon juice. For special occasions I would take the trouble to pat them dry of oil with kitchen tissue and then present them in a nice, gentle lemon juice and oil mixture.

Smoked oysters may be treated with a little more abandon than the ones which come canned in brine or stock. Minced or chopped, their flavour goes a long way to flavour sauces for garnish or filling puff pastry cases. You can make the most of their flavour to replace bacon on skewers of seafood for your grill or barbecue.

Smoked or brined, canned oysters which have been well drained are very good plumped and warmed very gently in a lemon-sharp white sauce, to serve with poached fish or chicken. They also make an outstanding stuffing for beef and are a simpler way to recreate the cornmeal and oyster stuffing which is so good and American with turkey. They perfectly add the proper touch to authentic Lancashire hotpot (well, all right, they shouldn't really be smoked for that, but you know what I mean) and nicely finish a steak and kidney pie the old fashioned way; best plan is to put them on top of the cooked meat mixture, so that their salt-savour is the first thing you smell when the crust is cut.

Pilchards: often described either as a type of herring or a type of sardine, the pilchard is cleverly both. A timid member of the herring family, it is actually an adult sardine, and thus by any measure good and fatty and delicious when fresh. They are a specialty of the Devon and Cornish coast between July and December but great care is needed when buying them, as they spoil extremely quickly. I'm not fond of tinned fish, a feeling particularly reinforced in the case of pilchards by seeing how many people buy them to feed to their pets.

Serving: the most famous dish made with fresh pilchards is the variety of stargazey pies of the West of England, which can be several shapes and sizes, all noted for being baked with whole fish whose heads protrude from their pastry cases. This is done to incorporate the rich oil from the head in the finished pie, without covering the heads with pastry, which would make eating difficult. You'd be lucky to get stargazey pies of any kind these days, dead lucky if they included pilchards, whole or beheaded.

We are most likely to eat canned pilchards whole as part of an Italian mixed antipasto. Otherwise, the type in tomato sauce, mashed with a little vinegar or lemon juice and soft butter, or cream cheese if you must, can make a fish paste of sorts that would go nicely on hot toast. A little chopped onion, capers, olives or anchovies, that enchanted saviour of the banal, might help.

Prawns and shrimps: although different from one another, prawns and shrimps look alike enough to be called by one another's name. In the United Kingdom you are usually safe calling little ones shrimps and big ones prawns. In America they are all called shrimp, but the giant Pacific variety, a favourite ingredient of many American menus, are often called prawns for the sake of alliteration.

Canned: I am constantly astonished at how good canned prawns can be, and how cheap. Perhaps those from Malaysia can be a disappointment for they are often shrimps, tiny and floury. Usually, though, tins are packed full of moist plump, pink, crustacea, their shells removed. The initial outlay might seem high for such a small object, but the value for money is comparable with frozen prawns.

Frozen: there are several pitfalls and pieces of advice to heed when buying frozen prawns. Some types are free-flowing, that is, each prawn has a protective ice-glaze. This means you are paying for water rather than seafood, and in the case of some Indian prawns, the water is highly salted. I have ruined a very fine sauce for 100 people by adding these prawns, liquid and all.

It is important that you defrost frozen prawns very slowly, or you will lose flavour, texture and moistness. The best way is to leave them in their bag in the refrigerator overnight. They will then be moist and plump and have retained most of their natural juices. If they are then to go into a hot sauce, first bring them to room temperature. Then they can be popped into the sauce just for the few minutes needed to cook them or heat them through. They do not need to be piping hot and the sauce should never be boiled.

I think you should carefully consider the size of prawn you want to use. Generally larger ones look better and they behave better if they are to be served hot. Prawns will inevitably shrink when cooked or when reheated. If cooked or heated for too long they will also toughen. Indeed, unless you are buying cooked prawns and they are to be used for stuffing something elegant, or puréed, or used as a garnish, bigger is always far better.

I do not understand the combination of avocado and prawns; both are bland and often even have the same texture. If you want something pink and green, then peel and cut some kiwi fruit into segments (not slices), soak those in Pernod for a while and serve your prawns on them with a mayonnaise flavoured with fresh lime juice and grated lime peel.

You can also extend prawns with cheaper seafood, especially mussels, as long as they have been canned in brine rather than vinegar. The two are especially good in pasta sauces, or in hot sauces to stuff vol-au-vents.

A PRAWN PÂTÉ

To make a truly excellent prawn pâté or spread, liquidize cooked prawns with half their weight of warm melted butter. Add white vermouth to taste. Let cool. Then whip some cream in the proportion of 300ml/½pt to 250g/½lb of prawns. Gently fold the two together, keeping as much air in the mixture as possible. Add a little white pepper if you like. Fresh or dried dill is a most refreshing addition, and you might also like a squeeze or two of lemon juice or a touch of brandy. If you want to use less cream, substitute half the amount for curd cheese, cream cheese, or cottage cheese you have sieved.

Other flavours which go well with prawns are horseradish, tomato, garlic, basil, ground cumin and coriander, sweet or hot paprika and, of course, cucumber.

Potted shrimps: the ones you buy commercially, are very good and easily copied at home, for they have simply been packed in butter flavoured with a little spice, mainly mace. But they should be served warm, with the seasoned butter in glistening pools. It makes me angry that rather famous fish restaurants, unable to make potted shrimps themselves, cannot read the labels on the ones they buy frozen and serve them ice-cold with limp toast made from plastic bread.

Roe: it will come as something of a shock to many a spinster to learn that her favourite supper of soft roes is not fish eggs but the milt or sperm of the male. Perhaps it is precisely this that explains their popularity. It's certainly a deliciously wicked thing to reveal as they are being enjoyed, and can quite spoil the most determined appetite, male or female. It is the hard roe which is the egg of the female fish.

Roe of both sorts are popular right round the world. In the Occident, the general agreement on flavour, in ascending order, is: mackerel, herring then shad and carp equal first. Most of the soft roe sold in fish shops or in cans is cod roe, but it can be herring, too.

Greeks are specially partial to the eggs of the grey mullet, and this is the proper basis for *taramasalata*. But try telling that to the shrill-accented debs in striped aprons behind a thousand deli counters. They'll dish out a pink paste by the hundredweight and swear it's better than they had in Corfu or Kos or Katerini. It'll certainly be *different*, for although the smoked cod's roe used is a good substitute for that of mullet, the *taramasalata* is really only an emulsion of low-grade bread and oil with some little amount of roe and a great deal of colouring. When we made it properly (albeit with cod roe) at my delicatessen we sold it as fast as it could be made until the cod war put up the cost of the roe astronomically. I didn't have the nerve of some Greek entrepreneurs in London who have made it down to a price rather than up to a standard. Pity. I'd never have needed to touch a typewriter again, for now they make virtually all that is sold in London – yes, even for the big stores and tiny delis that pride themselves on quality.

Much the most expensive of roe products is *botargo* (*botargue* in France) which is salted and pressed whole roe, again properly of grey mullet but sometimes of other fish. This is one of our oldest and simplest delicacies and, wouldn't you guess, inevitably one of the most expensive these days. It is found in many Mediterranean countries but belief in the disinfectant and protective qualities of the salting and drying process is ill-founded. When travelling companions of mine bought botargo from a street stall in Suez, there was no way of knowing where it had been; but we soon knew in which little room we would find them the next few days. As botargo is eaten uncooked, perhaps with oil and lemon, you also eat whatever contamination it has collected. This is definitely a case of buying only the highest quality from the most reliable source.

Serving: smoked roe, usually hard cod's roe, can be dipped in batter and fried, chilled and served sliced with light vinaigrette dressing, placed on toast and covered with a well-seasoned white sauce – but it really is rather too strong for most people's taste. It's better as an addition to a fish sauce or a garnish to something relatively bland of a fishy nature. There is one exception in my experience and that happened in New Zealand. There you can buy the firm smoked roe of both the schnapper and the blue cod (the latter when smoked was described by André Simon as being like Finnan Haddie gone to heaven). When served unpretentiously in thin delicate slices in a most successful small restaurant in Auckland called Cluny's, it was accompanied by a perfect light vinaigrette and a garlic mayonnaise. Quite worth getting off your jet to experience.

Salt cod: salt cod was the most important staple flesh of the medieval Catholic world, and continued so for much of the time after the introduction of Protestantism. During the long, universally observed Lent and the twice-weekly fish days, salt cod kept the wolf from the door. For the sake of Christian observance, millions of tons of cod have been pulled from the waters of the Atlantic and it was in search of bigger harvests that the first English colonies in the New World were established. In fact, so important was the catching and salting of cod to Massachusetts that they incorporated one in the design of their Great Seal of the State.

As Catholicism gradually lost its grip on Europe, and the great explorers introduced new foods, salt fish became less and less important in Britain. Just as well, when you ponder the problems caused by latter day over-fishing and the struggles for territorial rights which led to the unpleasant cod wars.

Now, the past importance of salt cod to our ancestors is hard to believe, considering the difficulty of buying it in the United Kingdom. West Indian communities usually have shops displaying the dried, crusty sides hung from the ceiling. And one enterprizing company is now prepackaging smaller amounts and these are available at supermarkets where there is an ethnic demand. Good Portuguese, Spanish, Italian and Greek shops should also sell it. Sadly, like herrings, it is considered too cheap to be fashionable. But it is well worth the attention of any true gastronome.

There is a Norwegian salted cod called *stockfish*, which is especially popular in Germany, Belgium and Holland; you may treat it as if it were ordinary salt cod.

Ling is the name given to the largest variety of cod, and as this is the type usually salted, salt cod was once known as ling, a point to be aware of when using old cookery books.

Serving: preparation of salt cod requires some forethought, as it should be soaked for a full 36 hours in several changes of water to hydrate and de-salt it. A 24 hour treatment will probably suffice, however. When soaked you drain off the last water, then put the fish in a saucepan with masses of cold water and bring the lot very slowly to the boil. It should now simmer, with the water barely moving, until the flesh flakes easily. It must never ever boil again, so if you have a large cooker like an Aga, even better results can be obtained if you simply leave the saucepan, once it has boiled, on the back where there will be just enough heat to give the desired results; that is how the Icelanders recommend you do it.

If you haven't planned ahead you can put the dried salt cod in cold water, bring it slowly to the simmer, change the water and repeat the process several times. But it won't be as nice.

The classic English way of presenting salt cod is predictably boring, for it is simply boiled and served with a sauce of hard-boiled eggs. It is only when you start looking at the kitchens of the Brazilians and Portuguese, the Spanish and Creoles, that it becomes remotely exciting.

Salmon: all salmon is not salmon, well not the same variety anyway. The Atlantic salmon, most famed as Scottish smoked salmon, is considered the best. But the four main varieties of Pacific salmon have much greater variety of use – nothing else cans quite as well as the Canadian pink salmon.

The major change in salmon in the past decade has been the extraordinary growth in farmed salmon, which in turn has meant smoked salmon and newly fashionable gravadlax are cheaper and available to more people than they used to be. That is a good thing you might think, but others hate the very idea of farmed salmon and consider it irredeemably inferior. There are differences between them and wild salmon, that's for certain, but I can't think it's all bad news.

You can generally tell one from the other if the fish are whole, for wild salmon will have bigger, wider tail fins with a deeper curve of the fan, the result of having to fight to swim harder and further. If wild salmon are caught in an estuary or only a short distance up a river they will be superb eating, rich with fat and fully fleshed. But because they do not feed in fresh water but live on stored fat and then their own protein, the further up the river the less good their condition, and the drier the flesh. Should they also have been caught early in the day, not instantly refrigerated and then battered in the back of a car, well, it's obvious they will not be as good as they might. Yet for many, this is all they have enjoyed and anything different is considered inferior.

Farmed salmon are only harvested in tip-top condition, immediately chilled and carefully shipped. They will invariably have a softer textured flesh than much wild salmon, but it can be argued this is because they are actually in better condition and that a fresh, farmed salmon is actually what salmon *should* be like.

The farmed salmon industry is still young, still learning the environmental effects of its activities on the remote waters they use. Some dreadful mistakes have been made, but monumental effort has made this a very important industry, bringing much needed jobs to otherwise barren areas. The farmed salmon's feed contains substances which replicate those in their natural foods which turn their flesh red; there have been scares about this, but they were exposed as wildly inaccurate.

The simple fact is that most smoked salmon is farmed salmon and much of that has been imported frozen from Norway.

Canned: I vividly remember the first time I saw salmon in cans in shops. It was from Russia and it must have been in the early fifties when the Russians were, to us in New Zealand anyway, something rather terrible. For them to be supplying us with luxuries was thought a bit much. Nonetheless it was with great relief that I found we were one of the first families to eat it, and it was wonderful. Later everyone was eating Russian salmon like mad and it seemed less appealing, even though it was only the finest red salmon being imported. Later still, the taste for tinned salmon rose to its pre-war level and cheaper pink salmon flooded the market. Shocked at its easy availability, I stopped eating both colours on the pretext that I was sick of it and never touched it for almost 20 years, when I found a Robert Carrier recipe for an Easy Tinned Salmon Soufflé. I was prepared to laugh – you may still – but it turned out to be excellent. Of course, one had to add a little of this and a little of that, but it remains one of my most basic stand-bys, is the bringer of some of my greatest compliments, and has the appeal of being all the better for the use of cheaper pink salmon.

If you come across little white crystals in your canned salmon that look like glass, they aren't. They are a harmless chemical called magnesium ammonium phosphate, which is the sort of thing that can occur naturally in man in the tartar film on teeth. You can check that these crystals are not glass by squashing one between a fingernail and a hard surface. Glass would not crush. The substance is also known as struvite and dissolves in the digestive juices of the stomach with no harm to the ingestee.

Gravadlax/Gravlax: what a meteoric rise this product has had, essentially a sweet-cured salmon flavoured with dill. When I prepared it on BBC television in 1982 only travellers to Scandinavia and food freaks knew about it. Today it is in supermarkets, well almost, for the commercialization of gravadlax has inevitably led to changes and some isn't the real thing at all.

The original product is sides of salmon smothered in salt and sugar and flavoured with crushed white peppercorns and masses of fresh dill. As the method was for preservation as much as anything, it was buried (the name means buried salmon) in the cold winter ground and the pressure of the soil contributed to the slow release of liquid and compression of the flesh. The released liquid would then dissolve the salt and sugar and their flavours and preservative properties would be carried back into the flesh. If you made it domestically you would merely put a weight on top of the sandwiched sides. The flesh becomes firm and translucent and is generally recognizable by its elongated shape when sliced.

Although much that I taste from pre-packs is certainly edible, it is softer than that I would make, presumably because a higher moisture content has been allow-

MAKE YOUR OWN GRAVADLAX

To make your own, a few ounces each of coarse salt and of sugar, a good scatter of lightly crushed peppercorns and a big bunch of dill will do nicely for two sides. Dried dill is very good and quite indistinguishable from fresh when it comes to it.

Most of the mixture should be evenly spread on the naked flesh, which is then sandwiched head to tail. Sprinkle half the remainder in a suitable container, add the fish and then the rest of the pickling mix. Cover with cling film and then a board or use another of the same flat-bottomed containers and then weight that: I reckon on two or three times the weight of the fish.

Leave at cool room temperature for 24 hours, turning the fish a couple of times and spooning the pickle which is being produced back between the sides. Then chill for two or three more days until all the pickle is dissolved and the fish is firm and evenly compressed. Scrape away most of the dill and pepper which is left, wrap tightly and keep chilled. It will keep well for a week or more.

Slice rather more thickly than for smoked salmon, and cut at a very steep angle right down to the skin to get the traditional shape, but should you wish to cut it like smoked salmon, nothing horrible will happen. Indeed this is easier to present. I twist the pieces slightly and form a ring on a flat plate with them. Into that I put some mixed salad leaves and a few shelled hard-boiled quail eggs. If the pickle is not too salty, a puddle of this is good, and then I sprinkle the lot with vodka. A pepper vodka or vodka in which you have macerated fresh green or dried black peppercorns and dill is particularly good.

Do not hesitate to substitute something else for the dill. Both mint and parsley are very successful, but not quite as wonderful as using rather a lot of finely sliced fresh ginger, an East-West marriage that I expect would once have earned me titles and country estates in both hemispheres. As it is, I give it to you, and you should make as much from it as you can.

ed, giving more weight to sell.

The product is eaten in Scandinavia with a sweet mustard sauce which I think is intrinsically disgusting anyway, and does nothing but harm to this most delicious of products. Dill cured salmon is best just by itself, with a little soured cream or with soured cream mixed with mild seed mustard.

Some recipes include cognac or vodka but they cannot overcome the amount of salt and sugar and are thus wasted; if there were enough to defeat the salt and sugar they would turn the flesh opaque and change the flavour. Sometimes spruce sprigs have been included and this is very good.

Smoked salmon: rightly regarded as one of the world's greatest delicacies, and the best is probably Scottish salmon smoked in London. The proper term is kippered salmon, as kippering is what is done to it: the salmon are beheaded and gutted, split, salted and then cold-smoked. The kippering process was only applied to herrings some time last century.

As with all old-established food processes there are many variations: some smokers will cook the salmon a little before smoking it (which is not true kippering). Some will hot-smoke it. Some will burn one type of woodchip and some will use others. I know of one company that uses Drambuie in its method, giving the salmon a most appealing golden brown colour and a definite extra flavour; but they won't reveal how and when the Drambuie is employed.

There are two traditional styles of curing and smoking, the Scotch (you are allowed to say that rather than Scottish if it is salmon or whisky) and the London. The London processing of salmon was long in the hands of European immigrants, usually Jewish. Because their market was on their doorsteps, they cured lightly and smoked lightly. Salmon from Scotland had to endure three or more days transportation by stage coach before it was sold, and for safety was thus cured and smoked much more heavily. Today, London curing can hardly be called traditional, because there are such strong laws about smoke emission; computer controlled mechanical smokers do it without exhausting smoke into the air. Mechanics rule in Scottish establishments of size too. What with that, vacuum packing and modern transportation it means anyone can smoke to any style they like. Yet there are many small smokehouses, in Scotland and Ireland particularly, that still smoke salmon and other foods by hand and eye, the old way, and you will generally find them more likely to favour a firmer, more savoury smokiness. If you find one, encourage them.

The best Scotch smoked salmon is pink-red and firm in texture; when it is cut, it should be slightly transparent and waxy. The smaller fish, the grilse, have a more delicate flavour and need to be sliced slightly thickly. Only the larger and more mature adults have enough flavour in them to be sliced finely.

Canadian smoked salmon you will find to be redder in colour, drier in texture, and denser. You might find it saltier, too, for it is expected to last longer, what with having to be transported here, and waiting for people to get over their natural inclination against it. The major difference is the variety of salmon. These are not Atlantic salmon but four varieties of Pacific salmon. Coho, pink, sockeye and king may all smoke well but the pink and coho are generally the ones you find. Think of it as smoked salmon, yes, but different smoked salmon. Really, there is nothing wrong with Canadian salmon other than being overcharged for it. And if you are catering for a lot of drunks, or family friends who haven't much knowledge of these things, it is a waste of money to serve the best Scotch smoked salmon.

To slice: mechanization has also taken over one of the most satisfying things I have ever done, slicing smoked salmon to order. Now it comes pre-sliced which is some guarantee of freshness and quality I suppose, but it's hell to peel the slices apart and generally much more oily. Slicing smoked salmon is not difficult; only getting practice is. When I was training people I found there are those who can and those who can't slice salmon, a gift easily discerned by watching those same people cut anything else. A man or woman who cuts a crooked slice of bread, or who always manages to crush bread while cutting it, does not understand knives. People like this think that pressure is what cuts and will not let the knife edge do the work. Try it. Hold a knife lightly and instead of pushing the blade through, let the blade slip through the bread as you go back and forth with only the lightest pressure. You'll get a thin, even slice and, unless you can do this, you'll never be able to cut smoked salmon finely, although frankly I have never understood the appeal of thin slices. Thick slices are much more rewarding to eat, but I suppose they cost more...

If you are presented with an unboned side of smoked salmon, this is what you do. First, cut off the fins and remaining bones at the bigger, gill end of the side. Now put the salmon on the edge of a table or draining board, skin side down, and using your fingertip, ease back the skin along the edges. If you can, peel it back under the flesh a little. Now slice off that peeled-back skin, including the soft foundations of the fins, all the way back to the tail. Next you have to attack the bones. Keeping a long, thin knife horizontal, take a thin slice off the highest part of the salmon, starting at the gill and working towards the tail. As you slice the smoked layer away you will, or should, expose the tops of the tiny white bones, which is what you are going to remove; if not, rub the back of the knife on the flesh from top to tail. The best tools are an eyebrow tweezer that has ribbed ends or a pair of pliers that have a long thin nose. So as not to tear the flesh, don't pull each bone out by yanking up vertically. Instead, pull gently in the same direction as the bones lie; you will be pulling towards the tail end. Once these are out you can start slicing and there are two ways to do this.

Short slices: in this method, which is the easier of the two, you start slicing about one third of the way along and slice towards the tail. (I *know* Selfridges slice towards the other end, but they are the only people in the world who do). The knife should be only very slightly angled and aimed so that you are cutting in towards the skin. Each time you take another slice you start a slither further back and keep the angle the same and soon you will have a slice that starts at the top, goes through the flesh and ends up at the skin. This is exactly right for as you continue this method you will have no wastage and the flesh close to the skin will be used at the same rate as the rest and not left, as is the case with...

Long slices: you start at the gill end and slice all the way along, with a flat knife trying to get slices that are as wide and long as possible. It is certainly very satisfactory to be able to slice a large salmon in thin tissues that could simply be laid one upon another to form the entire shape again. But this can only be contemplated privately or in catering when you know you can use all the fish. In a shop you tend to get left with the last ½cm/¼in of flesh, which, because you can see the skin through it, looks dark and unappetizing. Indeed, if it has been waiting for a customer for some time, it will be dried and possibly rancid.

Presentation: although it is the custom to serve smoked salmon with slices of lemon it really is too awful to spray it with such sharp liquid, for this immediately masks the delicate flavour that so many have laboured to create. Neither should it be too cold, for this will also mask the flavour. To get the absolutely best flavour from smoked salmon take it from the refrigerator about half an hour before you wish to serve it. Instead of allowing your guests to squirt lemon juice over it, rub each plate with a cut lemon wedge or a little grated peel, which is better. The perfume of the lemon juice or zest will soon penetrate the flesh with altogether more delicious results. An all together better idea is to sprinkle on neat gin or vodka, particularly if the latter is one of the flavoured types. You get just enough bite to contrast with the fish and the smooth texture of the alcohol is strangely complementary; many of the subsequent compliments will be equally weird.

I shouldn't have to say this, but the American custom of serving smoked salmon with raw onion is barbarity. It makes me seethe to see decent hotels and restaurants pandering to requests to serve it like this – perhaps they aren't such good establishments after all?

Of all the things that go well with smoked salmon, scrambled eggs are probably my favourite, hot or cold. HRH The Prince of Wales is said to be happiest of all when confronted by such a dish, a man of regal taste indeed. For a really marvellous starter for an important meal, roll smoked salmon around cold, creamy scrambled eggs to make a stuffed horn, and sprinkle the overflowing egg with black caviare, real or otherwise. For hot scrambled eggs, you simply slice the salmon into fingers and throw it over the eggs as you are serving them or lay it on the toast on which the eggs are presented. A very small amount of smoked salmon makes a wonderful addition to sauce for quite plain fish. It quite transforms cauliflower cheese, if there is not too much cheese in the sauce: better is to make a wine and cream white sauce instead, strew the cooked cauliflower with smoked salmon strips, perhaps with buffalo Mozzarella between them and the vegetable, pour on the sauce, sprinkle liberally with breadcrumbs mixed with lemon zest and chopped parsley and bake until browned.

Storing: smoked salmon freezes and defrosts extremely well and provided it is allowed to do the latter slowly can be as good as fresh, but, like all other frozen foods you only get out what you put in.

There are now a number of vacuum packs of smoked salmon on the market and they are an excellent way to transport salmon for they do not need refrigerating; however I'm told that refrigeration will extend the life of such salmon even further. Be assiduous in protecting the plastic from puncturing and only accept those that are tightly bound to the fish by vacuum. If there is the slightest looseness anywhere in the packaging or, worse, ballooning, the vacuum has been broken and the fish may be harbouring and nourishing a great number of organisms that may be dangerous before you can smell them. Otherwise a side of smoked salmon will keep for ages in a refrigerator if the air is allowed to circulate; ideally it should be hung. Even a cold larder is cold enough to keep smoked salmon sides good for weeks.

Sardines: for a while there you could almost forget sardines as a delicatessen product. I had calls from all round the world from people wanting me to get sardines in olive oil from Brittany. 'You know,' they would say, 'the ones you mature for a couple of years, turning them every few months.' There are very few traditional sardine canners left in Brittany, and for a long time the market taste moved. Thank goodness you can't fool all of the people all of the time. Although sardines do indeed come embalmed in countless horrors, they are increasingly available in olive oil and we must all buy as many as we can so they are not endangered again. The price range is tremendous, but all do improve with age and are the better for turning, which keeps the oil evenly distributed.

In fact, only refined olive oil is used, which is almost tasteless and even the very superior canners of Portugal have told me that after six months in the can, sunflower oil gives virtually indistinguishable results and flavour. There are three ways to test whether the sardines you have cherished have been worth the effort. When opened, none of the skin of the top ones should adhere to the lid; this means they were too fat and badly chosen or packed. When you scrape back a little of the skin you should see a wine-coloured layer, indicative of fattiness and flavour. Now turn back a fillet. If the flesh is white and creamy, the sardines were caught and processed quickly; if it is pink or red-tinged they were frozen before packing. The consensus is that it takes six months for sardines to mature in the can and they can improve for another six months. After that the packers say you should eat them up and replace them. Well, they would, wouldn't they?

Serving: eat them direct from the can on hot toast, mash with a tiny amount of sherry vinegar to do the same thing, or grill them lightly on thick, fresh white bread so it soaks up the oil and juices. Simple but splendid.

Sprats: not often seen, but when you find smoked sprats from Baltic countries, give them a try. They make a welcome change when arranging mixed seafood platters.

Sturgeon: traditionally, the sturgeon is 'royal'. The first one taken each season (August to March) is given to the sovereign, and someone did this in 1978 when one braved our polluted waters for long enough to get caught. It's a shark-like migratory fish, living in the sea but going into fresh water to spawn. Found from the Caspian Sea to North America, it grows to well over 6½m/20ft in the Balkans and Russia. Its female's roe is caviare; its air bladder makes isinglass, an archaic type of gelatine that the Swiss Family Robinson used for windows.

The royal status of sturgeons is both ancient and universal. Throughout Imperial China commoners forbore to eat it, reserving it for the palate of the Celestial Emperor, who then cunningly used it to tempt other parts of his favourites. The Roman Emperor Severus had it served honoured with coronets and serenaded with musicians; Alexandre Dumas suggests doing this, too. It needs razzmatazz, for the firm flesh is difficult to prepare and present tastefully. Strangely, one is counselled to hang it for some days. Then it tastes like veal and is often cooked in exactly the same manner, served with the same sauces.

We less-than-royal mortals are more likely to see it smoked, but rarely. The flesh is still very firm but tends to crumble, so it benefits from being served with a little excellent oil. I've only eaten it at a London West End hotel where their prices gave the impression that our small party was expected to reimburse the establishment for all the newly-completed redecoration! The smoked sturgeon was insensitively inundated with a too sharp vinaigrette. Voluble displeasure brought new, untouched slithers. With the merest whisper of oil and zephyr of lemon zest it was quite delicious – but not quite as delicious as smoked salmon.

There is a case for using expensive smoked salmon to make exorbitant smoked sturgeon go further. Arranged in rosettes of alternating colour, the pair make a luxurious start to a meal. Fresh dill weed and a delicate cucumber mousse would be better and prettier than parsley with either or both.

Trout: the trout belongs to the same group of fish as salmon and the many types of trout divide broadly into two groups – plus one type that devilishly spans both. Basically, either trout migrate to and from the sea, or they don't.

The pretty rainbow trout confuses these categorizations by living in fresh water lakes but migrating up their incoming rivers to spawn. It is a native of California but has now been established with enormous success in New Zealand, Chile and Britain. The American brook trout is actually a char, as is their Dolly Varden trout.

The smoked trout you buy in countries where they are taken in the wild and smoked naturally is superb. But I cannot help thinking the creatures we buy here, which are both farm-bred and then artificially coloured and smoke-flavoured, are a wee bit pricey for the pleasure they give. Still, they are an important basic component of many a menu and probably better than avocado and prawns, a mixture of blandness I've never understood. But you have to be very good at coping with tiny bones, and such difficulty can outweigh any pleasure the hard-won flesh might eventually give the victor.

Now there is something else of the same name in the shops; this is the flesh of farmed trout which have grown into comparative monsters and then been cured liked smoked salmon, kippered in fact. It looks the same and has very much the same texture and flavour as salmon, but there is a price advantage.

Serving: the small smoked trout I have been discussing are always hot smoked and thus cooked through. You should always peel away the skin and it would be churlish to serve less than one per person. A little lemon and freshly ground pepper is adequate accompaniment. If you have the time and skill you might like to take the trout off the bone and arrange it in strips with some of the more esoteric salad vegetables; I think raw fennel lightly dressed with oil and lemon excellent with trout. Flavoured mayonnaises go well too; perhaps present a choice of a tomato, fresh herb and horseradish flavours. Alternatively, serve the trout plain but with thin soldiers of brown bread spread with a variety of flavoured butters, which are simply made and keep for ages.

Tuna: now the world appreciates netting tuna kills dolphins and that canners have agreed only to line-fish, this truly delicious fish is back on the menu. Like sardines, tuna is subjected to all manner of iniquity in cans, packed in totally unsuited mediums. Go for brine packed rather than a vegetable oil and then you will get the best advantage from drizzling with olive oil, or incorporating it into a salad with a decent dressing.

The rarest type of tuna is the albacore, which has very pale flesh and is sold in the United States as Chicken of the Sea. This is no hype, for the flesh is quite as useful, more finely textured than other varieties and very delicious indeed. Spanish packers often include it in their range too, in smaller packs. I'm always grateful to find it in a specialty food store; indeed it is one of the first things I look for when I am making comparative judgments.

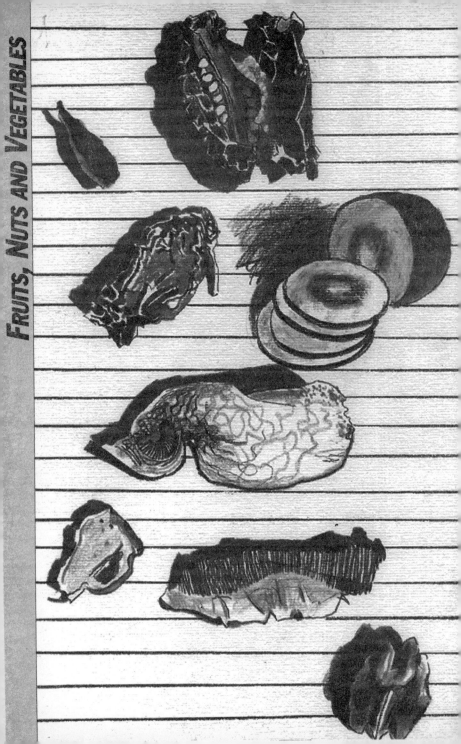

Thes are the goodies which make eating so much fun. And so they should, for we have had more practice with them than anything else. As hunters and gatherers the seasonal progression of wild fruits, nuts and vegetables kept us going between the feasts of meat, indeed without these we could never have gathered the strength to go hunting at all.

Modern transportation and genetic manipulation means more and more produce is available fresh all year round. But there remains a place for other types in every diet, every store cupboard. Canned or dried fruits and vegetables often offer flavours, textures and colours quite different from the original. And nuts are increasingly important as part of the vegetarian choice; luckily we no longer have to squirrel them away for a rainy day, but can enjoy them exactly when it suits us. If only to gather strength to shop for more.

CANNED & BOTTLED FRUIT

A lot of canned or bottled fruits are useful only for inferior fruit salads or for quick meals for children; the combination of sweetening and long cooking in the can changes flavour and texture too much for me. But some are extremely useful as a short cut to making unusual foods, ice creams or baked puddings. When you want a quick pie filling, look for tins which say 'solid pack'. Apples, peaches and cherries are all very good but need much added flavour, sugar, citrus and so on.

Apricots: strangely, canned apricots often have far more flavour than fresh. With a little lemon juice, and perhaps some crushed macaroons or amaretti, which are flavoured with apricot kernels, they can make an excellent pie or crumble filling.

Bilberries: usually found in bottles from Poland and that sort of country, bilberries grow wild in Britain but are neglected. They are related to the blueberry, but smaller. Use them wherever you see a blueberry mentioned – with waffles, in batters, on ice cream, in ice cream, in soufflés, or as a sauce for soufflés. They may need dressing up with sweet spices, with a little liqueur or citrus juice, and also like a combination with vanilla. Or simply thicken the syrup with cornflour, return the fruit and bake between layers of pastry, with thick slices of apple and lots of cinnamon and nutmeg.

Black cherries: such a bore to do yourself, and the higher quality canned ones, ready stoned, are just what you want for filling chocolate cakes, mixing with chestnut purée and whipped cream, or heating in red wine or brandy with bay and a little spice to serve with pork. Puréed and very slightly thickened with arrowroot or cornflour then flavoured with black rum, they make a sensational chilled sauce for profiteroles.

Cranberries: although some grow in this country they are largely ignored. We rely on imports from the United States, which are very good and not expensive. Fresh or frozen, they last for ages and are an excellent standby in the freezer or refrigerator. A handful in a stuffing for poultry, lamb or fish lends an attractive sharpness, and I've used them to add interest to apple pies and apple sauce.

Cranberry sauces made commercially are generally not bad but much sweeter than they need to be. To make your own, there are several simple rules. First, eschew water and use red or white wine together with some orange juice and a little very finely grated or sliced rind. Next, cook the cranberries only until they just begin to burst. Include some spice, preferably a cinnamon stick which can be removed, and add sugar only after the berries have begun to open or you will toughen the skin. That will give you a sauce so much nicer than anything you can buy.

It is a mistake only to have cranberries with turkey. The homemade sauce is excellent with ham, with duck, with well-flavoured, garlicky sausages, and it is perfectly marvellous with hot or cold tongue.

But why do most cranberry sauces find themselves served cold? Pop yours into the microwave or into a bowl over boiling water and it will be very much more delicious. And don't stop there. Add green or roasted black peppercorns, a cinnamon stick, mace or lemon zest. Add black rum, vodka or whisky. Add fresh or dried mint to serve with duck or lamb. Add juniper berries or gin (at the very last minute) for hot tongue, goose or guinea fowl. Stir in grated orange zest, a little cardamom and cognac – for almost anything. There, I'm sure you have the idea......

A perfect gift at Christmas time is uncooked cranberry relish: whizz up fresh or defrosted cranberries with an equal weight of raw unpeeled apple, oranges and lemons which are washed and de-pipped but still with their skins intact and a small amount of celery leaf. Leave overnight in a refrigerator, stir well and only then sweeten to taste, perhaps adding alcoholic spirit too. Then bottle and leave a week or so before use, still refrigerated. It will look pale but gets redder and softer as time progresses. I think it is best fairly rough, but you can make it as rugged or sleek as you like. It lasts up to a month or more, protected both by the sugar content and the very high vitamin C of the cranberries. Chopped toasted nuts, fresh pineapple, currants, or for really special friends, raspberries, may all be added.

Fresh or defrosted cranberries last for weeks and weeks in a refrigerator and thus make a remarkable treasure chest to plunder from time to time. They go directly into bread doughs, especially with nuts, stuff muffins and scones wonderfully, enliven any pâté or stuffing you can think of and can be popped into any number of sauces just before serving.

Gooseberries: they will have lost their colour and much texture but a purée of canned gooseberries, strained, is the basis of a quick fool especially when given a lift with cinnamon and grated lemon or orange. I never purée fresh gooseberries for a fool, preferring simply to mash them slightly, which gives a far more fascinating result – every mouthful different. The blander canned ones, and the strange texture of their skins, makes this version less successful, in my experience. The canned ones are too sweet to use as the base for fish sauces.

Greengages: occasionally seen from France. If they are very small ones (and sometimes they are savoury rather than sweet) they are interesting accompaniments to cold hams and other summer meats. Or they make an excellent purée for frozen or cream desserts.

Kumquats: fragrant, citrus-related fruits, eaten skin and all. They make unexpected garnishes, or fruit salad contents, when used with great discretion; particularly good scattered over or through soft red fruits.

Lychees: generally as good canned as fresh, with almost the same texture. Improved by being slightly chilled. If you liquidize a tinful of fruit and strain that, reduce the accompanying sugar syrup until just five or six dessertspoonfuls, mix them together and flavour with a little rose water, you have a show-stopping sorbet, all the better for being re-beaten during freezing and folded into a whipped egg white, which improves the texture. Drained of syrup and sharpened with lemon or lime juice, or soaked in vodka or dry sherry, lychees may be used as an ingredient of stir-fried Chinese dishes or served with roasted duck. But they are superb by themselves, helped perhaps by rose water, which has a similar flavour.

Mango: it is only worth buying mangos in tins if they are from India and are of the Alphonso variety – at least, that is so if you wish to use them as is. But for ice creams, fools, sauces and so on, other varieties, where the texture is less important, may be used. This most beguiling of all fruit makes the most bewitching of all drinks, which I call a Moghul Fizz – liquidize some mango, using lime or orange juice to get a light texture, whisk in a very small amount of clear honey. Put into champagne or sparkling wine.

Morello cherries: red and less sweet than black cherries, morellos are thought better by some for inclusion in chocolate cake fillings. They are tastier in their sharp way, it is true, and are certainly much better for making pies. Drained of most syrup, added to white wine, heated with spices and slightly thickened with cornflour or arrowroot, they make an attractive sauce for pork or chicken; sharpen with lemon juice at the last moment.

Paw paw: I'm trying not to be negative in this or any section, but I don't think canned paw paw works. However it can add interest to a tropical sort of fruit salad and work better when chilled and in combination with some fresh passionfruit pulp – bottled or canned passionfruit pulp is universally beastly.

Pineapple: although a world away from fresh, some canned pineapple products are most worthwhile when treated with interest and care. I think the yellower, sweeter pineapples from Hawaii and from Malaysia are well worth paying extra for, if asked.

Crushed pineapple, a standby of cooking and eating in Australasia, should be used more here. Drained (or otherwise) it can be used in cakes, in batters to make pancakes or fritters, or thickened with spices and butter to make sauces sweet or savoury. It can be set with gelatine in flans or on cheesecakes, or used in cheesecakes. Pineapple has a special affinity with gin, and drained crushed pineapple mixed with gin makes a very special hot pancake filling; you could even flame gin over the top, too. Butter-fried pineapple rings or chunks make an unusual but popular addition to bacon and eggs but are more likely to be found with baked pork chops, roasted pork or chicken, spread with a little mustard for more interest.

When decorating cakes with pineapple pieces, it is also an idea to drain and mar-

---

A PLUM ICE CREAM

A can of Victoria plums is the basis for perhaps the most successful of recipes I gave on BBC-TV Breakfast Time, at least judged by the number of requests we had for the recipe. You pour the contents of a 500g can of the plums into a sieve and save the syrup. Force the plums through the sieve using the back of a soup ladle. Now whisk a very well chilled small can of sweetened condensed milk for a few minutes and then add a small carton of double cream and keep beating until it looks like lightly whipped cream. Fold in the plum purée and flavour lightly with two or more tablespoons of lemon or orange juice. Cinnamon, ginger or cardamom make good additions. Freeze. The reserved syrup may be reduced over heat and served warm or cold as a sauce, but will of course be fairly pulsating with calories. The recipe works with 300ml/½pt of any fruit purée, and should you use canned apple sauce, cinnamon, some raisins and breadcrumbs fried in butter you will have made an apple strudel ice cream to die for, by which I suppose I mean, for which to die – but I promise you'll forget your grammar when you taste it.

---

inate them in gin. It adds much flavour and contrasts better with the sweetness of the cake and icing.

Plums: puréed plums, of any colour, make good bases for fools, ice creams or sauces. Spiked with a little red wine vinegar and mellowed with a little tomato purée, a slightly spicy plum sauce is tremendously good with any sweet meat, fowl or game. It's a sort of instant plum chutney in a way. Use brown sugar if you want it sweeter and include a little ground clove.

At the other end of the meal, even canned plums blossom for a dash or two of mirabelle *eau de vie* and a slice of ice cream or custard sauce. Canned plums are good for pies and sponge puddings and crumbles, but remember they are already cooked so keep cooking times to an absolute minimum.

Soft fruits: most soft fruits do not react well to processing. I cannot understand why anyone would want to buy canned strawberries or raspberries, which have artificial colour and little resemblance in texture or flavour to the original fruit. Some of the darker berries like loganberries and boysenberries are better. I once slightly thickened the contents of a tin of loganberries and served them as a hot sauce to a hot chocolate soufflé. There was rose water in one and black rum in the other, and they were superb.

White peaches: these are delicious and as few of us have ever eaten one fresh, can be enjoyed just for what they are. I had some on a slice of fresh foie gras but it wasn't enough really to taste. Expensive and seasonal, and apparently an appreciated Christmas present with the older generation.

DRIED FRUITS

An important source of sweetening and of sugar during winter for our ancestors, dried fruits are a most ancient food. Today there is some chemical assistance likely to improve colour or keeping qualities, and often they are dried without the aid of the sun, but the basis of preserving fruit by reducing the moisture content, allowing the natural sugars to act as a preservative, remains unchanged.

Apples: one of the most useful of dried fruits as they retain their Vitamin C content. ½kg/1lb of dried apple is the equivalent of 3-4kg/6-9lb of fresh fruit. They rehydrate nicely, often becoming rather fluffy and therefore good for purées. They are also a good stretcher of other fruits in pies, crumbles and so on. They are rather rubbery when dried but chopped into smaller pieces make a worthwhile addition to muesli.

Apricots: always dried without their stones, whether whole or halves. 3kg/5½lb of fresh fruit yield ½kg/1lb of dried. I once found them drying under trees in Ibiza, directed thence by the wondrous scent on the air. They were tended by one of those black-swathed Mediterran-

> **APRICOT SHEETS**
> In Cypriot, Turkish and Arabic shops you can buy something called armadine. This is sheets of dried apricot purée, and being made from Middle-Eastern varieties has a much bigger flavour than western dried apricots; it is sharper too, often because citric acid has been added. You can simply rehydrate armadine in a little water or wine, cook it smoother, watching it carefully, and serve it chilled with cream and almonds as a smooth apricot cream. I added eggs, black rum, sugar and vanilla, poached the mixture in individual containers, turned them out on a nut pastry and served them very cold with thin cream flavoured with more rum and vanilla. Very beaut.

ean women. Now that site is a hotel or two. Apricots are more often dried in hot air after having been exposed to sulphur dioxide which gives a brighter colour. My favourite dried fruit, it often tastes better like this than when fresh. The greatest of all snacks, pie fillings or breakfast fruit. Thin slices improve muesli more than anything else I can think of.

Bananas: these usually come from South America and are naturally sun-dried. 1kg/2lb of bananas make 225g/½lb of dried ones. Golden brown, very sweet and chewy, they are an addictive snack, but can lead to a fairly determined loosening of the bowels.

They may be soaked in water overnight and eaten with lemon and orange juice plus brown sugar – again black rum would find itself most welcome. They can be chopped and used as any other dried fruit in breads, cakes and puddings. Chopped or sliced they make a fascinating addition to any cereal, hot or cold.

Recently I have seen a new product which is long thin chips of crisp, dry banana, creamy coloured, and coated with honey. If you don't mind the extra sugar this is terrific at breakfast time.

Dates: Iraq alone grows 400 different types of date. They contain so much sugar that even the dried ones are sticky and moist, and they last for years after picking.

The Iraqi dates you most usually eat are the *Halawi* or the *Sayir*; from Tunisia or Morocco it is most likely the *Deglet Noor*, but it is not often you have a choice, so that may be useless information.

To many people dates are cloying and filling and so you should serve them in small amounts. They really are most enjoyed when offered as a sweetmeat after a meal, or as a very high energy booster snack when doing something exhausting like climbing a mountain or sailing. I don't much like dates that are filled with marzi-

DRIED FRUIT SALAD

Dried fruits should be thought of as treats in their own right, rather than as substitutes for the real thing. Apricots especially are used in all sorts of ways in the Middle East, savoury and sweet, and a dip into such cookbooks is always rewarding. Peaches can be used the same way but I think they are less satisfying, and so are pears.

One of the recipes you will come across when pursuing Middle Eastern food is simply to soak a mixture of dried fruits for 48 hours in just enough water, apple or orange juice to cover them. Add sugar, genuine almond essence plus a sprinkle of rose water and orange flower water. Serve with a contrasting scatter of chopped pistachios. It is amazingly good for almost no effort.

pan or cream cheese, but lots of people think they look nice. The only occasion I have used them in cooking was to recreate a Moroccan recipe that was also current here as a Lenten dish in medieval times.

You take a nice big baking fish and clean it thoroughly. Then cook some rice until it is just done. When it is good and dry, mix in some ground almonds, cinnamon and a touch of sugar. Stuff some dates with this mixture, and close each with a smear of butter. Put the dates and as much extra rice as will fit into the cavity of the fish and sew it up or hold together with toothpicks – sewing really is better this time. Put the fish in a baking dish with a little water, smear it with butter, and sprinkle with more cinnamon and bake under foil. You can sprinkle onion over the fish and lay it on a bed of onion, which will make a more savoury liquid for basting and for pouring over the finished dish. It is very good. Interestingly, this type of date is not that upon which desert nomads can live with the addition only of milk. That type of date, starchy, crunchy and with little flavour, is called a bread date.

Figs: I don't wish to pry, but if you think you have private problems, spare a thought for the fig. Figs have their flowers *inside* their fruit, and the palaver that they and certain wasps have to go through to get fertilized makes each fig a miracle of perseverance.

The Smyrna or Turkish fig is one of the most popular varieties for drying, originally named for the town through which most were exported from Turkey, now called Izmir. They are best known for their assistance to the constipated and useful as a snack but little used in cooking.

Peaches: generally the least common fruit in mixed packets. If they are soaked only in water they can seem floury, so I always use orange juice and that is a great success. They are especially good when subsequently grilled, which caramellizes them here and there. I sprinkle them with rose water and orange flower water whilst still hot and serve them with a decent vanilla ice cream.

Pears: there are two places I've especially enjoyed these. In Alsace they turn up constantly in savoury dishes of meat and game, and I often put them under chicken or game birds while roasting, so they swell with the cooking juices. The farmers market of New York's Union Square is particularly popular with the Amish of Pennsylvania and they also do terrific things with dried pears; they now have a permanent produce shop on the square.

Prunes: these are dried plums and now that the Californians have taken to producing them, have changed out of all recognition in the last few years. Rather than those hard, small things of yesteryear we have jumbo prunes and soft prunes and ready-soaked prunes and goodness knows what else.

If you must eat them for breakfast, then add a little orange juice or spice to the water you use for cooking, and serve them very cold.

The very finest prunes of all are the French Pruneaux d'Agen and it seems a pity to muck about with them, but people do. Carlsbad plums are actually prunes and, like the best of dried fruits, meant to be eaten at the end of the meal. They are available in wooden boxes but are so expensive they must be eaten instead of a meal. The Portuguese make a cheaper version called Elvas plums and the Poles provide us with something even better and even cheaper. They are called plums in chocolate and are stoned small plums (which is to say prunes), filled with a delicious soft toffee and coated with chocolate and decoratively wrapped. They make stunning gifts because everyone expects them to have cost far more than they do. Always a success.

Purées of cooked prune make excellent sorbets and ice creams; or you can flavour it with, say, orange or a little praline, add egg in the usual custard-making proportion and bake it in a flan case.

Prunes are common in stuffings but I prefer them thus, which is an idea I found in *The Guardian* many years ago, when I read it. Take some prunes and cover them with red wine; add some cinnamon, mace, a clove or two, a sliver of orange peel and, most important, quite a few bay leaves. Let this cook for a long while, gently, until the prunes are plump and the flavours have blended. Complete the flavour by adding some brown sugar or redcurrant jelly if you think some sweetness would be an improvement. Remove the prunes and strain the spices from the sauce. Serve hot or cold with

SWEET GINGER

Preserved or stem ginger in syrup is one of the great mysteries of Christmas. Everyone seems to be given it, but almost no-one knows what to do with it, other than to slice it onto some ice cream. In fact there are many uses.

Preserved ginger in slices, or chopped, together with a little of the syrup, is delicious on melon and far better than the silly idea of using powdered dry ginger. It is equally good with fresh or poached pears and can be used for baking in a host of ways, with apple, with peaches, with soft fruits in pies, sponges or crumbles. It is also very good with chocolate sponges; in fact if you put pears and ginger at the bottom of a chocolate sponge mixture you will turn out a memorable pear, chocolate and ginger upside down pudding... it looks better when baked in a ring mold.

Fine slices are a nice addition to any fruit salad, and can be added to homemade ice cream, especially when also flavoured with honey. The syrup itself is equally useful for dribbling onto hot fruit, pancakes or cakes as a moisturizer, or it may be used to mix an icing sugar.

Preserved ginger can rarely be used in savoury cooking, but might be included where there is already a mixture of sweet and sour in the sauce, or where the meat is very fatty, say with duck. But fresh green ginger would probably be better.

game, ham, duck or goose.

Vine fruits: it is thought the Egyptians discovered they could dry grapes in the sun, and what a good idea that turned out to be. Dried vine fruits have eight times more invert sugar than other types of fruit; as invert sugar is really pre-digested sucrose, the body is able to use it very quickly, and hence the usefulness of such fruit as snacks when you are labouring or having an adventure.

Generally, ½kg/1lb of dried vine fruit was once 2kg/4lb of fresh, and the types you will come across are:

Currants: these are not dried blackcurrants but a special type of seedless black grape. Originally they were from Corinth in Greece, hence the name, but now most come from Australia.

Sultanas: are made from seedless white grapes. They were a specialty of Smyrna, now Izmir, and were often called Smyr-

FRUIT VINEGAR PICKLED FRUIT

A few small bottles of spiced summer fruits, kept chilled in the refrigerator, take little time to make and are an excellent adjunct to meals both simple and super. Although I've specified fruit vinegars in the recipes, wine vinegar would give equally interesting results and cider vinegar is particularly good in this sort of thing. It is important to leave on the skins as they impart a pretty colour to the preserving liquid.

450g/1lb firm peaches, plums or pears
1 cinnamon stick
8 dstsp white sugar
2 dstsp pickling spice
300ml/½pt raspberry or strawberry vinegar

The fruit should be only just ripe and nicely firm. Rinse them under running water. Dry then cut into four, six or eight segments according to how big they are.

Put the other ingredients into a pan and bring to the boil very slowly. Simmer covered for 10 minutes. The spices can be strained out now but I rather like to leave them in. Add the segments to the pickle, bring slowly back to the boil, simmer for 5-8 minutes (depending on firmness), and leave to cool slowly.

Spoon the fruit into a screw-top jar, then pour in the liquid and spices. Store in the refrigerator for at least 3 days. These have continued to improve in flavour and appearance for as long as 4 weeks – after that they had all been eaten. Serve them solo or as a fascinating addition to salads and mayonnaises.

Options: if you want the fruit to last longer, cook them for only 3 minutes, which keeps them firmer, of course. You will need to wait 3 weeks before eating them but they will stay firm for some months – longer in the refrigerator.

Some vodka, brandy or peach brandy added to the cool pickle would also prolong the fruit's potential life, but add so much extra pleasure they may be eaten even sooner!

na raisins. I find these the most delicious of all in cooking, and when you want a rich mellow flavour in mixed fruit cakes and puddings, add extra sultanas rather than currants or raisins.

Raisins: these are dried red grapes of several types, sometimes seedless. The biggest and sweetest are the muscatels, which can be found without seeds if you look hard enough.

PENNSYLVANIA DUTCH PEARS

These are intended for use with cold meats and poultry, but are so delicious I also serve them with cheese as a pudding.

The quantity made will depend on the size of pears you choose. Whatever that is, ensure they are uniform so they are cooked to the same state at the same time.

1⅓kg/3lb white or brown sugar
1 tbsp whole cloves
425ml/¾pt cider vinegar
3 cinnamon sticks
300ml/½pt water
about 3kg/7lb firm, ripe pears

Combine the sugar, vinegar, and water. The cloves and cinnamon sticks – which should be broken into pieces – may either be added as is or put into a muslin bag. Simmer all together for 30 minutes from the time the syrup comes to the boil. Taste carefully and add more cinnamon if your sticks were not as strong as you thought – remember the flavour is going to be very diluted by the addition of the pears.

While the syrup is simmering, peel the pears but leave on the stems and do not core them. Brush them with a little water and lemon juice to keep them white if you are using white sugar, otherwise a little discoloration can be overlooked.

Put the pears into the syrup and cook gently until tender but still firm. Spoon the pears carefully into sterilized containers and cover but do not seal. Boil the syrup fairly rapidly for 30 minutes, pour carefully over the fruit, then seal. I would leave these a couple of weeks before eating them.

Options: thick slices of fresh ginger root would be a delightful addition to this fairly simply flavoured recipe; indeed, one day I intend to use masses of ginger as the only flavouring. Although not authentic as far as Pennsylvanians or the Dutch go, crushed cardamon pods add a wonderful fragrance.

GLACÉ FRUITS

These have always been a luxury, but now are very expensive indeed if made in Europe. Because of the current high price of sugar, glacé, crystallized or candied fruits mainly appear as presents at Christmas time but are excellent standbys in your store cupboard. We now import crystallized fruits from South Africa, which are relatively cheap because of lower labour costs, but I don't think much of the quality.

France is one of the better known manufacturers of luxurious sugar-preserved fruits and Apt in the Vacluse region is one of the oldest centres. It was not until the mid-19th century that glacé fruits were readily available in Britain, when they began regularly to be imported from France. The most popular lines are apricots and mandarins but pears, greengages, figs, pineapple, melon and cherries are quite common. Chestnuts *(marrons glacés)*, ginger and kumquats are rarer and more expensive. The manufacturing process is still barely mechanized. The fruit must be picked before it is fully ripe or it will be too fragile to withstand the processing. Once it is sorted and graded the fruit is generally stored in waxed underground tanks filled with brine. When required the fruit is rinsed, stalked and pitted and then subjected to a process called osmosis, in which all the natural fruit sugars are replaced by sucrose as a result of being soaked in increasingly stronger sugar solutions. Some fruit is then further coated with a sugar solution and lightly baked.

A light deposit of sulphur on such fruit prevents clouding and acts as a further preservative.

Moist, succulent and sweet, glacé fruits are the ultimate snack although explosively laden with calories. But I like to linger rather longer than the few mouthsful needed to demolish, say, a glacé apricot. So I slice them to use as an exquisite topping for fresh fruits – apricots or mandarins on strawberries, *marrons* on raspberries. Of course they are perfectly wonderful with ice creams or with cream, whipped and frozen together. Indeed you can make yourself wickedly ill simply by mixing some sliced glacé fruits into such excessively rich cream cheese as a Mascarpone and don't even bother to freeze it. A hint of rose water adds the ultimate touch of degeneracy and thus is urged.

NUTS

Nuts are fruits with a hard or leathery casing around an edible kernel. But not everything commonly referred to as a nut is one: for instance, peanuts are technically legumes, brazil and cashew nuts are seeds, and tiger nuts are tubers. 'Nuts to all that' you might say, but you'd be overlooking a very important source of protein, fats, minerals and vitamins, which is why vegetarians are so keen on them.

In Europe the fruit of the oak, the acorn, was part of earliest man's diet, Pliny called the oak 'the tree which first produced food for mortal man'. Remains of acorns have been found around the Upper Great Lakes in settlements dating from at least 2000 BC and the early Yosemite Indians made a porridge out of them. Almonds and pistachios are referred to in the Bible and right up until the end of the 18th century almonds and walnuts were blanched, pulverized and soaked in water to provide a staple milk.

As well as being edible in their own right, nuts are very important commercially in a variety of ways. The main such usage is in nut oils: the oil from the hazelnut is widely used in cosmetics and soap making, almond oil is used for moisturizing creams, and a rather nasty component of the whole cashew nut is actually employed in making plastics.

There's hardly a country in the world that does not have an indigenous edible nut, but here in the West we seem to have settled for rather a short list.

Almonds: probably the world's most popular nut. Britain imports about 15,000 tonnes annually, mainly from Spain. Other important producers are Italy, France, Portugal, Morocco and the Canary Islands. The United States is now largely supplied by the fast-expanding Californian industry.

The pretty almond tree, with its ornamental blossom, needs soil that is rich to a depth of 3.6m/12ft and that has very good drainage. It starts to bear useful fruit in its third or fourth year and increases its yield annually for 12-20 years. Harvesting must start as soon as the outer hulls are fully split open; if they are left too long the nuts stick tightly to the shell and are known as 'sticktights', a dreaded situation if you are into almond growing. Usually the nuts are dislodged from the trees with long thin poles but in California the pole has a padded mallet-like head and this collection method is called chubbing. Immediately after hulling the nuts are put in the sun to dry – if this is delayed the shells darken in colour. They're left to dry for two days to three weeks depending on the weather.

This is one nut where you need to know something about types:

Bitter: although very important in many dishes where just one or two round-out an almond flavour, these are very harmful if eaten in quantity. They actually contain the deadly-poisonous prussic acid, 'given away' in detective stories by its lingering smell of bitter almonds. Very hard to come by I find, but an excellent adjunct if you use almonds a lot in cooking; they work like lemons, orange or other fruit, bringing out all the essential flavour of the sweet almond yet without intruding. You can get something of the same flavour, without the intensity, by using cherry or apricot kernels.

Californian: a new type grown only in California with advanced techniques and irrigated orchards. Used mainly by confectioners.

Californian nonpareil: the principal variety grown in California, it is of medium width but quite flat.

Jordan: mainly grown in Malaga and Alicante and sometimes called the finger almond as their long, slender shape resembles the little finger. Jordan almonds are the sweet dessert kind and extensively used in cooking. Graded according to size, large Jordans are sold retail, and the small ones go to confectioners who need a long variety for making sugared almonds. These are the ones with which the eyes of Oriental beauties are compared.

Valencia: grown in Spain and Portugal, these are the flatter, heart-shaped nuts, with a rougher, tougher skin and less sweet flavour. Sold mainly for cooking, they are usually blanched and skinned and used widely for cake decoration, especially for Dundee cakes.

Whole blanched or unblanched halves: used mainly for cake decorating when they are all the better for being lightly toasted or roasted all through, and in some Chinese dishes, notably with deep-fried seaweed. If you are going to use them *in* cakes they really should be roasted first, otherwise they will soften during cooking. If you want to finish a sauce with whole or halved blanched almonds then they should be added only a few minutes before serving, again to conserve crispness.

Flaked almonds: one of the most useful of all ingredients in a kitchen. They are expensive but you need very few to add flavour and interest to an extraordinary variety of food. They should usually be toasted but for use in cream sauces can be left their natural colour.

Toasted or fried in a little oil or dry-fried in a non-stick pan, they finish off salads superbly and are excellent in sauces with rich fish and seafood, as their crispness complements the solidity of such flesh. Wonderful with potatoes, peas, beans and squashes. Creamy tomato sauces, white wine sauces and richer pasta sauces containing cream are all much the better for the addition of a few flaked almonds.

Toasted flaked almonds convert ice cream into something far more interesting and make a simple two- or three-fruit salad into a specialty of the house. An easy way to smarten up a simple cold pie or mousse is to whip cream, flavour it with orange flower water and then fold in toasted almond flakes. Almost good enough to serve by itself – or perhaps with a mountain of baby meringues. My newest use for them is incorporated into meringues: add some untoasted flakes to the mixture and cook a little longer than usual. The almond will toast and flavour the meringues, which are all the better for being flavoured with such liqueurs as Mandarine Napoléon or Crème de Cacao.

Slivered and nibbed: these fancier shapes, one long and thin, the other short and sort of fat, are mainly recommended for special decoration or where you want to add some texture – in a nut stuffing, for instance. In most cases flaked almonds would be as good, and probably cheaper.

Ground almonds: another invaluable standby and I'm sorry that soaring prices don't let me use them as lavishly as once was possible. They add wonderful richness and moistness to fruit cakes, make superb custards and tarts, transport stuffings into heaven, enrich sauces, and generally lift the ordinary into the extraordinary. I prefer to grind my own, for ground almonds can be very soapy and it's hard to know whether this is because of intrinsically low quality or staleness; it's not worth the risk. When seedless white grapes are in season spread some on a good short pastry shell and cover with a mixture of 125g/4oz of ground almonds, 2 eggs, some cream, and some sugar to taste. Bake in a gentle oven until set and serve warm.

Brazil Nuts: it may come as no revelation to you to be told that the brazil comes from Brazil however you might not know that it isn't a nut but a seed.

> ### MARRONS GLACÉS
> Made only with the marron chestnut, which is preserved by repeated boiling and soaking in syrup. But are they *really* worth the huge prices? No – unless you add brandy (even *more* expense) to the syrup. A better wheeze is to find very much cheaper bottles of broken marrons glacés. They too may be flavoured with alcohol and then used to sprinkle on ice cream and so on.

It's actually one of the 8-24 seeds arranged like segments of an orange inside a globular fruit 5-10cm/2-4in in diameter.

Other names by which it is known include butternut, creamnut, castanea, and paranut. The nut's rich flavour indicates a very high fat content and it also contains protein, iron and thiamine, one of the vitamins necessary to prevent you going nutty.

They are the only major nut which cannot be cultivated but must be collected from the tropical forest, produced by wild trees which grow up to 35m/115ft, and are thus altogether as resolutely and immutably organic as it is possible to be. The harvesting season is between January and June, which is how they get to us so nicely in time for Christmas. They are not much used in cooking, for no other reason than the expense I expect. They are very good with chocolate, a not unexpected thing when you consider their common birthright.

Cashews: native to Central and South America, the cashew was taken to East Africa and India in the 15th century and now grows abundantly along their coastlines. Related to the American poison ivy and the poison sumac, the tree and its fruit must be treated with great care. The nut – which isn't a nut but a seed – looks very odd on the tree, rather disturbingly like a worm eating its way into or out of a soft, fleshy apple. The cashew apple which surrounds the seed/nut in its shell is used to make jams and jellies and drinks.

The seed is enclosed in two shells between which there is a brown oil that blisters human skin; this oil can be collected and used as a lubricant, an insecticide, and in the production of plastics. After the whole nuts are detached from the apples they are left to dry in the sun.

The traditional method of extraction begins with the burning of the nuts amongst logs. This causes the tough outer shell to crack but the burning of the oil releases intensely injurious fumes. Modern methods get over this by roasting in enclosed cylinders. Either way, the inner shells still have to be broken open, usually by hand, and the kernels heated again to remove the remaining skin. I wonder who first bothered to cope with all this fuss and danger – they must have been very hungry.

The Chinese use toasted cashew nuts in combination with chicken and pork, at least those living in London do. I use them in stuffings for pork and chicken and they are my favourite snack. Otherwise I don't know of much specialized use for them in food.

Chestnuts: chestnuts roasting on an open fire are an essential component of any vision of old England – and Tin Pan Alley. What the songs don't tell you is that pieces of red-hot, burst chestnut shell fly in all directions, burning you and your carpet. If you wish to sin with Elinor Glyn – or some other kind of her – there are ways to protect yourself *and* eat your chestnuts. You can buy a small enclosed pan with holes in it with which to roast chestnuts, thus ensuring the safe pursuit of other traditional fire-side activities. The combination of fireside and chestnuts has also been used to tell amatory fortunes. Dorothy Hartley tells us in her seminal *Food in England*: 'It was a fortune-telling trick to name the row of chestnuts set along the top bar of the hot grate, and the first name to pop was to be the first lover to pop the question. If he jumped into your lap, you had him; if he popped into the fire and was burnt up... well, you didn't!' She doesn't elaborate on what *had* meant.

Chestnuts are different and interesting for a large number of reasons. They are the only nut we treat as a vegetable and, as they contain the least amount of oil and most starch of any nut, are the most digestible and the only ones that can be turned into a useful flour. Personally I find the shelling and peeling of fresh chestnuts a bore and for most recipes the canned or dried kind are perfectly adequate; and I wouldn't begin to try to make the wonderful commercial, vanilla-flavoured purée, the discovery of which converts any cook into a better cook as far as puddings are concerned.

If you do want to prepare your own chestnuts, the simplest way is to pierce the flat ends, put them into boiling water for five minutes or so and when cool enough to handle you can remove the shell and skin very easily. Everyone has their favourite method and if yours isn't the same as mine I won't argue. The important thing to remember is that chestnuts generally don't, in their natural state, have a great deal of flavour, and that without care even this can be diluted.

There are several varieties of chestnuts, which mainly differ by having one or more nut inside the shell. Only when there is a single floury nut in the shell can it be called a *marron*, and the best of these are held to come from the Ardèche, a beautiful French region of lakes, rivers, pine and chestnut-tree clad hills. It was once a centre of the French silk trade, but when there was a slump in 1882, a certain Clement Faugier set up a chestnut-processing plant in a town called Privas. Faugier is now the most famous marron producing firm of all, and still run by descendants of its founder.

Chestnuts can be bought in a wide variety of states, all of them worth your investigation.

Chestnut flour: mainly found in Italian stores and almost exclusively used in Italian kitchens. When mixed with water it makes a non-elastic dough (there being no gluten content) and this is made into fritters, porridges of various kinds mixed with cream, milk, water or oil and an extraordinary yeast-leavened cake flavoured with aniseed. It is also used for a chestnut-type polenta.

Dried (dehydrated): expensive but an excellent standby in the larder of any imaginative cook, so buy plenty when they are in the shops at Christmas. Provided they are stored in a cool place, dried chestnuts keep for at least 18 months. All you have to do is soak them in warm water until they can be bitten through or cut with a knife; but you can be more inventive than that.

I simmer the dried chestnuts gently in red or white wine spiced with cinnamon, nutmeg, a little orange peel and bay leaf. Or I'll cook them with red wine, a little garlic and some small pieces of fatty bacon, for chestnuts take to fat and smoky flavours like anything. Either way, reduce the liquid until it just covers the chestnuts. These reconstituted and reflavoured chestnuts are then ready for roughly chopping into stuffings and sauces, to add to brussel sprouts (a classic combination), or to serve by themselves with roasted meats and poultry. Another wonderful idea is to drain them after reconstituting then turn them in a hot caramel of butter and lightly-browned sugar – very gala, very simple.

You can also reconstitute them plainly to mash with sugar and spices and vanilla as the basis for sweets and puddings. If you want to use whole chestnuts or chestnut halves in any dish, I think the reconstituted dried ones have more flavour than those in tins (in fact I'm sure of it). As dried chestnuts are invariably from Italy it may have something to do with the variety used.

Chestnuts make excellent additions and stretchers to casseroles. In this case I often don't reconstitute them first but put them into the cooking liquid in the dried state. This way they make their contribution to the overall flavour and benefit in turn from all the flavoured fats and liquor; if you used ready-constituted chestnuts they would be more likely to give their flavour out and take nothing back. Chestnuts are especially good foils to the richer winter stews that include pieces of fat bacon, and are wonderful with pigeons and pork dishes of all kinds.

Purée, plain: not something you might use a lot of, but its concentrated flavour and delicious rich colour is useful. Mixed with breadcrumbs, chopped celery green, some brandy and a little onion or garlic it makes a simple moist stuffing for veal or poultry. Or it can be added to a pancake mixture to make fritters that will go with all manner of meat dishes. It's quite common to accompany duck with chestnut purée in some form; you might simply mix in some cream, salt and pepper, beat in one egg to each 150ml/5fl oz of purée, and gently bake this beneath the roast for 40 minutes or until it has a crisp brown crust. This would then be a superior chestnut polenta. You might also consider mixing in some whole, uncooked cranberries before baking.

Purée, vanilla: perhaps one of the most delicious things you can buy in a can. No, not perhaps – *definitely!* It's too rich and sweet for most people to eat as it is, so what you do is this: fold it gently into equal quantities of whipped cream, then add a tot of brandy or sherry for good measure. Simplicity itself, and truly heavenly.

Here are just a few of the ways I have used this mixture. It can be crammed into freshly-made profiteroles, perhaps with a black cherry in each that has been soaked in black rum for a while; stick the profiteroles together in a pyramid shape with light caramel. For a wedding at which 60 guests in formal dress sat down in candlelight to a ten-course dinner, I had to make a pudding which would also serve as the wedding cake. So I sandwiched one chocolate and one vanilla meringue together with this chestnut cream mixture, thus achieving a very pretty three-tone colour graduation. These were then built into a mountain some 90cm/3ft high and, having alternated the way they were presented, the mountain appeared to be made in stripes of white and brown. It created a sensation when brought in but nothing compared to that caused when served up, for each plate was sauced with a mix of puréed black cherries and black rum slightly thickened and glossed with arrowroot. The bride said it was worth getting married for.

Chocolate goes well with chestnuts and with the chestnut and cream mixture; next time you want to make a spectacular cake, bake a couple of chocolate sandwiches (use Betty Crocker mixes for something really rich and fail-safe), join them with 1¼cm/½in of the mixture then mix icing sugar with more of it. You might sprinkle orange or coffee liqueur onto a layer of the cake; you could also add a layer of fresh mandarin sections, or more black cherries, a combination which is also foolproof. If you make the mixture taste more of cream than chestnuts, you can serve it with almost any fruit, but it's fantastic with strawberries and raspberries.

I'm not going to give you all my best ideas but here's a last one worth remembering: make some millefeuille squares from puff pastry, split and rebake to crisp right through. When cool, spread thickly with the chestnut and cream mixture then arrange unsweetened strawberry halves which you have soaked in orange juice or liqueur (the juice is better) and then drained. Cover these with the top layer of the millefeuille, then if you have the time and inclination, glaze each with some lightly-coloured caramel which you should allow to run willy-nilly over the edges.

Coconuts: the coconut has been admired for countless generations, and relied upon for far more than food and romantic backdrops. Our earliest civilizations, in the Indus Valley, certainly ate them and the Chinese have included them in their diet for almost as long and are thought to have been the first to use coconut meat and milk in confectionery. The tree is probably native to India, the coasts of south-east Asia, South America and the Caribbean and could have got to the South Seas in several ways. In the first place the coconut is an extraordinarily hardy traveller and can survive in salt water for a long time then happily take root on hitting land. Alternatively, the Polynesians may simply have taken some along when they settled on the islands from various parts of south-east Asia; or later invaders from South America could have carried them as suggested by the great Kon-Tiki expedition. Those in the Bahamas were planted in the famous pink sands after Columbus had found them further south.

Every part of the coconut palm is useful and the Sanskrit word for it means 'tree which furnishes all the necessities of life'. The leaves are used for walls, thatching and packaging; the trunk is used for building; the hair covering the mature nut makes coir matting; the oil from the meat appears in cosmetics, soap and suntan oils; the meat itself is food, either fresh or dried *(copra)*; the milk is used for cooking or for making wine; the shell is an eating or drinking bowl, or, for centuries, the top-people's travel souvenir. In 14th century Venice, if you wanted to keep up with the Marco Polos, you would have to have had a silver-mounted *noce di coco* in your palazzo. As late as the last century polished coconut shells were still being mounted in silver and sent home by the adventuring scions of European families.

But there's always something new, even with such an ancient food. Clever – or lazy – men in Thailand now have trained monkeys to shin up the palms and carefully choose nuts of the preferred degree of ripeness and pick them, which saves their owners either (a) doing it themselves or (b) paying someone else. The state of ripeness of the nut is rather important, for although it will drop to the ground all by itself when nice and ripe, the milk contained in the younger, green coconuts is more plentiful and more delicious. When I stayed in a beach hut on an otherwise deserted 20 mile strip of burning white sand on the Gulf of Siam, I was impressed to find that our host had thoughtfully imported lads to shin up the trees to gather fresh coconuts each morning, so we could drink that cool and refreshing liquid. What he had overlooked was to tell us that it has a decided laxative effect – something we found ourselves learning *a posteriori*.

The name coconut is based on old Portuguese and Spanish words which mean 'grinning face', a reminder of the appearance of one end of the nuts, on which there are three darker spots looking like eyes and a mouth. Dr Johnson referred to it as the *cocoa*nut, which was an accident, but it took a long time for the spelling to revert to its original.

The coco-de-mer is a double coconut of enormous size found only on two islands of the Seychelles; polished specimens have become the new tourist status symbol and their undoubted resemblance to oiled and sun-tanned buttocks or voloptuous female thighs ensure they are noticed by the neighbours.

If you don't fancy coping with whole coconuts, the meat and milk can be bought in two basic forms.

Desiccated or flaked coconut: particularly popular in Australasia, where desiccated coconut is put into or onto more sweet and savoury dishes than Dame Edna Everage could ever poke fun at. Lamington cakes are squares of sponge coated with chocolate syrup and coconut and are as essential at a Down Under christening as the vicar. Coconut bumblebees, coconut ice and coconut-sprinkled fruit salads and curries will be as life blood to the newly named child. Actually, it is very good in all these foods, especially in curries with which it can also be served as a condiment.

Coconut cream and coconut milk can be made from desiccated coconut by covering, say, 150-200g/6-8oz with boiling water and leaving it to cool. Then put the coconut into a sieve or some muslin, and mash or squeeze it to extract the creamy-white liquid. If you leave it thick it is 'cream', or you can dilute this with water to make 'milk'. The liquid inside a coconut is called coconut water. It is often drunk but rarely used in cooking.

Cream of coconut: although you can sometimes buy coconut milk canned it has usually been adulterated and sweetened. Better to buy a solid block of cream of coconut which lasts for ages, is pure, and can simply be reconstituted by dissolving an amount in hot or boiling water. The thicker it is the richer, obviously, and as both thick cream or thin milk it can be used like the dairy product. Thick coconut cream curdles if heated to boiling point and this is done deliberately in West Indian and Malaysian cooking. Thick coconut cream spread on top of a grilled pork chop or roasted chicken gives an interesting and instant lift to otherwise ordinary food. Even such basics as vanilla ice cream, sliced oranges or grilled bananas are magically transformed; and used with care in association with finer fruits like strawberries or the wonderful mango, thick, chilled coconut cream makes child's play of creating new desserts during hot summer months. I always keep coconut cream in the refrigerator.

You don't always have to *eat* it; coconut milk is terrific in long summery drinks with rum and fruit juices – a hot evening, a barbecue, some friends, some coconut cream, assorted fruits and alcohols and you'll have a memorable party – or, if you are really lucky, a party that no one remembers!

I like to finish a spicy, gingery curry sauce by leaving the solid coconut cream to melt in the liquid, and it can add new dimensions of flavour to the most unexpected vegetables – I think you'll like sliced aubergine baked gently in coconut milk spiked with a few rings of green chilli peppers.

Gingko nuts: mildly flavoured and with a rather strange starchy-rubbery texture, these small buff coloured productions of the gingko tree are used as garnish or ingredients in all types of Chinese dish. Best bought canned in brine.

Hazelnuts: hazelnuts are cobnuts are Kent cobs are filberts; the only differences are technical and determined by the relative length of the nut to the husk, cobs usually being rounder and filberts somewhat longer. In the United States all types are called filberts, a name originally given because they usually ripen on or about St Philbert's Day, August 22nd. In Europe, filbert usually denotes a hazelnut that has been cultivated. The 15 species of shrub and tree from which this small and important nut come range in height from 2.7-36m/9-120ft and belong to the birch family. They need deep well-drained soil with plenty of sun, and thus Turkey, Italy and Spain are the chief producers. The finest nuts are said to come from trees best described as Eurasian – the European and the giant hazelnut. Hybrids of these with the American and Beaked Filbert are also excellent producers. Constantinople nuts is a trade name for Turkish hazelnuts, and those from Spain are known as Barcelona nuts. In New Zealand we call them monkey nuts...

From a culinary point of view hazelnuts are essential to a great part of the finest traditions of European cake making and confectionery, when they are usually used in ground form. Although there is some argument as to whether one should use hazelnuts, almonds or both to make praline, I think the purely hazelnut variety infinitely better (not that it probably matters one jot).

Like almonds, hazelnuts taste much better when lightly toasted, or, if you have the patience, slowly roasted until golden all the way through. Lightly crushed they are good to sprinkle over fruit dishes, in cereals, muesli, yoghurt, cream and with green vegetables. They are specially good with the aristocratic mangetout, or with broccoli, particularly if bathed with some garlic-ridden butter.

Toasted hazelnuts, whole or chopped, crushed or ground are quite one of the best additions to stuffing and make a fascinating addition to meat gravies and game sauces. I recently stuffed boned trout with a mixture of grated celeriac, chopped hazelnuts and garlic, baked them in a hot oven and served them with a dollop of chilled soured cream – perfectly simple and quite memorable. So too are strawberries served with whipped cream stiffened with ground or chopped hazelnuts.

Macadamias: a relatively new arrival on the international scene and virtually unknown in Europe, macadamia nuts are something of a cult food in America, particularly in Hawaii where macadamia shops are as shiny and well-staffed as service stations used to be. There they've done more things with macadamia nuts than you can – or would want to – imagine. Every kind of chocolate shape, every kind of jam, jelly and marmalade, every kind of cake, biscuit, cookie and character includes the macadamia.

The most extraordinary thing about this nut is that the tree upon which it grows is Australian, a native of Queensland and New South Wales. It looks something like a pale, fat hazelnut and has a slightly strange, fatty, waxy texture and a taste that can only be described as 'nutty', perhaps slightly buttery. The ones I've been sold as cocktail snacks were all helped with a little coconut milk oil, so perhaps there's not all that much unaided flavour. So why the fuss? Well, good marketing strategy excepted, they have a most valid claim to the world's very serious attention for they have an exceptionally high protein content and are being studied as a new and simple alternative protein source in remote tropical areas. If you manage to get some you will probably find them so expensive you won't dare use them. Best plan is to pop into a macadamia shop on Waikiki Beach and taste one or two of their confections for free.

And the name? It is associated with the man who pioneered the use of a tar mixture on our roads; the nut was one of Mr Macadam's later interests.

Peanuts: peanuts, which are not nuts at all but legumes, are also called groundnuts, earth nuts, monkey nuts... and goolers. Yes, that's right, monkey nuts and goolers. Perhaps because of such names, peanuts hide underground, the dying flower actually managing to burrow in such a way as to protect her offspring. At harvest time the entire plants, except for the deepest roots, are pulled up and left to wither in the sun for a day. Then they are built into large stacks around a stake with the pods towards the centre to protect them from the weather. In 4-6 weeks they are ready to be used to make all manner of goodies – peanut oil, peanut butter, salted peanuts, spiced or dry-roasted peanuts, or the peanut sauces that make Indonesian foods so original and full of flavour.

Traces of peanuts have been found in ancient Peruvian mummy graves and from their native South America they have now spread to India, Indonesia, China, West Africa and the United States.

Peanuts are very much more good for you than their usage as monkey food would suggest. Pound for pound, they have more protein, minerals and vitamins than beef liver, more food energy (calories) than sugar and more fat than double cream.

Pecan: native to North America where it was widely used by the Indians who called it *pecan*, a word describing all nuts that have shells so hard they need to be cracked with a stone. As well as eating its meat, the Indians ground it into a milky liquid for use in gruels and maize cakes, a combination which would be very good. It is now grown in a belt stretching from New Mexico to the Carolinas, and as far north as Illinois; South Africa and Australia also cultivate some.

The pecan is claimed to have the highest fat content of any vegetable food, with a calorific content similar to that of butter. The trees grow anything up to 48m/160ft high with a span of up to 21m/70ft and so harvesting is mainly by variations of beating branches or shaking the trees. Shelling is difficult, and a labyrinth of conveyors, blowers, reels, fans, graders, pickers, dyers and packers can take up to three days ultimately to separate the kernel from the shell and sort it into uniform grades; this complicated processing is the reason for its relative expense. Although most pecan trees are wild and grow on the banks of rivers and creeks, there is also a cultivated variety made possible by the experiment with grafting successfully carried out by a Louisiana slave in 1850. The cultivated tree produces a nut with a thinner shell and thus gives a better yield.

Whole pecans are sometimes available in markets in this country and recognizable by their red grey-brown shiny appearance, something like an acorn without its cap. They can be infuriatingly difficult to crack – using a hammer often disintegrates the shell and the nut, or forces splinters of one inextricably into the other. The best way is to hold two nuts on one palm and squeeze; one of them should crack right round the middle and the two halves can be extricated. Well, that's what should happen..:....

Pecan halves and pieces are increasingly available in the United Kingdom in specialty stores, and worth every penny. Good in sweet pies, vegetable purées or dessert pastries that include spices, they are often said to be interchangeable with walnuts, but in my opinion the substitution could only be made for reasons of economy. The pecan has a far richer and more elegant flavour, without the acidic bite of the walnut. If you ever want to bribe me, give me pecan pie: I'll do anything – before, during and after.

Pine nuts/pine kernels: these delicious morsels really are from pine trees, usually the stone pine, but other pines may be the source. Pine nuts are an essential for Middle Eastern food and are also widely used in Italy and Greece. Those seen in the United Kingdom usually come from China.

The small, moon coloured nuts are rich and oily and taste of the merest whisper of pine resin, but are perfectly addictive once you begin to eat them.

They are an important ingredient in the famed pesto of Genoa, pounded with fresh basil, garlic, oil and Parmesan into a pasta sauce. But generally they are browned lightly before being used, either in a little oil or in a dry non-stick pan, which is easier.

To convert any rice dish, even plain rice, into something Levantine, browned pine nuts with or without chopped pistachios is all you need. Added to a saffron or turmeric scented pilaff they are even better.

Once sweetened, I find they make a delicious and unexpected garnish for simple puddings like ice creams and lemon mousses; they go very well with fresh, lightly-flavoured cream cheese, too. The most spectacular way to sweeten them is first to brown a little butter (carefully) then to add some sugar and let that caramelize before you add the nuts. The sugar and butter will coat the nuts with a crunchy toffee; I first did this to top poached whole satsumas, served in their syrup with rose water flavoured cream cheese.

Pistachios: this is the most maddening nut of all – once you eat one you have to eat another, then just one more… until your fingernails ache and bleed from opening the shells, you cry out for liquid because of the salt, and your surroundings are littered with raped shells. But what bliss!

I've not been able to discover why pistachios are nearly always sold still in their shells, slightly cracked open and salted. Perhaps they keep better that way (as good a reason as any). They can also be bought shelled and unsalted, which is what you use for cooking.

This green nut, rich and decorative with its wine-red skin, is grown from Afghanistan to the Mediterranean and the United States, where it is particularly popular as a flavouring. It is expensive and has always been so, for there are records of complaints about its prohibitive cost from Ancient Rome. Of the more accessible places, Aegina in Greece's Saronic Gulf produces the most wonderful, and no visit to this island can be considered unless you are prepared to gorge yourself. Strangely it is the only place in Greece they grow.

They are invaluable for decorating, chopped finely over sweet or savoury food, hot or cold. Pistachios are essential, chopped roughly, in good Middle Eastern pilaffs which also include saffron and toasted pinenuts. Finely chopped pistachios are part of the fillings for Greek, Turkish and Arabic pastries and are also excellent in poultry stuffings. But Europe has never really taken this nut to its heart – or stomach – and it appears only rarely as the flavouring in specialized cakes or ice creams, usually in association with a muddy green colouring which has nothing to do with its natural state of affairs. In fact most pistachio flavouring is achieved by artificial means and tastes more like almonds, which is a terrible let down. I always send pistachio ice cream back if it tastes of almonds – especially if it is expensive and served in a restaurant with airs.

To get the really bright green colour which looks so good, boil the nuts for 30 seconds in water and then peel away the skin; if the nuts do not brighten they are not of the best quality.

Tiger nuts: these are the least nut-like nut of all, for they are actually tubers. Looking like a cross between shrivelled peanuts and extruded, dried dog food, they are perhaps better known under their Spanish name – *chufas* or *alchufas*.

Mainly eaten as a snack they have an extraordinary chewy texture and flavour, not unlike coconut crossed with brazil nut. Apparently they were very popular before the last war but disappeared with the corner shops. One supplier has told me that they have had letters from old people telling them how much they appreciate seeing them again.

In southern Spain you drink them rather than eat them, in a very popular beverage called *horchata*. This is made by soaking the nuts overnight (start with hot water) then putting them all into the liquidizer with the water. Drain well then put the residue back into the liquidizer again with a little more water. Drain again then put the residue into muslin, tighten that and squeeze the remaining milk. It is a really refreshing drink served chilled and if you've ever wondered what people do in a Spanish *horchateria*, now you know. Horchata can also be heated very slowly indeed in a double boiler and it will eventually thicken to make a custard.

Tiger nuts are rarely used in cooking, but when soaked, apparently go well in apple pie.

Walnuts: walnuts have been with us a long time and employed just as long. The Greeks used them lavishly, and still do in sweetmeats and pastries. The Romans spread walnut trees wherever they marched and may have introduced them to the British Isles; some can be seen preserved in the volcanic ash at the Temple of Isis in Pompeii.

There are several types of walnut. The black and the butternut grow in the eastern states of North America; the English or Persian walnut is common throughout Europe, the Middle East, China and has been introduced to the United States. The nut of the English variety is usually picked green and dried or ripened off the tree.

It's a particularly versatile nut, found successfully in sweet and savoury dishes throughout the world. It has a rather astonishing affinity with tomatoes and the Caucasian combination of tomato and walnut sauce is sensational. Perhaps the simplest 'gourmet' dish of all is a bowl of sliced tomatoes (but rich, red ones, needless to say), just slightly chilled and soaked in walnut oil. I also like them crushed together in butter with green peppercorns, to make a savoury topping for such tasty flesh as pheasant.

Walnuts were once crushed and soaked to make milk but the almond variety is the only flavouring of this kind now made. Vegetarians like walnuts and use them extensively, usually eating them in combination with cracked cereals to form their vegetarian steaks.

Pickled walnuts are increasingly hard to buy, and like so many traditional English foods they seem to be disappearing because commercial manufacture is *un*commercial. Some are made, but it is usually easier to buy them bottled from America; however, these are sweet pickled which is not to many people's taste.

The grading of walnuts calls for a mind besotted by minutiae and such a predilection would be of some help in buying them too. The best advice when buying walnut halves is that light is right – the lighter the colour the higher the grade. If you are being asked to pay exceptionally high prices, the half nuts should not only be pale, there should be no surface chipping and no smaller or broken pieces present, both of which are signs of a lesser grade.

Remember when you are making cakes or pies with walnuts, that if they brown they often become very bitter.

CANNED & BOTTLED VEGETABLES

Canned vegetables have largely had their day, well and truly replaced for flavour and colour by the frozen varieties. But there are some that are distinctly better, more convenient, or solely available when so processed.

Asparagus: although cooked to a softness we would never entertain in fresh asparagus, the canned green ones, perhaps because of their specific variety, are addictive to many. Rolled in thin, buttered white or brown bread, canned asparagus spears are as basic to Australasian entertaining as lamingtons and pavlovas. Asparagus rolls seem to be creeping into the repertoire of caterers in Britain, too, and are usually scoffed with unseemly greed. They are typically made with the green ones and even better if you butter the outside too and brown and crisp them before serving.

If you make a sieved purée of green asparagus, this can be folded into mayonnaise to serve with cold fish or poultry or you can stir it into a bechamel to make a sauce or soufflé base.

White asparagus, blanched in earth banks to keep the sun away from their thrusting stems, are not very much to the British taste anyway, and even less appealing when they are canned. But there are those who cleave to European tastes no matter what, and serve them with smoked or unsmoked ham.

Artichokes: artichoke hearts, *coeurs d'artichauts*, are an excellent addition to any cold hors d'oeuvres, and I like to slice them in half to add to hot or cold pasta dishes or potato salads. By themselves they should be served with a good olive oil vinaigrette, in which they have soaked for some time.

Artichoke bottoms, *fonds d'artichauts*, the little caps of solid, nutty tasting artichokes with no attached leaves, taste just as good from a tin as fresh – well, almost. They make good additions to mixed buffets, or sliced into salads. They may be sliced and dressed as a rather high class salad themselves, perhaps with a few cold peas, orange segments, some olives and a few anchovy fillets. They are best served at grander dinners when warmed and filled with a vegetable purée. Green pea is most traditional but anything with the bite of lemon or garlic will work... celeriac, brussel sprouts with nutmeg, carrot with allspice or thyme, and so on.

Bamboo shoots: sold in cans in chunks or large slices. Ivory-coloured. If the smell seems rather rich, rinse in cold water or blanch. Mainly used as a squeaky/crunchy contrast of texture but there is a definite deep woodiness of flavour which is useful too. Keeps a long time refrigerated in water.

Celery hearts: these are almost indistinguishable from braised fresh celery. Sprinkled with lemon juice, a little chicken or beef stock and some butter, they reheat wonderfully. They are also good braised in a little walnut oil and garlic and served with chopped walnuts.

Hearts of palm: only available here in cans. The central young stem of a special palm tree which dies when this

SEAWEEDS

Although very much associated with Japanese food or an unwanted reminder of unusual experiences with Welsh laver-bread, seaweeds are slowly demanding more and more attention, particularly from vegetarians, but also from anyone with a true interest in eating broadly. At food shows over the past years any stand featuring them, often as sea vegetables, has always been one of the busiest.

Except for laver, all seaweeds come dried and will rehydrate in cold water in five minutes, after which they may be boiled to be served hot or cold, although I should be very certain of your guests tastes before you dare either! Small amounts boiled up in water make very good stocks for cooking fish.

Agar-agar: this is a seaweed, and a vegetarian substitute for animal gelatin. Instructions are usually printed on the packet, which you are most likely to find in health stores. Generally you use about a tablespoon to a 300ml/½pt of boiling water. Required when making a set pudding with fresh pineapple or kiwi fruit, as they contain an enzyme which prevents gelatin setting.

In China this is also strips of processed seaweed which look like cellophane. After being soaked in water it looks and behaves like transparent rubber, and with various flavourings is usually served cold, which multiplies the comedic effect; it is a joke, isn't it?

Autumn dulse: dark red colour and very full shellfish/seaweed flavour. Once soaked, dredge with seasoned flour and deep fry, to make frivolous but arrestingly flavoured snacks or garnishes.

Dabberlocks/wakame: very accessible and un-seaweed like flavour, rather like combining green nuts and young peas. It's olive ▶

◄ green, good in chicken stews and soups.

Dulse: greenish red coloured and a definite marine/shellfish flavour, but less so than autumn dulse.

Fingerware/finger kombu: olive green with a meaty, beefy flavour which is also uncompromisingly marine. Rather limited in use by itself but good mixed into salads and other vegetable mixtures, or in stuffings. Interesting to boil it 20 minutes and then to grill it to crispness as a garnish for fish dishes.

Grockle/herb kombu: looks like a fleshy vine leaf and is much the same olive colour of cooked ones – a slight astringency behind a chestnut marine flavour. Fry in egg batter as tempura or deep fry in seasoned flour.

Kombu/konbu: dark green or brown sheets of the giant kelp which shows high quality if it has a sheen, a powdery surface and is thick. It should be wiped rather than rinsed. This is the seaweed one cooks in water very briefly with dried bonito flakes, *katsuobushi*, to make dashi, the basic Japanese stock.

Nori: essential to sushi. This is dried Japanese laver, and is usually slightly toasted before use; it may simply be crushed and sprinkled as a condiment. Can also be bought ready-toasted.

Sloke/laver/purple nori: can be red or black depending how it is cooked. Has an iodine-like back taste which is easily balanced by good vinegar or orange juice, but rarely is, which is why I find it difficult to countenance the favour in which Welsh laverbread is held. It is sold ready prepared after cooking for hours, and may also be bought in cans.

Sugarware/sugar kombu/girdle tang: a delicate looking and tasting seaweed, not unlike a salt-sea version of spring greens. You can do almost anything with it. Once rehydrated it makes a jolly good wrapping for fish which is to be baked, grilled or steamed.

heart is removed, hence the expense. They are found and enjoyed in many parts of the tropical world and the best are usually from Brazil. Serve chilled with vinaigrette or mayonnaise, as though asparagus. Better if you give a little tropicality, so flavour either type of dressing with lime. Sometimes the pieces can be woody and rather unpleasant, so if you are serving them for a special dinner it is wise to check each piece individually, and to have a spare tin on hand.

As a substitute for asparagus they always work, so serve with smoked salmon, with gulls' or quails' eggs, with smoked fish or with a barely-warm sauce maltese. One of the few times I have used toasted cashew nuts is to chop them over hearts of palm.

Lotus root: recognized easily as the slices with the holes in them. Crisp, crunchy and slightly sweet. Most usually bought canned.

Mushrooms: don't bother with canned mushrooms, whatever the ubiquitous home economists say. Bottled mushrooms are hideously expensive and unsatisfying. Do look however at the later section on dried wild mushrooms which are fabulous.

Peas: apart from mushy, or processed, peas which are a world unto themselves, canned peas have been cancelled out by the frozen variety. Petits pois à la française, which are cooked with baby onions and some lettuce, or should be, also retain a devoted following. I suspect this is based on nostalgia rather than inherent quality.

Potatoes: because they are generally small and waxy, canned potatoes are very good for making salads that do not fall to pieces. But heat them slightly before dousing with a vinaigrette and garlic or cloves, even if you are later to mix with mayonnaise. To ring the changes, mix only with soured cream and dill, or with a mixture of half yoghurt and half mayonnaise. Colour slightly with tomato purée, add horseradish sauce, some poached cucumber and a few prawns for something very special.

Pulses: all these are excellent from cans, but see the section on these for suggestions as to use.

Red peppers: these have generally been char-roasted and skinned and so are both sweet and convenient. Cut into strips they finish a salad far better than the raw ones, can be added to scrambled eggs, puréed for stuffings, added to pasta and fish sauces... they

---

SUN-DRIED TOMATOES

There are a great number of people confused about the explosive popularity of these over the past decade. I'm not surprised. Every time I have been part of a tasting panel there has been universally expressed horror at the low standard and extraordinary range of flavours – from burned caramel to vinegar. Excepting individual preferences, my recommendation is to avoid those which come hydrated in oil or any other liquid (they are hardly dried any more) and to buy dried ones with the greatest care, tasting first and avoiding anything with detached skins, browning or broken shapes.

The idea is simple. Tomatoes are fruits. Fruits can be dried for use later. So, sun-dry tomatoes. The Neapolitan cook who taught me about such things 20 years ago said her job as a child was to cut the tomatoes, lay them in the sun and bring them in every night. We luckier but sun-starved types can dry tomatoes overnight in a slow oven or domestic dehydrators, which are very good indeed. The trick is first to choose a tomato variety with excellent flavour, and then not to caramelize them by over-heating or do anything other than concentrate what goodness is there. I expect there are exceptions, but the only commercial ones which taste anything like tomatoes are from California: they are tomato-red, smell sweet, and are soft enough to cut and eat as they are, a texture somewhere between ready-to-eat dried fruit and old-fashioned hard ones, and even with your eyes closed you know it is a concentrated tomato when you put it in your mouth.

How you use them is as legion as the application of fresh tomatoes. They may be sliced and tossed onto almost anything, from potato salads to green ones, omelettes, pasta dressings, risottos, pilaffs. In all these they will give wonderful ▶

---

are one of the best things of all to have in your larder. And the opened ones last ages in a refrigerator.

If you really like peppers, simply drain well, dress with garlic and good olive oil plus a splash of lemon juice or vinegar for a simple but robust accompaniment to plain grilled lamb chops, chicken or pork dishes. Good mixed with slices of artichoke bottoms, too.

Sweet corn: whole kernel or cream-style, these taste just about as good as you would make – *(see GRAINS)*.

Tomatoes: good food is barely possible without tins of plum tomatoes processed in their juices. And now there is far more than mere whole tomatoes. We have chopped tomatoes, chopped tomatoes with any number and style of flavourings and we

◄ chewy explosions of flavour. If they are cooked in sauces, casseroles, stews, stuffings and the like they will expand and become softer, adding their flavour and some degree of colour. They are very interesting in tomato sauces, where they add fascinating levels and variations of the same basic flavour. I add them when I am reheating a ratatouille, for instance.

Of course, you can rehydrate them yourself and have different sorts of fun. Oil is a popular thing to flavour with sun-dried tomatoes and so is a decent vinegar. These techniques then give you both the liquids and the hydrated tomatoes to use. They make fascinating salad dressings and marinades; a strongly flavoured oil makes a terrific mayonnaise.

I like to put sun-dried tomatoes in alcohol. Soaked in cognac, vodka or black rum for a few hours they make the most perfect salad dressing, for instance. Do it longer and both improve immeasurably, making an ideal last minute addition to sauces, or a flavouring to sprinkle on grilled or simply cooked meats and poultry.

Every year I make a flavoured eau-de-vie for Christmas, ideally with a flavourless one bought from a French supermarket for remarkably little money. Last year's version was smoky red with sun-dried tomatoes, bright and clean with fresh lime zest and piquant with fresh peppercorns I had bought earlier in the year and frozen until I wanted them. It took about four weeks for the flavours and colour to develop and then I strained out the peppercorns or they would have added too much bite, the mistake of another year. It made the perfect welcoming shot for those who drink such things, but I tended to use it more as a dressing for foods such as smoked salmon, fish or game pâtés and the like, when it gave quite as much lift to the festivities, but discreetly.

have passata or cream of tomatoes, which is pretty much any of the above put through a sieve. They are interchangeable depending on whether you want texture or not and how long you intend to cook. The whole tomatoes generally do best with long cooking so they reduce and concentrate, and thus are a perfect medium in which to cook other food, from strongly flavoured vegetables to meat and poultry. If you don't cook them in such a medium it is also an excellent way to sauce them, cauliflower, parsnips, artichokes – even peas and beans. The only problem is the skin and seeds, but sometimes a certain disregard for such niceties can seem rustically attractive, at others it is delinquent.

Chopped tomatoes are a cook's dream. If you strain off some of the thick juice, and use them to finish a sauce or as part of a last minute sauce for pasta, say, they add terrific texture and there is a sporting chance someone will think you have been chopping all day, and neatly, too. Even when cooked longer they tend to keep a bit of texture and are also good for cooking things.

Passata or cream of tomatoes is basically what we cooked the other sorts to get. It is not at all like thinned down tomato purée or paste, for that tends to have a slightly caramel taste. Yet even though it seems thick and concentrated, it too cooks down even more, to give faster results for a Bolognese ragu for instance. If you cannot get a passata, squash a can of whole plum tomatoes, including their juice, and cook in an open pan until very reduced, liquidize and then strain, using the back of a soup ladle to squeeze maximum yield though the sieve. Only then flavour with olive oil, perhaps a few drops of vinegar or red wine, anchovy fillets rather than salt, and some herbs; if you use fresh mint (which is particularly good), basil or thyme, they will have scented the mixture in five minutes and may then be strained out. If you boil the sauce rapidly the oil (or butter if you like) will be emulsified and give enough flavour and body to make anyone think you had started from scratch.

> ### GREEN WRAPPERS
> **Banana leaf:** a common wrapping which, like lotus leaf, is used like the vine leaf. It is generally not used for or expected to give flavour, but long cooking will encourage in a leafy, tea-like flavour.
> **Lotus leaf:** an Oriental version of the vine leaf, used to wrap food and give a subtle extra flavour, especially to rice, pork and poultry. More likely to be used for steaming than boiling and thus flavour exchange will be minimalised. Usually bought dried, they should be soaked in warm water before use. If you grow your own, dip them in very hot water, both to wilt and to rid them of unwanted animal matter.
> **Vine leaf:** vacuum-packed, bottled or canned, these will have been lightly cooked and stored in brine. They are ready for use after a good rinse, and add a slight honey-like flavour to any food with which they are in contact for some time. Unlike the previous two, these leaves are eaten, but require fairly long cooking if this is your plan. But as a wrapping for fish, for roasts or for baked pâtés they may be allowed to add their flavour without being eaten. Fresh vine leaves from any type of grape may be used after quickly blanching in boiling water.

You might also reduce whole tomatoes without any squashing or sieving so that maximum texture remains. This is even better when made additionally rugged by the late addition of precooked bacon pieces, chopped garlic and ruggedly chopped parsley; it's a great way to top bean or root vegetable soups or pasta, of course.

Chopped tomatoes or passata also react well to the olive-oil-and-boil trick, which with a few herbs makes a tremendous tomato sauce – if you must have an onion flavour stir in chives just before serving.

Water chestnuts: a walnut-sized bulb covered by a tough russet coloured skin; the meat is white and crisp and stays that way whatever you do. Best bought prepared in cans. They are most usually sliced for stir-fries and such but are a boon when chopped to give stuffings and fillings guaranteed texture, particularly those based on Chinese mushrooms, which otherwise can tend towards unrelieved slime. Ground water chestnuts make a flour into which you may dip ingredients as you would ordinary flour for deep frying: it gives a really light and crunchy texture. May also be used to thicken sauces.

DRIED MUSHROOMS

The dried wild mushroom is an absolute must in my kitchen, used for everything from saving a mundane soup or stew to being served in homemade brioches or darkly to flavour a Venetian risotto which is perfectly *all'onde*.

It is sad they are so expensive, when Britain positively groans with most of the great wild varieties which could be dried by ourselves, but are not. It need not even require you to go down to the woods for a day. Some of us might merely stroll about the lawn a bit and collect any fairy rings fell upon, for when these mushrooms are dried they have a strong and aromatic flavour remarkably like that of cep, the most popular of dried wild mushrooms.

The most common culinary mushrooms found for sale (other than fresh) will be canned or dried. You must forget canned button mushrooms, indeed if you are reading this book I take it for granted you will have eschewed them anyway. Other canned mushrooms cannot really be recommended either, except Chinese straw mushrooms *qv*. But dried wild mushrooms are another world, indeed in the case of ceps, it is only the dried version which is worth using.

Cep, cepe (Fr), porcini (It), steinpilz (G): The most important of all. When fresh

---

CHINESE MUSHROOMS

Black: dried mushrooms which must be soaked in water for 30 minutes before cooking, so that they will resume their normal size and shape and become soft again. Rinse them off to get rid of the sand. The colour varies from a black to a speckled brown or grey. The medium-sized variety is the better tasting one. Use the stock for flavouring the rest of the dish. They can be breathtakingly expensive

Mo-er/cloud ears: a specialty from Szechuan province. A crinkly and thin tree fungus, which should be soaked for 30 minutes before cooking. Any hard core should be removed. Sold in dry chips. Adds a curious chewy crunch to stir-fried dishes and stuffings; the sort of ingredient that confirms you are not eating a fry up at the local caff.

Straw: small yellow mushrooms with pointed black caps, sold in cans. Use within a week, as their delicate taste is lost soon after exposure to air.

---

the cep can be bland and slimy; when dried it has a wondrous velvety golden brown colour and sensational earthy sweet flavour which is unmistakable. The best qualities are usually sold in dried slices taken through the cap and stem, but chopped segments or broken pieces are very much cheaper, especially in French and Corsican markets, and somehow seem to give a stronger flavour too. Check both carefully for too much damage by bugs, either before or after drying. If you pay the price you must be able to enjoy the way they look as well as their flavours.

Either way dried ceps must be rinsed quickly in cold water in a coarse sieve or colander to get rid of the inevitable grit. The liquid in which they then rehydrate is invaluable and should always be incorporated into something; if the mushrooms are to flavour a stew for instance, rehydrate them in that. Otherwise cover with liquid and put over a low heat which does it faster and gives the stock greater colour than steeping in cold liquid. I particularly like to use an amontillado or oloroso sherry or a dry sercial madeira, but something alcoholic is always better than mere water. When you use them in a stuffing for, say, chicken or roast beef, you might like to mix the ceps in dry so they are hydrated by the cooking juices. The same would go for vegetarian dishes, such as stuffed peppers or courgettes. If you want to give rice or barley pilaffs a lift, add dried ceps when you start to cook.

For really yummy sauces that are relatively instant compared to making bechamels and reductions and the like, rehydrate ceps in double cream. If you take 20 or so minutes while other ingredients are cooking, the cream will have reduced to the perfect consistency of a nicely made bechamel; finish with cognac. If you do not care for quite so much cream, rehydrate in sherry, white wine or vermouth, and when the mushrooms are soft and the liquor has reduced, add double cream and continue heating until the texture is to your taste.

The combination of potato, cep and cream is almost too good to eat, but here is something to do if you insist: rehydrate ceps in maderia, remove them and reduce the wine to a syrup. Layer the mushrooms and reduced madeira with sliced potato, pour over some thick cream, bake slowly, and then dare anyone not to eat it all. It makes cooking potatoes with truffles seem more insane than ever.

Morels, *morilles (Fr):* These are the pointy wrinkled ones, alarmingly like any image you might have conjured of the exposed brain of an alien. They are rather expensive but repay that with huge flavour, which is definitely mushrooms but also of meat and of bacon, particularly. Their appearance, flavour and cost mean they are usually used as garnish or to finish a sauce, which is fair enough. They take longer to rehydrate than ceps but the use of cream, wine or sherry rather than water is well recommended.

The rest: *chanterelles* and *girolles* and the very black *trompettes des morts* (we call them Horn of Plenty) all look good but have virtually no taste when dried, so I shouldn't bother, except for presentation. The very distinct contrast is the fairy ring mushroom which dries to give a really rich flavour almost as strong as cep, but you should discard the thin stems as they rarely become tender again.

Poland irregularly sends dried mushrooms to Britain, often in traditional strings or garlands, which are cheaper than the French or German, without being cheap. They are usually ceps but not always, so give them a good sniff, hoping to find a rich, almost wine-like scent, honeyed at first but finishing with a dusky earthiness. If you do, they will be the real thing.

TRUFFLES

When an author as august as Colette describes a fungus as the 'most capricious and most revered of black princesses' you can be certain it is rather more than a mushroom. The truffle, the black diamond of cookery, is one of the rarest of all the world's exotic treats.

Truffles have been popular and acknowledged as special for thousands of years and like all rare things have been credited with aphrodisiac powers, particularly by Francis I of France, but I suspect this was rather a matter of expecting more for your money than passing gastronomic gratification.

The flavour of black truffles is found in nothing else – indeed it isn't found in truffles most of the time. The delicacy is fugitive, easily overpowered and expected to perform tasks of which it is incapable. It is more a perfumer or catalyst than a flavouring and the true flavour is only passed on to other foods by standing together or cooking together very gently for a longish time. Truffle is best with other fragile flavours, such as exalted foie gras or creamy scrambled eggs. Although a standby of buffets, banquets and ballrooms, the practice of decorating with slivers of cold truffle is nonsensical and wasteful in the extreme – the truffle has not been brought to full flavour and the food will not be perfumed by it. Far better to use slices of black olive which have been blanched to desalt them. An extraordinary number of people will believe it is truffle if you tell them so, everyone will if you don't.

The 19th century was blessed by a boom in the truffle harvest, as is manifest in cookery books of the time which use truffles like we use tomatoes. It was nothing to be served a whole one as a starter, baked in an oven with a little Madeira and seasoning, and served on a crisp, white linen napkin. Now the harvest is around 100 tonnes a year when conditions are right. You need warm rainy summers to follow a spring in which the right types of breeze have encouraged the spores to travel, settle and germinate. Dry summer weather can reduce the truffle harvest by at least 25 per cent.

Truffles are gathered between the end of November and mid-March or so. They are probably at their best in January. Thus the rush to use truffles for Christmas cooking is generally pointless if you are using fresh ones, for they are most unlikely to have reached full maturity; and as preserved ones will not have anywhere near the flavour of fresh ones, the exercise is doomed anyway. I have decided only to use truffles if and when I can get them fresh or frozen.

Usually they are found under oak trees in 'burnt' areas, so-called because no other vegetation can or will grow there. They can only be found by being sniffed out by trained dogs or pigs, all of which contributes to the high cost. But if they grow under oak trees, are there no English truffles? Well, there is an English truffle, the Bath or Red truffle, but it has largely been lost to us by the creeping of our towns and cities into our fields and by a dearth of those who have the knowledge to train animals to find them. However, I once had a Lithuanian working for me who said regularly, 'Oh I know where to find truffles all over England'. Initial excitement gave way to inertia on my part, a dampening of disbelief. Imagine my face when he returned months later with a small paper bag full! There were black ones and white ones – and one extraordinary fragrant one the like of which I've never come across before or since. I knew rather less about truffles than I do now and probably ruined some of them in my experiments – but... truffles to *experiment* with. My friend told me he knew where to go because he had actually sown the spores all over England, having brought them from Europe after the war. I've not seen him for years now, but somewhere in England there are treasures as valuable as any Graeco-Roman silver hoards.

Others are trying to do this trick professionally and stories abound of success in Spain, but the only time I was treated to their produce was a grotesque pose of a do at The Savoy, where the kitchen had been instructed to do just about everything you should not do with truffles. None was a true black truffle and there had been no attempt to allow their wizardry to permeate and enliven the other ingredients.

The famed black truffle is **tuber melanosporum**. It is unmistakable when cut for it is indeed very black; there are many other truffles but only this type is so black and deserves anything like its reputation. Although widely known as coming from Perigord, this truffle grows in a number of places in an area ranging from there to Italy, including parts of Spain, Provence, Piedmont and Tuscany. Lesser types grow in other parts of France as far north as Alsace, but they aren't the same.

The black truffles of Provence have been amongst the very best I have ever tasted, but they were barely out of the ground, and only lightly preserved anyway. There, peasants were too poor to keep dogs or pigs just to find truffles and so they hunted with long sticks, indeed they still do. What you do is this: walk into the sun tapping likely ground far ahead of you with the stick. If you tap the ground over a truffle, a colony of midges will be disturbed, and as they fly furiously about in impotent rage, their tiny wings reflect the light. You have a truffle.

If you follow the truffle through history, and people do, you would find its abundance has fluctuated wildly but regularly. There are those alive who remember it was nothing to return home with many kilos of truffles each when they were young, and who were told by their grandparents that this was nothing compared to the harvests of their youth; for one person now to find a kilo in total throughout an entire season is thought fortunate. It was this bounty that made their flavour so appreciated: there was enough of it! It is idiotic to follow recipes which purport to recreate, say, the truffled turkey of last century. They used several pounds of fresh truffles to stuff a turkey, and buried that in soil for several days to allow the truffles to perfume the flesh. What possible effect can a single, ready-cooked truffle popped under the skin before roasting have?

With so few truffles about, you need to get maximum value, and canned or bottled ones really are not the way if you are choosing them for flavour rather than public display. If you can find someone who has sterilized a truffle in a small jar at home, this will have lost much liquid but kept rather a lot of flavour – but they may not sell it to you. It is best to pay extra money to buy a frozen truffle, to let it defrost very slowly in light olive oil, to which it will add some savour, and then to use it as many ways as you can. Seal it up with some eggs for a few days so it perfumes them or store it in rice, which is the way to transport a fresh one if you become its owner.

You can eat black truffles raw, one way to get a little flavour from the early ones; in Provence I was told they were grated over salads on Christmas Day, 'but only because they were the first, we did not cook with them yet'.

Whatever you plan eventually to cook with your truffle, it must be allowed at least a day in contact with the sliced fungus in a cool and moist place. Otherwise, to really know truffle flavour you must bake one whole, the way Colette and Alice B Toklas and others recommend. Each must be absolutely sealed. This might first be in thin air-dried ham, in turn in a crepe and then pastry: or if you had several they might be braised in wine or Madeira in a small sealed cocotte. It is less attractive but more efficient to use cooking foil which will then neither a lender nor borrower of flavour be. However you cook them, whole truffles should only be revealed in front of the diner so the accumulated scent can be gathered in a single huge sniff. Don't serve them on a white napkin, for you are as likely to smell the bleach which has made it so pristine. The curious flavour remains fugitive even when you have a complete mouthful, but there is a definite sense of bacon gone to heaven. If you are about when there are fresh black truffles to spare, bake one in a fine bread dough, will you, and let me know. I have always imagined that would be wonderful.

Black truffles are sold fresh, canned or bottled. After the laborious brushing and peeling and sorting, which can only be done by hand, truffles stay fresh for just three to four days and will be sold in the chilly winter markets of French villages whole or in pieces. Otherwise the truffles are preserved in one of two ways: they are either cooked before canning or bottling which gives some control over weight loss, or they are slightly salted and sterilized after packing which keeps all the flavour and bulk but converts 25 per cent of the weight into liquid. If you have a fresh truffle and wish to keep it, poach it in madeira and leave it in this liquid, itself a wondrous addition to sauces.

Frankly, though, I am disillusioned. I've never been knocked out by the flavour of a black truffle, even when it has been left for days to perfume a sirloin of beef. In fact the flavour that seems best is that of the madeira in which a truffle has been poached. Even the whole, baked truffle I enjoyed at the Ménage à Trois restaurant in London's Beauchamp Place wasn't such a thrill as, say, a slice of foie gras or a few spoonfuls of caviare. I'll walk a long way to eat freshly grated white truffle, but the black ones? I don't understand the fuss.

Tuber magnatum is the white Piedmontese or Alba truffle. It is very much more expensive than the black truffle, and has a penetrating smell and overwhelming flavour, redolent of every possible perversity and prohibition and impossible to describe because it is like nothing else: all you might do is relate what it makes you think about, and then, like me, you will probably keep that to yourself......

White truffle is never cooked but grated or very thinly sliced indeed over risotto, over pasta or onto hot brioche, which everyone tells me is a specialty of the sidewalks of Florence. It is even more difficult to cultivate than black truffles and such an idea can effectively be dismissed altogether. Such Italian enthusiasts as Antonio Carluccio imports them for use in the Neal Street Restaurant, and once brought over a kilo to my television studio, with a security guard too. A very high profile Labour MP refused to stay on our famed red sofa, nauseated he said by the smell and sickened by the thought of so much money being spent on luxuries. But he stayed when offered one......

They too may be frozen and defrosted most successfully and repay better than black truffles the ploy of storing them amidst eggs or rice or both, provided everything is very cool or refrigerated.

ORGANIC FOOD

Food labelled 'organic' now falls under EC legislation, apart, that is, from meat, dairy produce and wine, which are certain to be added shortly.

Traditionally, organic food has been described as that which is produced in harmony with nature, as far as is possible, using natural fertilisers such as animal manures and coping with pests by biological methods, such as attracting beneficial insects and by rotating crops regularly. Conservation of natural habitats is uppermost in the minds of organic farmers and farm animals are free ranging. Organic farming excludes the use of synthetically made fertilisers, pesticides, growth regulators and livestock feed additives.

The new EC regulations incorporate these general principles and lay out precisely what organic production systems can or cannot do. The body implementing these regulations in the United Kingdom is the United Kingdom Register of Organic Food Standards (UKROFS). Existing organic symbol setting organisations, such as The Soil Association and Organic Farmers and Growers (OF&G), now have to register with UKROFS.

Organic produce from countries outside the United Kingdom comes under the new regulations and these countries themselves have to register with the EC, provided that their own symbol schemes are recognised as bone fide by the EC.

Since January 1993, the EC regulations state that if the word organic appears on a foodstuff label, as in 'Organic Bread' (or more correctly, bread made from organic flour), over 95 per cent of the agricultural ingredients by weight must be accredited organic.

If the product contains organic ingredients comprising between 50 and 95 per cent of the total content, the label may not include the word organic in the name, or figure prominently in any description, but must be confined to the ingredients listing.

Products containing organically grown ingredients which amount to less than 50 per cent of the total may not be referred to as such at all. If interpreted strictly, products such as organic jam, which are made from non-organic sugar, may disappear entirely.

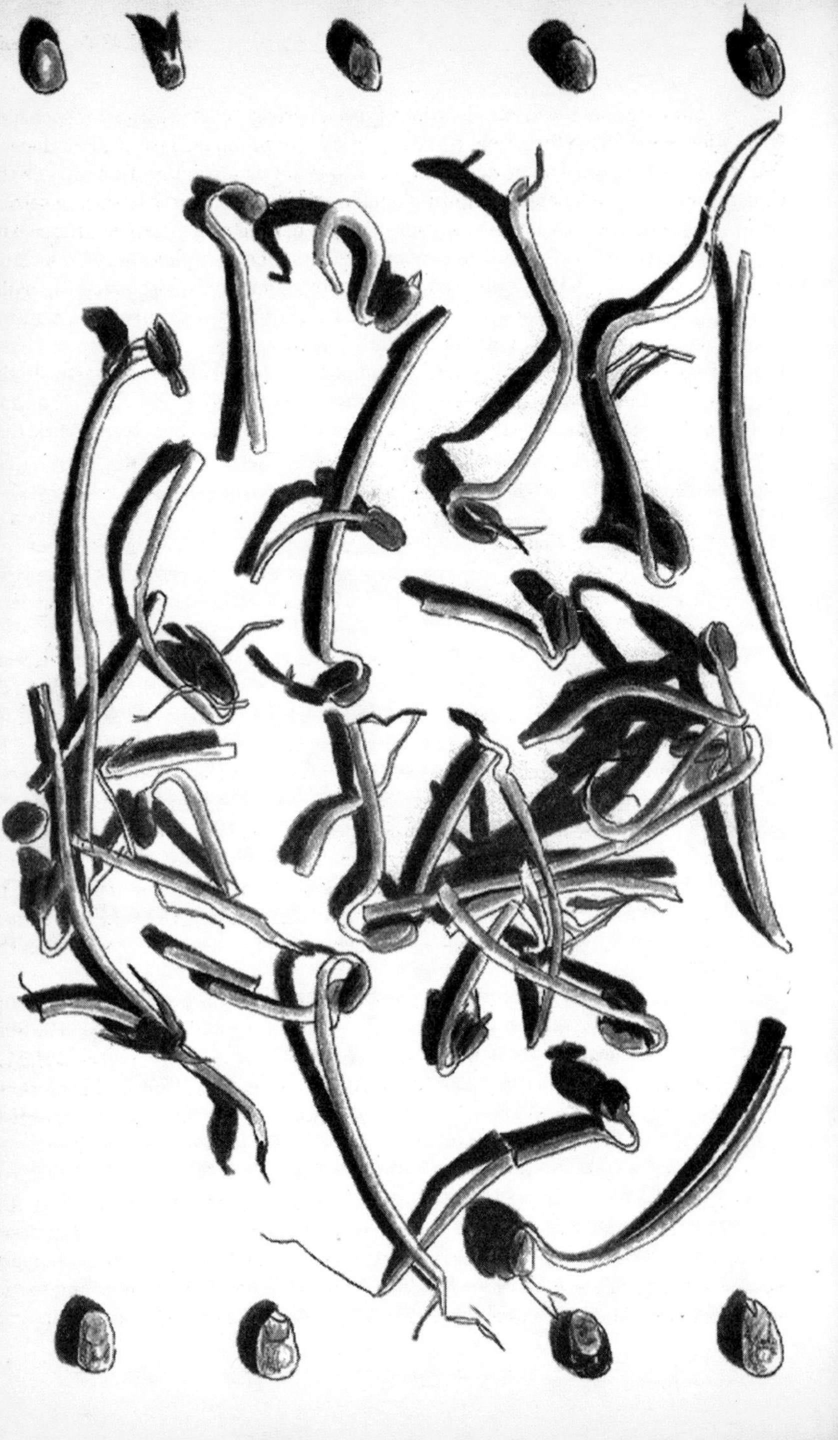

Grain is simply the seeds of various types of grass, yet it is largely responsible for man's long climb from primitive carnivore to his modern peak of dietetic sophistication. The switch from meat to grain as a primary food signals the change from semi-independent hunting and foraging on a nomadic basis to a settled community existence. Grain needed continuous care. The newly-formed groups who gave it, received in return new comfort and security plus a staple that could be stored for use in winter, when there was suddenly free time to explore emerging skills and interests. Meat remained an important part of the diet, of course, but hunting became less crucial to survival and developed as more of a recreation; in any case the mutually dependent and defended groups were also learning to domesticate the animals on which they liked to feast. While man ate grain, the cattle and other animals ate the straw that remained after harvesting. A balance had been struck that became the basis for civilization.

The new reliance on grains began about 10,000 years ago, and subsequently Babylon, Egypt, Greece and the Roman Empire were founded on the cultivation of wheat, barley, rye and oats; in the Far East it was millet and rice, in the Americas, maize. The villages, towns, cities and empires that everywhere arose through the decision to cultivate grain stimulated the cooperation that eventually shot men from the plains to the planets.

The leaders of those ancient civilizations had learned by observation or intuition what we know scientifically – that grains supply most of our nutritional needs – *(see THE VEGETARIAN OPTION)*. Even now, five-eighths of our teeth are shaped for grinding and crushing, as opposed to the tearing and shredding teeth required by natural meat-eaters. Our saliva contains the specific enzyme needed to begin the perfect digestion of grains and our relatively long intestines are adapted to derive maximum food-value from such a diet. One of the greatest advantages of eating grains is that their high proportion of starches is only slowly broken down into energy-giving sugars, providing a steady and sustaining flow of stimulation. The bran (outer husk) of whole grains is equally vital, contributing vitamins and minerals to the supply of necessary roughage, which keeps the digestive system healthy and active.

Thus grain is potentially the chief giver of health and energy. Whole grains supply significantly more nutrition than crushed grains or whole grain flours. For once a grain has been crushed or ground, the vitamin-rich oils in the germ *(see WHEAT)* begin to oxidize and lose food value, eventually becoming rancid and sometimes dangerous. Many commercial products made of grain are de-germinated precisely to avoid oxidization, giving long, trouble-free shelf life at the expense of nutrition.

It is worth soaking many kinds of grains before use, especially wheat and rye. The prime reason is not to shorten cooking time but to improve flavour and usefulness to the body. Soaking in water begins the germination (malting) process, activating a digestive enzyme similar to that in our mouths. This process converts starches into sugars – maltose particularly – making the grain sweeter and tastier and promoting fuller and more efficient assimilation. Once cooked, some grains continue to sweeten and improve in flavour, the result of a broadly similar process.

There can be a serious digestive problem with the grains that include gluten, which expands to contain bubbles of gas in bread doughs. Coeliac disease is the result of an inability to digest the gliadin in gluten. This malabsorption problem is of relatively recent discovery, but now there are many books on the subject – including those that tell you how to cook without gluten. Gluten-free wheat flour is available on prescription and some shops stock excellent substitutes.

With minor variations, all grains are constructed in the same way. The outer part, a fibrous container, comprises six layers of skin. This is the bran, only recently recognized as being a mineral-rich food as well as an invaluable source of roughage. The innermost bran skin, the aleurone layer, contains important additional protein and fat.

The germ is the embryo of the wheat plant. As it must sustain the early growth of the grain, it can be likened to the yolk of an egg. In wheat, its protein content, 25-33 per cent, is similar to that of dried milk or meat. The germ also contains significant quantities of essential vitamin E.

The endosperm makes up more than four-fifths of the wheat grain. It is mainly starch, which goes to make white flour (when sifted from the bran and germ). In its natural state the endosperm, ground or milled into flour, is a creamy colour. With ageing it slowly turns white. It is in pursuit of ever-more, ever-whiter endosperm ever-faster, that man has made his most remarkable advances in grain breeding; but it is in the treatment of such endosperm with bleaches and other chemical 'improvers' that some people consider excessive and even dangerous measures have been taken.

Flour milling: as you may already be aware, the endosperm is the starchy, major part of any grain. The purpose of milling is to break open a grain to expose the endosperm. Then once a liquid has been added the interaction with the starch and other components allows you to make a dough, batter or porridge. Man's first attempts at milling crushed the grain rather than shearing or grinding it, giving a very coarse meal contaminated with grit, stones and other foreign matter. After the laborious task of cracking the grain open by pounding one stone upon another, the meal was mixed with water and cooked in the sun. You had to eat the results hot, for once cold they would be as hard as the boulders on which they had been baked.

As refinements were slowly made to the process of the friction of two stones upon each other, crushing became grinding. The domestic hand mills, or querns, still in common use throughout the world, have always been tiresome and slow to use, whether employing a circular or up-and-down motion, and made a centralized grinding service impossible. It took enough time and energy to grind your own grain, let alone somebody else's. In Europe, the advent of the windmill changed that dramatically.

Considering that wind had long since been harnessed to propel boats and ships, it is strange that the water wheel preceded the windmill by over 1,000 years. Water mills originated with the ancient Greeks and were introduced to Europe by the Romans. But historians cannot agree as to who invented the windmill, or where; they are mentioned in 10th and 11th century manuscripts from Persia and soon afterwards were known in Europe. It is possible they developed independently, but either way wind and water-powered mills gave local people an extraordinary new social freedom; freedom to grow either more grain than they needed and sell it for profit or to grow and grind none at all. The control miller quickly became all-powerful as he bought, sold and, most importantly, stored grain. Mills freed men from the toil of absolute self-sufficiency and the centre of any thriving community had to be a miller and his mill – without them progress was impossible. Without them there simply wasn't the time to progress.

So it continued right up to the late 19th century. Then men perfected both the heavy-cropping Turkey Red strain of wheat and the first-ever, consistent, compressed baker's yeast. Next, the roller mill was introduced from Hungary, and that allowed milling on a scale undreamt of before. In the United Kingdom, once the first roller mill started operating in Glasgow in 1872, the old water and windmills were soon out of business.

Stone-grinding: the time-honoured system of grinding grain in a big central mill was based on two huge, circular stones of a special granite, each weighing well over one tonne. The bottom one is stationary and the top is revolved. Both are corrugated or grooved in such a way that the grain is sheared and the top stone may be raised or lowered to control the fineness of the grinding. The culmination of the movement and the corrugation of the wheels enable grain fed through a hopper at the eye of the upper stone to work itself gradually out to the edge, where it escapes through the apertures which are the ends of the grooves in the bottom stone.

This process, known as stone-grinding, can only produce a 100 per cent wholemeal flour (if whole wheat grains are fed in to it). The heat and pressure generated during the operation serve to distribute the vital wheatgerm and its vitamin E through the endosperm in such a way that they cannot subsequently be separated and

---

THE DAILY GRIND

The natural result of the awakening of the public to the goodness of grains and the badness of the majority of people who process them on our behalf is an interest in home grinding. Certainly you will get maximum dietary benefit from using freshly-milled flour. And you'll need it! For even the best of the small handmills requires exertion. You must take heed of the technique, instructions and set your mill to achieve a coarse grind first and then grind on with a finer setting. If you attempt to grind direct from grain to fine flour, you'll be too exhausted to cook with the result.

Food processors such as the Magimix/Cuisinart can't make flours or meals, but the big strong liquidizers such as that made by Braun are excellent. In the case of the harder wheat and rye grains, crush them lightly first in a mortar, which saves a great deal of time and ear-piercing racket.

Personally the effort of one method, and the noise of the other, makes me perfectly happy to belong to the 20th century, and to purchase my needs.

this is the great advantage of this system and of this flour.

To get white flour from a stone-ground wholemeal flour you must sift – or bolt – away the bran. It takes time and time has always cost money – thus the rarity and expense of white flour in the past, when only the rich and the clergy could afford it as a matter of course. It would not be considered as white by most people today, as there were always some tiny pieces of bran left. Even after being sifted of its bran to leave a high proportion of endosperm only, this stone-ground white flour would have been more nutritious than today's roller-milled version, for it was in full possession of its share of the vital wheatgerm and wheatgerm oil.

Roller-mills: roller-milling makes flour by gradually breaking down the grain in a series of processes, rather than the single operation of the stone method. First, fluted steel rollers gently crack open the grain. The endosperm is immediately separated and goes off to closer and closer set rollers which reduce it to flour; meanwhile, the bran and wheatgerm go their separate ways to similar processes. White flour made this way clearly cannot have an iota of the vitamin or mineral content of the germ or bran. In the United Kingdom legislation ensures that some of these are replaced; the replacement vitamins are usually synthetic, but not known to be less good for that.

In many countries, roller-milled flour has further indecencies perpetrated upon it in the interests of commerce and at the expense of nutrition; the worst of these is considered to be bleaching, which is specially common in the United Kingdom and United States. Freshly milled wheat flour is normally a lovely pale cream colour, but will gradually whiten if left for six to nine months during which other natural changes occur which improve its performance in baking. White, very white, flour is what the public has come to demand but having hundreds of thousands of tons of flour sitting about waiting to whiten is not the kind of idea that appeals to big business. In France, where food is second only to God in importance, they have managed to keep what might be called a healthy respect for the cream-coloured flour and no tampering is allowed.

But elsewhere flour is artificially bleached with a variety of highly technical, complex additives. There is no hard evidence to show there is any cumulative harm in these additives but the reverse has by no means been proven either. Increased consumer interest in commercial manufacturing processes has recently lead to the wider availability of both stone-ground wholemeal flour and of unbleached white flour.

BARLEY

Although it was among the earliest grains eaten and cultivated by man, barley is rarely eaten nowadays until, perhaps, the first, crisp, golden-leaved days of autumn put us in mind of the pleasures of steaming barley-thick meat soups and pottages. Yet it is much more important than this. Without barley we would not have our fine Scotch whiskies and there would be no Guinness. There would be no malted drinks, no malt flour and no malt extract, all of which are used to a greater extent than can be imagined. And half the world's barley crop feeds livestock, making us dependent on it second hand, at least.

Hardy and widely grown, barley has little changed over the centuries. It is really the same grain that was a staple in China over 4,000 years ago. It was popular with both the nobles and the workers of Pharaonic Egypt some 7,000 years ago, and was used in the training diets of the shapely Greek athletes. In Europe it was extremely important as a major bread grain right up to the end of the 18th century: it grew where the fickle wheat would not, and this was vital when most people were too poor to eat any food that had to be imported or transported.

Today, barley is a staple food in much of eastern Europe and in parts of Africa. Being almost gluten-free, it makes a heavy, moist bread, not at all to the modern palate. Its lumpiness dictated a round, flat form, perfect for use as the absorbent bread platters, or trenchers, that were so economical and filling in primitive and remote cottages where every drop of gravy counted.

Pearl barley: is the most common form, and is invaluable for thickening soups and stews as it has a natural affinity for fatty liquids, both in performance and flavour. It is the barley grain, husked, steamed and then polished to give the characteristic rounded shiny appearance. The dark line down one side is a remnant of the husk.

Pot barley: also called Scotch barley, has only the indigestible part of the husk removed, so it is extra nutty and nutritious. It is more commonly available in health or wholefood shops.

Flaked barley: is lightly rolled grains, usually of pot barley. This is my favourite for breakfast porridge, soothing, chewy and satisfying. Make it with milk rather than water and sweeten with a natural brown sugar.

Barley meal and barley flour: are difficult but not impossible to find. Terms are confused and transposed but generally the coarser meal is made from pot barley and finer flour from pearl barley. Country dwellers of determination could apply to their local animal foodstuffs dealer and sift the coarse ground barley meal they will find there. The best use for barley flour or meal in breadmaking is as the basis for a sourdough starter, otherwise simply substitute some for 15 per cent or so of your normal flour or flours, to add a sweet and wholesome flavour.

Barley sugar: twisted and golden, is increasingly hard to find and probably isn't the real thing anyway. It was so called because barley water was used in its manufacture and you would be hard-pressed to find companies prepared to go to such bother nowadays. Basically it was a superior boiled sweet, and saffron gave it its lovely golden colour, as well as a subtle extra flavour.

Barley water: to make this old fashioned treat, put 50g/2oz pearl barley into 600ml/1pt of cold water. Bring to the boil, simmer 15 minutes, drain, then replace drained liquid with 900ml/1½pts boiling water. Simmer until reduced by half. Strain. Sweeten or dilute according to taste, and add extra flavour with the traditional lemon, orange or lime juice.

Cooking: barley is always improved by being soaked overnight. And if you like a roasted flavour, first stir your barley in a hot pan with a little vegetable oil until it colours. Do this also to barley flakes. When cooking barley use three parts liquid to one of grain. I like to use good chicken stock or, failing that, try to put something fatty like a chunk of bacon into the saucepan. Pot barley will take about 45 minutes to cook, pearl barley considerably less.

The flakes can be added to muesli as well as being used to make porridge.

I think barley's most under-rated use is as a fascinating and unusual alternative to rice in pilaffs, something I first came across in Denver, Colorado. Made with either roasted or unroasted barley, such a pilaff is naturally wonderful with fat-rich lamb, mutton and chicken casseroles.

Barley excels with game birds. I like to pack cooked, roasted barley into individual moulds (ramekins will do) and turn them onto the plates just before serving. Then, dribble over all those mixed bird-and-bacon juices. Rich, I know, but I often think much of the best flavour is lost when you pour away the fat from a pan in which, say, a pheasant has been roasting.

Individual quails, pan-roasted with fresh tarragon sprigs and then flamed in brandy, should be perched in hollowed nests of barley pilaff, both for effect and for scrumptiousness. If you wished to add some fun, you might secrete a few peeled grapes at the bottom of each nest to imitate quails' eggs; but the inclusion of real ones, softly boiled then shelled, would be a *coup de table véritable*.

Storing: there are no problems in storing barley provided it is protected from heat, light and damp. Common sense, really.

BUCKWHEAT

Cooked and eaten as a cereal grain, buckwheat is actually the fruit of a herbaceous plant related to dock, sorrel and rhubarb. Its pretty pink flower is a great favourite with those devoted to the natural floral arrangement. Because buckwheat thrives in a harsh climate it has been a staple in northern Europe, Asia and Russia for untold centuries. Buckwheat and pre-roasted buckwheat are often called *kasha* but this is incorrect. Kasha is the collective name commonly used in eastern Europe and western Russia for almost any grain-based dish, whether porridge-like or dry and puffed up in the manner of a pilaff, it just happens that such kashas are usually made with buckwheat. Buckwheat has also been an important food in Japan for a very long time and the recent Western interest in the Zen-based macrobiotic diet has introduced some to its oriental usages; for instance, there is a Japanese buckwheat spaghetti called soba, which may be found in wholefood shops in the United Kingdom.

Buckwheat was also popular in western Europe right up until the end of the last century. Now we eat only ten per cent of what we did a century ago and it is really only popular in northern France and Belgium, where it is known as black wheat (*blé noir)* or saracen wheat (*sarrasin)* as it is thought to have been brought to this part of Europe by returning Crusaders.

It was the Dutch who introduced it to the American continent, when they founded Nieuw Amsterdam in the 17th century, and there it has remained very much in favour. The popular American habit of eating buckwheat cakes (pancakes) with syrup for breakfast is not one of their own ideas – this is exactly what you would have found in the breakfast rooms of the better-off gentlemen of the court of Elizabeth I.

Buckwheat cakes with hot maple syrup were, as a boy, as magical and romantic to me as Roy Rogers, Lois Lane and Lassie were to other kids. Somehow I just knew they would be terrific. I had to wait until I was 17 before I finally tasted the combination, on an American cruise ship, SS *Mariposa*, in Auckland harbour. Until that moment I had been the ship's agent's office boy. From then on I was their slave.

Although I've had many and varied American breakfasts since, and even enjoyed some of their more extraordinary combinations (would you believe blueberry muffins with ice cream and bacon) I always return to where I began. I like about five smallish buckwheat pancakes, preferably leavened with yeast, hot maple syrup and butter, two fried eggs with runny centres sunny-side up, and some strips of really crisp, hickory-smoked bacon. Once, in Washington DC, I ate this for breakfast, lunch and dinner – I could happily have gone to meet my Maker.

The small, whole grains are triangular-shaped and reminiscent of the beech nut: the Germans actually call buckwheat 'beech wheat'. The whole grain is mainly used in Russia and eastern Europe in as many guises and disguises as their politics. Buckwheat can also be bought coarsely-ground, when it is cooked in exactly the same way but with more speed. Both forms are available roasted or unroasted although the first is undoubtedly tastier; you can roast it yourself by stirring over heat in a pan with a little vegetable oil. Buckwheat is not usually soaked before using but there is no reason why it should not be.

The attractively speckled buckwheat flour gives a remarkable flavour to batters and bread doughs and complements such equally assertive flavours as game. In Brittany, buckwheat is the major ingredient of the famed *galette*, a huge, thin, savoury-filled pancake that is the staple of the peasants there – *and* of the cognoscenti of chic crêperies in Paris, London and... Brighton. The Russian *blini*, made to accompany caviare, is perhaps the noblest buckwheat pancake of all. But the English, with typical eccentricity, mainly give buckwheat to gamekeepers who feed it to pheasants, with excellent results.

Cooking: there is one basic way of cooking roasted or unroasted buckwheat. You seal the outside of whole or of coarsely ground buckwheat in a little hot oil, then cover it with water in the proportion of three-to-one. Replace the lid of the saucepan and cook gently until the liquid is absorbed. Made a little moister by the addition of milk or more water, it can be eaten with milk or cream and sugar. Or you can fry some sliced onions, garlic and bacon in the pan first and then use a wild mushroom or other flavoured stock to make a sort of pilaff. All these dishes can be called kasha.

Coarsely ground buckwheat (groats) roasted and then soaked, makes an interesting addition to crisp biscuits or cakes; the more finely ground version (not quite a flour) can be used similarly. You only need a few spoonfuls in a basic pancake or bread dough to enjoy its warm, haunting flavour. Buckwheat flour has no gluten content, so it must always be mixed with wheat flour in yeast-baking.

Storing: as with all grains, you should buy only in quantities that will last no more than a week or two, unless you have perfect cool and dry storage. Once you introduce warmth you induce the reproduction of creepy-crawlies, especially with organic produce which tends not to be treated with insecticides.

CORN

In modern English, corn means maize, but it was once used as a collective noun for all bread making grains, including wheat, and such usage may sometimes still be heard in unsophisticated areas. Corn is the only grain native to the Americas and was the basis of the extraordinary civilizations of the Mayas, Incas, Aztecs and other almost unknown peoples of Central and South America. The smaller tribal societies of North America also relied upon it and in all parts of the continent it was worshipped. Yet they all knew to grow and eat beans with the grain, to give full nutrition; when corn was taken to Africa in exchange for slaves the beans did not go too. Thus much of Africa's ills are actually exacerbated by the very food which is supposed to prevent them. Of all grains, corn is the least nutritious and most lacking in essential proteins.

Probably cultivated for over 7,000 years, it came to Europe only with the successors of Christopher Columbus, the Spanish conquistadors. It spread round the world like wildfire, and was known in China by as early as 1550.

Although we usually see only yellow corn, it can also be red, purple, orange, white or blue. Blue corn flour, muffins, chips, crisps and the like have recently enjoyed a spell of fashion, although it has always been the staple of many of the native American tribes of the south-west United States. If the fashion lasts you will doubtless enjoy the extra depth of slightly smoky flavour; but the inky-chalky colour is always a surprise.

There are essentially three types of corn – sweet corn, eaten as it is, maize grains used to make flours or as animal feed, and popcorn.

Sweet corn: known as corn on the cob in its natural state. Soft and succulent, it is eaten as a vegetable rather than as a grain. After picking, it degenerates in goodness and sweetness with breathtaking rapidity; native North Americans teach that you should walk to a cornfield and run back to the pot. Once you have eaten newly-plucked, freshly-cooked sweet corn, you may find difficulty in enjoying cobs you have bought frozen, or tinned, or shrink-wrapped in a supermarket.

Sweet corn, fresh and tinned, is very popular in Australia, New Zealand and America. The kernels stripped from the cob are often used in salads, especially when combined with green or red peppers or made into fritters, which are excellent with poultry and *de rigueur* with proper fried Chicken Maryland. Creamed sweet corn is also used in batters but more usually served as a hot vegetable, and is very good with pork. In Australasia you might be offered it on toast for breakfast; in Europe, though, sweet corn is largely unknown and confused with maize grain. When I, fresh from New Zealand, asked for some corn in a restaurant in Torremolinos, I was told with mixed horror and pity for my background that, in Spain, corn was for animals. Something similar happened to me at a high-class grocer in Hampton Court when I asked for pumpkin to roast with my Sunday beef. The reply was: 'In this country, sir, pumpkin goes *in* beef, not *with* it.'

Maize grain: which is gluten-free, has a tough fibrous outer layer, making it difficult to cook whole. It is better used in the traditional Indian ways, ground to a meal or flour. The coarsest meals are mainly used for fast, non-yeasted breads but also make a delicious addition to wheat bread. It is better to use them sparingly in yeasted breads as they tend to produce a crumbly, cake-like texture. This is why the American breads made only of cornmeal are usually eaten by the spoonful straight from the shallow pan in which they are baked, hence the name spoon bread.

Maize meal: is the basis of the Mexican staple bread, the tortilla. The maize is first treated with a solution of lime in water and the special meal obtained after grinding is called *masa harina*. It is now marketed by several of the giant United States food companies, mainly for American devotees of so-called Tex-Mex food, a mélange of Texan and Mexican cuisine.

Polenta: although the terms are interchangeable, polenta is not a type of corn meal, but a specific dish made from a bright yellow relative of sweet corn; it is so common in northern Italy that the chief ingredient has been given the name of the dish. Essentially it is a corn porridge, usually flavoured with Parmesan and butter or olive oil. It is very time consuming to make and splutters vengefully, landing the hottest and most blistering blobs all over your person – which is why it is traditionally stirred with a very long handled wooden paddle. But that effort is now behind us. Instant, which means pre-cooked, polenta is available, ready to eat in five minutes or so, but longer cooking does give a sleeker texture and is well worth doing.

Polenta is traditionally served three ways. It may be served as a thick mush, left to go cold and then sliced and fried or grilled, or baked with savoury ingredients which add flavour – small birds roasted in polenta is a great favourite of the Veneto. Polenta is also one of the trendiest of ingredients, a basic part of all-conquering northern Italian foods. Thus its possibilities are being explored. In New York I was served a very soft, almost silken, mush flavoured with Dolcelatte cheese with roast lamb. It is grilled as the base for everything from fish to roasted vegetables, and can be layered with many of the same good ingredients, covered with cheese sauce and baked again. Thin polenta mush is an excellent basis for cooking thinly sliced vegetables, finished with chunks of good Mozzarella or tiny chunks of Parmesan, and dribbled with a jolly good olive oil, one of those mushy, mucky one dish meals that can be so gratifying.

Yet most of those rely on lashings of fat or oil in one way or another and so are tremendously high in calories. I have found that a very light flavouring of rosemary in a warm polenta mush plus plenty of chopped black olives and only a touch of good olive oil when served is terrific: if allowed to cool and then baked brown under a grill the flavour intensifies. Sun-dried tomatoes, basil, pesto and almost everything else from the modern kitchen's lexicon of husky flavours can be served in, on or under polenta in some form or another. We have not heard the last of it...

Mealie-mealie: is finely-cut maize with most of the vital bran and germ removed and is an important staple food in Africa. It is cooked into a rather noisome porridge that has the advantage of being warming but there is little else to say for it, considering its importance.

Cornflour and cornmeal: are gluten-free, light and sweet and especially good for desserts like custards, blancmanges or baked puddings. Substituting cornflour for some of your soft white flour when baking cakes gives excellent results. Mix one part of cornflour to three of wheat flour and keep it aside as a special baking mix. The most important use of cornflour is in the lump-free thickening of sauces.

Although when first added it makes any liquid cloudy, cooking gives a nice clear sauce; thus it is much used in Chinese cooking. Instructions for use are always given on the packet. The white colour of cornflour is artificially induced. Its disadvantage is that cornflour sauces will eventually begin to thin again if cooked for too long.

Hominy: is whole dried maize without its yellow hull and was the chief food of the enslaved African-American. It was usually cooked in water until the white grains were very soft and swollen. Eaten with gravy and meat or with milk and sugar, or simply with salt and butter, it is still a great favourite throughout the southern United States. Cooked hominy can be incorporated into muffins and cakes or fried in lard.

Grits: is the name given to coarsely ground dried maize. Yellow grits are made from the whole grain, including the outer hull; white grits are most often served as a mush or porridge, boiled or baked in the oven and, like hominy, leftovers are often incorporated into the rest of the day's baking and cooking.

Popcorn: the kernels of this strain of corn have a skin that is under greater tension than the other varieties, hence its propensity to explode dramatically when heated.

Homemade popcorn can be cooked in hundreds of interesting ways, though this form of corn gives less nutrition than the others. Still, it's fun to run up a batch of garlic-and-herb-butter popcorn to serve with some roasted chicken and then watch

---

POPPING CORN

Just in case your popcorn doesn't have instructions for cooking, you cover the bottom of a saucepan with a thin layer of oil (butter burns too easily for this job) and a layer of popcorn. Cover and shake gently over a high flame until you hear one grain pop. Remove from the flame and continue shaking for another minute then put back onto the flame. Shake more vigorously until the popping stops then quickly turn the popcorn into a bowl and add the flavouring you've chosen, (for plain salted popcorn simply add butter and salt). Here are some other ideas:

■ Put 1 tbsp peanut butter (crunchy is best) in a pan with 2 tbsp butter. Melt together, add salt and mix with the popcorn.

■ Melt 3 heaped tbsp butter, then add 3 crushed

---

cloves of garlic, chopped parsley and salt.

■ Melt 2-3 tbsp butter and add several good squeezes of lemon juice and then a good pinch of dried parsley, sage, rosemary and thyme. You could call this Scarborough Fair popcorn and serve it to your folk-singing friends.

■ To 2 tbsp melted butter add 1 tsp coriander, 1 of cumin and 1 of turmeric. Toss together and add salt to taste. You could also add lemon juice and garlic to this – or you could cheat and simply reach for the tin of curry powder.

■ For dessert popcorn, melt 50g/2oz butter with 125g/4oz sugar and grate in the rind of 1 orange and half a lemon. Cook until it starts to caramelize. Add the juice of 2 oranges and a lemon. Stir to make a thick, smooth sauce. Add the popcorn and toss until covered. Serve with cream.

your guests' amazed faces. They usually can't decide if it is their first course or their pudding (and if it is either, what the hell is it doing on the plate now). Popcorn can appear during any part of the meal and between as well – not that you'd think so when confronted with the electric-blue stuff squirted at you in fairgrounds.

So-called Indian corn and Indian popping corn is close to being the original strain of corn grain and easily recognizable by its high proportion of bright red kernels. Although undoubtedly prettier, it is less good for popping than the newer, all-gold strains.

Storing: corn should, like any other grain, be treated with special care, for whole cornmeal still contains the fragile germ. In some cases you might be able to buy corn products which have been 'stabilized'. Achieved at the expense of a few of its nutrients, this stabilization prevents the germ oil going rancid and is higher in nutrition than products that have been de-germinated.

MILLET

To much of Europe, millet's *raison d'être* is to feed caged birds. But for almost a third of the world – from northern Manchuria to the Sahara and especially in north China, India, Pakistan and north Africa – it is their staple grain. It is the third most important grain in the world after rice and wheat and is actually a generic term for a variety of small-seeded grains. Sorghum wheat and Kaffir corn are other generic names, the first being used a lot in America, where sorghum syrup is sold as a substitute for cane sugar syrup. The millet we best know in Europe is yellow millet, which has many tiny, spherical kernels on each head.

African millet is usually Kaffir corn and is ground to a meal and cooked into a sort of porridge. It must always be very freshly ground because it goes rancid very quickly indeed. Japan and China use the grain like rice.

All millet has the unique property amongst grains of being alkaline rather than acid, and its blandness makes it an excellent foil for strong flavours and spices. It is blessed with another distinct advantage to the poorer nations – it hydrates astonishingly, so that ½kg/1lb of kernels will easily feed eight people when cooked.

Millet is nearly always eaten whole as the pilaff base for stews, curries and so on. It mixes well with oats for an interesting porridge and in English cooking you are most likely to find it used for a baked pudding like semolina. References to it can be found in the oldest cook books; I found one in a manuscript recipe book owned by my great-great-great-great-great-great-grandmother, a Senhouse of Netherhall in Cumberland and grandmother of Fletcher Christian, leader of the *Bounty* mutiny.

Millet flakes: are quite common and make simple additions either to porridges or to muesli where their alkalinity is an advantage.

Millet flour: is fairly rare but is gluten-free. It is easily made at home if you have a strong liquidizer. The flour itself makes a flat bread and one such product is the national loaf in Ethiopia.

Cooking: millet should first be browned slightly in a very little vegetable oil in a saucepan. In the meantime, put the kettle on and then pour the boiling water onto the pan-roasted millet in the proportion of four to one. If you have it, a stock or vegetable water would be even better if you are making a savoury dish. For a wetter, softer result you can add a higher proportion of liquid, but this is entirely a matter of personal taste. It will take about 20 minutes over a medium heat for the grains to absorb the water. Toss lightly with a fork then season with salt and a few herbs – even something as simple as fresh parsley, mint and garlic chopped together.

Perhaps, the best way of enjoying millet is to cook it in the same liquid as your vegetables or meat to create a main dish or substantial pilaff. This way you keep all the goodness of all the ingredients. And nothing could be simpler, cheaper or better for you. It's no surprise that most such recipes come from Russian peasant cooking. If you really must have meat with a meal, accompany a millet pilaff with a few slices of bacon, or some garlic-laden boiled Polish sausage – perhaps a couple of mazurska or some thick slices of zywieska. Plain cooked millet can also be sweetened with sugar or honey and mixed with fresh fruit and chopped nuts for a light delicious pudding. Yoghurt is a good foil for this, but if you are using sharp-tasting fruit then pile on the cream instead.

You can use millet flour as a thickening agent in soups and stews, but I prefer the whole grains to do this for less trouble and more interest.

Storing: treat millet of any type like other grains: keep it cool, dry and dark and buy in small amounts.

MUESLI

Where would the wholefood and healthfood trade be without muesli – even though such shops dislike being mentioned in the same sentence? It is muesli that has encouraged most people into their first faltering steps towards better, healthier eating; indeed, for some it is their only step. Invented about the turn of the century by the visionary Swiss Dr Bircher-Benner, it has become enormously popular in the past twenty years.

Like so many things that are good for you, muesli can be a bit of an effort to make, but make it you should for most manufactured mixes are far too expensive. The ideal balance is:

30ml/2 tbsp oats (or oats plus some other grain)
1 chopped hazelnut   1 small apple
honey or unrefined sugar   lemon juice
30ml/2 tbsp yoghurt   milk to taste.
Some people prefer to soak their oats overnight

in some of the milk or yoghurt, which makes them less chewy. You can experiment endlessly with combinations, so I recommend buying a few of the more serious (and less advertised) varieties for a start and then copying the one whose flavour you like best.

Whatever fresh fruit there is gets added, even the exotic peach and melon. If I had to give up every muesli ingredient but grains and one other, I would keep chopped dried apricots. Their acidity and colour work beautifully with the contrasted flavours and textures of the grain flakes.

But above all the key with muesli is to be bold. Start with flakes of oat, wheat, millet. Then add or substitute rye, rice and barley. Now all manner of seeds – pumpkin, sesame, sunflower and roasted poppyseed. Plus hazelnuts and almonds, peanuts, walnuts, fresh and dried fruits and even coconut.

OATS

Oats probably originated somewhere in the east and slowly worked their way westwards as a weed. Their hardiness and very high, sustaining fat content appealed to the hardworking and cold inhabitants of the northern regions, and thus it is to the Scots we must give thanks for nurturing them in this country.

Like rye or barley bread, oat bread was made where wheat would not grow; but even when bigger crops and better transport made wheat flour more widely available there were many who preferred the way the heavy oat breads lay longer in your stomach, warming and strengthening you as you toiled in mines, fields and highlands, certainly an advantage in colder climates.

Oats are bought as whole grains, rough cut (sometimes called groats), medium or fine meal, or as flakes. Grains are best for porridges, groats are best for thickening stews or broths and for oatcakes. Medium oatmeal is the one for mixing with other flours to make scones, bannocks and such; fine oatmeal is best for pancakes, for flouring grilled herrings or making a thin, gruel-type porridge.

Quick cook grains and flakes have been partly pre-cooked; in the process of husking, oats are steamed, and an extension of this process followed by kiln-drying gives you this time-saving version with only little loss of dietary value. Jumbo oatflakes are rolled whole flakes; all others have been cut into smaller pieces. Oatmeals which are 'steelcut' are considered superior nutritionally as they have not been subjected to any heat during processing.

Oat bran: while a fibre-rich diet is good for you, not all fibre is the same and so a little discernment is required when choosing bran as a 'cure' for your health problems. Wheat bran speeds up the passage of food through the digestive tract and primarily consists of insoluble fibre. Oat bran however contains a large portion of soluble fibre and therefore is capable of lowering cholesterol levels. Additionally it provides protein, energy-giving carbohydrate, and the B vitamin thiamin as well as maintaining normal glucose levels in the blood of diabetics. Making oat bran part of your daily diet can help lower both total cholesterol and the harmful LDL cholesterol while not depleting your stores of the protective HDL cholesterol. The easiest way to consume it is as part of your breakfast cereal (several commercially manufactured oat bran cereals are now available in supermarkets) but you can also incorporate it in muffins, breads, cakes, biscuits etc.

Cooking: when cooking whole or flaked oats for breakfast there is no doubt they are better if allowed to simmer gently overnight. But with the cost of today's fuel this is sadly impractical other than for very special occasions, or unless you have an economical Aga or similar stove of that nature. Best alternative is to soak your oats overnight and then cook as long as is practical in the morning. For a change, roast your oat grains or flakes first. This can be done over low heat in a pan with some oil or in a tray in the oven. They should only just turn colour.

Another way to make porridge overnight is to bring it to the boil with five times its volume of water and then leave it overnight before cooking again, for twenty minutes in the morning. Scots may well blanch at the thought but the inclusion of dried fruits such as apricots or peaches adds a great deal of interest and further nutrition. Some say that sliced fresh bananas are good, too – yes, with *hot* porridge!

Be bold with your porridge and mix the same ingredients as go into your muesli – all sorts of other grain flakes, sunflower seeds, dried apple, coconut, chopped nuts, soaked whole grains. Then top it with molasses or treacle, with a choice of unrefined sugars and, of course, plenty of salt. The only food that goes with muesli that I don't like with porridge is yoghurt. You may think otherwise.

In fancy baking for high teas and special occasions, oat flakes have long been used as a sweet addition to scone and cake doughs. To take regular advantage of the rich food value, you can sprinkle flakes over bread dough before baking, sprinkle meal into the greased baking tins or knead some soaked oats into the dough. Other traditional uses include stuffings and sausages. White pudding should include a measure of oatmeal and Cumbrian oyster sausages rely upon it; indeed, where the Manx and Scandinavians would use oatmeal to flour the humble herring, the English feed it to the aristocratic oyster.

Incidentally, if you always include citrus juice or vitamin C in any meal in which you eat oats, you will get far more of that important iron content into your blood.

Storing: keep your oats calm by keeping them cool, dark and dry and don't go wild and buy in large quantities.

RICE

As well as being the most important grain, rice has the distinction of being probably the single most important food source in the world. It supports the cultures of China, Japan, India, south west Asia and much of the Middle East. Its origins are in the Far East, and one ancient Sanskrit word for it means 'sustainer of the human race'.

The beauty of whole grain (or brown) rice is its ideal balance of essential nutrients – carbohydrate, protein, oil, vitamins and minerals – in a soft, digestible bran which allows it to be cooked and eaten as whole kernels, with only the husk removed.

Mainly grown on submerged land, the romantic paddy field, there are as many varieties of rice as there are climates to which it is adapted. Although expected by travellers in Asia, the shocking, violent green of young rice shoots is a surprise when encountered outside Valencia in Spain, in northern Italy or southern France. Louisiana, the Carolinas, Arkansas and California grow great quantities of rice of extremely high quality, and so does Australia. Once it was grown in England, but as an increasing population caused the draining of marshy areas, the rice-fields became more suited to pasture or other grain crops.

Rice is the one grain where the layman can easily identify and enjoy a variety of whole grains, thereby ringing dietary changes with ease. The basic choice is between brown and white, short or long grain.

Brown rice is whole rice, with only the outer husk removed. Once the bran has also been removed by milling, you have **white rice**, which is usually polished with a mixture of glucose and talcum. When such naked rice became fashionable amongst the Eastern rich, as white bread did in the West, the masses clamoured for it. Eventually they got it. And ghastly endemic diseases followed, including beri beri and pellagra, caused by deficiencies of thiamin (vitamin B1) and nicotinic acid respectively. Even in brown rice thiamin is fugitive, being quickly leached out into cooking water; up to 30 per cent can be lost even when using the technique which absorbs all the cooking liquid (see page 207).

Slowly the lesson is being learned and whole rice is replacing white rice as a staple food in those countries where rice is often the only food available.

Today, in the West, brown and white rices are available in a wide variety, each with flavour and cooking performances peculiar to themselves. The new interest in brown rice has stimulated a remarkable range of imports, from the elegant, pale, true long grain of Surinam to a variety of shapes and flavours from California.

The size and shape of rice grains usually tells you how it will cook and how best to use it. Long grains give the separate, fluffy grains enjoyed as an accompaniment, in stuffings and in pilaffs and birianis, where the rice is cooked with other ingredients. Medium grains are nearly always used for dishes where the starch in the grains is expected to lend a creamy richness to a sauce made from its own cooking liquids, as in the true risotto. Short grain rices are particularly suited to the long slow cooking of milk puddings.

Arborio: the proper rice for a risotto, something too often confused with pilaffs. The risotto of northern Italy has its roots in the addition of rice to soups; the balance is now reversed and a risotto is rice cooked in stock. To be absolutely correct, the rice must first be turned in rather a lot of butter (but no onion, as that should be in the stock, at least that was my instruction from the Venetian chef of The Cipriani, who should know). To that is gradually added boiling stock or broth and the mixture should be whisked *all* the time it is cooking, so the liquid, the butter and the starch of the rice form a voluptuous emulsified sauce. Vegetables and other ingredients, notably seafood, may be added towards the end so they do not break up and a true risotto is always finished by having a mixture of butter and Parmesan cheese whisked in finally to polish and thicken the sauce. The rice should retain a bite in the middle and the dish should be almost too wet to eat with a fork: the Italians call this *all'onda* or wavelike. Because risotto must be eaten the moment it reaches perfection it is properly a first course, or a main course with nothing to precede it.

The alternate and easier method of allowing a series of additions of liquid to be absorbed can make a sort of risotto, but this dangerously runs the risk of becoming a dry-grain pilaff and the sauce will never have the velvety texture which comes from constant whisking. But this and the microwave method can be helped by a last-minute whisk, perhaps with extra liquid, and certainly with butter and Parmesan cheese.

In general, the simpler the better: a wild mushroom risotto using the soaking liquid from dried porcini, fresh sweet peas to make *risi e bisi,* squid ink to make a black risotto scattered with other seafood, finely chopped fresh vegetables and herbs to make a *primavera.* There is a slow move to sweet risotto too, cooked in sweetened and flavoured milk, or vanilla and spice flavoured sugar syrups; some have fruit beaten in and then more stirred in to serve, others are served cold as a variation on rice pudding, or layered with fresh fruit and whipped cream as parfaits or pies.

Basmati: one of the world's great rices, from the Himalayan foothills. It has an elegant, some would say dainty, long grain and an unmistakably appealing fragrance. Its inherent sweetness is the perfect foil and balance to spiced foods and also makes it an excellent choice for stuffings and rice salads. All kinds of Indian dishes seem better with basmati, even those which include rice, like birianis. Brown basmati is commonly available, but the husk somehow seems to mask the very flavour one has chosen this rice to appreciate. The addition of bay leaf to the cooking water, especially for rice salads, underpins the flavour of the basmati beautifully. If you cook by the absorption method, basmati rice needs only 1½ times its volume of liquid; the brown version needs two times.

Brown: all rices could be brown, for it is merely rice which has been dehusked, leaving behind the layers of nutritious, fibrous bran. It is altogether a healthier food, with more protein and vital ingredients than white rice, as you would expect, but in spite of its nutty, sweeter flavour it is bland to many and also requires both longer cooking and more chewing. If you always cook it in stock, or add soy sauce to the cooking liquid, you'll will find it more readily accepted.

Brown rices should always be cooked by the absorption method so you lose none of the vitamins and minerals and generally need 2½ times their volume of liquid, to allow for the inevitable evaporation.

Although the basis of macrobiotic and vegetarian diets, any belief in brown rice as a complete food is seriously misguided: to be so it must be eaten in balance with pulses and legumes or as an accompaniment to vegetarian full-protein sources such as eggs, milk, cheese and soy-based produce.

Carolina: once a specific but now rather a generic for American long grain rice, very much a New World version of the Patna rice. Can be used for sweet as well as savoury dishes.

Converted/par-boiled: it sounds a lesser rice but is quite the reverse. It has been part-cooked before being husked and milled. This forces thiamin and nicotinic acid into the grain so that even though it looks white it is closer nutritionally to brown rice, at least where it matters so vitally, satisfying both society and sense.

Cristallo: is par-boiled arborio rice.

Fragrant: a variety of rice with a truly wonderful fragrance, and often also called jasmine rice. It is thought of as a special occasion rice, and unless you eat rice every day there is no reason to be stingy. Once quite difficult to buy, but now marketed widely, for which we should be very grateful. The best flavour comes from cooking it by the absorption method, but note the proportion of liquid to rice should either be equal or 1¼ times at the most and that this rice cooks up to one third faster than other types.

Glutinous/sticky: these are types of rice which go slightly jelly-like when cooked and thus stick together. They contain no gluten, so glutinous is rather a misnomer, but merely have a very high starch content. The savoury ones are specially liked in Asian countries because the stickiness means they are easier to eat with chopsticks. Sweeter ones are much used in puddings and cakes of great variety, often fluorescently coloured and flavoured with coconut or jasmine and wrapped in banana leaves. One of the highlights of the Thai year is eating sharp and nutty slices of green mangoes with cold mounds of sticky rice.

Sticky rices are sometimes called sweet rices and they are a little sweeter. The unpolished or brown version is very dark, almost black, rather like wild rice. The most usual preparation method is to part cook them in boiling water and to complete the process over steam.

Louisiana: an undistinguished long grain rice grown in the State and essential to the gumbo, a local style of soup served over a tightly packed mound of rice. It is also cooked in rich brown stock to make Dirty Rice and with mixed meats and vegetables in the one-pot jambalaya. Cooked Louisiana rice is mixed with peppers, onions and celery and the flesh of the famed local crustacea to make crawfish pies.

Patna: a generic term for basic long grain Asian white rice. It is pretty much all-purpose and well behaved, except it will not make wet risottos. Increasingly less used as a phrase in favour of the all-encompassing 'long grain'.

Pecan rice: a variety of rice from the United States which claims to taste of pecans. It is certainly a little different, and delicious, but I have yet to be reminded of pecans.

Pilaff: often confused with risottos, but they should not be. A pilaff is a pulao, pilau and a plov. All are what you might call dry rice dishes in which the rice is separate even if cooked in a stock. It might be flavoured with spices, and will contain other ingredients. The rice is always a long-grained variety. India's birianis, in which rice is cooked in the liquid of stews to make a one pot dish, are in the same general culinary vein, and so are Spanish *pollo con arroz* and *paella*. Fried rice with leftovers might conceivably be called a pilaff, but must never be thought a risotto.

Popcorn: a local name for the sweet and appealing new flavoured varieties of rice being developed in the southern states of the United States, especially in Louisiana.

Pudding: a nice comfy term for white short grain rice used for slowly cooked rice puddings. It swells and joins up and feels wonderful to eat but never goes sticky if cooked slowly enough. Although traditionally done in the oven, the same result can be achieved slightly faster on the hob. If you take your time, pudding rice cooked in skimmed milk and sweetened with a sugar substitute tastes just like the real thing but has almost none of the calories. Such famous culinary rice dishes as Rice a l'Imperatice are usually made with long grain rice, first blanched in water then cooked in milk.

Risotto: a medium to short grain rice known generically in Italy as superfino. They are all rather fat and chunky with a hard white core you can see: this stays firm when cooked properly, whilst the rest of the grain leaks starch into the liquid to make a velvety sauce which is the sign of a proper risotto. Arborio *qv* is the best known risotto *superfino* but *carnaroli* and others are also found in Britain as risotto becomes more and more popular... *semifino* rices look the same but do not perform quite as well and are best for drier dishes or as an accompaniment – *vialone* and *nano* are the ones most often encountered in Britain

Valencia: another generic for a number of varieties of medium grain rice grown on Spain's east coast and which are particularly absorbent. The one to buy when you are on holiday in Benidorm, where you will find some of the best supermarkets in Europe, is rice from Calasparra with a DO stamp on the pack. Because it will absorb three or four times its volume of liquid it yields far more food for your money; when it is cooked in the highly flavoured liquids of a paella the concentrated savour of the result is unbelievably delicious.

I wonder which came first to this area, the paella or this kind of rice? A paella is actually the name of the flat round metal cooking pan in which dishes of rice, stock and other ingredients are made and thus arguments about what should or should not be in a paella are fatuous. The best paella, like bouillabaisse, will be cooked over a wood fire, so some smoke is absorbed by the rice.

Wild rice: the immensely beautiful, deep mahogany to black seeds of an aquatic grass and not related to rice at all. But who cares?

Wild rice is less romantic and much more common than it used to be, for it is no longer truly wild, only collected by hand from wee canoes in a few northern US states by native Americans. Wild rice has been tamed. It is farmed in northern California, amongst other states. Just recently Poland harvested its first crop – they will sell it as Indian rice and it should, or better, be relatively cheaper.

Wild rice has a deep nutty flavour and can take about the same time to cook as brown rice, depending on size and quality; the finest quality will be the darkest, longest, most lustrous and evenly graded grains. The grains are cooked when butterflied, the skin has split, the grain has slightly burst and opened out from its central seam. Native Americans used to do this by adding hot stones to rice and water, and modern Americans often cook it by bringing it to the boil and letting it cool several times, which does give wonderful flavour and results if you have the time – several hours. Otherwise the absorption method will do and you can expect it to take 30 to 40 minutes. Unfortunately, chefs who cook with their eyes rather than their palate often serve wild rice undercooked, because you see more of the attractive brown skin I suppose. It is then starchy and chewy and if really raw will be sharp enough to puncture tongues, gums and throat: I saw this happen to two people at my table at a supposedly smart restaurant in Kensington. But as the hostess was intent on retrieving a cork from an expensive Burgundy with a pencil at the time, she failed to notice and subsequently refused to believe.

Wild rice is frequently extended by being mixed with white rice which is always cooked separately. It can be cooked with brown rice in the same water, but that should be added ten minutes after the wild rice has come to a simmer. Wild rice in commercial mixtures of rice will have been scarified, scratched so the water can more easily penetrate and cook the grains, shortening the time considerably.

Nutritionally, wild rice has a much higher protein content than true rices and an excellent range of vitamins. But it does not have the equivalent of the complete protein spectrum of meat or soybeans.

Rice flakes: like other grain flakes, are the result of a steaming and rolling process; they can be made either from whole or white rice and used for a faster cooking porridge, for baking and for muesli.

Rice flour: may be used in bread and cake making but gives a dry, rather flat product. It is better combined with wheat and cornflour mixtures in this context. Otherwise it can be used to set interesting milk and fruit puddings and delicacies, the like of which fragile Victorian women could just manage to absorb at tea time.

Cooking: personally, I *refuse* to listen to one more person telling me how they cook rice. Everyone thinks they know best. In case you don't, read on – otherwise, skip the next few paragraphs.

Here's how I cook rice of all kinds. First I gently sauté the rice in butter or oil until it is opaque but not browned. My experience is that this is the best way to neutralize any stray starch, talcum, glucose or whatever else might cause stickiness; I *never* wash rice. Then I add some sort of liquid in the correct proportion according to the type of rice, using the same cup or plastic bag or measuring jug, plus salt and a bay leaf or two. This is brought to the boil and simmered at a steady pace with no lid on the pan until the water is level with the rice and a few bubbling holes can be seen. A folded tea towel, clean and dry, is put over the pan and the lid clamped very firmly on. If cooking with electricity I then turn the heat off and put the pan on the edge of the element; if gas, I put it on an asbestos mat over the lowest possible heat. Either way, the rice is left for seven minutes exactly and is then ready. That's it. You may find your saucepan is thicker or your burners are hotter and have to adjust the final timing. Otherwise it is simple, unfussy and easy to do at the last moment, avoiding the horror of soaking, washing, rinsing and reheating, all of which reduces or loses altogether what vitamin content there might be. My way conserves the maximum possible.

If you can be bothered to go to a little trouble, the Iranian method is fun too. Use about one-quarter less water than normal then, when the rice has absorbed all the water and is still a little hard, transfer it to another saucepan in which there are a few spoonfuls of water plus 25-50g/1-2oz of butter. Put more butter over the top, cover with a cloth and lid as above and let steam over low heat for 15-20 minutes. The rice will then be cooked and separate but have a crisp golden coating on the bottom. They call this *dig* and it is a great honour to be served it.

To cook brown rice I use exactly the same method as above. But I cook it uncovered, and it can take up to 45 minutes. But, white or brown, *you must never, ever, stir rice when it is cooking* for this more than anything else will make the grains sticky. The sole exception to this rule is risotto; this must be whisked all the time. And remember when making rice for sushi, the stirring is done when cooking is completed.

Rice is easy to keep hot if covered with foil and kept in an oven with a few dabs of butter. But it's better to do it over steam, which is the way to get those really light and fluffy grains that are so maddeningly delicious in good eastern restaurants, especially if they have used basmati rice. If in spite of all precautions you end up with sticky rice unintentionally, a 15-minute steam should save the day if you have the time. Simply put the rice in a strainer or colander over a saucepan of boiling water, cover with a cloth and a lid and keep over gentle heat. Once you see the grains start to separate – after, say, ten minutes – you can fork it over gently.

Leftover rice, brown or white, makes an excellent addition to yeast-leavened baking. If it has also been allowed to sour slightly, by being kept at room temperature, it is remarkably good in the heavier 'health' breads favoured by followers of grain and vegetable-based diets. *The Tassajara Bread Book* is good on this type of recipe.

Even in the United States it can be prohibitively expensive to serve a pilaff or stuffing exclusively of wild rice. But used to flavour a rice-based stuffing it is a memorable experience, especially with poultry or game. As the flavour is so strong and pervasive you can mix it with up to two or three times the amount of white or brown rice and it will still be fully appreciated. A sprinkling in a salad of cold chicken mixed with a flavoured mayonnaise is terrific and I once incorporated some into cream with which I decorated a cucumber mould to be served with poached salmon. Another time I topped wild rice with some quickly-cooked chanterelles and morilles and arranged this salad in a scooped-out pumpkin. This rich, earthy-tasting mixture was dressed with olive oil and lime juice and the glistening browns against the bright orange receptacle were a wonderful sight, made even better by a ring of poached cucumber crescents, almost transparent and fluorescent. I really think it is better to serve wild rice in such combinations than on its own, whatever your finances; besides it's tiresome to eat solo as it requires major mastication.

Coconut rice: the cooking of Indonesia, Thailand and all south-east Asia is full of fascinating ideas for using rice. One of the simplest you'll come across is coconut rice, made simply by cooking long grain rice in coconut milk. Fabulous. It can also be flavoured with the addition of a curry leaf and some lemon grass, both of which are available at Oriental food shops. But a good squeeze of lemon or lime juice is equally rewarding. It may also be coloured and further flavoured with some yellow turmeric powder. Either way it is very good with curries and other spiced dishes, or simply with cooked chicken.

Pudding rice cooked in coconut milk and sugar is an idea I found on Pitcairn Island. It became a firm (but sticky) favourite of my expedition, especially when served with a little hot orange, lime or lemon juice. A sprinkle of black rum is wonderful too.

Fried rice: the left-over standby of many provincial Chinese takeaways but which rises to greater heights in Indonesia: there it's called Nasi Goreng and should be accompanied by or include strips of beef, chillies, prawns and soy sauce, topped with soft-fried eggs, or sliced omelette. They also do it very well in the Indonesian restaurants of Amsterdam. In Thailand fried rice would include pork and the inevitable chopped green coriander leaf.

But there's no great secret to making fried rice. You simply fry cooked rice in hot oil until nice and brown, then stir in all manner of bits and pieces, especially crunchy and colourful goodies like shrimps, bits of bacon, cubes of ham or flakes of fish, sliced up omelette, green or red pepper, herbs, garlic, green ginger, chillies, apple, pineapple, leftover vegetables etc. When well heated through, dish onto a platter and serve accompanied by soy sauce, and an Asian hot sauce or Worcestershire sauce.

All fried rices are strangely improved by the inclusion of cucumber cubes, sticks or slices. But don't ask me why.

Savoury rice: this is what supermarkets and small-town restaurants would call a *pilaff, pilau* or *plov*. There are so many recipes in so many books I won't bore you with any more. For hot or cold buffets I always colour rice with saffron or turmeric and mix it at the last moment with chopped pistachios and some pine kernels that have been gently turned brown in a little oil. Both these nuts are expensive but a little goes a long way and make a considerable and luxurious difference. You could serve rice the Middle Eastern way simply by preparing your favourite stew of meat or poultry and then adding rice for the last half hour of cooking, which will then absorb the liquid. That's all there is to it really. And this is also the basis for the famous Creole jambalayas.

RYE

A very important bread making grain in Scandinavia and the former USSR, rye can be cultivated in conditions where other grains fail. Once it used to be sown with wheat as a matter of course, so that if the wheat failed there would still be something to harvest. The mixture of wheat and rye which was thus the usual crop was known as maslin and used as it came with little regard to the proportions of each grain; but as this added interest to an otherwise repetitive diet, the inconsistency was probably welcomed. For some genetic reason, wheat and rye never crossed with one another; this has now been achieved by science and the new grain is called triticale.

Bread making is by far the most important use of rye but a loaf made with 100 per cent rye flour is dense, dark, nutty and dry, for there is not enough gluten in rye to allow a high absorption of moisture or a good rise. This dark, so-called black bread is often further coloured and flavoured, especially if made with a mixture of rye and wheat flour. Caraway seeds are the most common additives but others are molasses and caramel. One American recipe I saw advocated the use of instant coffee powder.

In many rural areas a dry loaf is actually preferred for its long keeping qualities and ability to sop up gravies, and far more of Europe makes such loaves than I first thought. I best remember sawing chunks off a huge, low, round rye loaf of this type at Hautfort, near Perigord, though it had been bought at a village some distance away. The sur-

prise of finding such a loaf there was somewhat diminished, overwhelmed perhaps, by eating it in the huge kitchen of a magnificently-restored château, accompanied by homemade foie gras, local truffles, omelettes of scorzonera flowers and a wine called 'charming fart'. Not, I imagine, such a bread's usual milieu.

It's commonly accepted in eastern Europe and Russia that dark or light rye bread is better if made by the sourdough technique. Pumpernickel breads are usually based on rye and other whole grains but the name is loosely applied to a range of breads.

In the past, rye straw was invaluable for thatching, packing and brickmaking. But for all its positive uses, rye was also a potential killer as it is subject to attack by a fungus called ergot. This extraordinary mould is responsible for a disease of the nervous system called Saint Anthony's Fire, which was specially prevalent during the Middle Ages in northern Europe, but huge epidemics caused by infected rye bread were common before and after this. The last small epidemic in England was in Manchester in 1927, but in France it was seen as late as 1951 in the aptly-named village, Pont-Saint-Esprit. The medieval epidemics must truly have been frighten-

peas, mung beans, whole lentils, peas, soybeans, beans, whole rices, wheat, fenugreek, barley and sesame seeds. But chick peas and fenugreek usually give the fastest results.

This is what you do:

■ Put 50g/2oz of seeds or grains into a jam jar.

■ Cover the seeds with luke-warm water.

■ Tie a piece of muslin or very coarse cotton over the mouth of the jar.

■ Let the seeds absorb the water overnight, adding more water if required as some seeds will more than double their size. Chick peas swell so fast they get jammed, so free them gently.

■ After 8 hours, drain off the excess water and leave the jar to stand.

■ Twice a day rinse the seeds with cold water. Then invert the jar and gently shake it to prevent sprouting roots tangling. Leave for a few minutes to allow water to drain thoroughly, then invert again.

■ When the shoots are three times the length of the seeds but before tiny leaves appear, the sprouts are at their peak. If you don't want to eat them immediately, put them in the refrigerator to inhibit (but not stop) further growth.

ing, as the uncontrolled dancing, trances and hallucinations could only have been explained as witchcraft. Ergot-infected rye was actually used as a human abortive, its effect presented and disguised with the mumbo-jumbo of black or white magic. Interestingly, in learning how to control ergot-infestation, we have learned how to turn it to advantage as well. It helps induce labour in difficult or late child-birth and, not surprisingly, is a source of lysergic acid, LSD.

It was ergot problems that lead to rye bread being dropped like hot cakes whenever wheat became a viable alternative. For some, though, old habits die hard and in most towns with a Jewish or eastern European community you will easily buy rye bread. In the United Kingdom, London, Manchester, Leeds and Edinburgh are good bets. In the United States rye breads of all kinds are a staple of the delicatessens – well, who hasn't heard of salt beef on rye?

Rye flakes: good in mixed grain porridges or in muesli. For general use I think they are best when used in or on bread doughs, after soaking and cooking.

Rye flour: quite easy to obtain and only useful for breadmaking. Most countries like a mixture of rye and wheat (say 15 per cent rye to 85 per cent wheat for a light-coloured and tasty loaf) and other than making such a flour mixture you might use rye flour for your sourdough starter and then use wheat flour for the rest of the dough. I don't know of any other major use of rye flour, other than for the unleavened Scandinavian crispbreads.

Cooking: it is unrewarding to serve cooked whole rye by itself but it makes a worthwhile contribution when added to other grains or as a bulker in casseroles. Treat it like wheat berries, by soaking overnight and then cooking for about 12 hours. Even so you might have to cook the grains on in a soup or casserole to get them really tender.

Storing: keep all rye products cool, dry and dark and they will store well. Ideally, buy only as much as you can use in a relatively short time. Buying in bulk has distinct disadvantages, especially in summer when the hotter weather encourages the reproduction of all manner of grain pests.

TRITICALE

Until quite recently, although wheat and rye almost always grew together, they never crossbred. This was finally achieved scientifically in Sweden in the 1930s, when the resultant cross was called triticale, a combination of the Latin names of both grains. Work on further development continues in Mexico City and Manitoba.

The main advantages of this artificially inseminated grain are nutritional, for it seems that triticale can always be relied upon to give a higher yield of protein, amino acid balance and general food value than any wheat strain under the same conditions. Triticale has a gluten content higher than rye but lower than wheat. It is also somewhat fragile, so treat triticale lightly and never knead its bread dough other than with feather-light fingers. Otherwise you can use triticale like other whole grains to add interest and nutrition to pilaffs, porridges, mueslis, breads and biscuits.

WHEAT

Over 90 per cent of the flour consumed in western Europe, the United States and the countries of the old Commonwealth is made from wheat. It is without doubt the western world's most important grain, and always has been.

Archeological evidence shows that wheat has been cultivated since about 7,000 BC, which suggests its use for a much longer period. It is a grass of the Triticum family, the true origins of which have never been determined. Recent research has come closer to breeding it back to its very early forms, which will be used to strengthen or create new strains. For nearly 9,000 years man cultivated wheat in exactly the same way, introducing new varieties rarely, and usually by chance. But it was never cheap or plentiful enough to be a universal food; neither would it grow in northerly climates. Until the 19th century wheat products and wheat bread were a status symbol in Europe and America. Then the strain known as Turkey Red was introduced into North America. It began to produce such mammoth crops, so easily, that the wheat farmers of the world all wanted part of this bounty. So did the public, keen to establish their improved social position by eating only wheat bread and forgetting the barley, oat and rye breads of their forefathers. Soon Russia and Australia, too, had developed heavy-cropping wheat strains that were specially suited to bread making (the so called strong wheats). In just a few years the world's wheat growers had to change every agricultural, cropping and manufacturing technique so they could cope with the size of the crop and the demand.

Burgul or bulghur: is known commonly and incorrectly as cracked wheat but is quite different from that above. It's actually a processed food, probably the world's oldest. Berries of the local wheat in Middle Eastern countries are cooked to a mush which is spread out to dry, sometimes having first been strained. When crisp and dry it is broken down into varied textures. To use it you simply pour twice the quantity of boiling water over it and eat it plain or flavoured when the liquid has been absorbed. It is a delicious alternative to rice, especially wonderful in stuffings, and used throughout the Middle East in highly individual and often exciting ways. Simplest is the salad made with cracked wheat and masses of very finely chopped parsley and onion, known as tabbouleh; the most esoteric use to our taste is probably kibbeh, which is a wheat and raw lamb concoction of great popularity. I thoroughly recommend *A Book of Middle Eastern Food* by Claudia Roden (Penguin) which is packed with ravishing tastes and ideas of all kinds.

GLUTEN

This Chinese standby of vegetarian cooking is the extracted protein of wheat. The process is simple. You make a dough of strong (bread making) flour with water, salt and baking soda and after kneading well leave it to stand until the gluten has swollen and the dough is light and pliable – just as you would for pasta or bread dough. The lump is then washed in water to dissolve away the starch, leaving you with the protein. This is shaped in many ways and offered for sale fried at the same shops and stalls which sell bean curd. But you can easily tell the difference for unfried gluten is a profoundly depressing shade of grubby grey. Whereas even fried bean curd will fall to pieces if boiled too long, gluten will stand long braising and simmering.

Couscous: the national dish of much of north-west Africa is based on a fine semolina which is then rubbed patiently into a very fine flour so that every grain is coated with a film that helps keep them separate during steaming. To me the appeal of couscous lies entirely in the wonderful sauces and stews by which it is accompanied, redolent of cumin and coriander and saffron, glistening with fats and butters, burgeoning with exotic vegetables and meats. Without these it is fairly boring considering the amount of effort and care required to make it. But look at the label. More and more couscous has been pre-cooked and all you need do is to add liquid, as with burghul. If you want it faster and want it hot, it will swell, and steam to perfection in a microwave in minutes.

Kibbled and cracked wheat: are generally considered the same thing in the United Kingdom, but there is a difference, and the latter is also very much confused with burgul or bulghur. A kibbler is a machine that pricks the whole grains, splitting them into small pieces; cracked wheat is crushed under light pressure. In both cases the object is to split the grain to enable faster cooking, at the same time as preserving the nutritional values of the whole grain. Either can be used like whole grains and I like them soaked, cooked and then sprinkled over or incorporated into bread doughs. This makes a good basis for stuffings, too, far more interesting than boring, pulped-up plastic breadcrumbs.

Semolina: is probably one of the most widely known but least used wheat products, loved or hated depending on the standard of puddings at your school. It is often, but not always, made from durum wheat and is the boltings of flour – that is to say the hard unground pieces of wheat endosperm that do not pass through the sifter. At least that would have been the case before the roller-mill. Now, semolina

SPELT

Once, and not that long ago either, spelt *(triticum spelta)* was commonly the staple grain grown throughout Europe. Although of the same genus as common wheat *triticum aestivum*, spelt has a different genetic structure providing more protein per grain, a greater concentration of minerals and vitamins, and a propensity for making specially flavoursome bread which does not crumble when sliced.

Modern farming, commonly at odds with good food, changed that ancient dependence. For although the close fitting husk of spelt gives it superior protection against pest and disease, it is difficult to thresh mechanically, and thus the winning appeal of modern varieties which have looser husks.

Today organic farmers are more impressed with the disease resistant qualities which guarantee a decent harvest, and don't mind the extra work in husking.

There is also a view that the protein in spelt does not cause as many problems to those who are gluten-intolerant, and may indeed allow those sufferers to eat wheat produce, provided they introduce it into their diets slowly. Spelt is being grown again in Britain and, should you see it or spelt bread offered, it will be well worth your interest.

is simply de-husked wheat that is rollered to a state of coarseness that allows it to perform as expected. Semolina is simply a sort of coarse wheat flour.

Trahana: What? I hadn't heard of it either, until the 1993 International Food Exhibition. It is a rustic, wheat-based product from northern Greece, looking rather like a dessicated crumble mix. Perhaps that is as well for it is made from a paste of flour, goats' milk and eggs. You cook it in water to make a creamy but textured porridge. If you make it quite thin it is a sort of soup to which Feta cheese, herbs and olive oil are added, more of a broth I suppose. Made rather more thickly it may be treated as a rude polenta of sorts, either as a mush onto which you put other foods or as a cooking medium which I especially like: small pieces of mixed green vegetables will cook in the prepared trahana in five minutes or so, and then I add cubes of Gruyère or Feta. There is a sweet version too, and between them they offer a new style of food to explore. Like burgul, this is a wheat product which even the most inexperienced cook can conquer.

Wheat flakes: are the result of steamed and softened berries being gently rolled under pressure. They are best used to make a delicious wheat porridge or as a major component of cold-grain breakfasts – the ubiquitous muesli. As with all flaked grains, I also like to use them to change the daily flavour of mixed-grain winter porridges, for no matter how good a flavour is, I cannot abide eating or drinking the same thing day after day.

Wheat flours: it is thought that there are now over 30,000 varieties of wheat, each with its own local advantages. Today's crop is estimated to be in excess of 300 million tonnes annually, broadly made up of just two types, the strong and soft wheats.

The grain of strong wheat has a relatively higher proportion (13-14 per cent) of gluten-producing protein, essential for bread dough. When water is added to wheat flour, the protein hydrates to form a continuous web of gluten throughout the mixture. The elastic gluten can be expanded by gas (yeast or chemically produced) and, being strong enough to trap that gas, thus causes the mixture to rise. The risen mixture can support both itself and the addition of whole grains, fruits and so on. The grain of strong wheat is frequently red and always long. It flourishes in hot summers and snowy winters, but cannot abide humidity.

Soft wheat grows in more temperate climates and is lower in protein (7-10 per cent) than strong wheat and thus will not give a good rise when leavened with yeast. But it is higher in starch, which contributes to the light foamy texture desirable in cake and scone making, when chemicals are used to give the rise. Soft flours also absorb less moisture, so baked goods with a low-fat content will quickly become stale. French bread, especially the well-known long shapes, are made with soft flour but this makes only a minor contribution to the special flavour and fast staling of these loaves. A long slow rising gives the characteristic holes and flavour, and the special crisp crust comes from being baked in commercial ovens with controlled bursts of steam: they were never produced domestically and cannot be.

All French bread is made with French soft flour, giving the characteristic sweetness and fast staling. You cannot reproduce the flavour of an authentic French loaf in the United Kingdom without proper French soft flour, as enthusiasts will have discovered; but if you use soft, unbleached white flour and eat the bread almost immediately, you will get close.

Most commercial plain white flour is a mixture of soft and hard wheat blended to produce an average taste and average performance, hence the description 'all-purpose' seen on some packets. A fuller discussion of flour of all types will be found under the section on milling, (page 190).

There is one other major strain of wheat – the durum – which, as its name implies, is the hardest and strongest of all. Its special use is in the making of pasta of all kinds and it is suitable for semolina, too.

Wheatgerm and wheat bran: are usually used as additives to bread doughs or sprinkled over other foods. Take great care in the buying and storing of the former; indeed, only buy it if its packaging and provenance are impeccable, or it will be rancid. The term wheatmeal has now been phased out in the United Kingdom and, indeed, may not be used.

Wholemeal and 'wheatmeal': these terms are synonymous and indicate a flour made from the whole grain, with nothing added or taken away.

Much confusion is caused by the term wheatmeal, which is *not* a 100 per cent wheat grain flour, much as manufacturers would like to have you believe this. It is what is called an attraction flour and is often also sold as 'farmhouse flour'. Such a packet also tells you it is an 85 or 81 per cent flour which simply means that 15 or 19 per cent of the original grain has been sifted out, giving you a flour that is subsequently lighter in colour than wholemeal and which also gives lighter results in baking.

Remember, if you are making bread with 100 per cent wholemeal flour the dough should not be kneaded, as this increases the deleterious effect of bran on the gluten.

Cooking: perhaps because wheat is so ancient and universal it is sold in more forms than other grains. Wholewheat grains, known as wheat berries, are not often used domestically, but when soaked overnight and then cooked in water for an hour or two, make a mild and nutty contribution to bread dough, to soups and stews or to mixtures of cooked pulses or rice. If during the final minutes of cooking, you let the water almost boil away, then add milk and let that thicken up, you will have a specially chewy type of porridge that is excellent when flavoured with natural muscovado sugar. Moist, freshly harvested wheat treated like this becomes the traditional English furmenty or fruminty (or dozens of other names), once a most popular dish, which, if you believe Thomas Hardy, was

THE VEGETARIAN OPTION

The only people who could possibly think vegetarian diets less nutritious than meat ones are those who produce meat. The vegetarian diet is absolutely sustaining and healthy. But only if you do it right.

To live healthily you must eat a protein source with the complete amino acid spectrum found in flesh – meat, poultry or fish. With one exception, no vegetable product has the complete proteins of animal flesh. If you are vegetarian and do not know this, believing it is enough to eat lots of vegetables, perhaps with rice, pasta or other grains, you are increasingly malnourished, day after day, week after week.

Milk, cheese and eggs are complete proteins which can replace meat, but quickly become boring and have little to offer those who want to reduce fat. A diet based on low fat and skimmed milk produce cannot be said to make getting out of bed worthwhile, and if eating is not enjoyable, life is not worthwhile.

The only complete vegetarian protein source is the soybean. As a bean it is tasteless and curiously textured and thus almost no one eats it. The Orient converts it to tofu, a white curd made from soybean milk. It is basically flavourless and requires considerable cookery knowledge and skill to be enjoyed on a regular basis. This is why Orientals tend to use it as part of their protein spectrum rather than as an alternative. Anyway, switching to soy products is not simple. Of all beans, soy creates the greatest intestinal gas problems and converts quickly learn to avoid it for they find themselves bloated and uncomfortable or relieved and embarrassed.

Thus vegetarians turn to grains and pulses, if only for variety. They also provide welcome texture, a spectrum of vitamins and minerals, vital fibre and are generally fat and cholesterol-free. Unfortunately none is a complete protein. Grains lack the vital

often laced with rum or other liquor and then could lead to the sale of spouse and offspring. With suitable caution against such consequences, it makes a time-honoured accompaniment to venison. The jelly-like result of allowing it to sit and cool is an unusual refreshing summer treat.

PULSES

Pulses are how the British lump together peas, beans and lentils when they are dried, but that term is little understood elsewhere. These most ancient of foods, cheap and nourishing, are looked upon in this country with much disdain, largely for reasons which are difficult to argue against.

Perhaps the most common complaint about dried peas, beans and lentils is that they are boring and associated with sandals, long hair and beards (and that is just the women). There is much basis for this prejudice and the serious perpetrators of characterless lentil rissoles have only themselves to blame for the failure of their regimen to grip our imaginations. If only they knew they could be as original with these foods as they are with their clothes

The other oft-heard complaint is wind. This is a very real and sometimes painful problem for many people, but a little sound knowledge and advice will sort this out in most cases. First concentrate on the thinner skinned varieties of pulses, which cook faster, as they seem responsible for fewer side

amino acids lysine and tryptophan; beans and pulses have those but lack methionine. Yet as nature is a good and beneficent provider, should you eat the two together the essential balance is achieved. The theory is simply told and easily remembered. You should aim for 60 per cent pulses or beans to 30 per cent grains and make up the remaining 10 per cent with green salad or vegetables; baked beans with a couple of slices of wholemeal toast is an almost perfect substitute for animal protein, so is an Indian meal of lentil-based dhal served with chapati.

The combination must be made within the same meal or the benefits can be lost, and it is a good idea also to include something high in vitamin C, as this helps release iron, often harder for the body to obtain from vegetables than from meat. The wind problems will not always be lesser, but if you introduce these products to your diet slowly, as side dishes rather than main courses, you will find the bowel will adjust and in a month or so you can be fully vegetarian without it going – or blowing – against the grain.

Moderation and time should be observed if you decide to include more grains and pulses in your diet. The digestive system needs time to adapt, but if you increase your intake slowly and regularly it will do so and you will find bloat, flatulence, wind or whatever you like to call it will cease to be a problem.

Thus with a little knowledge it is possible to eat spectacularly well as a vegetarian, almost thoughtlessly obtaining the high fibre, low fat, low sugar ideals of modern nutritional theory. Milk, cheese or eggs each day, or some soy product, or a proper mixture of grains and pulses and you are safe and very well indeed. Is it not worrying that virtually no vegetarian cookery books tell you such facts? Is there just the slightest possibility they might cynically be exploiting a confused market and thus putting the health of many young people at risk?

effects. Then, always soak *and* rinse *and* parboil them before cooking.

Our digestive systems will adapt to new diets in an extraordinary way if we give them the chance. If you think you would like to introduce more peas, beans and lentils into your diet – and there is every culinary and health reason to do so – start by regularly including some in moderate amounts in other foods. In just a few weeks you will be able to enjoy red kidney beans, or a chick pea salad with rarely a grumble.

All the pulses are excellent sources of protein and carbohydrate but are slightly unbalanced in protein content and for balance need always to be eaten in conjunction with other types of protein, cereal, seed and nut, or dairy. This is generally done without thought, as eating baked beans on toast, or scooping hummous with pitta bread.

Pulses have no fat content but it is difficult to find many enjoyable recipes that do not add this in some form or another. They have the advantage of containing a high degree of dietary fibre, and this is most important, especially as we get older, when the general trend towards eating softer food means food might take many days to pass through the alimentary canal, and this unquestionably exacerbates any illness and contributes to general ill-health. Even small amounts of pulses (or whole grain cereals) in the diet can make a major difference to health in the elderly, and is good practice for all others.

There are many famous bean, pea and lentil dishes to be found in the cookbooks of the world but I have to say that I often end up cooking beans the same way – with tomato, lots of garlic, fresh herbs in a bundle and lots of fat – bacon, goose or butter. Often the fat, bacon and garlic will come largely from

GENERAL COOKING ADVICE

Cooking times are given under individual entries. These are just a few words about methods of cooking.

There is continuing discussion about whether all these products need to be soaked, and certainly if the soaking is not done properly fermentation can begin, which gives an unpleasant flavour. My experience is that soaking in cold water can enhance the flavour by starting the germination process (the same as the malting of grains) and it certainly cuts down on cooking time, a saving of expensive energy. Generally speaking, overnight, or from morning to afternoon, is enough – allow plenty of room for expansion, especially for chickpeas, and keep fairly cool.

If you have forgotten to soak your pulses in cold water it is possible to plump them faster, by bringing them up to the boil in water, simmering for five minutes then turning off the heat and leaving until cold – for at least two hours.

Soaking water should not be used for cooking any pulse if you are afeared of wind problems. Either drain it off and put the pulses into fresh cold water, or rinse them very thoroughly under running water.

If you have persistently bad digestive problems you might try the equivalent of blanching at this stage, bringing the soaked pulses to the boil in fresh water, simmering for five minutes, draining and rinsing before cooking in more fresh water.

It is essential that salt should never be added to the cooking water until the beans are thoroughly cooked or they will be tough.

Acid in the water can also toughen beans and thus it is not a good idea to cook them in a tomato purée, for instance. Better to cook them first then add them to a rich stock or vegetable-based liquid that has been prepared separately. Cook on to let the flavours mingle.

Onions are also acidic and thus better added towards the end of cooking, after the beans have softened.

Pressure cooking is really the way to get your beans tender or cooked in a short time. My advice, gleaned from Rose Elliott's The Bean Book, is that you should use 8kg/15lb pressure, cook for a third of the usual time and always include a few spoonfuls of oil as this prevents foaming up, which might clog the valve.

chunks of Polish boiling sausage. But be brave with peas, beans and lentils. With chickpeas, use cumin and coriander and tomato paste and olive oil when they are warm – just enough tomato to bind them together – and serve sprinkled with chopped chives as a salad.

Serve cold tuna fish with cannellini in vinaigrette as a starter. Mix leftover butter beans with chilled orange slices, black olives and segmented tomato.

To make a succulent sauce for any hot beans, take up to a quarter of cooked ones from the saucepan, add water, stock or tomato purée to them and cook to a mush (you might even purée them then). Return to the drained beans and cook on. A real chili should have a sauce of softened purée-like beans like this. Beans in their own sauce are excellent hot or cold, and reheat well, too – witness the famous _refritos_ of Mexican and Tex-Mex cooking.

Whenever a bean recipe fails to excite you, and you have added enough salt and extra fat and more garlic, then add red wine vinegar teaspoon by teaspoon. The difference will be wondrous, and fast.

Neither should you overlook the flavouring possibilities of oil. Olive oil is almost _de rigueur_ unless you have very fatty bacon or a tin of goose fat. But beans cooked simply with tomatoes and then finished with a splash of walnut oil make a superb accompaniment to poultry and, after setting in a refrigerator overnight, the most memorable cold salad. Better with garlic, it goes without saying.

Lamb, especially the cheaper fattier cuts, goes well with beans. I like to cook neck of lamb in tomato with garlic sausage and some fresh thyme, then to add in cooked haricot or butter beans and cook on for enough time to allow the beans to melt into the sauce and absorb the fat. Just put the pot on the table and let your family and friends help themselves.

But for all I have said about the boring way these foods are generally seen, nothing can quite equal the feverish grip with which lentils hold our great chefs in thrall. From something to sneer at, lentils have become an essential accompaniment. A affinity with fish is the most surprising discovery, pigeons and every type of bird seem naked without them and even aristocratic beef is served with lentils perfumed with herbs and glistening with pork fat. Of course, it's not any old lentil, but the blue-green _lentilles de Puy_, which have an Appellation d'Origine Contrôlée.

In canned form they are more expensive, but a few tins of cooked beans are a godsend standby. Heated and drained and dressed with oil and garlic as a salad base, puréed, or drained and reheated with a herb-rich garlic-laden tomato sauce, they make a fast vegetable stew appear to have taken you days to make. Of course, they instantly bulk out a soup, casserole or ready made salad, too, if someone should come knocking upon your door whom you do not wish to send away. I think beans are good hot or cold but never at room temperature.

Storing: although good keepers, all peas, beans and lentils will toughen with age and many reach a stage where even the most determined soaking and cooking will never soften them. It is better to buy them in smallish quantities from shops that you expect sell enough to have a regular turnover of stock. Do check, if they are in bulk, for excess dirt or insect contamination, but expect some. And don't bother with stock that is broken. Store them cool and dark.

ADZUKI OR ADUKI BEANS

Small, ochrous-red and sort of pillow-shaped, these are an Oriental bean and have long been regarded as the best of them all in Japan, China and Thailand. Unknown to the West until George Ohshawa introduced the macrobiotic diet earlier this century, they are now much favoured here because they are the most 'yang' of beans, and because they have an appealing, strong, nut-like flavour.

I've always preferred them eaten as sweets covered with sugar or made into a paste for those luminous and often glutinous sweetmeats of the East. But they are also served savoury: the most famed version is Serkhan or Festival Rice from Japan. Rice is tinted with the pink cooking water of adzuki beans, then the two are mixed together.

The bean is the seed of a bushy plant which grows up to about 75cm/30in high. Juice made from adzuki beans is still prescribed by Oriental herbalists to help kidney problems.

Cook at least 30 minutes, perhaps longer. When mixing with cooked rice, begin with a proportion of about one part adzuki to eight of rice. This mixture is similar, by the way, to the rice and peas of Jamaican cooking. In macrobiotic cookbooks you will find suggestions for soups and desserts; I like the sound of one that cooks together adzuki and dried chestnuts, makes a purée of the mixture flavoured with cinnamon, and bakes that in a pie crust. The pie is served with cream and almonds.

BLACK-EYE BEANS

These beans are actually peas, a variety of cow pea and this is why they are also called black-eye peas in the United States. To add to the confusion, they are the seeds you find in the yard-long bean. I find I like the rather savoury flavour and interesting appearance of these more than the plain haricots. They cook comparatively faster too and I believe many people find them lighter on the stomach. Essential to Creole cooking and the related soul food.

Soaked beans take 30-45 minutes to cook.

BROAD BEANS

Not very common in their dried form, and unrecognized by most because they are brown rather than the expected green. But I like them for their bigger size and flouriness. Although it is nice to have a bit of a chew sometimes, the skins of these take expectations of mastication too far. You either have to skin them after cooking, or buy the more expensive ready-skinned variety.

These should have a good long soak and will then need about 1½ hours cooking – but less, of course, if you are using those without skins.

BUTTER BEANS OR LIMA BEANS

Many books divide butter beans from Lima beans but I'm sure they are the same thing. If they aren't, it doesn't matter for they are both large, white, flat and aristo-cratic of flavour. They should not be cooked until pulpy, but must be very well cooked and pre-soaked for they have some rather unpleasant constituents.

Baby lima beans are pale green and usually sold fresh or frozen. Opinions vary but I think fresh baby limas are quite the best for mixing with sweet corn to make succotash, even though I have seen recipes which require cooked, dried ones.

Smaller ones will take 45-60 minutes; bigger ones will take 15-25 minutes longer.

CHICKPEAS OR GARBANZOS

With their spicy, peppery flavour, appealing golden colour and hazelnut shape, these are amongst the most attractive of all dried pulses from any point of view.

They are the main ingredient in hummous, that standby of Middle Eastern, Greek and Cypriot restaurants, but one also found in Spanish and Latin American cooking and make excellent additions to soups as well as fascinating salads. They mix well with other vegetables, too, and I always like to have some on hand.

Cooking times can vary enormously. Older types may take up to three hours or more but newer types, the ones most likely to be bought here, should be cooked in something over an hour. They rarely go out of shape and are much nicer, I think, when rather floury, for then they absorb somewhat more easily the oils, spices and flavours with which they can be mingled.

FUL MEDAMES

Fundamental to Egypt for countless centuries, these are round and brown. Like broad beans, they have a tough outer skin and a rough but enjoyable flavour that welcomes the vigour of garlic, oil and onion.

KIDNEY BEANS

This is the biggest group of beans and one which causes much confusion. Simply, all beans which are kidney shaped without being flat are kidney beans. There is a variety of colour and flavour – but they *are* all kidney beans. The average time for cooking these beans is one hour, but haricots can be stubborn and need longer so be prepared to exercise patience.

Black beans: very popular in the Caribbean and in the southern United States, these shiny, very black beans are the most similar of all kidneys to the better-known red kidney beans. They cook to a firm satisfying texture and have a meaty, full flavour. Used by themselves or with other beans they make an attractive change to the look of your cooking.

Borlotti: (also known as rose cocoa beans) streaked with rose or crimson, and all the better for being pale of colour these are specially popular in Italy and excellent tinned examples are available. They seem usually to require little soaking when dried, and they have a rather sweet, soft texture.

Cannellini: a small white kidney bean that is absolutely interchangeable with haricots. In Italy cannellini might mean other white beans, too. These are almost always the right bean to use with rugged Italian sausages and with lots of garlic and tomato of some sort make excellent cold salads dressed with good olive oil.

Flageolet: these are very young haricots removed from the pod before they are ripe. Thus they are a delicate green, sweet and tender. By far the most expensive and a very special accompaniment to fatty birds, to young lamb or to hot ham.

Haricot: these creamy kidney beans are perhaps the best known of all, for they are the beans for baked beans. In this country in 1979, 850 million cans were consumed. Extraordinarily adaptable, they are the basis for the varying versions of cassoulets in France, cooked with bacon or goose fat. Some say they are called haricot because the French included them in their stews called haricots, but the late food writer Tom Stobart says 'haricot' is really a corruption of the Aztec word *ayecotl,* which I am inclined to believe.

In America they are known as navy beans; and just to add to the confusion they are often shaped more like a cushion than a kidney.

Pinto: a shorter, fatter, squarer version of the borlotti, speckled and savoury of flavour.

Red kidney beans: because delicatessen counters discovered they were nice to eat cold as a salad, and because chili con carne has proliferated, these are as well known as white haricots now. Their rich colour and texture and full flavour make them worth the popularity, but they can kill. Red kidney beans must be very well soaked and very well cooked until really soft; during cooking they should actually boil for 15 minutes.

Their uses abound throughout Central and South America and the Caribbean; they are the basic chili bean and, like their black brothers, add considerable spice when mixed with whites or other beans.

LENTILS

One of the first-ever crops in the East, lentils are richer in protein than other pulses, except for soy. They have a very high calorie content too, so even though lacking some of the essential amino acids they make an important food staple, especially in Third World countries.

There are two basic types but both have many names:

Green or brown lentils: also called continental lentils. It is generally these lentils that are mentioned in European cookbooks, old or new. They keep their shape when cooked and have a stronger, earthier taste than the red ones, which blends very well with smoked meats, fatty pork, herbs and onions.

You would have to be a particularly zealous hermit not to know that from their long standing social association with wierdos, lentils have moved up to spearhead trendy cooking, well, in restaurants anyway. They will generally be green ones, and inevitably *lentilles de Puy,* a greeney-blue variety from central France which have an especially delicious smokey-sweet tang, plus the snob appeal of AOC protection. Nonetheless, well-cooked lentils provide a surprisingly wonderful way to make all kinds of fish more gratifying for big eaters, indeed they were part of *kitcheree* which ended up as kedgeree. They make far more sense of game than those infuriating crisps, and when really soft and lightly puréed make a sensationally good sauce for vegetarian lasagne. But, and it is a big but, they must be well-cooked and not served crisp and individual, no matter how aesthetic this seems. The point of lentils is rich, comforting smoothness, with some of them mushed and emulsified with rather more fat or oil than you care to know about. Green lentils take much longer; soaked ones 30-45 minutes, unsoaked 1-1¼ hours.

Red lentils: also known as Egyptian or Indian lentils. These look reddish but are the ones that cook into a yellow-gold mush. They are vital to all sorts of winter soups and go extra well with contrasted sharper vegetables like garlic, onion and green peppers. Unsoaked red lentils take 20-30 minutes to cook, and soaked ones will cook in about 15 minutes.

MUNG BEANS

An entrancing dark, frosted-olive green, mung beans are one of the basics for making into bean sprouts but can be cooked as any ordinary pulse. Like the red adzuki, they are quite soft and sweet when cooked.

Cook between 25 and 40 minutes.

PEAS

Provided you can suspend both belief and memories of what other people may have done to them, dried peas can be an excellent, honest and sustaining food. They are available whole or skinned and split, green or yellow; the green seem harder to find but I prefer them. Peas rarely hold their shape which is why they are put into soups or made into soups. It is always a surprise to taste how sweet they are, which is why they are a natural accompaniment to salted meats.

Cook for about 45 minutes. If you want to keep some semblance of shape, use a minimal amount of water and watch carefully.

SOYBEANS

God's worst joke. That's the verdict on soybeans by the late Tom Stobart, surely one of the great but least rated food writers. In *The Cook's Encyclopedia*, he acutely points out that on one hand soybean is the richest and most sustaining vegetable food on earth; on the other they are terminally boring to the point of being inedible. The only exception I ever found were small green ones available for just a few weeks in early July around and about Nanjing, and thus unlikely to change the world's perceptions.

But what I want to know is, who bothered to work out that if you made a milk from soybeans you could make almost anything else? Which Chinese worked out it was so good for you it should be called the meat plant? We'll never know that and are still finding extraordinary facts, most importantly that soybeans are the only vegetable product which replicates the complete spectrum of the proteins (amino acids) of meat. In fact, the soy is a far better provider even than meat. Stobart says an acre which grew soybeans would keep a man alive for 2,200 days, but the same acre would sustain him only 75 days if he ate the beef it produced.

The United States is now the world's greatest grower of soybeans, mainly for oil for margarines, but the East is still the greatest consumer of soy products, as bean curd or tofu and myriad other products including soy sauce. In the West, we are also beginning to take soy milk seriously, use soy flour to add protein to breads and baked goods, make non-dairy ice cream-style products and, less successfully, spin its protein into threads which we stick together and pretend is meat, but less than we used to do, thank goodness.

There are thought to be a thousand varieties of soybeans, in most colours of the rainbow and sized from petits pois to cherry size. Their oily blandness makes most of them pretty awful to eat, for they neither absorb other flavours nor contribute anything of their own, no matter what their culinary companions. But once they are cooked, probably after chopping, and then pressed and drained the result is soy milk and that opens a new world. Soy milk may be made instantly from dried pre-cooked soy powder or other products of the beans, but the end result will look like milk and have rather less soy taste than the beans. But not always.

Some soy-based products are frankly inedible, others good enough for second helpings. In some cases the cause of the horrors is bad production techniques, but it is much more likely to be the result of using inferior varieties of the bean, which leave a lingering, raw, green bean taste. At least that is how the problem was explained to me in Japan, where I tasted wonderfully creamy tofu and in Sweden, where an ice cream-type product comes without the slightest clue to its soybean origin.

Bean curd: probably best known as Japanese tofu, but this is actually an invention of the Chinese, as most things seem to be. They call it *dau fu*. Like dairy milk, soy milk can be curdled with lemon juice or vinegar, giving a slight welcome acidity and flavour. Commercially the curd may be set with a spectrum of substances. Calcium sulphate, gypsum, also increases the calcium content but can give a slightly chalky consistency – hardly surprising as the substance is related to plaster of Paris. Calcium chloride may also be used and this is often accompanied by emulsifiers which bind in the liquid whey which would normally separate out, thus giving a higher yield and softer, wetter curd; the addition of simple sugars (not sucrose) add sweetness and a smoother mouthfeel. Full of Beans, down Brighton way, use a Japanese extract of sea water and there are other ingredients which will do the curdling. As with dairy cheesemaking, the exact texture and firmness of the curd can be affected both by the amount of curdling agent and by pressing and draining the curd. Generally the softer curd is used for steamed dishes or for adding at the last moment to wet dishes. The firmer curd is chosen for frying, often done to add extra strength to pieces of curd before they are added to a braising or boiling stock.

Although made from a liquid which has been boiled, bean curd must be treated as though it were a fresh milk product and kept submerged under water and refrigerated for safety, where it will be fresh and safe for a few days – up to a week if the water is changed daily. It should be virtually odourless and tasteless, but has the invaluable chameleon virtue of absorbing other flavours; it may be used as a protein to replace animal protein, or, as is more common in Asia, used as a complementary extender of meat.

Apart from its invaluable protein content, bean curd is high in B vitamins and iron, but the latter is in a form difficult for the body to absorb. Vegetarians are recommended always to eat or drink something containing vitamin C with bean curd, as this helps unlock the iron.

Fresh bean curd is still not a product found in the classic European delicatessen, not least because it has been too associated with the weirder outposts of vegetarianism. But the growing interest in Asian produce and flavours has brought it firmly out of the cold and into the chilled cabinets of many supermarkets. In an effort to broaden the market, soy sauce supremo Kikkoman has marketed in Europe several styles of bean curd which are pasteurized in vacuum packs and thus have a long shelf life at ambient temperature, which is an invaluable addition to the choice.

It is important to introduce bean curd slowly into your diet and best to mix it with other foods rather than eating it in large quantities or on an empty stomach. When you are used to it, treat it as a bland white cheese, and serve it with bright condiments, or add it to highly flavoured foods, giving it time to absorb its surroundings. It may be fried, deep-fried, roasted, toasted, marinated, microwaved, crumbed, stir-fried, chopped, cubed, sliced, whisked into 'cheesecakes', whipped into creamy desserts, frozen into ices. Iced tofu/bean curd products run the gamut from beany to amazing.

There are, famously, food writers who claim they would put anything but tofu into their mouths. But as the choice of products and standards increase it is increasingly difficult to avoid doing so. Bean curd is no longer an alternative, but has become a pleasure in itself.

Bean curd sheets: also called bean curd skin, because this is how they begin and how they can feel in the mouth – like skin. They are made from soy milk rather the way clotted cream is manufactured; the milk is heated until a skin is formed, which is taken away and dried flat. They must be soaked to soften before being used as a wrapper for other foods, and are then deep-fried or fried and poached in a rich stock of some sort, which is when they soften up to the texture of skin. Funny thing for vegetarians to want in their mouths, but there you are.

Bean pastes and sauces: beans are the basis of three types of important Chinese ingredients. Brown (sometimes yellow) and black bean sauces are made from different varieties of fermented soybeans and are largely interchangeable as a pungent but generally acceptable flavouring for fish, poultry, meat and vegetable dishes.

Brown/Yellow: if the label simply says Bean Paste or Bean Sauce, it will have been made from a yellowish variety of soybean, and be rather smooth, thick and brownish, not unlike Japanese miso. The flavour and use is rather like that of soy sauce but the thick texture and rich colour are such that it will change those of a sauce as well as adding distinct savour; very much part of Northern cuisine. A Szechuan variation adds crushed chilli peppers.

Black: these products will come as whole beans, pastes or sauces. They are based on salted and fermented black soybeans and although largely interchangeable with brown bean sauce, seem particularly popular in the West on fish and seafood, for although resolutely savoury, black beans also have a residual sweetness which is always appreciated with fishy foods. If you buy a bag of the fermented beans, they should be rinsed and chopped before use. They are said to last a very long time without refrigeration. All but the manic purist generally find it simpler to use black bean sauce, in which fermented beans are crushed and extended with soy sauce and other flavourings, particularly orange or tangerine peel and ginger; you may add further ones, sherry or ginger wine, fruit juices, chillies, or garlic, a particular affinity. There is a sweetened version, which may be used instead of Hoisin sauce.

Red: this pink paste is made from adzuki beans and used as a filling to spoil nice dumplings and steamed buns or to stuff those relentlessly dull and leaden Chinese desserts.

Milk: soy milk is a godsend for thousands, for it is cholesterol free and lactose free. But it can have a vegetal flavour that is either disconcerting or downright horrid, to say nothing of the internal problems caused by those indigestible leguminous sugars, problems which are not a million miles away from those of lactose malabsorption which many are trying to avoid; of this I speak with first hand experience.

A comparative taste test of soy milks in *Good Food Retailing* magazine was not flattering on the whole: many manufacturers over-sweeten their product to counteract intrusive soy flavour and, unsurprisingly, the soy milks liked best had no soy aftertaste. Still, at least soy milk is taken seriously enough to be listed by supermarkets and manufacturers are trying hard to get it right, offering a choice of organic sweetened, sweetened and unsweetened. It's a product worth watching, but in the meantime, you are more likely to enjoy using it if you prefer sweetening in hot drinks.

Miso: a Japanese product which looks like thick, dark, grainy honey but is a paste of soybeans fermented with malted grains. The precise grain added determines the colour and flavour of the result, and some versions are traditionally more salted than most. The most important basic use is for miso soup, miso diluted with dashi or plain water, a highly nutritious and delicious soup with a malty, salty flavour, which is basic to the Japanese diet. In my experience, it is much more digestible and causes far fewer intestinal problems than such other soybean products as bean curd: indeed a bowl of miso soup seems to settle everything down.

The basic flavour of miso is warm and sweet, with overtones of honeyed fermentation and when diluted there is a nuttiness rather than beaniness. Once you discover miso there are thousands of ways to use it to flavour food before, during and after cooking, as well as to enjoy it for itself. Excellent for making marinades. Chinese (brown/yellow) bean paste is related but not as comfortingly flavoured. Miso should be refrigerated when opened.

Aka: a red, rice-based miso, generally highly salted and will last without refrigeration; any mould may be removed and ignored.

Hatcho: made only of soybeans and aged in wood for at least three years. It is rich, dark and complicated in flavour and although it may be mellowed with shinsu-miso, may be used by itself as a tonic drink or in a soup.

Mugi: made with barley to give a peasanty and gratifying flavour, but is said to be more popular in the West than in Japan these days, where it is expensive.

Shinsu: yellowish, young, all purpose and cheapest.

Shiro: made with rice, white and rather sweet.

TVP: Textured Vegetable Protein is an entirely Western product, essentially the protein content of soybeans spun into strands, which are like meat fibres and may be shaped this or that way to imitate meats. Like bean curd, TVP is characterless but absorbs any flavours with which it is cooked and thus conveniently extends meat dishes, especially chopped or minced ones, to reduce costs or increase profits. That seems reasonable if labelling rules are strictly observed.

What makes me uncomfortable is the use of TVP as a meat substitute for vegetarians, and flavoured with all manner of unusual things, as we find in some frozen foods for instance. Are manufacturers so devoid of creative ability? Or vegetarians so uncertain of themselves? There are hundreds of millions of the world's inhabitants who would share proper vegetarian recipes using soy products, if that is the problem.

I would encourage both vegetarians and meat eaters to enjoy more soy products of all kinds and for many reasons. Growing soy for human consumption is clearly an excellent use of natural resources, offers countless fascinating ways to vary the diet, helps balance our budgets – and you do get over the wind problems. But vegetarians eating fake meat? That seems very second rate.

Tempeh: essentially, yet another form of fermented soybean. Generally made with cubed bean curd injected with a specific yeast which creates a white mould and turns the curd into a creamy texture, like ripening cheese. May also be made with cooked and lightly crushed whole soybeans. Like cheese, it should be avoided if ammoniacal.

Time to set matters straight. Herbs are always leaves and usually green, and everything else is a spice, which includes seeds, fruits, pods, buds, bark, stalks and roots. There are many books which will give the fascinating lore about herbs but I'm sticking mainly to culinary information and including some more unusual items that may puzzle you when you come across them on your delicatessen shelf or in foreign books.

The one golden rule for herbs and spices is to buy as little as possible and store for as short a time as possible. Although convenient, the storage of herbs and spices close to a cooker is rather silly as the heat will hasten their deterioration. Light does too, so although it is very pretty and homely, it's not a good thing to hang sprays of herbs in a warm kitchen. Find somewhere cooler and darker and they will be longer lasting, better tasting and more rewarding.

Both herbs and spices can be used to make a remarkable number of interesting drinks, hot and cold. The rule is that leaves and flowers are usually infused in boiling water and roots, barks, stalks and so on are usually boiled for a few minutes. The former should always be brewed in a cup with a saucer over the top or in a pottery tea pot; the saucer or lid keep in the essential fumes and keep the drink hotter.

If you don't like the look of leaves in your cooking, and many people don't, then brew some strong liquor from your herbs and use that instead. Commercially, most herb flavours are obtained from essential oils. These are proclaimed as the true flavour of the herbs, pure and unadulterated. And that is the trouble. Being unadulterated with the vegetable matter and minute trace fragrances, the oils don't reflect the essential flavour of their parent herbs. But obviously it is simpler for commercial interest to add a small amount of oil than to cope with fresh or dried herbs, and once again the customer loses out, having to make do with second best.

Herb vinegars are a wonderful way to utilize fresh bunches of summer herbs and details of how to make a variety of these useful condiments are given on page 332. Once you've made them you'll find them perfectly invaluable.

Allspice: one of my favourite devices for giving a lift to all manner of food, allspice is the dried, unripe berry of a myrtle-related tree discovered in the New World by Christopher Columbus. Its hot spicy smell and taste is similar to a mixture of the sweet spices of the Eastern world – cloves, cinnamon and nutmeg. And thus its name, a single spice which tastes the same as all the others.

If your mixed spice is too sweet or has lost its flavour, add some freshly pounded allspice berries. Freshly pounded or ground allspice goes very well in rice stuffings for poultry and lamb and is essential in pork or veal based pâtés, sweet root vegetables like carrots and parsnips; fruit pies and sauces, pickles and curries can also benefit. The whole berries are nice in pot pourris and ground allspice can be used for pomander-rolling mixtures.

Sometimes allspice is called Jamaica pepper or pimento or pimento pepper, but it must not be confused with pimiento, which is a vegetable.

Angelica: a member of the parsley family, the lovely angelica bush was once a mainstay of herb and flower gardens; its handsome foliage can grow as high as 1.8m/6ft and you can make it into a perennial if you keep its flower spikes cut.

Every part of the plant has been used, and the celery-flavoured leaves are still popular as the base for a tisane (herbal tea), sometimes in conjunction with a little juniper berry. The root may also be boiled for tea, and root or seed oil flavours both liqueurs and wines. But the best known use for angelica is in the form of candied stalk and leaf stem for cake decoration. If you have an angelica plant or know where there is one (masses of them grow wild, usually close to rivers where there are rich, moist, shady conditions) try making your own glacé angelica.

Cut the selected stalks and stems into lengths of 10-12.5cm/4-5in, place them in a glass or crockery dish and pour over a boiling solution in the proportion of 600ml/1pt water to 100g/4oz salt. Cover, leave for 24 hours, drain, peel and wash in cold water. Boil a syrup of 900ml/1½pt water with 700g/1¼lb sugar for ten minutes, add the angelica and simmer for 20 minutes, then remove and drain on a wire rack for four days. Reserve all syrup. After draining, reboil syrup and angelica for another 20 minutes, then allow the angelica to cool in the syrup. Drain for another four days, sprinkle well with caster sugar and store in air-tight containers.

Angostura bitters: originally a fever cure, these get their bitterness from the inclusion of quinine, but are said also to incorporate tropical spices, citrus and some rum. Of course, most of us know them only for the pink they give to pink gin, but they can be far more useful than this, if used with great discretion.

Perhaps the most fascinating assistance they give, apart from beefing up a variety of cocktails, is to fruit salads, especially where there is a good proportion of fresh orange. Add it to the sugar syrup early on.

Angostura bitters are quite good with creamy things and I have found them useful for finishing sauces for fish, for chicken and for pork.

Anise/Aniseed: Once used to pay taxes and a supposed bringer of good luck when included in wedding cakes. The plant is an annual which grows about 60cm/2ft high overall, a native of Asia Minor and probably one of the oldest known aromatic seeds. It has a sweet, liquorice-like taste with a broad spectrum of uses, from marinades to fruit salads, cakes and pickles, and is very good with cabbage dishes hot or cold, or scattered on bread dough. The tea, made by steeping the seeds in boiling water, is a good digestive after a large meal; but then so is aniseed liqueur – *anisette*. Anise is the flavouring of all the pastis drinks and these are a simple way to flavour fish dishes and many dried fruits. A discovery of mine is sliced kiwi fruit marinated in Pernod and served with prawns and a lime-flavoured mayonnaise.

Annato: this seed gives a flavourless colour similar to that of saffron and is used for such purposes throughout South America. Here we use it to colour our butter and such cheeses as Red Cheshire and Red Leicester.

Arrowroot: the anglicized name comes from the belief that the tree's root was an antidote to the poisons on the arrowheads of the natives of the West Indies. The arrowroot we buy is the finely-ground root of a tree grown in tropical Central America. The industry was the mainstay of income for Christian missions throughout the

South Pacific during the last century, and it's still not difficult to find communities who perform the tiring grinding procedure by hand.

I think it's far better as a thickener than either cornflour or flour, giving a cleaner, more translucent look to sauces and gravies without imposing a colour change. It has the additional advantages of making no alteration to taste and being particularly easy to digest. Milk puddings made with arrowroot are very good indeed for invalids and children and can be flavoured to suit the individual.

If your skin is allergic to talcum powder (which is a mineral) you can use arrowroot instead, perhaps slightly tarted-up with a little cinnamon or some other warm spice.

Asafoetida: a gum with a perfectly horrid and persistent smell, not unlike rotting garlic. Must be used in the tiniest amounts, and is most commonly found in vegetarian dishes, especially dals. I should let someone else struggle with the problems of keeping it in their kitchen.

Basil: to me, the very essence of summer. Once fresh basil starts arriving in the shops, the pungent warm smell seems to attract people from miles away, and it's sold in hours. Actually a native of India and Persia, basil nowadays is particularly associated with Italian cooking, but is also important in south east Asia, Thailand in particular.

Basil's peak of culinary achievement is its simplest use – freshly chopped on slightly chilled slices of rich, red, knobbly tomatoes; it is an insult to something so regal (to say nothing of the palate) to combine basil with those woolly orange bullets sold as tomatoes in the United Kingdom. Use basil with any tomato dish, hot or cold, including pizza and spaghetti sauces. Although some people wouldn't add herbs to ratatouille, I think a combination of basil and sweet marjoram gives a quintessential element of hot Mediterranean summers to this glorious vegetable mixture. Its peppery sting is surprisingly good with parsnips.

There is also a bush basil which has a smaller habit and leaves, and is rather more like marjoram in flavour. It seems easier to grow if the summer is not hot enough to encourage the full-sized plant. Basil grows well in a sunny window and should always be grown under cover if you only have one or two plants – once they discover basil, birds become besotted with it and can devour a large specimen in days.

The darker, smaller leaved variety (holy basil) is much used in Thai cookery. It has a slightly more focussed flavour, but European sweet basil can be substituted – _(see PESTO)_.

Bay: this is the leaf with which Olympic heroes and poets were crowned. I think it indispensable in any red meat dish or the sauce that goes with one; I regard it as the boards of a stage upon which every other flavour must perform. Knowing cooks use three or four times the number normally specified in recipes. But one shouldn't forget it has a remarkable flavour itself; try it stuffed under the crackling when you roast pork or under the breast skin of a chicken. Prunes, simmered with bay leaves, red wine, spices and a little brown sugar become the most unctuous accompaniment for game dishes; simmer until there is just enough juice left to cover the fruit, then remove the leaves and whole spices.

When you add a little wine or stock to a roasting dish, add a little bay to pull together the gravy flavours.

As the prime ingredient of a bouquet garni, bay also lends its flavour to many of the great sauces, particularly white ones, and I like to use bay when I am cooking fish; it is essential in all but the most recherché marinades. But perhaps the most interesting way to appreciate the individual perfume of the bay leaf is to use it to flavour rice; use 1 big leaf to 225g/8oz or 1 cup of uncooked rice. Served with both plain or spiced food it adds a truly individual touch (but too strong a flavour can be cloying). Bay-flavoured rice is particularly good when it is to be eaten cold in salads.

There is a much rarer golden leaved bay. Not only is this more ornamental to have about the place but its flavour is much more fragrant and elegant. The only place I know to buy a tree is the Duke of Cornwall's nursery.

Bay-flavoured custard is an old favourite and very elegant when chilled; get the depth of flavour by simmering several leaves in the milk, removing them and proceeding in the normal way.

Bay rum, beloved of 'gentlemen's hairdressers' is made of bay oil, plus essences of orange and clove, plus black Jamaican rum.

Powdered bay is very useful in pâté mixtures and in spaghetti sauces, but generally the leaves are more reliable. When using them fresh, check the underside for nasties, as my tree regularly plays host to all manner of them.

Bergamot: also known in 'olde worlde' gardens as Bee Balm, because its scarlet flowers are very popular with honey bees. The crushed leaves give off a citrus-like fragrance that has unmistakable overtones of the exotic, and the flowers are very good to eat in salads. The leaves can be brewed into a tea of sorts and it was this with which American patriots comforted themselves after the Boston Tea Party deprived them of tea from China.

Oil of bergamot, which flavours Earl Grey tea and is the main ingredient in the new suntan oils that tan you faster, has nothing to do with this plant. It comes from a variety of eastern bitter orange and is so named only because its perfume is like that of true bergamot. The kumquat liqueur you will know from holidays in Corfu has somewhat the same flavour, even though it is only distantly related.

Borage: the cucumber-like flavour tells you what to do with it; sprinkle it over salads, use it in sandwiches, layer it in gelatin moulds, put a sprig in long, cold summer drinks – especially in Pimms. A salad of finely sliced borage leaves and fresh strawberry halves is extraordinary and as good as it is unusual – very. But if you do not chop or slice it very thinly, you will be distressed by the hairiness of the leaves; better to use only the vivid blue flowers.

Camomile: although not, as far as I know, used as a flavouring herb, camomile is one of the most commonly used bases for a tisane. The yellow liquid obtained by steeping or boiling the dried or fresh flowers is a natural tranquilliser and used extensively as such in Spain, Italy and Greece. It is also very soothing to upset stomachs and can help relieve diarrhoea. Blondes use it to rinse their hair, to which it adds golden highlights.

One of its oldest uses is as a strewing or treading herb, grown in the cracks of paving-stones to release pleasant smells as you saunter through herb and other gardens. It has the distinction of being a fighter; the more you tread on it the faster it grows and it has thus become the emblem of humility. If you have space for a lawn but not for lawnmowers, plant camomile and you'll soon have a lovely and practical ground cover – which you can also drink. Vast stretches of the garden party lawns at Buckingham Palace are camomile.

Capillaire: this rather extraordinary flavour is actually that of the maidenhair fern, and was very popular towards the end of the last century but quite unknown now.

Dorothy Hartley in *Food in England* says it was used to garnish sweet dishes in the same manner parsley is used on savoury ones. The black ribs of the fern when boiled with sugar make a thick aromatic syrup, which was usually improved with orange flower water and saffron.

Capillaire syrup was mainly used to flavour drinks, and was thought to be a tonic – the sort of thing to take 'on rising in the morning'.

To make your own, stew 50g/2oz freshly-gathered maidenhair fern in water for several hours, strain and boil the liquid with sugar in the usual proportion of 450g/1lb to 600ml/1pt When thick, add a good spoonful of orange flower water and cork or bottle tightly. Miss Hartley suggests the following uses: put a dozen cherries, pounded till their kernels are cracked, into a large glass with crushed ice and a wine glass of capillaire, and top up with iced plain water (soda might be nicer). You will probably never want to make or drink capillaire, but when you come across it in a book you will now know what it is.

Caraway seeds: you love or you hate these, the tiny grey sickles of sharp aniseed flavour that populate seed cakes, and some rye breads. They can be rather interesting if they are used in moderation on hot vegetable dishes and cold salads; a few sprinkled on buttery carrots are very nice and they seem to suit coleslaw and beetroot salad very well.

Caraway has a certain affinity with apples, both raw and cooked. The nicest combination for a baked apple pie is to grate half an orange over roughly sliced raw apple and then add brown sugar, butter, nutmeg and few, very few, caraway seeds. A casserole of liver and sliced apple cooked in cider is all the better for a sprinkle of caraway.

The popular Kümmel liqueur relies on these seeds for its flavour and digestive qualities. Aphrodisia, a surprisingly good herb and spice shop in New York's So-Ho district, recommends you to make your own thus: steep 2 tablespoons caraway seeds and 225g/8oz caster sugar in 450ml/16fl oz of brandy for at least 1 week, shaking vigorously each day. Strain and use. I think you can make this even more interesting by using gin or vodka and by adding some thin slivers of orange peel.

Cardamom: quite one of the most aromatic spices of all, native of India and introduced to Scandinavia by the Vikings, where it remains the saviour of their otherwise bland food. Cardamom is the spice which gives that elusive extra appeal to good Danish pastries, but can also go into meat balls, marinades, curries and fruit dishes. Crushed cardamom cooked with the syrup you make for a fruit salad, and then strained out, adds a sensationally exotic lift.

Cardamom is one of the most important flavourings of Indian and Middle Eastern sweets and is also used in drinks. A tiny sprinkling over hot coffee at the end of a smart dinner party is often the cause of more comment than the most complicated and original dish.

If you like your curries fragrant rather than hot, add cardamom to your garam masala or curry mixture and go easy on the ginger and chilli/cayenne. Cardamom is also widely used in salamis.

The most common way to use cardamom is to bruise the pod, slightly cracking open the fibrous casing and crushing the seeds. Otherwise you must remove the seeds and crush them very well indeed; if you do not your dish will look distressingly as though a thoughtless rodent has passed that way.

White cardamom: from the Middle East and sun dried, it is especially suited to hot drinks.

Green cardamom: usually from Central America and not as aromatic as the white.

Black cardamom: the least spicy but most common.

Ground cardamom: although available is not recommended. Cardamom is so expensive you should get every last bit of goodness by crushing your own whole seeds and anyway, it loses its strength quickly.

Carob: this is a substance made from the abundant locust bean and used as a substitute for chocolate by those who want such a flavour but little of the accompanying fat, calories or caffeine. The pod of the locust bean is cooked and then roasted and ground. The roasting caramelizes the natural sugars present and gives a cocoalike reddish brown colour. The flavour is definitely like chocolate, but with fudgey, caramel overtones. Mainly available in health food stores, carob can be used in cooking as though it were cocoa; to replace chocolate, use a couple of dessertspoons per chocolate square. But remember, because it is naturally sweet it cannot be used as a substitute for dark or bitter chocolate.

Cassia: the bark of the cassia tree is sold as 'Chinese' or 'bastard' cinnamon and can be used as a substitute for the real thing, but it is stronger and coarser. Cassia buds are sweeter and tangier (like cinnamon and cloves combined) and especially good with cherries; you may well see them specified in recipes for Hungarian cherry soup. The use of cassia precludes that of true cinnamon, and I am indebted to the late Tom Stobart for learning that in a chemist shop, cassia is another name for senna pods.

Even when preserved in salt and sugar, its tiny yellow flowers have a wonderful fragrance, presumably because they are from a member of the jasmine family. Traditionally used for scenting teas and wines and otherwise for sweet dishes, but I remember it creatively used in the sauce for a duck dish at The 1993 Hong Kong

Food Festival.

Cayenne pepper: and chilli powder are the same thing. Cayenne and paprika all come from the basic red pepper or capsicum but different climates produce different degrees of flavour and pungency. Cayenne is the hot one, sometimes sold simply as red pepper. Named after the area in South America whence it came, it is now widely grown and used in Asia. It gives colour to a garnish but adds bite rather than flavour so should be used very sparingly. Cayenne pepper proper is the ground pod and seed and should be a dingy red-brown; brightly-coloured cayenne has been tampered with. I don't approve of very hot food, so prefer hot paprika which is milder and more flavourful – *(see CHILI POWDER).*

HOT STUFF

A certain hot tang in the mouth can be very appealing, but it is an effect rather than a flavour, and there is research to say that if you eat so much chilli you feel as though your tongue has been burned, it takes over 24 hours before you can taste properly again; you have subjected yourself to mouth trauma rather than a taste thrill.

But why do we think hot food so wonderful? After all, anything really hot prevents the mouth tasting other ingredients so any expense or subtlety is lost. The simple fact is that chilli is actually the refuge of the poor, who rely on mouth trauma to give their boring diets any sense at all. Thai food very hot? Only for the workers. So-called Royal Thai food is exactly the same dishes, but uses more expensive proteins and leaves out chilli most of the time – those with enough money to buy decent ingredients want to taste them, and so should we.

It is essential to understand that what you eat abroad does not taste the same to us as it does to the locals. Indeed, any idea that because food tastes hot in Thailand or Sri Lanka, you must make it as hot to be authentic is nonsense – it simply does not taste that hot to people who have been eating it all their lives. The more you eat chilli, the more the tongue becomes immune to its vices, literally a burned out case. What tastes hot to us, even those who eat chilli several times a week, will be nothing like that. Thus to be authentic, really authentic, you are absolutely right to ask for minimal chilli or none at all in restaurants, and to refuse anything that burns your mouth. Very hot condiments to add or subtract as you like, yes, but eating very hot basic foods contradicts the realities of the choice and comparative comforts we have in the West.

Celery seed and salt: the seed, when ground in a pepper grinder, can be used as a condiment and is good with fish, soups, tomato, potato salad, eggs, cheese and vegetarian nut dishes. It can add an interesting lift to a marinade if you heat the liquid slightly to stimulate the extrusion of fragrant oils from the seed. But never include the whole seed in food: the flavour is really rather coarse and you are better off with chopped celery greens or the more subtle flavour of dill weed (even though not quite the same).

Celery salt is a mixture of salt and ground celery seed, much beloved of vegetarians and drinkers of the Bloody Mary. It is common to use too much and this is why many delicate vegetarian dishes all taste the same, but it is nonetheless a very handy helpmate when bland dishes need to be saved from death.

Chervil: really a delicate parsley, to which family it belongs. Often called French or (in America) gourmet's parsley. The subtle difference is lost on most people and in most dishes... but it sounds good.

Chili powder or compound: this is a mixture of ground chilli pepper (cayenne) plus spices, the most important of which is cumin. Without cumin you cannot have real chili or chili con carne. Real chili powder is an interesting mixture which can also be used with great delicacy and to much effect in egg cookery. Correctly, chilli should mean the pepper and chili (with one 'l') means the compound.

When you buy chili to flavour foods check to see it is a mixture, or insist on tasting it. There are some packers who call a powder or compound by the simpler and incorrect name of just 'chili' or, worse, 'chilli'; and there are scoundrels who simply grind hot chilli and call it chili powder which it is not. You have been warned.

Confusion about this is why so much chili con carne is only chilli con carne and thoroughly disgusting up and down this country – undercooked watery onions and grey mince have been sprinkled with chilli rather than chili, nothing but a bit of heat and no flavour.

Chilli powder: – *See CAYENNE PEPPER.*

Chives: although billed as the mildest member of the onion family, I still doubt the place of raw onion flavour of any kind in serious or subtle cooking. If you disagree, you'll find yourself using it chopped over chicken soups, on sour cream garnishes, in omelettes and cheese dishes.

But I will concede that chives work very well as a relatively subtle onion flavour in a fish stock or cooked into a soup for a few minutes or in a poultry stuffing.

Chrysanthemum: you'll come across these petals in a most regal Japanese soup; I recommend you try it for they give a spicy fragrant flavour. One or two flowers infused also make a delicious tea, hot or cold; they can also be added to your usual tea.

Cinnamon: the spice for which the New World was discovered. Introduced to Europe in the 15th and 16th centuries from the East, mainly by returning Crusaders, it soon became one of our most popular spices. Demand was so high the ruling families knew that if they could find an alternative way to the East Indies, by sailing westwards, they would be rich and secure. Hence Christopher Columbus.

Cinnamon is actually the inner bark of a fragrant type of laurel. Cinnamon sticks are rolls of this soft bark and make wonderful swizzle sticks for coffee or hot wine, for hot chocolate and, surprisingly, for hot tea, a combination which is soothing and delicious. Sticks are important ingredients in curries but should be removed before serving.

Ground cinnamon is multifarious in its usefulness. We Occidentals frequently use it with fruit and with cakes and pastries; try cinnamon sprinkled on thick, chilled slices of a blood or navel orange – strikingly simple and unbelievably good. The Arabs are rather more voluptuous with it. They sprinkle it over poultry, with rose or orange flower water. Egg dishes, sweet or savoury, also go well with this warm, comforting flavour as is seen in the American breakfast combination of cinnamon coffee cake with eggs and bacon. Rice stuffings for lamb or whole fish benefit from

DUTCH SPICED RICE TART

This is a late eighteenth century recipe I have adapted. It's delicious eaten with apple sauce or a crisp apple.

For a 25cm/10in pie dish
1 pre-baked shortcrust base
115g/4oz short grain pudding rice
300ml/½pt milk, cream or mixture
½ cinnamon stick
4 eggs, lightly beaten
50g/2oz butter, melted
150ml/¼pt single or double cream
85g/3oz sugar, white or brown
2tsp orange flower water
Grated nutmeg, be generous
Soak the rice in warm water for half an hour then drain. Cook covered with the milk, cream, or a mixture of both, plus the cinnamon stick, until soft. Allow to cool a little then remove the cinnamon stick.

Stir in the eggs and remaining ingredients, except the nutmeg. My preference is for brown sugar as it better suits the spicy taste of the tart.

Put the mixture evenly in the baked pastry case and sprinkle quite freely with nutmeg - freshly grated or scraped is noticeably better in flavour.

Bake in a preheated (180°C/350°F/Gas 4) oven for 30 minutes, by which time the rice mixture should be nicely set and lightly browned on top - if not, a few extra minutes won't hurt. Serve warm or cold.

the addition of cinnamon, especially if some ground almonds and a little, very little, sugar is also included.

The best cinnamon is thought to come from Sri Lanka, and it should be yellowish rather than reddish brown and slightly pliable. A good tree can go on producing for almost two centuries.

Clover blossoms, red: dried or fresh, the honey-like flavour of these flowers makes a delicious tea and can be employed to make sensational but delicate creams and ice creams.

Cloves: two thousand five hundred years ago, Chinese courtiers were obliged to have cloves in their mouths when addressing their Emperor, to sweeten their breath. Our name comes from the French *clou* meaning nail, for these unopened buds of an evergreen tree from the Moluccas look like shrivelled nails and seem as hard. They are grown commercially in the West Indies and on the islands of Madagascar and Zanzibar (or the Malagasy and Mozambique Republics, as they're now mundanely called).

I regularly reach for ground or whole cloves when I'm cooking pork, rubbing some into roasts or incorporating either form in casseroles and pâtés, where I think them most important. With fruit, marinades, spiced biscuits, rich fruit cakes and mulled drinks it always works better in combination with sweeter spices such as cinnamon. I also think that orange has a special affinity with cloves, so in hot cross buns, Christmas puddings and Christmas cakes, I always add extra ground cloves to the mixed spice and incorporate grated fresh orange peel. The classic pomander is, of course, an orange covered entirely with cloves.

Coriander seeds and leaves: the orangey bite of freshly ground coriander seed is something I'd like to see used more in British cooking. I mix equal quantities of coriander seed, black and white peppercorns for a taste better than either one or both those peppers. In fact I now keep one grinder full of that mixture and one filled just with coriander as it makes an unobtrusive but satisfying flavour change to a huge variety of foods, sweet and savoury. It can be used in rather greater quantities than most spices. I use it with apple in pies and with anything that is remotely citrus-like; it is good on a salad dressed with lemon juice rather than vinegar. Pork goes very well indeed with ground coriander seeds, and this spice is a favourite of mine when making interesting marinades. Coriander is very nice in breads and biscuits, or in custards and is commonly used in sausages in Europe. Peas, carrots, lentils and pumpkin are other vegetables that go well with it.

Coriander is a prime requisite in curry powders and if you decide the commercial one you have bought is rather boring or just plain horrid, you can improve it by adding a generous amount of a mixture of coriander and cumin powder in the proportion of two to one. A sterling tip, that one; sometimes you might even reverse the proportions.

The green leaves look like flat parsley but are something else entirely, with a bitter and haunting flavour which is endemic (some would say epidemic) in countries as diverse as Thailand, Mexico, Spain, Greece and Cyprus. It is used as a basic flavour or an almost inescapable garnish in the first two former countries where life can be very difficult if you don't like it. I must say I didn't mind it when balanced by, say, a lemony coconut milk which bathed a large steamed fish, but it is aggressive enough to become boring when served too often. I know one man who banned its use in his Bangkok kitchen and immediately lost his entire staff.

It was once used extensively in Britain but I expect the story of the Latin name for it got about: apparently they called it the bed-bug plant, for the smell of the leaf is that of crushed bed bugs.

Fresh coriander is sometimes sold with its roots attached (one way to tell it from flat leaf parsley). Although the stems can be rather tasteless, the roots are a powerhouse. They are pounded with garlic and black pepper as a basic flavouring in Thailand. I do the same but poach the garlic first and also add coriander leaf: it is then a wonderful pomade to use as a marinade, to fold into mayonnaise or other sauces or, best of all, to spread over fresh white dough instead of tomato as the base of a Thai-style pizza, topped with sliced lemon grass, tiger prawns, coconut and so on.

Cream of tartar/tartaric acid: made from powdered dried grapes, it is a basic ingredient of baking powder. The combination of baking soda and tartaric acid together with liquid and heat is what causes the manufacture of gas and the subsequent rising of cake mixtures. If you only have baking soda, you must use something acidic in the mix, such as sour milk or milk and lemon juice.

Cream of tartar is also used in making sweets.

Cumin seed: together with coriander, the basis of curry mixtures, and one of the most important spices throughout the tropical belt of the world, New and Old alike. Most of ours comes from Malta and Italy.

Cumin works very well with tomatoes in sauces and goes surprisingly well with seafoods: prawns bathed in a pink sauce of tomato and cumin are wonderful. The Moroccans combine cumin, sweet paprika and tomato, which is magical. It is also found on yoghurt and bean dishes. Its special tang goes very well with the bite of chickpeas, cooked whole or made into a purée.

See the coriander section for advice on how to zip up a boring curry powder mixture.

Cumin and coriander make a good flavouring for rice salads, and I think that whereas coriander and clove work extra well when orange is present, cumin reacts well with lemon – and this marriage should always be arranged when possible.

Toasted cumin seeds are invaluable to have about. Toss them gently in a nonstick pan until they smoke lightly; it is very like burning old rope or the sort of smell which came from fat, hand rolled cigarettes in the sixties. You can crush them of course, but these slightly crunchy sickles of bright flavour are perfect strewing material, on salads, sandwiches, fish, poultry and meat.

Curry: the word curry is almost certainly based on a Tamil word *kari* which means a spiced liquid. The basic ingredients are cumin, coriander, cayenne and turmeric: the first two for flavour, the third for heat and the last for flavour and colour. From

READ BETWEEN THE LINES

We are increasingly lucky to find more and more small family companies making authentic Indian spice mixtures and sauces in Britain. Not everyone will agree the precise definitions of their descriptives, but the following might help point you vaguely in the right direction.

Bhuna: up to 20 spices make a mild mix for meat and chicken.

Biriyani: principle flavours chilli, pepper and ginger. Medium spiced. Best used in rice dishes with meat, fish or poultry.

Delhi: generally indicates a mild degree of spicing.

Dopiaza: from northern India, this is based on onion and tomatoes and a preponderance of cumin.

Jalfrezi: a Kashmiri combination based on sweet peppers and coconuts.

Kabuli: medium spiced with cracked black peppers and almonds originally from Afghanistan.

Karai: medium hot with the classic combination of cumin and coriander plus fennel seed and tomatoes.

Korma: the real meaning is braised dishes but the word is commonly used for any sauce which is lightly spiced and creamy, often because it is finished with coconut. This makes it very popular.

Madras: one of the hottest and so it matters little what else is included.

Makhani: medium spiced and buttery with fennel seeds dominating.

Moglai: must be very aromatic and should contain expensive saffron and thus be mild to medium in heat.

Pasanda: generally favours the fragrant spices plus the richness of almonds – very good with lamb.

Rogan: tomato and cumin based sauce commonly used for lamb, and thus rogan josh.

Tikka: medium spiced and flavoured with ginger and turmeric.

Vindaloo: the hottest of all, making western-style eating perfectly pointless. Food flavoured like this should properly be eaten in very small amounts with a proportionally huge helping of rice to dilute the fire.

then on it's up to you: ginger, cinnamon, cloves, garlic and cardamom can also be included. Fenugreek adds a certain something but is over-used in many commercial mixtures, and responsible for that ghastly sour smell that hangs around cheap Indian restaurants. Green ginger root, the sharp juice obtained by soaking tamarind in hot water, coconut cream or milk, and sliced limes or lemons are also excellent ingredients. There are no rules and the mixed spice mixture which curry is, is so widespread you can have authentic African, Jamaican and Thai curries.

Curry shouldn't be thickened with flour; the use of coconut cream or a tomato and onion paste is usually enough. The latter technique is well

GROUND GARAM MASALA

A heady mix you might make up from ground spices if they are very fresh. 1 tablespoon each of ground cumin, coriander, black pepper, cardamom, cinnamon, fennel and ginger plus 1 teaspoon of ground cloves: you may add salt and sugar, too. In some dishes, usually so-called white curries, such a mixture would be added as whole spices.

It is important that good curry making technique is always followed. After cooking the onions long and slow, until they are devoid of liquid and just beginning to brown (30-40 minutes for 450g/1lb), the spice mixture must also fry to agitate and encourage the flavoursome oils. Only then may wet ingredients or liquid be allowed in the pan.

The following are all for a jointed medium-sized chicken or a couple of lbs or kilo of meat, and added after any onion, garlic or fresh chillies

In each of the following mixtures, the spices should be lightly roasted before grinding, but you may use the sweet contents of a garam masala as they are.

For meat or vegetables: 2 generous tablespoons coriander seeds, 2 teaspoons cumin seeds, 1 teaspoon aniseed or fennel seed, 1 teaspoon cardamom seed (out of the pod), 1 teaspoon black peppercorns, 2 teaspoons poppy seeds, 2 teaspoons mustard seeds, 6 cloves, cinnamon stick, 10 dry chillies: the cloves, cinnamon and chillies do not need to be roasted, and you should add turmeric if you like it when finishing the masala. When you have finished pounding your spices, rinse out the mortar or rinse off the board and save and use that liquid, known as masala water, of course.

worth noting. Fry a lot of chopped onion in oil until it becomes a mush, then stir in the curry powder and cook on until it has released all its odours. Put the meat in, seal it, then add tomato purée or canned tomatoes slowly and the mixture will gradually thicken.

You should always heat curry powder before use; it is almost pointless to add curry powder early to a stew or casserole in the hope of beefing up a boring curry.

You probably don't need to be told that prepared curry mixtures are not really the thing, and that you should roast and pound and mix your own. Those who do not will probably get better results from using pastes rather than powders but both are infinitely more useful if they are regarded as a starting point, and you add individuality as you choose. Anyway, these days, it is as common for city dwellers throughout India and its associated countries to buy spice mixes as it is for us to use them: the difference is they will buy small amounts and use them only as a

For a chicken: 1 teaspoon cumin seed, 1 dessertspoon coriander seeds, ¼ teaspoon (ground) turmeric, 1 inch fresh ginger root: use tomato as the cooking liquid. A commercial garam masala mixture might also be added.

SRI LANKAN BLACK CURRY:

Some cooks will roast only the whole coriander, cumin and fennel, others roast them all. It is acceptable to roast whole spices and keep them for some time before grinding.

50g/2oz coriander seeds	1 tbsp fennel seeds
25g/1oz cumin seeds	1 cinnamon stick, about 5cm/2in
½ tsp fenugreek seeds	½ tsp whole cloves
1 tsp freshly grated nutmeg	1 tbsp dried curry leaves
½ tsp cardamom seeds	

Start the coriander seeds off for a few minutes at low heat in a non-stick pan, then add the next two. Let these colour until quite a dark brown then add the rest and continue only until they are just beginning to colour.

Keep the heat low and stir constantly. Cool thoroughly, and store in a cool dark place. Grind finely to use, when you might add chilli or ginger for heat, turmeric or saffron for colour and background flavour, garlic, lemon grass and cinnamon; tamarind water, whole bruised cardamoms and coconut cream to finish would be typically Sri Lankan.

In India, spice mixtures are masalas, garam masala is generally a mixture of sweet spices without chilli, which is used both at the beginning and the end of a dish.

starting point.

Virtually every mixed spice in countries east of Greece will begin with some mixture of coriander and cumin. The first is sweeter and lightly orange-flavoured; the second is more peppery, lemony and sharp. Thus either may be added to any curry powder or paste to change its basic appeal; both are likely to have been roasted in a dry pan, especially cumin seed, but even ground spices may be lightly coloured.

From then on, the choice is from every possible spice, but the best results come from using those with most fragrance and going easy on chilli, which has negligible flavour anyway: if you really want to add extra heat it is much better to add lots of black

pepper or ginger in some form. Cinnamon, cloves, paprika and cardamom, particularly, are the basic lexicon: it is unlikely you will wish to add more fenugreek or turmeric, for instance.

Curry leaves: leaves which smell and taste of curry, funnily enough. Available both fresh and dried. Fresh leaves are lightly fried at the start of cooking. Dry ones are added once the cooking liquid is in. Arguments rage over whether or not bay leaves may be substituted, and I think the consensus is not.

Dill seed and weed: The famous standby of Scandinavian cookery, but also found unexpectedly in Turkey and Greece. The seed, lightly crushed, is sharper and more pungent than dill weed, and can be used in rice dishes and breads, with fish and cucumber. It is used as a condiment in Russia.

The feathery fronds of dill are absolutely wonderful to use, quite different from anything in the basic English repertoire of flavours. When dried (it is sold as dill tips) it has almost the same flavour as when fresh. It is superb with fish of all kinds, and on anything to do with cucumber, yoghurt, vegetables and, surprisingly, with meat. The Turks make delicious stuffed courgettes and aubergines, filled with dill-flavoured mincemeat and cooked in a sauce of tomato and butter. Dill weed is basic to *gravad lax*, the Swedish dish of lightly pickled salmon, and the Swedes also cook their crayfish feasts with festoons of the weed. It goes well as an unexpected flavouring with spinach, particularly in a filo pastry-covered spinach pie.

Elderberries: like elderflowers, these usually find themselves made into wine. Provided you use a recipe that incorporates spices like nutmeg and cloves, you will, after several years of patience, be rewarded with a wine that in my experience has all the elegance and nobility of a fine Burgundy.

I've never eaten elderberry jam, but believe it to be very good. What I have done is combine elderberries with apple in a pie and that was very successful.

Elderflowers: honey-scented elderflowers make the most sensational muscatel-like wine. It improves dramatically with keeping and then serves as both a stunning wine accompanying puddings, and an irreplacable flavouring agent. Classically, elderflower is cooked with gooseberries, but gooseberries ripen just as the flowers fade and you can miss out (muscatel wine is a good substitute). When cooking gooseberries for a fool, one or two heads of rinsed elderflower will be enough to add the required flavour. Gooseberry and elderflower jam or jelly is particularly recommended.

Cream perfumed by soaking elderflower in it overnight is a lovely surprise with all sorts of summer fruits, strawberries and raspberries included. And by the way, although the recipes for elderflower champagne are terribly easy to make, the result is more a children's drink – very sweet, only slightly fizzy, and probably filled with clouds of dead yeast.

Elderflowers apparently pick up lead easily so should not be gathered beside busy roads. Each flat head should be smelt as it is picked for some have a distinct catty smell which, like all bad things, dominate the rest no matter how much or little you have. You can mix the florets into a cheesecake mixture or stir them into a pancake batter.

Fennel: in New Zealand I was constantly chastized as a child for chewing the stalk of both fresh and dried wild fennel. No one knew in Auckland that the fabulous fresh fish hauled out of the harbour would have been even better if cooked with fennel stalks burning under it or fennel fronds in it. I had to get myself to the Mediterranean to find this out and now regard my early habits as the first sign of a natural ability to find good things to eat.

Similar in taste to the liquorice-like anise and dill seeds, and somewhat interchangeable, fennel seeds are especially useful in cooking oily fish such as mackerel as they help cut the richness, and they are good in the butters which go with snails. I think the frond and the stalks should be used lavishly: red mullet and other oily fish should be stuffed full and if you have a barbecue, the dried stalks should be put onto the charcoal to smoke and smoulder just before the fish. You can put the sticks to burn under the mesh of a grill-tray, if you do not have a barbecue.

Root fennel (F. *vulgare dulce*) is a different animal and quite one of the world's most delicious vegetables; its name in Italian is *finocchio*, which is also a vulgar name for flaunting homosexuals, presumably because both are highly perfumed.

Fenugreek seeds: its name translates as 'greek hay' and there is a distinctly hay-like quality. The bittersweet taste is used in the curries of southern India and Sri Lanka and over-used in many commercial powders – (*see CURRY POWDER*). Very little, ground and sprinkled over vegetables, can be rather appealing. In Greece fenugreek seeds are eaten raw or boiled with honey. The seeds are also recommended for sprouting.

Fines herbes: in contrast to the mixture of herbs in a *bouquet garni*, which should be robust, fines herbes should be a combination of three or more sweet delicate herbs, such as parsley, tarragon and chervil or chives. They go very well with eggs. The mixture sold as mixed herbs, and used to excess by those who know not how to cook, is much more rugged, often contains sage and is better consigned to the back of the cupboard or, in extremis, to assist an ailing stuffing or sausage mixture.

Five Spice/Five Fragrance Powder: a powerful mixed spice with a predominantly anise and cinnamon flavour but which may be any combination of star anise, cinnamon, cassia, fennel seeds, cloves, liquorice, nutmeg, Szechuan peppercorns and ginger. You can make your own mixture, from as many as you like, but the flavour of the first two must predominate. Especially used in marinades, but I like it in poultry and pork stuffings, or rubbed well into their scored skin before roasting.

Food Colouring: generally, if you can do without food colouring, I think you should. The exceptions are two – children's food and absolute disasters. I suspect many people rely on colouring to cover overcooking, especially where cucumber-based food is concerned. Most colourings are very artificial and contain ingredients about which the long-term effects on the human system are totally unknown. Every year a different yellow or green, or red or blue is suspected and this is enough reason not to use colouring for children's food and drink on a *regular* basis. For fun, and from time to time, should be the rule.

At medieval banquets even quite ordinary food had to be brightly coloured. Sandalwood made food red, saffron made it yellow and spinach made it green. It was gilded with egg and gold leaf, silvered with silver and most spectacular it must have been. For very special occasions I think such presentation is worthwhile and a few years ago I experimented to find out how one could recreate coloured pastry without having to find sandalwood and so on. It turned out to be frightfully easy. Once you have made your pie, you simply paint on it with undiluted food colouring of which there is now a vast range. Once it has dried, you cover it with the usual egg glaze, let that dry and bake away. Lighter colours are fugitive so if you are using light greens and yellows only glaze for the last few minutes. The simplest stripes look good; try diagonal stripes of bright green and saffron yellow on, say, a chicken, lettuce and cucumber pie.

Artists can really go to town. At a recent wedding I cooked a ten-course banquet for 60 people in evening dress (them, not me). The *pièces de resistances* were hot game pies, gilded and decorated and painted. One of the guests was a fairly well-known artist from Paris, so she came to the kitchen and made each pie crust into her own brand of picture. A sensation. Another time I made a fresh peach and rose geranium pie for Glyndebourne. I decorated the top (over-decorated some might say) with roses, leaves and vines of pastry and painted them carefully, leaving the crust its natural colour and only glazing the flowers and foliage. Others on the Glyndebourne lawn came to take photographs and it is still mentioned with awe. It is far more fun for a child to have their name or portrait on a cake than to be presented with blue, yellow and green striped parfaits. A damn sight less trouble, too.

One of the most commonly used colourings is caramel or gravy browning, but good cooking technique should make this unnecessary. Use minimal flour and make sure your meat is very well browned before adding liquid. Commercial gravy browning is the result of an extraordinary process that incorporates ammonia and some authorities recommend it should not be used. It is simpler to brown some sugar, dilute it with water and keep that bottled until you wish to use it.

Galangal, kha, laos root: a highly aromatic root, with distinct overtones of camphor. It looks like a thinner, paler, pinker version of ginger root, and has a crisp, much less fibrous texture, so is sliced rather than chopped or squeezed. Must be used with moderation, even though the flavour lessens when heat is applied.

It is specially important in Thai cooking, pounded into pastes with other basic flavourings. My instinct was always to combine it with fresh ginger, but my Thai mentors said you never mixed the two, so there. Galangal is indeed galingale, which so often appears in the sumptuous ingredient lists of medieval cookery, but it was then used dried and ground.

Garlic: like the onion, was the chief nourisher of the slaves who built the pyramids and the common food of Roman labourer and legionary. Slowly it is becoming more acceptable in the United Kingdom and can be used with more foods than you could imagine. All meats do better with garlic and all birds should be rubbed over with a cut clove whatever else you are going to do with them: duck a l'orange is far better when the crisp skin has the tang of garlic. When frying garlic, though, beware of browning it too much for this gives a bitter flavour.

Bitterness is also a common problem with the fashion for roasting garlic. Commonly this is done by slicing the top off a whole bulb and slowly roasting it, often in a bed of coarse salt, not that that does anything. Otherwise unpeeled cloves of garlic are slowly roasted until browned through. I cannot think of a time I thought this good, although they might all have been overcooked. I always poach garlic cloves with their skin on. The flesh goes the most wonderful creamy colour and develops an unctuousness close to mayonnaise; they may be tossed in olive oil and lightly grilled to give the skins a little cosmetic colouring and then used in warm salads, or as a condiment – you squash out the flesh and mix it into other foods and sauces as you go. Otherwise you simply throw whole unpeeled garlic cloves into the liquid of stews and casseroles as they cook and serve a few to everyone, so they enjoy their cream of garlic as and when they like.

The simplest use of garlic is to flavour butter, melted or otherwise. I also usually add lemon juice and chopped parsley and this is wonderful with hot cobs of sweet corn, as a dip for artichoke, with fresh asparagus and with broad beans. Hot vinaigrette sauce with garlic and parsley is a specially good idea with simple salads of hot or cold pulses, potatoes or mixed vegetables. If you make your garlic butter too strong, melt and cook it a little and that will reduce the harshness. Once you get the idea there's no limit to what you can do… I even use garlic with fresh salmon.

If you are saddled with someone who says they loathe garlic, use it anyway and simply say it is 'a secret ingredient from Turkey (or Brazil)…' It's astonishing how many people do not recognize garlic when it is used with subtlety.

Wild garlic, which brightens up many a corner of an English wood, is perfectly usable – the green tops sliced finely make an interesting addition to salads.

Credited with amazing medical powers, garlic seems to be accepted as good for the blood and strengthening to the throat, so is beloved by opera singers. It keeps witches and devils away, too.

Dried minced garlic/garlic powder: these never quite work in my opinion, usually giving an unwelcome bitterness.

Garlic salt: useful for final hints of flavour but you must remember it is largely salt – you'd be amazed at the number of people who don't. Make your own, if you like, by mixing three or four parts salt to one of garlic powder and use it to flavour mashed potatoes, gravies or seasoned flour.

Smoked garlic: once you had to go to Boulogne for this, but now oak-smoked garlic is made in Britain, and very useful it is indeed. Try it anywhere you would expect the flavour of smoked bacon – in stews of beans or pulses – but be unexpected too. I like it in mashed potatoes and in salad dressings.

Geranium leaves: scented geraniums usually have rather small leaves and these have many uses in the kitchen for someone who likes exotic but traditional effects without fuss.

My favourite is the rose geranium (_Pelargonium graveolens_ and _Pelargonium capitatum_). The musky rose flavour of the leaves has dozens of uses, the oldest of which is to flavour plain or chocolate sponges. Spread the leaves over the base of the baking pan before you add the cake mixture. A little rose water in the icing completes this transformation of a basic cake into something very special. Rose geranium leaves can be left in caster sugar and after a week you'll have a scented sugar that is good on soft fruit or in baking, far more interesting than vanilla sugar.

I like to chop a few rose geranium leaves into soft fruit salads just before serving, and when pressed on the side of pats of cream cheese or unpotted Petit Suisse and left overnight, they make a wonderful accompaniment to raspberries. Orange-, lemon-, mint-, nutmeg-, apple- and coconut-scented geranium can be used too.

Ginger: grown all round the world, ginger is one of the spices that is very different dried from when it is fresh. Indeed, whereas many herbs are used dry and fresh, it is rare for spices to be so used. Fresh ginger is now more easily available in the United Kingdom and is well worth exploring. Peeled and sliced thinly, the combination of pungency and perfume is fabulous with stewed rhubarb, wonderful with beef, excellent with chicken and almost indispensable with fish of all kinds, particularly when poached. Always use a little more than you think for the pungency soon cooks out. I chop ginger root and squeeze it through a garlic press and often use this juice to refresh the flavour of any sauce just prior to serving. This green juice can also be put on the table for people to use as they wish. Use a garlic press to extract juice when the ginger is too fibrous to use in slices or to chop. Ginger root keeps very well in the bottom of the refrigerator, although it might dehydrate a little. I've read you can bury it in moist earth and keep it for ages by watering occasionally. You simply dig it up when you want some, and replace the unused piece afterwards.

Dried ginger root and ground ginger have more fire but less fragrance, and I do not use dried ginger very much as it often seems to add a dimension that is medicinal rather than culinary. But of course it is _de rigueur_ in cake making and then I like it enormously. Gingerbread can be many things – from a rich treacley dark cake to the thin, almost crisp, Grasmere gingerbread still only made in the village of that name in the Lake District.

Preserved ginger is dealt with in more detail elsewhere and can be used in ways that its sweetness would seem to belie. Elizabeth David recommends its use in white dough to make ginger tea breads, and it certainly goes well with ice cream of several flavours – vanilla, chocolate and coffee for example. The syrup in which it is preserved is very useful and far more elegant an accompaniment to chilled melon than the awful eye-watering dust of sugar and ground ginger usually served.

Ideally, use fresh ginger root wherever you have used dried or ground ginger before and you'll discover a world of subtlety that makes the simplest and most familiar dishes different again. It is very good with many vegetables, especially green beans. If you have made some nice stock, cook it for five minutes with matchsticks of ginger plus four or five other contrasted vegetables – cucumber, green pepper, celery, carrot, radish and so on and you'll have an elegant oriental soup.

To put an authentic Oriental flavour into Chinese, Thai or other dishes add chopped green ginger and garlic in equal quantities, a few minutes before serving.

Although specially associated with Eastern food, whence it originated, the best ginger comes from Jamaica.

Thinly sliced young ginger, lightly pickled in Chinese white vinegar with a touch of sugar is used as a condiment and as you would any other pickle.

Golden needles: dried tiger-lily buds. They have to be soaked, rinsed, and the knobby ends picked off. Beware, oversoaking can soften too much.

Grains of paradise: often called for in older recipes but I've never seen it in shops. It is apparently a fairly strong sharp flavour and the best substitute is a good quantity of cardamom or black pepper or a judicious mixture of both. If you know anyone or any place associated with voodoo you might be able to put your hands on this spice, for it is integral to such charms and love potions.

Gum arabic: this natural, edible gum has virtually no scent or flavour but is used as a fixative and binding agent in scented foods and beads, as below.

If you are sybaritic enough to want scents wherever you go, you simply mix one part (a tablespoon, perhaps) of powdered gum arabic to three parts rose water, almond oil, vanilla extract or something equally aromatic. Mix until a thick paste forms, then use your palms to roll small beads which are then left to harden overnight. They can be threaded and worn close to the skin or carried in a warm pocket from whence they will dispense their headiness. A few drops of your favourite commercial scent can also be added and you can experiment with powdered spice mixtures. To crystallize flower petals, mix one part gum arabic with three parts rose water, brush them all over with this solution, sprinkle with caster sugar, and dry on a rack in a dry, warm place.

Honeysuckle flowers: the woodbine's heady perfume can be captured and used to flavour creams and syrups, including ice cream. Dried honeysuckle can usually be bought in Chinese food shops.

Horseradish: this habitué of English railway cuttings is used more as a condiment than a flavouring but once you start to experiment it has many uses. Of course, when freshly grated, the root is very hot, the fumes alone making your eyes water and nose run. Thus I'm not too fond of it in its common guise – freshly grated and mixed with vinegar or a little milk to accompany roast beef – as it seems to overwhelm the meat's flavour. I recommend you look out for packets of imported horseradish from Germany or Sweden. They may be mixed with milk or cream and make a far nicer sauce. The best way to use prepared horseradish cold is to fold a little into whipped cream and then leave it for some hours for the flavours to mix. This is rather good with fish, especially smoked fish like eel or mackerel. Or, you simply buy a tube of _pepparots visp_, which is a preparation of horseradish and cream the Swedes use to smear on thin slices of reindeer meat. Next time you serve cold meats, make a very gentle horseradish and cream sauce and just see how good it is. Once you get used to using it with discretion try it in seafood sauces, hot or cold; in the former some of the heat will cook out, making it more delicate and hard to discern. I first ate horseradish with fish at the Red Fox Inn in Middlesburg Va, said to be the first 'pub' on the United States East Coast. If not for the iced water, the huge portions and low prices, the low ceilings and panelling might have created an atmosphere just like an English inn. But I wouldn't have been served split Pacific prawns with horseradish cream sauce in the Thames Valley, I bet.

If prepared with a very light hand, horseradish and cream sauce can be served very successfully with grilled salmon.

Irish moss: also known as carrageen, this seaweed-based product is very good for you, and is used to set liquids in the same way as agar-agar.

Jasmine essence: called _mali_ in Thailand, where it is used to perfume sweet syrups and custards. You should do the same. Add it to thick coconut cream and serve that instead of dairy cream with tropical fruits or, wondrously, with strawberries. But it can be used in anything milky or creamy, in ice creams, cakes, icings and biscuits. Wonderful stuff. It is sold in Thai shops in Britain, where you might also look for essence of _pandan_, which is as seductive and suggestive as its other name, screw pine.

Juniper berries: their ancient reputation as an appetite stimulant is probably what made the English and Dutch flavour raw spirits with the juniper berry, thus giving us gin. The unique flavour of juniper – half bitter, half perfume – is very important in marinades, especially for game or when you want to add a gamey quality to anything. Pig's liver, usually too strong to eat by itself, becomes very good indeed if soaked overnight in milk and then marinaded in white wine with juniper berries and baked whole. The berries can help make rabbit taste like hare and lamb like mutton (although I'd rather have the flavour of those untampered with). Better to use the berry to complement the natural strong flavours of venison etc.

The juniper-based flavour of gin is not used a lot in cooking, possibly because it is fairly fragile. But if it is strengthened with crushed juniper berries you get some delicious results. Gin and pineapple have an astonishing affinity, which is very appealing when hot. A layer of thinly sliced fresh pineapple doused in gin should sit for several hours, and then be cooked beneath a soufflé flavoured strongly with Galliano. To call it smashing is only to describe the effect; the flavour is wonderful.

Katsuobushi: shaved flakes of dried bonito (tuna), a basic of Japanese cooking, used with kombu seaweed to flavour dashi, the basic stock. Although sold in such a form, if it is loose it will lose its flavour very quickly: keep them well sealed and buy only as much as you expect to use quickly. Can be tear-jerkingly expensive.

Katsuo dashi: liquid bonito extract – a simple way to make fishy stocks, either by itself or with kombu dashi, which is liquid kelp extract, to make the Japanese staple cooking liquid.

Lemon grass: although particularly associated with Thai food, this fragrant citric grass is also used in Sri Lankan, Mauritian and many other tropical cuisines. Its fragrance is closer to lemon balm than lemon and there is thus a hint of sweetness. It really only works when fresh, although dried versions are available. The best flavour is in the fleshier bulb end, and precisely how much and which part you use depends on the dish.

When used fresh, perhaps to finish stir-fried prawns or to flavour a Western-style salad, the bulb end only is crushed and very thinly sliced, but even so it can be woody. In long-cooked dishes, the whole stem is more likely to be bashed flat and used whole, and then removed before serving; but thinly sliced fresh lemon grass might be added for the last few minutes to freshen the flavour. Thai cooks usually combine lemon grass with other citric flavours, including lemon zest and lemon juice, lime juice and kaffir lime leaf *qv*. In Sri Lanka it is likely to appear in their sensational white curries, based on coconut milk and cream and gentle spices.

Lemon grass is a natural companion to fish of course, but its extraordinary new popularity in the West means its full range of affinities is still to be discovered. Essentially it does anything and goes anywhere lemon or lime might. It is terrific on tomato salads and a welcome change from the inevitable basil. In Sydney it is apparently going into everything – you can even buy a lemon grass chocolate. It makes a terrific flavoured custard, I'm sorry, should that be *crème anglaise*? I am happy to stop with the Mauritian habit of stuffing lots of bruised lemon grass into a tea pot with boiling water and drinking the resultant tisane.

Lemon grass grows in warm windows and gardens in Britain, but supermarkets also sell it. You may freeze excess stocks, but it loses its crunch and is then best used for cooking rather than salads. Store slightly damp whole lemon grass in a sealed plastic bag or tall screw top jar in the refrigerator and it lasts weeks.

Lavender: I use lavender quite as much as I do rosemary. It has an extra, musky perfume that is quite addictive. The spikes and leaves can replace rosemary in almost any recipe, especially with fish and veal. Lavender and carrot soup is very special, and you can use the flowers or the spikes. Lightly, lightly is the rule and perhaps one of the best ways to use lavender is to incorporate it in your favourite sweet herb mix; it comes as a surprise to many that it is often included in that delicious mixture Herbes de Provence. Some of those most surprised are suppliers of traditional mixtures. They say the lavender has been added to disguise the poor quality of the other ingredients and I still don't know which side to take.

Lavender flowers and rose water mixed into cream cheese make a most elegant chilled cream pudding for hot summer evenings.

Lemon balm: regarded as a weed by many for it is even more prolific than the proverbial pet rabbit. But that's a good thing, for then you can use it in greater quantities. It is one of the greatest bath perfumers. Strew great bunches in your bath while it is running and you'll be rewarded with a heavenly smell that would normally cost an astronomical price. It makes delicious tea, too. But otherwise, like so many herbs, its very smell and flavour dictate its use. Use it instead of, or in tandem with, lemon: in stuffings for poultry or fish, finely sliced in salads (very good) and to add a tang of taste and colour to fruit salads.

Lime leaves/Kaffir: the fleshy, dark green, shiny leaf of a knobbly variety of lime used almost exclusively in Thai cookery, but with a great deal to offer to others. It lends a full, rich citric flavour which has overtones of sweet brilliantine and thus must not be overdone. It is especially good when used in conjunction with lemon grass. The flavour reward is in direct proportion to how thinly the leaf is sliced, presumably because this releases more of the oils. Scissors are better than knives for the slicing. Like lemon grass it is common to use slightly crushed leaves as the base of a stock or sauce and to finish with finely sliced leaves, which may be left in or strained out.

Extraordinarily, kaffir lime leaf has a spectacular affinity with lamb. Stuff rolled leaves under the skin, the way you would rosemary, roast the ordinary way. It is one of the most delicious things you can imagine and even better when cold. What picnic sandwiches it makes, but remove the leaves as you slice. And then resolve to do something similar to chicken or duck or turkey. Young leaves, shredded or chopped, are excellent on such as tomato salads and can be whizzed up into all kinds of sauces, pesto alternatives and the like; in all such cases, remove the central spine and ignore older leaves which will be coarse.

Kaffir lime leaf is regularly available in Thai shops, and freezes very well, so buy a bag when you see it.

Liquorice root: a natural sweetener that contains no sugar, it can be used to stir drinks or made into a sweetening brew by boiling in water. Chewing this instead of sweets is said to have helped many give up smoking, but it's also said to be an infallible aphrodisiac, especially for women.

Locust beans: – *see CAROB.*

Lovage: looking like a huge celery and having something of the flavour, all parts of the lovage plant can be used. Mainly it is added to soups and stews. In the West Country they make a cordial with it which, mixed with brandy, is said to be the best soother of upset stomachs there is. You can make your own simply by steeping the root in brandy. It's supposed to be very good in baths, too (the leaf I presume).

Mace: the outer covering of the nutmeg kernel and altogether more elegant. Mace is essential in fruit cookery and in pork pâtés, in chocolate dishes and with vegetables. Use it as an alternative to nutmeg, or as a way to add individuality to any spice mixture. It is extra good in a crumble topping over rhubarb or apple. Some say it has a special affinity with the cherry, and a dusting is good with hot shellfish sauces. Mace, in whole blades or ground, should be a very pale yellow-ochre – the paler the better.

Maidenhair: – *see CAPILLAIRE.*

Mahlab: these are cherry-stone kernels and can be bitter or sweet. Available in this country in Greek stores (and probably Turkish and Middle Eastern ones, too) it gives a great density of almond/cherry flavour, and is a standby of Turkish Delight. Russians use it to make cherry *kissel* and the Greeks flavour their large Easter loaves – *Tsourekia* – with it.

Marigold: not commonly used nowadays but the dried petals are recommended as an interesting alternative to saffron for colouring stews and casseroles, soups, breads and buns. The slight flavour can be rather exciting with poultry dishes and the fresh petals make an excellent addition to mixed salads.

Marigold flowers should be dried fast rather than slow – do it in a low to middling oven. To use them either grind the dried petals and use the powder, or brew a few petals in hot milk or water and use that.

If you are a butter or cheesemaker, marigold was the original colouring before annato began to be imported. It can still add life to cream or cottage cheeses.

Marjoram: closely related to oregano, sweet or knotted marjoram can be used in exactly the same way, with grills, tomatoes, poultry and fish. The flavour is reminiscent of thyme, but warmer, slightly spicy and definitely sweet. Although an important part of flavouring strong vegetable dishes such as ratatouille, I don't think it works with red meats like beef or game. Instead, I use it when making smoked mackerel pâté, where it seems to complement the flavours perfectly, possibly helped by the inclusion of tomato purée. It is quite fugitive and should only be added to hot dishes shortly before serving. Wild marjoram is usually the much stronger pot marjoram, and when this is grown in dry sunny places it becomes oregano. The Greek *riganis* is also wild marjoram but may be other species.

Mastic gum: another slightly liquorice flavoured substance but with the resinous overtones you would expect from the natural gum of a tree; the precise tree is the lentisk, a type of Pistacia. The flavour is fascinating when used in moderation – it is amazing in rice pudding. And it is also used in cakes and breads.

Although related to the flavours of ouzo and retsina wine, mastic is a different substance. The Greek island of Chios makes a rather special liqueur called mastica, flavoured with the gum from their variety of lentisk, which is unique to them; the Turks use mastic to flavour their fire water – raki.

Mint: the large family of flavoured mints provides a simple and accessible way to start experimenting with herbs and herb teas. Any decent plant nursery will have a variety of them, most of which can be used for culinary purposes.

Spearmint is mellow and usually has a green stalk. Peppermint, thought to be a hybrid, has a definite extra fizzle on the tongue, has a reddish stalk (the darker the better) and is the proper one to use to make a good mint tea. Either can be used in basic cooking, but peppermint is less usual.

These basic mints tend easily to overpower a salad, I find, so only add them at the very last minute and in whole leaves (cutting or chopping gives bitterness).

Other mint flavours include pineapple, lemon, orange, apple and champagne. These smaller, whole leaves are perfect for salads, for decorating or perfuming cakes and fruit dishes – (see *GERANIUMS*). Eau de cologne mint is pungent and needs to be used with great discretion but is wonderful in summer salads and drinks.

I loathe the idea of mint sauce in any form; the idea of dousing sweet lamb meat in sugar and vinegar is appalling, and certainly not traditional, well, not for long anyway. Lamb was always served with jellies or sauces made from the berries which grew on the same hills it did. In fact it was rarely eaten; mutton was the thing and the fore-quarter considered infinitely better than the hind leg. But, once New Zealand began to send Britain cheap frozen lamb, budgets and good sense persuaded a national change of taste. At the same time the growth of the cities meant it was more likely you had a patch of mint at the door than a rowan tree. Thus convenience rather than culinary sense meant that the acidic mint sauce which perfectly complemented the strong meat of mutton was thoughtlessly served with the sweet flesh of lamb. Horrid.

But stuff lamb with sprigs of mint, roast it on a bed of mint, and serve it with a spoonful of the juices you have pressed from that bed and you have something quite superlative. This works sensationally with chicken too, and cold minted chicken is the most marvellous picnic food.

Dried mint works rather well in grain-based stuffings and when added to the sweeter Eastern combinations that also include currants, dried fruits and nuts, makes its own tantalizing original contribution.

Mint teas, the subsistence drink of millions of Arabs in tea shops, are also beloved of the French, the Italians, the Greeks, the Austrians – they must be the most popular of all tisanes – and can be made in many ways. The Moroccans make it by plunging stalks of peppermint into a pot of brewed gunpowder green tea, and very nice it is too; in Egypt they simply brew up with fresh bunches of leaves. But in all cases they sweeten it rather too dramatically for my taste. Like them, you can use whole bunches, leaves or chopped leaves on their own, or you can combine mint with any other black or green tea. You can use them fresh or dried. It is always refreshing and enormously soothing.

Mint is used in cold drinks, too – in the famed mint julep of the southern United States, or in a wonderful Pimms, which is doubly good and dangerous if made with champagne rather than lemonade.

Pennyroyal, a member of the mint family, has extra dimensions of flavour that I recommend. It also grows wild, even more of a recommendation.

Mirin: a sweetened Japanese rice wine which is never used for drinking. Instead it adds flavour, especially to marinades and grilled dishes and thus can be combined with soy and other sauces; Chinese rice wines, like Shao-Hsing are equivalents, but these are also used for drinking. There are processed and flavoured varieties, generically known as **aji-mirin**.

Mixed spice: although generally a mixture of cinnamon, nutmeg and cloves or allspice, a really decent mixed spice can include far more than that, so don't be afraid of experimenting to get a really good spicy taste rather than just a sweet and aromatic note. Dill and fennel seeds give a liquorice flavour, which is good in conjunction with clove overtones. Coriander and cumin both give warmth and can be added together or individually. Ginger adds bite as well as flavour. Cassia serves to heighten the cinnamon taste. Fenugreek can also be used, and Elizabeth David added pepper to her spice mixture (and if she said it's all right it must be). Finally, mace adds elegance, and cardamom an unmistakable touch of the exotic but it can easily overpower, so be careful.

MSG(monosodium glutamate): don't stop reading! MSG is potentially one of the most important and useful ingredients in your kitchen, particularly if you have a heart problem. Like salt, MSG does not alter the flavour of food but stimulates the flavour buds of your tongue so that it can taste. Unlike salt it has no flavour of its own. Those who say they can taste MSG are quite wrong, but they may well be able to detect the effects of over-use of the substance, for then the tastebuds will be stimulated to such a frenzy of sensitivity they will be tasting aspects of the food, even of their own saliva, never encountered before; if salt stimulated such a reaction all you would taste is the salt, and probably be sick, too.

So, you can forget that mainly American posturing about MSG allergy. Provided it is used properly it is perfectly safe, even for babies according the United States FDA, one of the world's toughest food safety agencies. There will be a few who have unfortunate reactions but this is particularly rare and orange juice is more likely to be the culprit. The problem is that we in the West misuse it. A large amount of MSG on an empty stomach upsets in some way almost 50 per cent of the world population, including Asians. When we order a Chinese soup as a first course we put ourselves right in line for a problem, for these are likely to have the highest amount of MSG on the menu, to make weak stock taste stronger. Yet, eat the soup in the middle of the meal and those who might well have had some reaction will have none. That's where the Chinese eat their soups. If they didn't, they would have problems, too.

Of course, bad chefs do over-use MSG, and that is to be deplored. But would you want to ban chips because they were served too soggy or oily and made you feel sick? Of course not, you would only eat them when they were cooked properly. Of the many surprises about MSG, one of the biggest is that glutamates are manufactured by our own body, and contained in many popular savoury foods, tomatoes and roasted meats in particular. Indeed it may be their very presence that makes them so enjoyable and differs us from animals. There is a serious school of thought that appreciation of the specific glutamate flavour of roasted meats was one of the first steps from ape to man...

The particular savour given by glutamates is called *jian* by the Chinese and these may be added to the five basic flavours of their cookery – sweet, sour, bitter, hot and salty. *Jiang* is a seventh, translated as fragrant or aromatic flavours, especially the effects of wine and spirits, garlic, spring onions and spices.

MSG is very widely used in processed foods as a flavour enhancer because of its ability to make the tongue taste more flavour when less is actually there.

One of its greatest contributions is to anyone with a lazy tongue or with heart problems. Each of us has a tongue which works at a different pace, hence it is arrogance of the highest plane to tell another how much or how little salt they should have on their food; saltiness and taste can only be a subjective absolute.

Those unfortunates with lazy taste buds require more salt to get flavour of any kind, and often end up using so much that salt is all they taste, but at least something is happening in their mouths. Take the salt away, perhaps on the recommendation of a doctor, and they get so little gratification from eating they are bound to slip from their diet. The secret is judicious amounts of MSG. It has far less sodium than salt and is, anyway, used in far smaller amounts; by helping the subject to mouth gratification they will be likely to stay on their diet.

A broad rule is to use a quarter to half the MSG you would of salt; for those who merely want to cut down a little, a mixture of MSG and salt works wonders.

Even for those with no health problems, MSG can be a boon. If you have created something you know tastes terrific, but is fairly light on that flavour, you will not want to add other ingredients and change it. Sprinkle in small amounts of MSG, and that will greatly enhance what you have created. But remember, that is only in your opinion. To some it will be over-flavoured, to others it will still require seasoning to make their tongue work. But at least the MSG will help prevent your food tasting only of salt.

Manufactured monosodium glutamate is made from dried fermented wheat gluten and/or soybean protein often enriched with powdered dried shrimp or seaweed, and available named just as MSG or under a variety of brand names.

Mustard: there are three types of mustard seed – white, brown and black and all three are from plants of the cabbage family. Combinations of ground seeds (flours) or mixtures of the coarsely-crushed seeds together with a variety of liquids are what give the broad palette of mustard flavours.

Although introduced to us by the Romans 2,000 years ago and thought of as basic to English cookery, we actually use it for very little other than on our plates and for devilling. And I think the introduction of the rather sweeter American mustard, that coincided with the invasion of the hamburger, has done more to create interest in the United Kingdom than the tiers of gaudily packaged prepared mustards that come from everywhere and contain everything.

Mustard flavour only develops when the crushed or ground seed is in contact with water; both salt and vinegar inhibit the development of flavour, as will very hot water. Mustard powder, even when used to flavour, say, a cheese sauce, should first be mixed with water and left for ten minutes.

It is also important to remember that the hotness and flavour of mustard disappears with time and cooking; thus you should add mustard to any sauce or casserole only five minutes before serving. The seeds, or lightly crushed seeds, keep their virtue relatively longer than does the powder.

Having a germicidal action, mustard is used as a preservative, which explains its use in piccalilli.

As well as the types of mustard listed below, there is a mustard oil, more easily available in Indian shops. Very hot, it is a good way to get a controllable heat plus interesting base flavour into curries if you use it instead of a blander oil.

English mustard: sold as a powder or ready-prepared and usually made of brown and white mustard seeds, with the addition of wheat flour if it is for the United Kingdom market. The English mustard sold in the United States is pure ground mustard seed. Mix with cold water and leave to stand for five to ten minutes, which allows the pungency to develop. Personally I think this is quite horrid and the use disguises any flavour the food may have. But if you then mix it with milk, cream or a mixture, the flavour is mellower and more of a complement. Those who insist on ruining their food *and* their palate might mix mustard with malt or wine vinegar and even add horseradish, which is what they do to Tewkesbury mustard.

Prepared English mustard is not quite as strong as the freshly-made kind.

French mustard: a broad term this, covering many mustards which in general are far less strong than the English type, mainly through being mixed with other aromatics, thus lessening the proportion of heat to flavour. Dijon mustards are mixed with grape juice only, whereas the Bordeaux usually have herbs added. Either are excellent for spreading on steaks or other meats before grilling or roasting, and give a touch of interest when mixed into a good mayonnaise. Currently popular to the point of swamping the market are French mustards made with whole or crushed grains, the red-wax-topped Moutarde de Meaux being first and best known. Although I've seen some people in print say they are not much use for cooking, I think they are most useful for they add visual interest as well as flavour. Use them liberally in stuffings (the heat cooks out, remember) or in vegetable purées.

German mustard: this is usually mild and sweet, often with an important herb content. Austrian mustard is often tarragon-flavoured (at least the one I buy is).

American mustard: sweetened with sugar and made only with the milder white mustard seed, this is made into a creamier consistency than we are used to. Thus it can be spread with a nonchalance that would strip your mouth if it were the English type. It's the only mustard to eat with hamburgers or frankfurters, and an interesting base for sauces. It can contain a lot more additives than other mustards, which are largely unnecessary in view of mustard's own preservative abilities.

Making your own mustard is easy with a pestle and mortar: try and get a variety of mustard seeds and grind some into powder, some into pieces. Honey goes very well in mustard mixtures, but isn't a good idea if you are going to coat meat or fish for grilling, as it will caramelize and burn.

Nam pla: – See FISH SAUCE.

Nutmeg: must be used sparingly and should always be grated from a whole nutmeg for it loses its flavour and develops a soapy, thin flavour when ground and left. It is extraordinarily flexible, equally at home in sweet and savoury dishes. There are very few cheese dishes, for instance, that do not benefit from the addition of nutmeg (although perhaps those which include tomato, like pizza, are better without it). But fondues, soufflés, sauces, rarebits, cheesecakes, salads and sandwiches all benefit. Nutmeg is a prime ingredient of mixed spice and thus important to cake and biscuit cooking, particularly in association with apples. Hot green vegetables are good with nutmeg, specially green beans and spinach. It is very good with many meats and excellent in pâté; fine-textured sausages like frankfurters and

---

BAKED SPICED ROLLMOPS

This recipe will appeal to those who cannot abide the thought of eating uncooked fish. I particularly like it because it doesn't contain onion. Perhaps these aren't really rollmops at all?! Never mind. They are delicious hot or cold. You can start with fresh herrings or with salted ones which have been soaked overnight in cold water. You need to end up with a nice row of neat, boneless fillets of herring, perhaps twelve, to make the effort worthwhile.

Rub a little salt, pepper and mustard powder into the flesh of each fillet. Grate onto that some fresh nutmeg, then roll up each fillet and hold each together with half a toothpick. Arrange them in a dish which will just contain them and cover with a mixture of two-thirds wine vinegar and one-third water. Sprinkle on any roe you found inside the fish plus some bay leaves, some whole garlic cloves (a big one for every three fillets) and a generous scattering of whole coriander seeds. A couple of dried chilli peppers could be crumbled in for some tang.

Cover the dish with some foil and bake in the lowest heat of your oven for one hour. Turn off the oven and leave to cool, without lifting the foil. Once they are quite cold they are ready to eat but will keep in a cool place for three or four days if you turn them over every day. In a refrigerator they will last well over a week, turned daily.

As with most herring dishes, soured cream makes a perfect sauce, particularly if it includes some horseradish. On cold days, heat some gently in their liquid and serve with hot or cold potato salad.

bologna invariably include some.

You can buy nutmeg graters, but it's just as simple to run a kernel up and down the finer side of a grater or to scrape with a knife. Once upon a time the gentry used to carry their own nutmeg and a pocket-sized silver grater partly to flavour hot chocolate and partly for swank. Because they were so common they were little valued and few were preserved: now they are among the rarest small pieces of silver. I've seen only one in 20 years of looking, but I presume there are more.

The large evergreen nutmeg tree looks like the pear and is distinctly sexed; only the female produces the fruit, which looks like a small yellow plum. Beneath the flesh lies a hard case surrounded by a membrane, which dries and becomes mace; inside the case is the softer fragrant nutmeg.

Orange flower water: a standby of my kitchen, as it was in every British kitchen until well into this century. For some inexplicable reason (perhaps the increasing victory of mediocrity?) both this and rose water suddenly fell from favour after a reign that lasted from the days of the Crusaders, who first brought them to Europe.

Distilled from orange flowers, the liquid has a sort of brilliantine scent which can be off-putting. But once it is sprinkled over food this softens and becomes as fragrant as moonlit nights in orange groves (yes, it is romantic). The Arabs still use it lavishly on every conceivable type of meat dish, in breads, pastries, cakes – and you. In Morocco, for instance, it is frightfully good form for a host to have his guests sprinkled with orange flower water by servants after dinner. If it happens to you and you're also drinking good wine, I suggest you quickly clap one hand over your glass.

With peaches or strawberries orange flower water is extraordinarily wonderful. Even simply mixed into cream and used to top almost any dessert it will be a wow. It will be more difficult to convert you to sprinkling it over lamb stews, over chickens and over roast kid, but once you've tried it...

The variety we buy here in Britain is often called citrus flower water and comes from Greece where I suspect that lemon blossoms are also used, giving the brilliantine effect. In Egypt or Morocco there is a water that is softer and richer and I recommend travellers to get some, or ask friends to bring some back for you.

Orange flower water combined with almonds, pistachios, rose water and honey is what gives such flavour to the range of Arabic pastries now available in London. In eastern Mediterranean countries, it is diluted and served as 'white tea'. This is said to be a soporific, especially for young children.

Palm sugar/jaggery: a rich, dark, caramel-tasting and rather soggy sort of sugar made by boiling down the sap of a few very specific palms. It gives very special flavour wherever you might choose to use dark sugar or molasses. When mixed with coconut and a few spices, the way they do in Sri Lanka, it makes a sensational filling for pancakes. Keeps forever, but is best sealed and refrigerated, for it attracts moisture, and then will become a syrup and seep any and everywhere.

Paprika: there is more ignorance or confusion about this spice than any other. Although there are dozens of flavours of paprika, they all come from two basic plants which you would recognize as capsicums or red pepper. One is a native of the west-

ern hemisphere and one a native of the east, and their product equally can be simp-
lified into two categories, the hot and the sweet.

A recipe that includes paprika as an ingredient but that does not say whether it
should be hot or sweet is no recipe at all. In fact, in most countries where it is indigenous to the cooking there is usually not a choice as most houses actually mix the
two to get a taste to their own liking. The combination I like most is three parts of
sweet paprika to two parts of hot.

In Hungary or Spain you can buy both hot and sweet paprika but here, where
even some of the spice distributors seem not to know there are two types, you will
generally find that so-called Spanish paprika is only marginally sweeter than so-
called Hungarian paprika, which might be slightly hot. The difference in flavour
can be obtained several ways. Usually paprika is the dried and ground flesh of red
peppers, which avoids the bite of including the seeds. Hotness can be obtained by
the inclusion of a proportion of the seeds and sweetness is often added with sugar,
which is why the Spanish or sweet paprikas tend to caramelize easily.

If you wish to add a little heat to paprika at home, judiciously mix in some cayenne pepper, which is also sold as chilli powder (don't buy chili powder or compound
for this as they are different things).

Don't be alarmed at the amount of paprika called for in some recipes, you *do* use
a lot – 20-30ml/3-4tsp for 900-1200ml/1½-2 pints of liquid is nothing. I usually only
put in half the specified amount when starting to cook and add the rest ten minutes
before serving.

Paprika of both types is excellent with tomato-based sauces and in Morocco is
used in conjunction with cumin powder, an unexpected but excellent combination.

Just to show how easy it is to be wrong about the cuisine of other countries, here
is an official Hungarian definition of the basic types of food flavoured with paprikas.
Note that the beef goulash in a rich tomato sauce, flavoured with soured cream,
that we all know and love doesn't exist. What's more, paprika only became popular
in Hungary a century ago.

Goulash or Gulyás: more a soup than a stew, made with onion and chunks of potato as well as small pieces of pasta (*Note* – no sour cream).

Pörkölt: a stew with masses of finely chopped onions, braised rather than boiled,
and with a thick sauce.

Tokány: less onions and little paprika, finished with mushrooms and soured cream.

Paprikas: all the dishes made with paprika and finished with soured cream or
sweet cream. Always made with white meats – fish, fowl, veal and lamb (other red
meats and fatty birds like duck and goose are never used for these dishes).

Parsley: The only things you may not already know about parsley are:

■ The best flavour is in the stalk so use that for flavouring stocks, soups and so on.

■ Chewing parsley neutralizes the odour of onion or garlic on the breath.

■ Don't use dried parsley; it nearly always has a hay-like quality that is the antith-
esis of its appeal when fresh.

■ Flat-leafed parsley, also known as French parsley or petroushka, tastes the same as curly parsley; but green coriander leaf looks similar, so beware as both are more readily available than previously.

Peppercorns: possibly the most important spice in the world, certainly the most widespread in use. Native to India and the Far East, they were the basis of the earliest trade between East and West, and at one time all manner of public debts, dowries and rents could be paid in them – hence the origin of the peppercorn rent.

All colours of peppercorns, black, white, and green, come from the same climbing vine, and the variations are due to the manner and timing of harvesting.

BLACK PEPPERCORNS: aromatic, sharp tasting, and beloved of food writers who demand freshly ground black pepper with everything. These are the whole peppercorns picked when slightly under-ripe and dried and sold in their entirety. Black pepper is indeed very good but it is dangerous in the hands of those frightful people who *will* screw it all over everything before so much as even asking if the food in front of them is seasoned. When used in cooking it is better not to add it too early for it tends to go rather bitter; whole or coarsely ground pepper put into a casserole about five minutes before serving is *much* better than the same added at the start of cooking. Try it and see. Of all the uses for black peppercorns, I like them ground onto thick slices of slightly chilled red Moroccan or beefsteak tomatoes. Ground black pepper is also very good on strawberries; it takes some nerve to try this one but I do recommend it.

Brazilian: this is both hot with piperine, the flavoursome oil found in pepper, and aromatic. A good, robust, all-purpose pepper.

Indian: a hot pepper with rather less aroma and character. Thus useful in cooking for heat but not satisfying to use fresh on food.

Sarawak: the mildest, sweetest and most fragrant and by far the most rewarding to use freshly ground on vegetables and salads, and for tossing into sauces just before serving, which really dramatizes the flavour.

WHITE PEPPERCORNS: these are the whole peppercorns left to ripen fully on the vine and then soaked to remove the outer husk. The creamy corns underneath are hotter than black pepper but do not have its extra perfume and full flavour. The main use for white peppercorns is in fine stocks (but black ones taste better I think) and for flavouring sauces that would look nasty with black pepper pieces floating about. Thus you would use white peppercorns in béchamel sauce, in scrambled eggs, cream soups, quiche mixtures and so on (you can always put some black pepper on afterwards). A combination of white and black peppercorns is rather interesting to have in a peppermill, and sometimes I add coriander seeds to this mixture. In France small allspice berries are often added to white and black pepper, and that is very good indeed.

For some reason white pepper has always been more popular than black on the English table and it's only since long frocks, sandals and scrubbed pine have come back from continental holidays that the latter has become popular. I can only imagine that we've preferred the simpler, hotter flavour because it was less perfumed and foreign tasting.

GREEN PEPPERCORNS: these have made a strong impact on the fine food market over the last ten years. Mainly from Madagascar, they are exactly what they say they are, underripe peppercorns, and really most delicious. Being quite soft they crush into butters or marinades; the colour is useful and the flavour has heat and a truly wonderful aroma that is quite unique. Be very careful only to buy green peppercorns which are packed in brine; those packed in vinegar lack elegance and usefulness.

The brine from green peppercorns is actually a useful flavouring agent itself, just right for adding a dash to a stock or sauce, particularly for fish. To keep green peppercorns once you have used some, turn the remainder out of the tin into a screwtop jar and just cover them with extra medium strength brine solution. They will last for months in the refrigerator and that brine will soon take on their flavour. It may go black, but the peppercorns will be fine once rinsed; make more brine and recover them. It is simpler to use vodka, of course.

Steak au Poivre made with green rather than black peppercorns is delightful: I'm tempted to think this is the proper way to do this overdone and often palate-searing dish. Green peppercorns go very well with fatty meats and thus complement well a duck or goose.

Dried green peppercorns need to be ground or crushed and don't have the subtle overtones or flavour of the tinned ones.

RED OR PINK PEPPERCORNS: let the colour warn you – these can be dangerous. Pink peppercorns, which quickly became the *ne plus ultra* of nouvelle cuisine in the United States, never caught on in the United Kingdom, and just as well. Still, when I tried them, I found the flavour perfectly wonderful, something truly new, and my excited broadcast had hundreds of people scouring the shops in vain. Although suspicious of why I could not determine their exact provenance I decided to use them in a tight-security dinner for five very highly placed politicians. Just two days later I discovered the ghastly truth: pink peppercorns are not peppercorns at all but the processed berries of a pesky plant known as Florida Holly, a relation of poison ivy. They can cause nausea, giddiness and fainting, and can stimulate the eruption of excruciatingly large and painful haemorrhoids. It will be many years before I dare ask for, or tell, the secrets – political, medical and physical – of that dinner party. Why, I may have wiped out a whole generation of our future leaders, so to speak.

Pickling spice: this mixture of spices, with a few herbs like bay thrown in, has more uses than for pickling onions. I use it to flavour vinegar for my red cabbage, use it to flavour wine or cider when sousing mackerel, sprats or sardines. There is no agreed recipe for pickling spice, but a quality blend would have mustard seed as its main component and fragrance and interest can be added with most of the following: coriander seeds, peppercorns, ginger root, allspice, dill seed, chillies, fenugreek, whole cloves, mace and cut bay leaves.

Sousing is a good way to do fish, especially the sardine; long slow cooking lets the vinegar dissolve the bones which in turn act with the liquid to form a jelly.

Poppy seeds: you'll have to take my word for it, unless you are quite mad, and have

---

SPICED CHEESE

450g/1lb soft cheese   salt
50g/2oz butter, softened   brandy
2 dstsp mixed whole pickling spices   2 mace blades
vine leaves

Salt the soft cheese then work in the softened butter. Wrap in sterilized muslin and shape into a disc about 2.5cm/1in thick. Turn daily for a week until the surface is dry. You can unwrap it for the last few days.

Brush the surface with brandy and grind the mixed pickling spices together with the mace. Press all over the cheese, wrap in vine leaves and tie securely. Then wrap in waxed paper. Leave in a cool, airy place for two weeks, turning daily. Once softening, it may be transferred to the refrigerator. If you leave off the waxed paper you will get a much drier cheese.

---

unlimited time: there are 900,000 tiny blue-black poppy seeds to the pound. The mild, nutty flavour is very rich when mixed with such other ingredients as egg, almonds and sugar as a filling for middle European or Russian cakes and breads. I find the seeds often have a strange, bitter taste that stays on the tongue for ages, but am told this never happens if you first roast poppy seeds by baking them in a moderate oven for five to eight minutes until a light golden brown. Roasted poppy seeds are quite nice when incorporated in salad dressings or in dips. They can be added to rice or included in cream sauces for noodles or other pastas.

Commonly they are sprinkled, unroasted, over unbaked bread, bread rolls and savoury biscuits, in which case they are usually first mixed with salt or sprinkled with strong brine to add extra flavour. There is a white poppy seed which is used in Indian cooking.

Originally from Asia, poppy seeds, *Papaver rhoeas* are now widely grown in Europe, especially Holland. Those who are weak of will should not worry about possible addiction; opium and morphine come from the different *Papaver somniterum*.

Quatre épices: a great standby of the French and available commercially there. I'm told that it is made up from equal amounts of ground white pepper, cloves, nutmeg and ginger. But, like our sweet mixed spice, there is room for considerable variation of proportion, usually to do with the amount of cloves. It is used on sweet vegetables like corn and squash, with bacon, beans, dried peas and mushrooms. It can also be used over grilling meat and should then be mixed with a little salt as this will help spread the flavours more evenly.

Quatre épices, like all ground spices, should only be made in small quantities, kept dry, cool and airtight and used quickly.

Ras el Hanout: you won't come across this spice unless you go to Morocco, one of my favourite countries from a food standpoint, but you could make it. Ras el hanout is the ultimate mixed spice, a culinary guide to the countries conquered, visited or lusted after by the Muslim nomad, soldier and proselytizer. Its name means 'top of the shop' for that is where the spice merchant will keep it, far from robbing hands. Many of the contents are strange to us and its claim to be aphrodisiac as well as fragrant is based on the inclusion of something I thought was apocryphal – the Spanish fly or cantharides. You can buy ras el hanout ready ground but then you might not get the best quality and certainly won't have the best fun. This comes only with watching an expert put together the unground ingredients, weighing this, counting that, wrapping each one separately. A good ras el hanout customer is honoured and treasured.

There are five different peppers included – Guinea pepper, long Indian pepper (*Piper longum*), black pepper, grey cubeb pepper and monks' pepper, which comes from Morocco. Fragrance is given by cardamom, mace, galingale, nutmeg, allspice, cinnamon, turmeric, cloves, ginger, lavender flowers, rose buds, cassia and fennel. Orris root, cyparacee, ash berries, bella donna and quite a few untranslatable things will also be included. Then to top it all, the metallic glint of whole cantharides, counted more carefully and tellingly. When you get them home, grind and mix them; the perfume is quite intoxicating, and although meant to be used in winter dishes to heat the blood, hands, feet and other extremities, I find it does very nicely all through the year. So far the libidinous effects of Spanish fly, although carefully monitored, have remained undetectable. Either that, or my guests aren't letting on.

Rosemary: the thin spiky leaves of an attractive bush, rosemary has a camphorous, piney, smoky flavour, particularly liked in Italy but often hated elsewhere. Lots of food writers don't like rosemary and some cooks worry about the spikes 'getting' everywhere; I can't understand either point of view. The warm, smoky flavour of rosemary is quite unlike anything else and when used discreetly makes an incomparable contribution to good eating. If you are worried about the spiky leaves, then grind them. Or, like me, stick a whole branch of the fresh stuff into a sauce for 10-15 minutes; this is more than enough for its perfume to be transferred, then I yank the branch out leaving only a few potentially offensive bits.

Rosemary twigs are also extraordinarily good for perfuming barbecued or spit-roasted food; this was dramatically demonstrated to me when I arrived in a thunderstorm at a converted medieval nunnery in the South of France to ask if I could stay for an unspecified time with two people I had never met. One was a morose Swedish writer, the other a Frenchman, and both were caretaking the magnificent house during the winter. They were as pleased to see me as I them, for life was lonely. They decided on an indoor barbecue and that night I dined on spit-roasted breast of lamb cooked over masses of rosemary. Conversation was tricky as none of us spoke each other's language to a noticeable extent, and there was the complication of a large and incontinent pet ape of some sort who shared the banquet.

The most common uses for rosemary are with all cuts of lamb, with chicken, shrimp and prawns, in bread, in sauces that contain tomato, and in conjunction with lemon or orange to finish simple butter or grilling sauces. Some dried rosemary or a small sprig of fresh is excellent when brewed with Indian tea – very good for relieving tension headaches.

Rosemary is for remembrance and where it grows it is said to show that the woman rules the house. I think it should be grown far more, especially as hedges, when it makes something dense, aromatic and useful. Many holy places in the Mos-

LAMB STEAKS WITH ORANGE AND ROSEMARY

A very simple way to serve lamb steaks. If you leave them marinating longer than four hours before cooking, keep them covered in the refrigerator, but bring them to room temperature before cooking.

Serves 2

2 lamb steaks, boned	juice of 1 lemon
wholegrain mustard	5 tbsp white wine
1tbsp fresh rosemary or 1 tsp dried rosemary	
juice of 2 oranges	
1 small garlic clove, crushed	
salt and pepper	
watercress or fresh rosemary to garnish	
1 tbsp butter	

Spread the steaks on both sides with the mustard and put them side by side in a shallow dish. Sprinkle with the rosemary and add the citrus juices, garlic, white wine and seasoning. Leave the meat to marinate at room temperature for 4 hours.

Thirty minutes before you plan to cook the steaks, drain off the marinade into a small saucepan. Boil over medium heat until it is reduced and syrupy. Heat a non-stick frying pan and cook the steaks quickly over high heat for 3-4 minutes on each side, depending on how pink you like your meat. Keep them warm, covered on a plate.

Strain the reduced sauce into a clean pan and over low heat beat in the butter a little at a time to give some shine and thicken it a little. Make a puddle of sauce on two heated plates, arrange the steaks on top and garnish with one or two watercress leaves, or a tiny sprig of fresh rosemary.

lem world are surrounded by such protection for there rosemary is credited with powers of purification.

Rose buds and rose petals: dried or fresh, these are the bases of all manner of wonderful things, but not, it seems, in Britain. You need to go to India or to Turkey to get the best jams and preserves made from red rose petals and I think those of the latter by far the best. Roses make an extraordinarily good wine, and petals can be used to perfume sugar in the same way as vanilla beans or geranium leaves. Crushed rose petals ground into a fine powder are a delightful flavouring for fresh fruit and are incorporated in a lot of Arabic mixed spices. Crystallized rose petals make nice cake decorations or garnishes for puddings and soft fruit dishes.

Whenever using roses for culinary purposes it is advisable to cut off the white part of the petal. Red damask roses are traditionally best but there are now so many strong-scented varieties that rules are pointless. If it smells, eat it. A few rose petals in a salad look and taste good, rose jam is great with a traditional cream tea, and pink petals are wonderful on summer pudding.

Another way to enjoy the flavour of roses is with Rose Pouchong tea *qv*, and in authentic Turkish Delight.

Rose water/eau de rose: is *really* the way to use the glory of the rose. Distilled from red roses, it was hardly possible to cook throughout the Moslem world and Europe right up to the death of Queen Victoria unless you used this. Now almost forgotten here, it is still vital in the Moslem world, sprinkled into everything and over you.

Do, I beg you, go out and get a bottle and start experimenting. It is wonderful with milk-poached pudding grains, especially barley and rice, goes surprisingly well with poultry, and is really best with things chocolate and fruity. If you bake a chocolate cake with several rose geranium leaves underneath it, mix a chocolate icing with plenty of rose water for something out of this world. Or flavour a particularly rich chocolate soufflé with rose water, serve it while very runny in the middle, after only 20 minutes baking, and with a little hot soft fruit purée (loganberries would be very good). Soak dried fruit overnight and then serve them with chopped pistachios and lavish sprinklings of rose water and orange flower water – people will think you have done something expensive and difficult.

Rose water goes very well with cream cheese or cream and, as with orange flower water, you can make much of ordinary puddings by using it. I once made a banquet pudding out of profiteroles stuffed alternatively with orange and rose flavoured creams, and held together with the lightest caramel. Pouring cream was chilled and also flavoured with rose water and the whole concoction was finished with a scattering of rose petals. The scents were bewitching and the flavours tantalizingly difficult to identify. Rose water-flavoured cream or syrup goes especially well with raspberries and fresh peaches.

Florentine curd pudding is an old English curd cheese, egg and spinach custard tart with the addition of currants, spice and rose water and a 'talking point' end to a meal – well, when did _you_ ever have rose-flavoured spinach for pudding?

Rose-flavoured vinegar is excellent too.

After all that I suppose I should tell you what the stuff tastes like. It tastes like it smells, very rosey but surprisingly spicy and slightly smoky. There is no rule about how much you use, sometimes I like to use very little and other times find I can get away with making the flavour very strong indeed – for instance to flavour a syrup for sliced oranges or with raspberries. I repeat, get out and buy some, and give yourself the pleasure not only of recreating the food of our forefathers, but also of inventing new ideas with the broader range of ingredients at our disposal today. Make sure it is triple-distilled or it will be useless.

Rue: this bitter aromatic herb is not very fashionable in the kitchen nowadays, but if you come across some it should be used with great moderation with the lighter-flavoured red meats and poultry and perhaps with potatoes. The only time I've actually enjoyed it is in combination with _grappa_, the fiery Italian equivalent of _marc_, which in turn is a fairly rough spirit distilled from what's left after wine has been pressed – skins, pips and pulp. The Sardinians put a long stem of rue into each bottle of their grappa, for rue is thought to be a digestive aid. _Grappa con rutta_ turns a pale green and has a most appealing extra perfume and flavour.

A man, whom I was assured was a _bandito_, walked into a bar in Alghero and ordered a _dynamite_ (with Italian vowels of course) and was poured a huge glass of grappa con rutta. After I had expressed a liking for this drink, the same man agreed to send me some made illicitly by him in the mountains. Its arrival was accompanied by checking of windows and doors, two cars full of very big men, and a number of hissed sentences which I presumed promised death either through drinking too much at one time, or revealing my source. Apparently the punishments for bootlegging are as severe as for kidnapping, which was their other interest in life. You have to be careful to whom you talk in Sardinia.

Safflower: this flower can give the same colour as saffron and thus is substituted for it but it doesn't have the same subtle flavour. It was used by native Americans to colour breads and porridges, by Japanese courtiers to dye their lips, and is used in Mexican food. It is also known as American, Mexican or fake saffron. Safflower is more important as a source of a low cholesterol cooking oil.

Saffron: delicate and very expensive, for saffron comes only from the stigma of a certain crocus. They can only be picked by hand and it can take almost a quarter of a million stigmas to make just one pound. It has been used since time immemorial and the Phonecians used it to colour the crescent-shaped cakes that were eaten for Ashtoreth, goddess of fertility. Her rites and name have become our Easter and our hot cross buns are directly traceable to these earlier Phoenician offerings. Saffron goes particularly well in doughs, and saffron cakes and scones and breads are specialities as far apart as Sweden and the West Country, Russia and Spain, Italy and Armenia. With fish it is superlative; both bouillabaisse and the Spanish rice dish paella are impossible without it. The Milanese use it a lot with rice in their lovely moist risottos.

Saffron is available powdered and in stigmas. Some say the powder is often made of ingredients other than true saffron. If so I don't think it matters for I've not been able to tell the difference and I think the desecration to be imagined. When you use stigmas, dry them gently in a warm oven, crumble them and then pour over a little boiling water to draw the colour and flavour. It doesn't look good to include the whole threads in a dish.

Next time you make a white wine and cream sauce for seafood stir in one or two sachets of powdered saffron. The warm, slightly sweet, slightly bitter flavour and the wonderful colour transforms something quite ordinary into a treat. You need so little to make such a large difference I really can't think of it as expensive. If you think your sauces wouldn't stand saffron – for instance because it would change the colour incorrectly – there are other ways to use it. I often mix it into an egg yolk and use this as the glaze on pastry coffins or vol au vents in which seafood is going to be served. You get a glorious golden glaze and a tantalizing flavour. Saffron also gives an intriguing lift to rich tomato-based sauces – try it with tomato-casseroled lamb, perhaps also adding a mixture of hot and sweet paprikas.

Sage: the time-honoured flavouring in the true blue British sausage, but you'd be hard pushed to find many that do actually contain it. Pork and veal together with goose, tomatoes and cheese, are the best foods with which to combine sage. Fresh sage tucked under the crackling of pork works very well and the classic veal dish is *saltimbocca*, in which thin slices of veal are wrapped around ham and fresh sage.

Sage and onion stuffing is traditional for poultry but I can't think why the commercial variety is so popular – possibly because so few people have tasted the fresh leaves? Most dried sage tastes distinctly like a musty damp room smells, and that is not what the fresh herb does. The worst perfidy thrust upon sage is the use of its name in association with Sage Derby cheese, that stuff with the green marbling. They use sage oil and colouring and you can read what herb oils are all about in the introduction to this section. I can't think why people bother to eat it. Especially now there is a Sage Lancashire and a Sage Cheshire on the market in which rolled sage leaves are incorporated. No colour, no oil and perfectly delicious; a good way to convert someone to the pleasures of sage, as I had to be.

The affinity of sage with tomatoes is why some people suggest you crumble a sage-flavoured cheese over a tomato salad.

Sarsparilla: the root of a plant indigenous to tropical America from Mexico to Peru, sarsparilla is used to flavour a drink with so-called tonic properties. Certainly sarsparilla tastes as though it should be good for you, rather like combined winter green and chewing gum if early teenage memories serve me well. Then it enjoyed a brief vogue as a soft drink flavouring, but the emergence of Elvis Presley shortly afterwards quickly returned us to Coca-Cola, which is flavoured by berries from the cola plant and once also included extracts from the coca plant, source of cocaine; *its* instant success was hardly surprising. If you want to try sarsparilla, look in Jamaican communities; the best root comes from there and they still drink it as though it were life's blood.

Salt: the simple name for sodium chloride, an essential part of our body chemistry but, like so many things we take for granted, its role can be misunderstood, and it may be used to our detriment.

The problem is that salt can be addictive, or at least the flavour can be, and too high an intake is thought to be dangerous to the heart. To begin with, do you know how it works? Salt does not alter or improve the flavour of food one iota, other than to add its own, or in the case of salt-preserving to hinder or help the development of flavour-giving bacteria.

What salt does is to stimulate the taste buds of the tongue to discern what flavour is inherently present, and the more salt present, the greater the stimulus and the greater the flavour reward. But – the more salt you use, the more you taste the flavour of the salt rather than of the food.

It does not necessarily follow that someone who uses more salt than you has a saltier flavour in his mouth; his tastebuds might need a higher degree of stimulation to experience the *same* taste as you. But the risk of a high salt intake is that eventually the salt taste becomes paramount, and that is bad for you and boring for the cook. Like sugar, salt is present naturally in a great deal of the food we eat, especially that which is processed, and it is worth taking a really hard look at the amount added and the amount really needed. Are you really tasting the food? or are you tasting salt?

There is a difference between the salts you can buy, a matter of how they are made, whence they come, and with what traces of other chemicals each is mixed.

Rock salt: this is mined in ready-formed crystals, and is the deposit of a long-gone dried sea or other waterway. It is invariably mixed with a great number of other tastes, some of which you may not like, so it is an idea to taste rock salt before you buy. It can be even better than the more common...

Sea salt: evaporated from the sea and thus bound to include a number of other trace elements and chemicals. Yet it is perfectly safe and free from anything nasty.

The broad spectrum of ingredients which complement the sodium chloride is what recommends sea salt to the health experts. I simply prefer its flavour. It is not that simple, of course. Slaves to salt go to extraordinary lengths to find *fleur de sel*, the first and finest flakes which have been whipped by the wind onto the shore or the edge of the salt pans. They say that different weather conditions, tides and temperatures will all produce different flavours.

Bay salt: is a cruder form of sea salt, often rather greyish as it is less likely to have been purified in any way. It will be flavourful and is commonly the salt used for preserving and brining.

Common or kitchen salt: this is made by extracting salt from the earth by dissolving it in water, pumping this brine out, and evaporating the liquid.

There are various forms, and this is what used to be made into the solid blocks. Vacuum salt, that is salt that has been extracted and purified in a vacuum, is 99.9 per cent sodium chloride, but this is usually then turned into...

Table salt: the purity is interfered with by the addition of starch or other chemicals to promote free running. The combination of such essential purity and additives makes its flavour pretty boring and perhaps this is why so much is used.

Iodised salt: salt to which iodine salts have been added as a necessary dietary supplement in some countries as defence against goitre. It has a definite taste of its own, but is vital where needed.

Flavoured salts: sometimes called seasoned salts, these are traditional for flavouring meats but were usually made at home with preferred mixtures of cloves and nutmeg, peppers, and some of the sharper, sweeter herbs. Garlic salt is increasingly popular but beware when you buy it – check the label and you might find it also contains monosodium glutamate.

Celery salt is beloved of vegetarians and can be very delicious if used with infinite restraint. Quite simply, it is salt pounded with celery seed. Hickory flavoured salt is a favourite in the United States. You can try pounding any fresh or dried herb with salt, and they keep for a long time.

If you wish to dry-salt fish or meat, salt with large crystals gives better results.

Although a fine preservative, salt behaves rather strangely when deep-frozen. Whereas salted butter keeps far longer than unsalted butter in a refrigerator, salted butter should only be frozen for a month. Unsalted butter can be stored three times as long. The salt content is why dishes containing bacon cannot be frozen for very long periods. Strange, isn't it.

Sansho: the most common Japanese condiment, used rather the way we use pepper (they don't use it) and related to the Szechuan peppercorn. It is only available ground, and only used by the Japanese.

Sassafras: one of the very first exports from the United States to Europe, the root and bark of the aromatic sassafras tree can be made into a warming drink and it is the root from which American root beer is made.

In Creole cooking the leaves are ground and made into *filé*, a strange green powder that has a thickening effect on hot liquids, but which must be used with great care or the results can be most unpleasant and stringy. It is the most important ingredient in some gumbos, the important rice dish of Creole food. If you don't have *filé*, you can replace it with a little cornflour, which will do the thickening but won't add the strange flavour which I would describe as a cross between eucalyptus and marijuana.

Sassafras isn't very expensive and it is worth asking someone travelling to America to bring you back some.

Savory: often confused with thyme. Summer savory has a slightly more peppery taste and the leaves are longer. It is particularly good with beans and often grown between rows of broad beans for it repels the black fly which normally attacks the latter. What grows together gets eaten together and the French are very fond of savory with broad beans; I think you should try it too, otherwise use it where you would thyme. It is generally used much more on the continent than in England and there is a good but expensive *mi-chèvre* (half-cow, half-goat milk cheese) coated with savory, which is called *sarriette* in French. Winter savory is inferior.

Sesame: extremely versatile and used in the Near, Middle and Far East for aeons, the sesame seed has only recently become popular in the west, mainly due to increased travel and the growing influence of Eastern diets.

Raw, the seeds have high nutritional value and a sweet nutty flavour and can be made into a milk, but are generally used as a sprinkler over breads, in casseroles, sauces, pie crusts, puddings, and so on. When browned lightly in butter they are excellent on almost every type of vegetable or on plain noodles. Sesame seed bars make terrific snacks as long as you have good teeth.

We are probably more familiar with sesame in halvah and as tahini. Halvah is a Turkish/Greek/Israeli confection made of ground sesame seeds, honey and flavouring. It can have all manner of other ingredients including dry milk powder and dried fruit. The Poles make excellent halvah, for some reason, and their chocolate-flavoured one is particularly good.

Tahini is sesame butter, ground sesame seed with nothing added or subtracted; it can be used just as you would peanut butter and is also used to flavour salad dressings when thinned with a little oil and lime or lemon juice, or to flavour dishes like hummous, a paste of chickpeas. Vegans can use it as a substitute for butter in pastries and bread, for it makes one of the best oils of all for cooking. Marco Polo was one of the first to extol its virtues in the West, but he probably didn't know it was so good for those on low-cholesterol diets.

If you wish to cut down your salt intake, *gomasio* may be the answer. It is Japanese, but not so strange it can't appear on your more ordinary table. Toast sesame seeds, mix with salt in the proportion of five-to-one, crush or grind and keep in an airtight container. I like it sprinkled over food rather than in it.

If you are offered a tahini that is rather darker than you expect, this may be because it has a lower oil content; some Greek storekeepers say that a proportion of commercial tahini is made from what's left over after the seeds have been lightly toasted and crushed to extract the oil. I can only surmise there are several ways to make it, and you buy and use the type you like best.

Shao-hsing wine: a delicious yellow wine made from rice which is not unlike sherry and is always drunk slightly warm, even when of the highest possible quality. It is used extensively in cookery, sometimes first to intoxicate prawns – that really is getting the flavour through the flesh. A specially good use is as a final sprinkle on those Chinese greens which are always slightly bitter, but knowledgeable Western chefs will sprinkle a sweet wine into many fish sauces and dishes – dry white wine is actually the last thing fish needs.

Shichimi: a very interesting Japanese mixed spice with a fascinating flavour if it is not made too hot. It should include sesame and poppy seeds, tangerine peel and a number of untranslatables, plus chilli. Noodle dishes are commonly served with this on the side but it is also used in stews.

Shrimp, dried: the great divider, and one of the principal flavouring agents of south east Asia, although used elsewhere in the East. Like all dried fish they have a penetrating cheesy smell which nauseates many, although in mitigation they never taste as bad as they smell. Generally used as a base flavouring, they must be soaked in water for 30 minutes before using, but may also be soaked overnight; sherry or rice wine will make them more innocuous. Dried shrimps are often pounded and are commonly the basis for the flavouring pastes of Thai cookery.

Sorrel and wild sorrel: if you were a horse and called a sorrel, you would be a bright reddish chestnut colour. If you were a plant you would be green, and bear acidic leaves which can be steps to rare gastronomic heights. You would also be as rare as hen's teeth in stores throughout the British Isles even though you grow wild. Sorrel looks a little like dock or anaemic spinach; the cultivated leaves grow quite big but the wild is sometimes not much bigger than a man's thumb. Some shops sell it fresh but I earnestly recommend you grow it; in California it is sold in supermarkets. Although used raw in salads for contrast, it is mainly a superb flavouring for sauces; I personally don't like the sorrel soup which is every other book's basic sorrel recipe.

To make a sorrel sauce you first melt the de-stalked leaves over gentle heat in lots of butter. They shrink prodigiously, a couple of handfuls of small leaves end up as a puddle on the bottom of a saucepan. Try not to brown them. Now sprinkle over a little flour and some more butter and cook gently for a few minutes, which gives you a strongly flavoured roux. Add liquid that suits your dish to make the sauce. You can use white wine or milk or cream, but be careful about curdling. Stock is good, especially vegetable water, for although the sorrel is strong it can end up just being acidic and having its flavour overshadowed by strong sauce ingredients.

Now, how do you use your sorrel sauce? Well, it's outstanding with fish, especially eel, salmon and sea trout. It is excellent with sweetbreads, giving a wonderful contrast of sweet and sour and is very good with eggs and with young green vegetables. I like to make this sauce and then put it into the choke-free centre of baby or teenage artichokes, so you dip into it with the cooked leaves. Provided it is not too strong, sorrel sauce also makes a nice change on asparagus spears, too.

One point: it isn't worth simply chopping sorrel and putting that into a white sauce or hollandaise; unless it is reduced the flavour isn't strong enough.

Szechuan peppercorns/fagara/brown peppercorns: nothing to do with peppercorns, but the berries of a Prickly Ash. They have a pungent, slightly anise smell and are always bought whole and then roasted and crushed before use – only the petal-like husks have flavour. They have a unique effect in the mouth, for they numb rather than burn.

To roast them toss lightly in a dry non-stick pan until smoking slightly; when cool crush roughly. Some will strain out the kernels but this is a little fanatic. A common seasoning used as a dip for deep-fried food or anything else which needs a little zip of flavour is mixed roasted Szechuan peppercorns and salt: mix one teaspoon of the peppercorns with three tablespoons coarse salt and dry-fry over low heat until the peppercorns are lightly smoking and the salt is lightly browned. Cool, crush and keep in an airtight bottle.

Less common but terribly useful for adding imprecise fascination to bland dishes, is to steep roasted Szechuan peppercorns in vegetable oil; a few teaspoons to a half-pint is about right and the process is considerably speeded if you add the oil to the pan after the peppercorns are roasted and apply gentle heat for another 10-15 minutes; it's either a frying medium or a discreet condiment.

Tamarind: essentially an Asian and Indian way to add the sourness for which we would use lemon juice. Dried tamarrind should be soaked in very hot water and then strained. A walnut-sized lump in 300ml/½pt for 20 minutes is about right. Excellent in all curries, otherwise throw in a halved or quartered whole lemon.

Tangerine peel: a common but sometimes very expensive Chinese flavouring ingredient; its expense means it is often never used in enough quantity to taste, but as a menu come-on. Thus although you can buy it, you may as well make your own, by drying in a slow oven or by following the instructions which came with your microwave. The slightly bitter pith is usually scraped off. The Chinese product is likely to made from an orange or what we would call a mandarin, but the sharper Sevilles give a better ultimate result than, say, sweet navel types. It will slowly darken to black, but this is an advantage, as provided it is kept dry, it will improve in flavour for several years, at least.

The dried and aged peel is commonly used as a flavouring for sauces but discarded before serving; if it has been chopped finely it may also be used as a final flavouring for a stir-fry, especially of vegetables. If you plan this, soften the chopped peel in a rice wine or sherry first. Can also be used to flavour sugar.

Tarragon: a necessity in every herb garden and kitchen, basic to French cooking, and to anyone who cares about fine flavours. It is warm and aromatic but must have both bite and an air of liquorice. There are two sorts, the Russian and the French, but I recommend you only use the French for the Russian will add a flavour not much more useful than fresh lawn clippings.

Tarragon's great affinity is with all dairy products and with eggs, hence its appearance in classic sauces, and I always try to get some into savoury soufflés. It is extraordinarily good with melted butter over virtually every vegetable but does have a special relationship with courgettes. This also applies to chicken, and chicken roasted only with butter, a little lemon and fresh or dried tarragon is really hard to beat. When you cook chicken, courgettes and tarragon in the same dish the result is... well, try it for yourself. A lesser known affinity is that of tarragon with lamb, another recommendation; so is lobster baked with tarragon.

Tarragon is essential to sweet, mixed herbs and wonderful in a herb mayonnaise for serving with cold fish, especially salmon, when the bite of the tarragon is a good foil for the smoothness of the flesh. Tarragon vinegar is one of the finest of all the flavoured vinegars and adds instant elegance to almost anything. Vinegar is often overlooked as a finisher for casseroles and sauces, but shouldn't be.

Tarragon is better for being grown with lots of sun, but its flavour is very changeable, being affected by the slightest variation in soil and climate. No two plants taste the same so always test the strength on your tongue when using tarragon.

Thyme, lemon thyme and wild thyme: a favourite herb of such long standing that the ancient Greeks used it as an incense to purify their temples and Greek thyme honey from Mount Hymettus is regarded as the best in the world. Certainly thyme is one of the all-time favourites of bees.

There are many different types of thyme, most of which are useful in cooking. Basic and wild thyme are related in flavour, with the wilder being the headier. Lemon thyme is more citrus than thyme but has a lovely flavour and gives a clue to one of thyme's greatest affinities – lemon. Other rarer thymes have the flavour of caraway and should only be used with great discretion.

Thyme loves tomatoes and tomato sauces, goes well in savoury sausages and stuffings and indeed is fairly basic in my opinion. Dried thyme imported from the Mediterranean may be very much stronger than the fresh but weaker stuff from a damp English garden. You have to be careful. White flesh, rabbit, veal and poultry go well with the slightly sweet-sharp flavour and it is good with garlic. Nearly all vegetables like thyme but carrots are its best and prettiest companion.

Turmeric: the brilliant yellow colour and pungent flavour of turmeric is basic to piccalilli and curry but well worth exploring in its own right. Related to the ginger, it is the plant's ginger-like root that is used. The flavour is mellow, perhaps peppery; used as a saffron substitute there is no similarity in flavour and the practice can have unfortunate culinary consequences. Use it on rice dishes, in stews, fish dishes and in kedgeree; mixed with a little butter and garlic it can make an interesting enlivener of vegetables.

Vanilla bean: This is the fruit of a climbing orchid native to Mexico but now grown throughout tropical areas. If stored in a closed (*not* airtight) jar, it improves with keeping. So widely used it is barely regarded as a flavour at all – how often do people refer to vanilla custard or ice cream as 'plain'? You shouldn't use the bean itself to eat, and I don't agree with some people who grind it to mix with sugar.

Its basic uses are to flavour milk or sugar syrups in fruit or pudding dishes; the classic ploy is to store the bean in a closed jar with caster sugar and to use the flavoured sugar (also good in coffee or tea drinks). If you use a piece to make a syrup, don't throw it away, rinse and dry it and it will be good for a dozen or more times.

Don't worry if you see what look like long fine white hairs on a vanilla pod, this is a sign of high quality.

There are many substitutes for vanilla so when you buy liquid vanilla flavouring, ensure it says vanilla essence or pure vanilla essence.

Vanillin is a white powder used to give vanilla flavour and although it has the same chemical formula of the ingredient that makes vanilla beans smell, it is only half the story. If it means anything to you it is $C_8H_8O_3$.

Wasabe: one of those Japanese ingredients particularly associated with their most sophisticated dining, but which does not stand up to close scrutiny. This is a very hot green form of horseradish, either grated fresh or dried and mixed with water to form a paste. Although aromatic and delicious it is very hot indeed, yet served almost exclusively with exceptionally delicate raw fish (sashimi) or sushi, both of which are considered best when almost flavourless. If sashimi is soaked in soy sauce and then dipped in wasabe it may as well be a slice of white bread for all else you will taste.

Wasabe seems the Japanese equivalent of serving onions and eggs with caviare, an ancient way to conceal all possible shortcomings of age and condition. In the modern world it is not needed with sashimi and sushi except in the most minimal amounts; but as an ingredient to combine with more rugged flavours it is well worth exploring.

It can't have been long after man first learned to cook food that he looked around for tasty accompaniments or methods to preserve fresh and cooked foods. With salt, with vinegar, with oil and with smoke he accomplished both and we still look to simple methods of salting and pickling when we want a savoury snack or condiment.

OLIVES

The silver-gnarled olive tree – its leaves a symbol of peace, its fruits of resurrection and renewal, its oil used at baptisms – thrives only on a narrow border of sea-lapped land. It can't grow at heights, won't grow very far inland, but where it is suited it is utterly reliable, which is why early civilization could trust it. Nothing short of dynamite can guarantee an olive tree's death. Snows, fire or brigandry merely destroy it above the ground. They live an average of 600 years, but many are reputed to be thousands of years old.

The olive is one of the foundations of western civilization. Together with wheat and wine it formed the triumvirate of produce for food and for trade in the Eastern Mediterranean which supported the first civilizations – Crete was cultivating them at least 5,000 years ago.

There are thousands of varieties of olives, with infinite variations of flavour and perfume. Rather like apples, some are harvested early in autumn, and some are not ready until the raw depths of winter. Dirk Bogarde's harrowing story of harvesting his Provençal olives in freezing winds rather changes one's view of olives as somehow being a fruit of indolent, sun-sodden pastorality.

Green and black olives are not necessarily different varieties. Some olives are better harvested early and used green, others must be fully ripe and black, and some super-useful trees produce an olive suited to being used as both. Less common are olives harvested half-ripe, usually called violets because of their colour and seen particularly on the North African coast. From these come three types of culinary olive, the green, the natural black and processed black.

The olive knocked or pulled green from the tree is generally inedible and must be relieved of its bitterness, if it is to be eaten rather than crushed for oil. The simplest way is to soak the fruits in brine, but there are few varieties inherently sweet enough for such simplicity. Most are first put into a soda (lye) solution, which whilst neutralizing the unpleasantness generates heat and thus also softens and slightly cooks the olives. After washing they are then put into brine and fermented for up to three months. Ripe olives, which may be anything from violet and purple to brownish but are rarely truly black, are sometimes sterilized but not otherwise processed before going directly into brine. The fermentation process is based on yeast action rather than the lactic fermentation of green olives; they are exposed to air to oxidize and darken the skins.

Processed black olives combine something of both the other processes. They do not need to be fully ripe and are alternately immersed in lye and then in water, during which time compressed air is bubbled through to oxidize them throughout. Once you know, you can recognise these, for they are shinier and blacker outside and much more uniformly dark inside.

Once cured, olives may then be stored in any combination of light brine, oil or vinegar. Generally only the very finest qualities, such as the wondrously fleshy Greek Kalamata, are stored in oil (pointed with superior wine vinegar), even though such a ploy would greatly improve the flavour of inferior types.

Each country usually adds another type of olive to its natural green, natural black, assisted black and its violet olives – the old and wrinkly olive. These are the raisins of the olive world, left on the tree over winter so that both cold wind and new season sun dessicate and concentrate their flavours.

Pitted and stuffed olives are a great favourite, if not to eat then for decorative purposes. The most popular are those stuffed with red peppers but there are others. I particularly like those stuffed with an almond and particularly dislike those stuffed with onion or anchovy. Orange and lemon peel are sometimes found in eviscerated olives and both are marvellous but more likely to be encountered at a *tapas* bar in Spain than in Ilkley. The stones that have been extracted, mainly by machine nowadays, are often used for low grade olive oil and the resultant pulp is an animal feed. Now, you didn't know that before did you?

Knowing your olives is a lifetime occupation. To that I have no simple solution other than that which is the secret of most really good eating. Choose what you like, and remember which ones you liked best.

SPAIN: although dozens of olives are used for making Spanish olive oil her soils have a special affinity with a few green eating olives. Her best known are the queen (known as the *gordal* in Seville and the *sevillano* in the rest of Spain) and the *manzanilla*, both from Andalucia. The queen is large, deep-green, fleshy. The small manzanilla is paler, finer textured and silky skinned, especially good for cooking. Incidentally, it is only a pitted manzanilla olive which properly belongs in a martini cocktail. Pimiento, anchovy or almond stuffed, or intact manzanillas, are, well, they are just not right…

FRANCE: the south of France grows a bewildering number of olives in both colours. And as well as plain black or green the markets of Nimes make a specialty of stuffed olives. The best black olives in brine are from Nyons and Carpentras; Mentons are especially big and luscious. But this is only whence, and local varieties are just as important to know. Amongst green ones, *la picholine* is deliciously savoury and generously fleshed even though small; *la lucques* is curved, pointed and parts easily from the stone; *la saloneque* is often broken and especially good in cooking where a reserved bitterness is welcomed. Round heart-shaped *nyons* (sometimes *tanches*) are the best French black olives, actually a rich plum-black. Although rarely seen outside Provence, the *cailletier* or *olives de Nice* are small but very perfumed, and the proper olive to use in Niçoise cooking.

There is a fascinating museum of olives in a chateau at Cagnes sur Mer and another, private one, at Ampus, open in the afternoons in July and August.

GREECE: the majority of olives are black and these include some extraordinary varieties sweet enough to eat direct from the trees; the island of Mitilini is reputed to have the best of these. In Greece it is especially easy to detect differences of flavour given not just by variety but by soil and climactic condition, however their rather violet-coloured *kalamata* olives are widely thought to be amongst the very best from any source. *Thrumpa* are considered amongst the very best of the wrinkly, over-wintered type of eating olive.

Flavouring: flavouring olives your own way is terribly simple. A few minutes in the markets of Fez or a stroll through the Thursday market against the ancient walls of Aigue-Mortes will give you dozens of ideas. Sliced lemon with dried oregano is basically good. Crushed cloves of garlic, crushed coriander seeds (particularly), bay leaves, peppercorns (black, white or green), thyme branches, parsley stalks, sliced peppers, and sliced dried chillies are what I usually use to start. Of course many of the things you would expect to find in olives go with them too, anchovies and crushed nuts particularly. Oils made by soaking dried tomatoes, dried mushrooms and the like give very superior results.

Cooking: if you fancy cooking with olives there are a few tricks. They should have been brined rather than oiled, must be blanched quickly in boiling water, and then stored in cold water for a few hours. They are generally rather better added towards the end of cooking, too. Or you could use prepared olive purées, one of the few really outstanding new products on the market.

Olive purées are often flavoured with nothing much more than a touch of decent vinegar, and all the better for such modesty. I find them terrific with fish – they wonderfully hide the brown membrane that is so difficult to remove from monkfish tails – but are excellent with anything of a Mediterranean persuasion, including roasted chickens and tomato sandwiches. They make an instant all-covering sauce for hot pasta, and might be swirled into mayonnaise for cold pasta salads. If all this is too much trouble, you won't do better than toast fingers spread with black olive pâté, a couple of soft-boiled eggs and something decent on the telly. Incidentally, although olives are an important ingredient in Provençal tapenade, they are not the most important ingredient: the word is based on local dialect for capers, *tapeno,* and it is the flavour of these which should predominate.

Flavoured, oil-enriched, herby or spicy, olives make excellent additions to food which may be warm or cold. Chop them into vegetable purées, sprinkle them on salads, stir them into pasta sauces or toss them on pizza after cooking. They have an unexpected affinity with oranges, with highly flavoured cheeses (think of them with Feta in Greek salads) and with many fruits. I remember a plate of black figs, Kalamata olives, properly spicy rocket leaves and curls of parmesan cheese. You would too.

Storing: if you live in a small community where bulk olives are unobtainable, don't hesitate to buy in quantity elsewhere when you can.

Olives sold in bulk look better and more inviting than bottles and jars and are generally cheaper. But there is a paradox. Keeping them dark is more important than keeping them refrigerated; a good display of bulk olives is precisely what puts them at risk. Once at home you should assiduously keep the level of brine or any other preservative just above the olives: a slice or two of lemon usually stops the formation of mould on the brine. It is as well to pop some lemon into large bottles of bulk olives once they have been opened, too.

Even better is to drain the brine and to moisten the olives with olive oil, or a mixture of olive oil and a tasteless vegetable oil, or with vinegar and olive oil. And once you start doing that, the fun really begins.

PICKLES & CHUTNEYS

A pickle can mean any food preserved in acid (vinegar) or salt.

It is well known that salt in solution with water is a preservative, because in a strong brine bacteria cannot multiply and cause putrefication. But too much salt in food can mean an unacceptably hardy flavour to many. Luckily, a process called lactic fermentation can be employed to preserve vegetables with rather less than a saturated brine – (see FRUITS, NUTS & VEGETABLES).

All fresh vegetables contain sugars and have a skin covering of micro-organisms which can be controlled to our advantage. If you quickly put freshly-gathered vegetables into a brine that contains only 8-11 per cent salt, the putrefactive bacteria will be inhibited but those which act to ferment sugars and make lactic acid proceed – it is the same process that sours milk naturally, of course.

Lactic acid is a preservative, too, does not have a marked flavour but it is not powerful enough to be a sole preservative. So once lactic fermentation is complete, the lactic brine is replaced by a brine of 15 per cent salt and about one per cent lactic acid, then neither fermentation or putrefication is possible. Lactic acid is often combined with acetic acid, the acid of vinegar, to dilute the latter's sharpness, especially in pasteurized packs.

If vegetables are placed directly into a 15 per cent brine solution or into a mixture of brine and vinegar, this is called non-fermentation brining.

The degree of lactic fermentation, presence of herbs and flavourings, temperature of brining and quality of the initial produce, will all flavour these products. The presence of air causes the growth of bacterial moulds on the top of lactic-brines, but are harmless and can easily be scraped away. The produce, though, should always be kept below the surface of the liquid and away from light as much as possible.

Products which are pasteurized in liquid are likely to have a lower lactic or salt content, because of the additional sterilizing action of heat treatment.

Preserving in vinegar or acetic acid alone works because it short cuts lactic fermentation by providing from the start a high enough acid level to kill or inhibit all bacterial action. Some items require a mixture of salt and vinegar to control their unique infestation. Onions are pickled by being cooked in vinegar; and when this process also includes fruits, spices and herbs you get spreadable pickles and, by including sugar, chutneys. Make the same products smooth and you have sauces, and ketchups.

Chutneys: Indians would not recognize our chutneys, even though the word came from there. Our chutneys are hot and spicy, based on fruits, always contain both vinegar and sugar and should be quite coarse in texture. Often the major fruit has been brined separately, and is added to the cooked base sauce at the end of the cooking process. Mango chutney is the best known, but peach is very good, too. Chutneys mix well with mayonnaise and can also make quick, interesting hot sauces for cold meats; for instance, heat a few spoonfuls of mango chutney, splash in a little citrus juice and the merest touch of brandy.

There is an entirely different type of chutney, which is uncooked and much more encountered once you are in countries with an Indian influence. One of the best I tasted was in Mauritius, a whizzed-up mix of coriander leaf, garlic and coconut with a tiny amount of chilli and fresh ginger.

Mustard pickle: what the Americans call piccallili, a word that almost no one can spell anyway.

Piccallili: this is a law unto itself. First the vegetable content should be crisp, and so it is lactic fermented or brined rather than being boiled in a sauce like other pickles. The sauce itself is thickened with cornflour and made from onions, garlic, spices, vinegar and, of course, mustard, according to each manufacturer's specific recipe. The usual vegetable content is silverskin onions, gherkins and cauliflower florets. The yellow colour is turmeric, or should be. Some commercial manufacturers use colouring instead, because turmeric fades in sunlight.

Pickles: this is really quite a broad term when you think that olives, onion, piccallili, beetroot and cucumber can be called pickles. Mixed pickles vary from the delicious Italian examples of crisp mixed vegetables in a light, vinegary brine, which are excellent as hors d'oeuvres, to the Oriental bottles of lime pickle, mango pickle, and so on. As pickles last so well, buy one or two really excellent examples to use from time to time to give a welcome lift to ordinary food. Although I love pickled walnuts, I can't think of a commercially available English mixed pickle that is better than those made by such Indian companies as Patak's or Ferns; but English pickled peaches, oranges or pears, occasionally available, are very good.

Beetroot: bottles or tins of small pickled beetroots, usually from Scandinavia or Germany, are very useful indeed, cold as a garnish or hot as a vegetable. Drained of their preservative liquid (those from Scandinavia are less sharp) and heated in some orange juice and butter, with a little lemon for accent they become quite special. Excellent heated in sour cream which is spiked with horseradish, with garlic, with parsley or with paprika – or any combination. Didn't know they could be such fun, did you?

Gherkins: what the French call cornichons. These are usually baby or dwarf cucumbers, and they make nice decorations when cut almost through their length several times and then fanned out. I find their flavour too determined even when they are real gherkins, which are not baby cucumbers at all but a relation and native to the Caribbean.

Capers: Tom Stobart described these as tasting 'goaty' – they are certainly unusual

---

CUCUMBERS

Cucumber products are generally lactic fermented.

Salt cucumbers: are treated the most simply of all and after fermentation are put into a plain brine. No other flavouring is incorporated.

Sweet and sour cucumbers: have extra flavour added to them by mixing vinegar or acetic acid into the second brine. A variety of other herbs and spices might also be used. But these are more usual in:

Dill cucumbers: these rely heavily for flavour on the fresh fronds of dill but the brines can also contain peppercorns, red peppers, garlic, grape, blackcurrant, oak and cherry leaves, bay, parsley and horseradish.

New green cucumbers: are simply lightly salted and ready to eat in a few days, whereas dill pickles can take up to three months to taste right.

The secret of retaining crispness and developing flavour in pickled cucumbers is to allow low fermentation to progress at a low temperature. New green cucumbers are usually cured in a warm spot and must then be eaten quickly whilst being stored in a cool place or they will soften and lose flavour, colour and texture.

The techniques and ingredients are accessible to anyone, so when the markets are flooded with ridge cucumbers, have a go at making some of your own pickles. Traditionally, pickled cucumbers are sliced lengthwise or diagonally and eaten as a relish. Very good with salt beef, hot or cold, and I also like dill cucumbers with smoked fish, especially salmon. Any hot or cold smoked meat or sausage is transported into a different part of heaven by the addition of some slices of a crisp cucumber pickle.

and can be unusually awful if not used with the greatest discretion. They are the unopened flowers of a Mediterranean plant that grows like a creeper. Good ones are expensive because the gathering cannot be mechanized – I believe that the life of the flowers is so short you must gather each morning or miss out altogether. They are not lactic fermeted, but put into jars of a vinegar brine, which preserves by the joint action of acetic acid and salt.

Use? On the few occasions I have enjoyed eating them they were always first soaked (in water or milk) and used with great restraint – cooked gently in a sauce as a flavouring rather than served as something to be eaten in its own right. Mr Stobart, who was enthusiastic, says he always combined them with grated lemon and garlic and I can imagine how good that would be with fish. Perhaps I'll give them another try, when I've saved some money. Two things I'm certain about – you should never buy cheap capers, and they must always be covered with liquid, or they develop a taste that makes goats seem positively fragrant. Caper pods are like small green footballs, rarely seen but very delicious.

Onions: almost everyone knows more about onions than me, because I dislike them very much. Onions seem to me to represent all the worst of British cooking, onions with everything and vinegar on your chips. I simply do not believe that every sauce or stew or soup needs onion as a base and I know that Cheddar cheese, caviare and tomatoes, among other things, are far nicer if they are not massacred by the acidic sharpness of raw onion which then stays on the palate to disfigure the taste of your wine or pudding. Pickled onions are worse. Eat them if you like, but keep your distance.

Red Cabbage: with or without apple, this is a very cheap canned vegetable that goes a magically long way. Always cured on the day it is gathered, red cabbage can stand a lot of cooking – allowing you to improve it at home so that it tastes homemade. Sliced or chopped apple, bacon and spiced vinegar make the usual combination – make the vinegar by simmering a few spoonsful of good wine vinegar with a dessertspoonful of pickling spice, drain and add. Garlic and orange juice with hot and sweet paprika is another wonderful combination; so is garlic and juniper berries and gin. A touch of molasses give colour and body. Red cabbage is first choice with any hearty meal, especially game dishes or fatty continental sausages.

Sauerkraut: the truth about sauerkraut is no less astonishing than that about soft roe or salami. It is made the same way a farmer makes silage for his cattle, indeed the smell can be distressingly similar. Sauerkraut is white cabbage that has been subjected to lactic fermentation but it is rarely drained and re-brined. The sauerkraut you can buy in tins is very good but has been cooked, of course. If you are lucky enough to buy it uncooked (we manage to get a few barrels from Holland each year) you can eat it like this but it is more usual to drain and rinse it and then to flavour it with bacon, onion, garlic, apple, carraway, wine – even champagne. You cook it for up to an hour; it should not be mushy but have absorbed the cooking water or liquid you have used, which should have equalled half the original volume of the sauerkraut. Cooked together or separately, sauerkraut and rugged pork sausages, bacon or starchy vegetables all belong to one another. The choucroutes which are served in varying ways throughout France are nearly all more filling and rich than expected; and a version into which champagne is poured really does exist. I ate it in Cognac, where they know a thing or two about food – it was delicious but I don't think I'd do it again; I had a conscience about doing that to champagne.

Walnuts: picking the young green walnuts that go into pickled walnuts is dangerous work as walnut trees have extremely brittle branches and each nut must be picked individually, unlike ripe walnuts which are shaken from the tree. The green walnuts are hand-selected and trimmed before being pickled, in typically, malt vinegar, but around Christmas time in particular you may also find them packed in luxuries such as port. Best used the old-fashioned way, as part of ploughman's lunch – *(see FRUITS, NUTS & VEGETABLES)*.

SAUCES

Brown fruit sauce: the HP sauce and relations. Good for flavouring mayonnaise into which you may wish to incorporate poultry or vegetables. Date syrup is the base for many, especially HP sauce, but vinegar, onions and fruit of other kinds are also essential. It is easy – and right – to make fun of those who use these and other sauces with no thought for the cook, but like every product that has survived on the market, fruit sauces have their place and time. Give me a good game pie or pork pie and I'd much rather have such a sauce than a mustard; I like them slightly cooled, too, which removes any unnecessary sweetness.

Fish sauce: although best known as the *nam pla* of Thai cooking, fish sauces are also used in China. They are a result of the fermentation of fish, a direct cousin of the Romans' garum. But be calm. None smell or taste of fish if they are any good, but are a lightly coloured and flavoured seasoning, more salty than anything else. Used to finish dishes or as a table condiment.

Hoisin sauce: this is the one for Peking Duck. Also known as Barbecue Sauce even though its name means fresh flavour of the sea. Made from soybeans, flour, sugar, salt, garlic, and chilli peppers it is a dark reddish brown in colour, has a creamy consistency and a sweet aftertaste. Particularly associated with roasted duck and pork and the like but, as the name suggests, also with seafood and fish. It may be used as a simple dip, too.

Whatever you do with it, experiment. Make it sweet and sour by adding citrus or vinegars, make it aromatic with sherry or ginger wine, add tomato ketchup to make it more like a Western barbecue sauce. With crunchy peanut butter, sesame seeds, sesame oil and a touch of chilli it gives an interesting variation on satay sauces.

Mushroom ketchup: few people make this or any other type of ketchup at home now, but a well stocked larder once always contained a selection of sauces made from ingredients as diverse as cucumbers, oysters, fruit and vegetables. Mushroom ketchup is one of the few that survived and when you can find it (made commercially) buy it more as a flavouring than a sauce to lay on the side of your plate. It is made by an interesting process using salt, which when sprinkled on mushrooms will extract the liquid from them. This is heated, flavoured and bottled. Commercial mushroom ketchup often contains soy sauce nowadays, which makes the apparent salt content even higher; it is so high that mushroom ketchup becomes interchangeable with anchovy essence, but that is no bad thing. Use mushroom ketchup only at the end of cooking to strengthen or add interest, in the same way that celery, salt, soy sauce, anchovy essence or garlic and ginger juice might do.

Oyster sauce: a rich brown condiment or dipping sauce made by fermenting oysters and soy sauce, and thus related to fish sauce and soy sauce, but meatier tasting and more expensive than either. Use to finish a dish rather than as a cooking ingredient. Like fish sauce, only poor quality oyster sauces will taste or smell fishy.

Pesto: pesto has become unavoidable but that's no bad thing. This sauce of fresh basil, pine nuts, garlic, parmesan and olive oil is bright, pungent and just what tomatoes and pasta need. But it is also an excellent condiment with steak, roast lamb and poultry and fish – that goes for hot or cold. If you make it yourself you can even consider using it in stuffings or marinades before cooking, which will, it is true, injure much of the special appeal of basil. But take heart. Commercial bottles of pesto have been pasteurized and most of them don't taste too bad: otherwise, if you do not have the half acre field of basil needed to make even a small amount of pesto, buy a jar and chop into it some fresh leaves and keep your mouth shut. No one will know. If they do, it's because they do it too.

Plum sauce: like a smooth plum chutney, made from a particular type of sour yellow Chinese plum. It is essentially sweet and sour and widely used as the start for other sauces: equal amounts of this and tomato ketchup make a basic sweet and sour sauce mix. Sometimes known in America as duck sauce, for they were served together rather than the more usual Hoisin Sauce.

Rouille: essentially a mayonnaise or an aioli with chilli. Sadly rouille is increasingly served with bouillabaisse in the belief that it is traditional and correct. It is not, but becoming so. Rouille properly belongs to the simple and bland bourrides made west of Marseilles; bourride is mixed white fish poached in stock which is then thickened with aioli. It is simple and coarse and the chilli helps cut the richness of the oil.

But bouillabaisse is made from far finer fish and, anyway, flavoured with saffron, the world's most expensive spice. Do you really think traditional cooks used saffron and then added chilli so you couldn't taste it? The problem apparently arose through restaurants in Marseilles employing chefs and waiters from the poorer west, who brought with them the custom of rouille with everything. Once again proving that very hot food is a refuge of the poor with nothing but bland food otherwise to eat.

Soy/shoyu sauce: the quintessential flavouring and condiment of Asian cooking. Shoyu is the Japanese name but is often used by food writers to indicate a naturally brewed product rather than the artificially produced product, but this can seem nothing better than precious.

The real thing begins with steamed soybeans mixed with malted wheat kernels, that is they have been allowed to sprout and then roasted. A special yeast is added to start a natural fermentation and precisely developed yeasts give this or that manufacturer their particular flavour and style; they are jealously guarded secrets. After three days the mixture grows a mould or culture on the surface, and then it is blended with brine and put into fermentation tanks.

Over a period of a few weeks the mixture bubbles gently as the soy bean protein changes to amino acids, the basis of its flavour and colour. Wheat starch changes to sugar, and the sugar content changes to alcohols, giving a distinctive aroma and other types of flavour. Some of the sugar and alcohol transforms into acids which give sharpness to the final flavour. Natural glutamates are also formed, the basis for the sauce's ability to enliven other tastes. After six months maturing, the mixture is drawn off into cloths

> **LU SOY**
>
> This is what Cantonese call a basic simmering sauce or master stock; it gives wonderful colour and flavour to poultry and is the secret of Lu Shui, the famed Chiu Chow goose dish. To 300ml/½pt of light soy sauce add 250g/¼lb each of salt and sugar, ten or more slices of fresh ginger plus five-spice powder to taste. Ideally these spices should be in bouquets which can be removed once the liquid has come to the boil, or soon after if you want a stronger flavour. It does not need to cover the beast being cooked, but should be spooned over from time to time, as indeed you should turn the contents of the sauce.

to be pressed. A deep, reddish brown, clear liquid is funnelled from the pressing machines to be pasteurized and bottled.

Well, that is the classic process, indicated by the words 'naturally brewed' on a label. Commercial processes make an approximation in a few days by hydrolising soy protein using hydrochloric acid, diluting with salt water and then adding corn syrup, colouring and other additives; there is also a process, semi-natural, semi-chemical, which combines both methods.

The Kikkoman Company has been making naturally brewed soy sauce in Japan since 1630 and also makes a special brew just for the Imperial Household. The beans for this are hand-picked for quality and size and everything else is done the ancient way, including a three year brew in huge oak casks, which give added complexity of flavour and colour to the result.

Once opened soy sauce keeps its virtues for about a month, after that it will begin to oxidize and lose most of its subtle complexities; this happens faster and more noticeably if it is exposed to extremes of light or heat. Provided it is well sealed, refrigeration will not harm it. Many Oriental ingredients last forever, but not this one.

Light soy sauce: is brewed purposely to give 25 per cent of the usual colour, so it will not discolour dishes when adding flavour; it is often slightly saltier than dark soy sauce.

Dark soy sauce: has a rich dark concentrated flavour, that is both sweet and salt. It will colour sauces and foods and this is part of the consideration when using it. Often both dark and light are combined to get precisely the flavour required.

Tamari soy sauce: is made only with soy beans, and is used in sushi restaurants, but rarely in the home.

Low-salt soy sauce: is increasingly marketed.

Sukiyaki sauce: soy sauce mixed with rice wine and sugar, added to water and boiled up as a stock for cooking beef and vegetables: if you make such stock from scratch it's called *warashita*.

Tabasco: some people have all the luck. Can you imagine owning an island with its own variety of hot red pepper plus its own salt mines so you can make a world famous product without leaving home? The McIhenneys do just that, making millions of bottles of hot Tabasco sauce from the products of their backyard, Avery Island in the bayous of Louisiana. The yearly harvest of red peppers is mashed, mixed with salt and then fermented in oak barrels for three years. The resulting liquid is mixed with a special vinegar for further aging and then bottled. That's it. Provided the local alligators, hurricanes and such keep their distance, you are in business.

In fact, the operation is now so big the peppers are grown in other parts of the world too, notably South America, but in carefully selected soils to give exactly the same flavour as Avery Island.

Because it comes with definite flavour, Tabasco is a much more acceptable way of adding heat to food and food sauces than cayenne/chilli pepper.

Even better is to serve it at table and let people make food as hot as they prefer, averting your eyes if it seems too much.

Although recommended by the McIhenneys for every type of food, I think it particularly good with things creamy, including dishes with cheese, or cheesy sauces.

If you can buy only sweet paprika for a dish which requires both sweet and hot, as most do or should, a few drops of Tabasco will right the balance.

Tabasco will last for years, if it is stored away from heat and out of the light for these will eventually lead to deterioration.

Teriyaki: a Japanese barbecue and grill marinade, baste or dip. Essentially soy sauce flavoured with wine, sugar and spices; you can make good but individual equivalents by mixing soy sauce with pineapple juice, with mirin and five-spice powder or with plum sauce and ginger wine. Some of these mixtures will be more like sukiyaki sauce.

Worcestershire sauce: this is one of the few good things to come out of the Indian Empire, and is also an echo of everyday life in the Roman Empire. The Romans would have been lost without their garum, a sauce made by fermenting and maturing the liquid that small fish give off when salted and left in the sun in barrels. It sounds awful, but after much maturation it ends up being only slightly salty and barely fishy; nothing similar remains in the West, but in the East similar fish sauces are used as freely as we use salt.

When such sauces are mixed and matured with extra ingredients – vinegar, molasses, garlic, the bitterness of tamarind and much more that is secret, you get something like Worcestershire sauce. There used to be many of these spicy, hot, salty sauces, made from recipes brought back by gourmand colonels from the India of Queen Victoria. Some were manufactured for distribution and some were kept as private stocks. Lea & Perrins Worcestershire sauce was first made as a private stock but forgotten about by the owner. Eventually the barrel was about to be thrown away by the custodians, some pharmacists, who bravely decided to check on the contents. They discovered that the long sojourn in their cellar had transformed a sharp and unpleasant liquid into something with possibilities, and started to make it commercially. Thank goodness.

In Thailand I noticed it used with great abandon by much of the populace, and in Australasia it is used as often as dessicated coconut, which is saying something. But it *is* extraordinarily good for pepping up boring food and for adding unrecognized piquancy and interest to mayonnaise, soups, aspics, sauces for fish, herb butters and mince dishes, especially hamburgers. I like to use very little on a lamb chop, rubbed in both sides and left to sit an hour or so before cooking. You know, of course, that a Bloody Mary is bloody awful without Worcestershire sauce.

Even though an Italian word, pasta is about as exclusive to Italy as palaces and royal families are to Great Britain. Marco Polo did *not* bring it to Europe from China – that is a 19th century American fabrication. And firm, *al dente* pasta is better for you than well-cooked pasta. Now, having shattered the basic misconceptions, here are some facts.

All pasta is based on a kneaded paste of strong (usually durum) wheat flour and water to which eggs are sometimes added. Its origins are the same as those of cheese – no one knows when, where or by whom. Ancient Etruscans, Greeks and Romans enjoyed it – indeed the *noodles, nouilles* and *nudeln* of modern Europe are clearly rooted in the Roman *nodellus,* a word which means little knots and describes what happens to long strands of pasta when on your plate. Even the Arabs have their own noodles, the *trii,* which they introduced to Sicily long ago, in sumptuous recipes. More surprising than pasta's long history is that it was only rarely eaten in post-Roman Italy until the middle of the 19th century, and even then those who ate it all lived in the south. The people of the north used rice as their staple starch product.

Pasta products seemed spontaneously to have become popular again with pockets of populace of southern Italy around the 13th century; they had been known there since the Greeks colonized this part of the Mediterranean. This was all well before the appearance of the tomato, so pasta was served with sharp fish or vinegar-pointed sauces or with the voluptuous flower-scented creams and cheeses that dominated European cooking after the return of the Crusaders. When the tomato arrived it was found to flourish most fulsomely near Naples, and soon the inventive proprietors of the rumbustious Neapolitan inns and *vermicelli* stalls were offering a rich reduced tomato sauce as an optional extra dressing for their pasta products. In 1860, when bearded Garibaldi led the One Thousand into southern Italy from the rice-eating north, this army learned to like the combination and when they returned home they took their new tastes with them, permanently altering the style and flavour of northern Italian cooking. At about the same time, new strains of wheat made wheat flour more readily available and both north *and* south Italy ate more pasta than ever before. Now the north claims as its own several of the most popular pasta sauces – *pesto* and *salsa Bolognese* in particular.

Many European countries have used long thin noodles in one way or another for centuries, often with or instead of vegetables. The smaller, cut shapes, called macaroni generically, were more often made into sweet puddings. But almost always the pasta was cooked for hours, reducing it to a muciferous mush. This would be horrifying to the Neapolitans who like their pasta not *al dente* but *verdi verdi,* which to us would seem barely warmed through, let alone cooked. But you are wrong if you think this would be dangerously indigestible. Quite the reverse. Firm pasta encourages you to chew more, breaking it into small pieces and mixing them with the important digestive enzymes of the saliva. The well-cooked stuff slips down the gullet in great dollops, landing heavily in the stomach with no such enzymic help to assimilation. Thus the digestive trouble begins. But if your trouble is other than of the stomach, you may care to know that a decent meal of spaghetti and tomato sauce is said to supply significant amounts of vitamin E, which is of specific benefit to the reproductive organs (trust the Italians and French to know this). Still, they *have* given us a clue. Both know the tomato as the 'love apple': *pomo d'amore* and *pomme d'amour* respectively.

In other parts of the world, broadly similar food has been known for aeons. Think of the Orientals with their noodles, steamed or fried, and the tiny steamed parcels of dough, the wonton. The Russians' *vareniki* are like ravioli, little pillows of pasta, stuffed with cheese, with cabbage, with fish or strawberries or poppyseeds or almost anything. And in Thailand they make all manner of white or transparent noodles in a fascinating manner which I saw in a jungle village in the infamous Golden Triangle. They don't make a dough which is rolled out and cut. They make a thick sludge of

ORIENTAL NOODLES

Chinese: A staple of most parts of China, and thus made from a variety of flours, reflecting local staples.

Bean Thread or **Cellophane:** made from mung beans, these are first soaked and then cooked a maximum of ten minutes, often with other foods to extend leftovers. They are transparent as the name suggests and considered a type of vegetable rather than a true noodle.

Handmade: a basic entertainment, like flinging pizza about. Wheat flour dough is pulled, stretched, thrown and twisted like mad until very long noodles are obtained. I can't decide whether to learn how to do this or to juggle should I decide to moonlight.

Rice: sheets of steamed rice flour batter are sliced to make rice sheet noodles; rice stick noodles or rice vermicelli are very much thinner and when deep-fried, expand enormously, which makes them very absorbent but a bit unsatisfying to eat.

Wheat: thick Shanghai noodles are made from

mixed rice and soy flour, which is ladled into what look like huge icing bags with a much-pierced nozzle. From some height and with considerable dexterity, thin strands are extruded directly into a vat of water aboil over open charcoal fires, in which they congeal immediately. In seconds they are looped out and hung to drip dry under teak-leaf-thatched roofs in great opalescent skeins. They don't last long in the humidity so the agile villagers had their work and their fortune cut out for them to supply, as they did, nearly all the local district. But the concomitant pigs, scabrous dogs and mucous-choked children cut them right out of my diet.

There seems to be no end to ingenuity when it comes to making noodles. In Vietnam a particular type of cellophane noodle, thin and transparent, is made with a flour of dried mung bean and in other parts of south east Asia, gram flour, made from a type of pea, is used. The Chinese make a batter of whatever flour they can get, spread this on an oiled platter and steam until transparent; it is rolled and eaten with chopped green onion and revived dried shrimp. In Japan the great pasta speciality is *soba,* a spaghetti-type product made with a proportion of buckwheat; you can buy this in the United Kingdom.

Hungarian egg drops – *tarhonya* – are well worth finding. These small pellets of egg pasta are fried a golden brown before being covered with water to cook. The

wheat and eggs and sold fresh or dried. Cook like European noodles, or cook, steam dry and fry. Thin Shanghai noodles, usually used in soups, are generally whiter and contain no egg.

Japanese: increasingly available in Britain thanks to our awareness of the macrobiotic diet, and the growth of noodle bars and Japanese supermarkets.

Soba: made from buckwheat, usually with wheat flour and egg, too. Surprisingly they are generally served cold, but dipped into a hot broth and other flavouring agents as they are eaten.

Somen: fine wheat flour noodles.

Udon: thick wheat noodles usually without eggs. Generally eaten in a hot broth into which almost anything from sliced roast pork to raw eggs and every imaginable vegetable or flavouring might be tipped; they were a perfect reviver at a street stall at 5.30am after a freezing visit to Tokyo's cavernous fish market. It takes longer to learn the appropriate rude slurping noises than to master getting more into your mouth than you leave behind.

nuttiness is delicious and once you have eaten them with a paprika-rich goulash, mashed or boiled potatoes will never do again.

Then there's America. It is the United States that has led the march of pasta so steadily to the top of the post-war popularity poll. It was they who popularized the idea of eating Italian pasta as a main course, which it never was: Italian purists would also say it should only be eaten as a first course at lunchtime and never in the evenings. It was almost certainly someone in the United States who invented *canneloni*, *tagliatelli* with cream, ham and peas, *carbonara* sauce, and the notion of cold pasta salads. But the chances are that these innovators were also of Italian extraction, and not *all* progress is a bad thing. When thousands of Italians emigrated to the United States it was pasta they wanted more than anything, and it had to be Neapolitan. It was this export demand that allowed the great pasta families to mechanize and then sell their products all around the world.

As you might expect, mechanization has had some effect on commercial Italian pasta. Eighty years ago you could find 250-300 different shapes, but now the number is probably closer to only 50 or 60 and that includes new monstrosities like spacemen and flying saucers.

But the phenomenal amount of pasta sold these days means old standards and quality have had to be forgotten, and there must be many who cannot understand the fuss. Take the trouble to buy old-fashioned pasta just once, and you will. It is easy to spot, for it will be dull rather than shiny and, if you can get to it, slightly rough to the touch.

Much modern pasta is made with softer flour than used to be the case. Once moulded it must be assisted to dry with heat, which adds a give-away glaze. Proper durum pasta dries naturally to a dull glow. The roughness comes from the use of traditional bronze tools in the moulding machines. Modern nylon extrusion moulds make absolutely smooth surfaces but the metal ones mark each piece of pasta with minute scoring and this is actually the most important of all differences. This scoring dramatically increases the surface of each piece, and thus, once it is cooked and has steamed dry *(see COOKING)* it is capable of absorbing very much more olive oil or sauce than the lesser area of smooth, glazed pasta.

That absorption of flavouring is why traditionally made pasta sings in the mouth, and probably why Italians use about 20 per cent of the sauce we would in any dish. They know how to combine the two, to enjoy the flavour of both: we use rather tasteless pasta to bulk out a sauce which is usually far too diluted anyway.

To those who have not been brought up with pasta it can be an extraordinary experience to discover the amazing range of flavours pasta can have, all obtained by varying the thickness and shape of the same combination of wheatflour, water and, possibly, egg. Spinach juice or tomato purée can be added to make green, *verde,* and red, *rosso,* pasta. Pasta is very simple to make and doubly delicious when fresh rather than dried. The fun of making it can be as addictive as the pleasure of eating it. But before you dash into the kitchen, here's an attempt to guide you through the maze of the most common categories and shapes of Italian pasta.

PASTA FAMILIES

Flavoured: with black pepper, beetroot, squid ink, pumpkin purée, orange, walnuts and almost anything else, these have cerebral appeal rather than culinary. Once they are plunged into the requisite boiling water the flavour you have paid for is dissolved away: the only way to rescue this is to flavour the water highly with the same ingredient. Only in King's Cross, Sydney did I find this, when I enjoyed mussels on saffron linguine, which had been cooked in saffron seafood stock. It's much more rewarding to use decent pasta and a good sauce.

Pasta all'uovo/pasta with egg: here the flour is mixed with a proportion of egg that varies but should never be less than one per 500g/1lb of flour. It is nearly always made into *pasta lunga* products but every type of pasta may be made with eggs. Much of the very good pasta that comes from Israel is made with eggs.

Pasta corta/short or cut pasta: the best known in these categories are the rounded, hollow pastas, usually cut on the bias and which may be smooth or grooved. These include *macaroni, rigatoni, penne* and the comparative newcomer, *canneloni.* This category also includes the shapes and shell types, so wonderful for holding sauce-juicy chunks of meat or seafood. *Lumache* (snails), *conchiglie* (shells), *gnocchi* and the elbow-shapes also come into this category.

Pasta lunga/long pasta: from the tiniest *cappelli d'angelo* (angel's hair) to thick and broad *lasagne,* with every type of *spaghetti, vermicelli, liguine, ziti, fettuccine* and *tagliarelli* or *tagliatelli* in between. With or without holes. Once nearly all the thinner *pasta lunga* was made up to 1½m/5ft in length and looped to dry like wool. Now it's usually cut into 20-32cm/8-12in lengths.

Pasta ripieni/stuffed pasta: *ravioli* in all different sizes is the best known, I suppose, but *tortellini* which look like belly-buttons are much more delicious, I think, as are *cappelleti* which look like head scarves tied on the chin. There are varieties of stuffed dumplings, called *angolotti,* but these are rarely seen commercially.

Pastina: these tiny pieces of dried dough are specially made for serving in soup and are most usually seen as egg drops, squares or bow ties *(farfalli);* then you must also include novelties such as alphabet pasta, tiny animals and the aforementioned visitors from outer space.

Pre-cooked: just what it says, and a special boon when it comes to making lasagne, but make the sauces a little wetter for the liquid to soften them has to come from somewhere.

Sweet: it's in New York. Jelly bean flavoured and coloured pasta shapes to serve sweet. And a British company is threatening pasta stuffed with chocolate and nuts and stuff. Lovely idea, but wouldn't you have to cook them in a sugar syrup and/or serve them with a sweet sauce? I hope we will be told.

Wholewheat: a century ago most pasta would have been like this, but by the time it became internationally popular, white flour was easily available. The Veneto, around Venice, still offers *bigoli,* a thick type of spaghetti made from whole flour.

PASTA SHAPES

Spaghetti is generally known as being round and thin but without a hole; the diameter (and subsequent flavour) varies enormously without any change of name. So the following can only be arbitrary, and is based more on what you might buy easily rather than what is being made in the village kitchens of Italy.

The basic rules about choosing a pasta are these: the smooth or ridged shapes are best with smooth but thick and clinging sauces; those with major ridges, crevasses, folds or holes have been planned for very thin sauces or for lumpy sauces, which will be caught and held. Tortelloni are usually served in a cream sauce or tomato sauce, but ravioli might be served in butter, especially browned butter.

Bucatini: a thick, hollow version of spaghetti.

> ### ORIENTAL WRAPPERS
> Spring roll and wonton wrappers are both pasta and pastry, and may be thought of as Oriental filo. The difference between the two is in size and use.
>
> Spring roll wrappers are big enough to roll up into a sausage-sized parcel of ingredients; they are then deep-fried.
>
> Wonton wrappers are only 7 or 8cms/3in square and are as likely to be steamed or boiled as fried.
>
> Both are available frozen; after defrosting you may peel away the number you want and then refreeze the remainder.
>
> Bean curd skins, *qv,* made rather the way we would clotted cream, are just as useful.

Capellini: very thin, flat or round noodles *(capelli d'angelo* being the thinnest).

Cappelletti: 'little hats'. This is a stuffed pasta, like a small peaked and tied head scarf.

Conchiglie: seashells. Available large or small, smooth or ridged. Excellent for trapping the tastiest bits of seafood or meat sauces and attractive in cold pasta salads.

Farfalli/farfallini etc: a bow-tie shape often with crinkled or diamond-cut edges. Made by pinching the middle of a square of pasta.

Fettuccine: a blood brother of *tagliatelle, fettuccine* originates from Rome, is usually made with egg, and is narrower and thicker than its relation.

Fusilli: a spiral-shaped pasta.

Gnocchi: this should be made with starch or a purée of something other than wheat flour. Dry mashed potato or pumpkin are the most common but flour is also included. The proper shape is a small oval that is slightly folded and serrated.

Lasagne: the broadest pasta noodle, smooth or ridged. *Lasagne verdi,* like all green pasta, is coloured with spinach. Lasagne is one of the few pastas not dressed with sauce at the table. Instead it is layered with *béchamel* and *ragú* sauces and returned to the oven to be baked *(Lasagne al Forno).*

Linguine: another flat, thin noodle.

Macaroni: a generic term for all commercially-made dried pasta. But in general use is often used to mean only the well-known cut, tubular pasta. There are many lengths and sizes of such macaroni.

Orecchiette: these 'little ears' are shaped just like that, and suit salads and chunky sauces.

Pansotti/panzerotti: a triangular, stuffed pasta.

Penne: specially used to indicate a hollow short pasta cut at an acute diagonal angle – up to 2½cm/1in long. The shape is reminiscent of the end of a sharpened quill, hence the name.

Quadrucci: these little squares of noodle are used in soup and in today's prosaic times are liable simply to be labelled 'egg squares'.

Ravioli: best known of the stuffed pasta, they are square-shaped and can sometimes be found quite large.

Rigatoni: ridged and tubular, sometimes curved, but without the pointed ends of penne.

Spaghetti: thin strings of pasta, without holes. Called *vermicelli* (little worms) in southern Italy. There are thinner varieties called *spaghettini* and *vermicellini.*

Tagliatelle: a long, thin egg noodle, the speciality of Bologna, one of Italy's greatest food centres. There is also a green one – *tagliatelle verdi.*

Tortellini/Tortelloni/Tortelli: a stuffed pasta, more or less of a twisted ring shape which look like perfect belly-buttons. Can be bought fresh or dried in many English cities; in London they are available deep-frozen, having been imported from Italy. They are a good ingredient for a timbale – the rich pie of pastry and pasta.

Cooking: the manufacturers don't necessarily know best and often tell you to cook your pasta longer than is necessary. The Italians say 'pasta likes friends', meaning you need to keep an eye on it when it cooks. The slightest variation in thickness, humidity or amount of water will affect the time it takes for your pasta to be to your taste. There is a tradition that says some Italians reckoned theirs was ready when a handful flung onto the wall stuck there; I've never been able to find necessary details of type of wall, distance thrown or style of delivery and so have gone for the more mundane tooth test. Boring but effective.

Fresh pasta tells you it is cooked by floating to the surface, sometimes in just a few minutes.

You must use as much water as possible so that each pasta piece can swell unhindered. I always put some oil in the cooking water as this stops the pasta sticking together when drained. Classicists say you should never pour pasta into a colander but take it out of the water with a large fork or spoon. Do what you will, but don't rinse it in cold water and then expect to reheat it without it going sticky. Correctly, cooked pasta should be drained and then allowed to steam dry; it happens very quickly, almost magically, and the dry surface will then hold or absorb sauces. The exception to the rule is lasagne. When lasagne is cooked, run cold water into the cooking pot and gently move the lasagne sheets until separate and cool in the running water. Then take them out and lay them on a tea towel to drain and dry.

Generally, it is regarded as bad practice to toss your cooked pasta in its chosen sauce. Rather you should put the hot pasta into a dish, let it sit for a few minutes, when it will almost miraculously absorb the moisture on its surface, then pour the sauce over. The mixing is then done at the same time as the serving, which looks better and protects the pasta's texture and shape.

Complicated shapes, like shells, should be drained in a colander, and gently turned so the water caught in the interior drains away.

Serving: because it is a simple food, pasta particularly suits simple accompaniments. But which sauce goes with what pasta? Every sauce goes with every pasta. But some are better than others. For example it can be pointless to serve a *pasta lunga* with a very thin sauce or with a sauce filled with large chunks of meat or seafood; in both cases the sauce will slide from the pasta and need to be eaten separately. Such sauces are enjoyed more when served with the complicated shapes of *pasta corta*, which can catch the sauce in pools or trap the morsels of flesh. But even this rule can be ignored if you have the wrong type of pasta in the cupboard.

Butter sauces: melted butter flavoured with chopped garlic, herbs and a dash of olive oil makes one of the best and clingiest dressings for pasta lunga. If you want to ignore the above advice, some seafood, snippets of cheese, cubes of ham or salami, croûtons or lardons, black olives or cornichons might also be added. It is correct to serve some ravioli and gnocchi with melted butter; often the former is served with butter that has been allowed to brown slightly.

Cheese: yes, Parmesan and other cheeses do go nicely with pasta dishes. But please don't add it regardless. Such piquant cheese is to be considered an alternative to salt and pepper, and so on some dishes, especially the creamy seafood sauces, the additional flavour of cheese is quite wrong.

The use of grated Cheddar cheese, spongy and stringy, adds little but bother, unless it is dissolved into a sauce completely. Even so it is pointless using something mild as you spend more trying to get flavour than if you simply bought less of a biting Parmesan, for all its expense. I blame the Italian restaurants themselves for the propagation of Parmesan-with-everything; at least eating chips with everything does not mask flavours which some chef has, or should have, been creating for hours.

Cream sauces: the simplest cream sauce is simply a reduction of double cream. For two, reduce 300ml/½pt double cream to half its volume and then flavour according to your store cupboard. An excellent way to proceed now is to add some of the juice from a tin of baby clams or Danish mussels which have been preserved in brine or their natural juices. Add also some tomato purée, until there is a rosiness rather than ruddiness. Continue reducing until a coating consistency and only then add salt and, if you have some, a teaspoon or two of brandy.

When your pasta shells or *lumachine* or *penne* are cooked and well drained, serve onto hot plates, then quickly toss the clams or mussels in the sauce before serving. A little oregano is good with this. So is a sprinkle of mixed hot and sweet paprika.

Should you want a creamy sauce for noodles, then reduced and flavoured cream is really the best way. This is also true when preparing any sauce for *tortellini* or *cappelletti*.

Meat sauces: the basic tomato/beef sauce or *ragú* does not need complication or expense to be good. First you must brown the minced meat with onions and a little celery. Then cover the meat with plum tomatoes canned in tomato juice, including all this juice. Add some bay leaves and then let this simmer gently for several hours – the larger the quantity the longer the time. No garlic, no herbs, no red wine and definitely no expensive cuts of meat.

At the end of the long cooking the meat will almost have dissolved into the reduced sauce, the flavours will have combined and the colour will be wonderful. Finish with some black pepper and salt if you think it is necessary. Should you wish a higher colour or even stronger tomato flavour then use tomato purée as your cooking liquid, diluted only slightly, or add some, in the way outlined under my piece on that subject, towards the end of the cooking. This is the sauce which is also the basis of lasagne making. But for that layered and baked dish, the *ragú* is mixed, swirled rather, with equal quantities of a thick but simply flavoured béchamel sauce. Do not accept as lasagne layers of pasta and undercooked or watery mince; without the texture and contrast of the béchamel sauce it is horrid and dry or greasy.

Tomato sauces: the simpler the better. If you have tomatoes in your garden which are rugged and red and sun-ripened then simply chop them up and cook them gently with some olive oil, strain them or liquidize and strain, then reduce further. But don't bother to attempt this with the orange bullets you buy in the guise of tomatoes. If you don't have the goodies in the garden and you can't buy the wonderful *marmonde* tomatoes now being imported, then open a couple of cans of plum tomatoes and reduce them into a sauce as above. Onions and bay leaf are the only additions to consider.

But you have to be quite patient about reducing the liquid enough, and also take care that it does not burn or caramelize. A few minutes before serving, add some sprigs of fresh herbs, like basil, thyme or mint, let the flavour draw, drain and serve. Dried herbs work as well, but I recommend you strain them out, too.

See OLIVES, PICKLES & SAUCES.

ODD WAYS WITH LEFTOVER PASTA

I often find myself with some leftover pasta, cooked or uncooked. The latter is often hard to find a use for though, as it keeps so well, perhaps this is only a problem of space rather than economy. Here are some ideas for using small amounts of cooked pasta and appearing to be creative at the same time.

Casseroles: cooking dried pasta or reheating cooked pasta in the juice of braises, stews and casseroles gives you a meal in one container. And you retain all the vitamins of the dried pasta instead of throwing some away in the cooking water. Liver and bacon is good with pasta in it; so is goulash, with added paprika and sour cream. Braised steak that is too wet and sloppy can be saved by cooking noodles in the liquid.

Fish: leftover fish incorporated into a rich white sauce with a sharpening of green pepper, cheese and Tabasco is a nice combination with small macaroni shapes. Bake until a crisp golden brown in the oven. Smoked fish would probably be better.

Fried: it is not only noodles that can be fried. Simply ensure that your leftover pasta has been well and truly dried and dump it into deep, hot oil or fat, cook until brown, drain and serve. It is particularly good mixed up with masses of fried onion or crisp-fried onion rings.

Fruit: provided they are not oily, cooked pasta shapes make interesting additions to cooked fruit. Toss the cooked shapes in a little sugar and cinnamon or in some syrup. They are particularly good with puddings made with dried fruit and with apple – you'd be surprised how good is a layer of small, buttered macaroni at the bottom of, say, an apple crumble. I'd be inclined to pour a little cream or milk over the pasta, so it could be absorbed with the dripping juices of the apple whilst in the oven.

Salads: cold pasta in salads is very popular. It can either be the basis or an ingredient. As the former, consider adding a few highly-flavoured ingredients to pasta tossed in good olive oil and lemon juice whilst still warm – some smoked sausages or frankfurters, some rollmops and sour cream with onion, salami and gherkins, for example. Pasta is especially good in the classic *salade Niçoise*. When incorporating pasta with a poultry salad, use the Polynesian idea of including fruit, too. Mix pasta with chicken, avocado and pineapple, or with turkey, apple, nuts and celery plus some orange segments.

Vegetables: almost any hot vegetable dish that includes a sauce or is in itself rather wet can be extended with pasta shapes. Ratatouille becomes even more filling and nourishing. Cauliflower cheese, brussel sprouts or leeks in a cheese sauce plus pasta make a snack a meal; it looks good if you've used wholemeal pasta.

Pies have long been a mainstay of the British table. Their ancestors were mixtures of meats, herbs, spices and dried fruits baked in coffins or huffs, crusts of varying composition, often painted and gilded, but not meant to be eaten. Once pastry making was perfected, the idea of baking meats in edible containers quickly became universal, for not only were they easy to store and transport but the crust gave you more of a meal to enjoy.

Raised pies are a peculiarly British preserve, and the closest thing left to us of those medieval coffins. Indeed, the hot water, flour and lard based cases of raised pies hold a pretty uneasy position between the old and new styles of pie crust – the inedible and the edible. Classically the warm pastry is shaped over a wooden mould and sets in shape: domestically something like a preserving jar is often used as a mold, but I treat it like any other sort of pastry and bake it in a loose-bottomed pan.

Pork pies are the best known raised pies, yet even their greatest admirers agree there is a reliably distressing layer of greeny-cream raw pastry between the admittedly succulent outer crust and the meat. This, as you might expect, seems largely to be the result of commercial compromise, for I have made, been offered and bought raised pies with thin, beautifully cooked-through crusts, so it is more than possible. But just because the outside was once absolutely inedible and today only just makes it, must modern contents vie also to be so bland?

The fillings of raised pies are, largely, a sort of pâté, minced meat with a high content of fat, vital for flavour and as a guarantee of long life – life-threatening bacteria generally do not grow on fat. Thus it seems extraordinary to find them so plodding and bleak. Even the beautifully made pies from a famed farm shop I know, generously packed full of pork and game or duck, taste like damp cardboard, for the meat is utterly unseasoned, and the ill-advised low-fat, low-moisture content means it has also steamed in its own juices, inevitably producing the damp, flabby flavour not even a good stock poured through the cooked crust can balance. Bad raised pies are a sad opportunity missed, but could simply be recovered. It's not the fat content driving customers away. There's just too many other things to buy these days which taste better.

Of course standards vary up and down the country and so if you know better you have a terrible dichotomy – do you keep a tasty raised pie to yourself or broadcast its appeal and run the risk of commercialization and all that this so often means?

Here is what you might find in stores and how they could be.

Gala: the frenzied pinnacle of British commercial invention, it seems, a pork or veal and ham pie baked in a long oblong with an extruded egg-substitute through the middle. The original, with real eggs, is terrific.

Game pies: ideally, these should contain the minced dark meat of game birds mixed into a pork farce plus layers of the sliced breast meat. Bacon and fillet or rump steak were once thought essential, too. Old recipes include cayenne and mace with the salt and pepper but unless a really rich stock was made from the bones of the birds and poured into the spaces left by shrinkage after cooking, the result would not have been as tasty and gamey as expected.

If you are making such at home, the meat mixture should be allowed to rest overnight before cooking; thyme is quite the best herb for these compounds and juniper berries always help. Even a small amount of wine, cognac and garlic make a terrific difference.

More of the same must be included in the stock, which should be almost too strong to enjoy by itself: remember it will be greatly diluted once in the pie and thus no matter how stiffly it might set by itself, will undoubtedly also need extra gelatin added. I use flavoursome aspic rather than gelatin and alcohol rather than water and reduce that before use too, so that concentrated port might make the aspic for a pheasant and walnut raised pie, and so on.

Another version, just

MY PORK PIE

Although by no means traditional, my recipe for pork pies does at least introduce you to what the possibilities might be, and were once. The proportion of meat to fat commonly recommended was two to one. Minced belly of pork approximates this, but if you wish to be more exact, combine lean leg with hard back fat. Although sage is a more British thing, thyme is a far better friend to pork and more universally liked. A centre layer of cognac-soaked prunes rolled in cinnamon makes a voluptuous thing to discover as you slice and eat.

To make a 1½kg/3lb pie
For the filling:
875g/1¾lbs minced pork
50g/2oz onion, very finely chopped
150ml/¼ pt dry white wine
2 tbsp cognac
½ tsp dried sage or thyme
1 generous tbsp Dijon mustard
1 small dessert apple, peeled and grated coarsely
½ tsp freshly ground nutmeg
½ tsp ground mace
½ tsp freshly ground black pepper
1 tsp salt
1 packet aspic powder
beaten egg for glaze
For the case:
375g/12oz plain flour
1 tsp salt
150ml/¼ pt water
125g/4oz lard, cut into small pieces

Mix the pork with all the ingredients, except the aspic powder, and

as authentic but more domestic, uses just mixed game, first casseroled together (on the bone of course), and then boned, layered and baked in a rich gravy of the cooking stock with added gelatin in a pastry case. Wonderful, and even better if you can bear to leave it uncut several days.

Mutton pie: you'll most likely find these in Scotland, but once they were the wares commonly hawked by Simple Simon and other itinerant pie sellers. They're small raised pies based on minced mutton (now probably lamb), brown sauce, or stock and such spice as nutmeg or cloves, but minimally. They might once have had red

leave at room temperature for a few hours or overnight in the refrigerator, thus ensuring the flavours fully blend.

To make the pastry, first sieve the flour with the salt onto a board and then make a well in the centre. Heat the water with the lard until the lard has melted. Pour the mixture into the flour, mix into a dough and knead until smooth. Keep it covered with cling film when not subsequently working with it, so it keeps warm.

Take a 15cm/6in loose bottomed cake tin. Reserve about a quarter of the dough and cover with cling film. Press or roll out the remaining dough into a large circle – hands are faster and keep the dough warmer. Fold the dough over a rolling pin and transfer to the tin, and then ease it into shape using your knuckles, ensuring it is neither too thick nor too thin over the base or where that meets the sides: allow an overlap.

Add the filling. Roll out the reserved pastry so it is just bigger than the tin, transfer and fix in place with a little water. Trim neatly, angling the knife outwards from the tin so there is a slight overhang, and then crimp by hand or using the handle of a wooden spoon which gives a deeper, bolder look. Make a slash in the top of the pie and pull back the edges so there is no chance of them closing during baking.

Bake at 200°C/400°F/Gas Mark 6 for 30 minutes, then glaze with the beaten egg and reduce the temperature to 180°C/350°F/Gas Mark 4 for another 90 minutes.

Let the pie cool and then make up the aspic powder with half the recommended liquid – you could use more white wine rather than water. Pour the liquid in through the hole, slowly and in stages. You need patience for it takes longer and the pie absorbs more than you can imagine. Once the pie is indeed filled, let the aspic set then wrap the pie and keep for several days before cutting. The addition of coarsely chopped parsley or grated lemon zest to the meat mixture, as you would in a veal and ham pie, both work well. Expect the cooked meat to be pork-coloured rather than pink.

currant jelly poured into them, too, and on market stalls were topped with mint leaves, to prevent a mix up with pork pies.

Modern thought finds these also made with short crust pastry, of course, and sometimes topped with mashed potato, like a combination of mutton pie and shepherd's pie.

Pork pies: yes, these could be only minced pork with salt and pepper, and give good porky and peppery results. But only if you are able to use the more flavoursome, naturally raised, old varieties of pig. Modern recipes I have seen suggest mixed spice or all-spice but the usual instruction that there should be but a pinch or two for 1½kg/3lbs of fatty meat is laughable – a good sneeze would give more flavour.

There is no good reason for pork pies not to be flavoured with mustard and herbs, wine and onion and garlic or, best of all, plenty of spices, in the style of British potting. Pork pies seem to be a major surviving victim of the Puritans' ban on the use of spices and flavourings in food; before that pies were aswirl with all the flavours of Araby and with its dried fruits, too. Even after that they had more character than we might believe from the general standard of today's offerings.

Pork pies have traditionally had a particular association with Leicestershire, Melton Mowbray chiefly, because local pigs were specially well fed on whey, a byproduct of cheesemaking; the bakers of this town also once added butter to the pastry and cayenne to the filling. And Dorothy Hartley in *Food in England* says anchovy essence was essential to their mixture because it made the cooked meat pink whereas everyone else's was grey; personally, she put a sage leaf plus marjoram into each pie, which all sounds very encouraging. But there's more. She says the gelatinous stock which finished each pie, filling the space left by the shrunken cooked meat, was highly flavoured with herbs plus the cores of the apples which had been used for sauces since the pig had been killed. They have a slight almond flavour plus a welcome acidity. Even that inspired idea would give only a poor reflection of the once commonly manufactured pork and apple raised pie, now rarely seen, in my experience.

Other centres baked their pork pies in other styles which equally deserve to be better known – Market Harborough used to add apple, sage, onion and sugar; those of Lincolnshire included stock made from the trotters; in Yorkshire they included sage and nutmeg, which sounds good; and in Derbyshire the meat was cooked with its bone before being added to the pies, an even tastier idea.

Although most commonly seen eaten cold, pork pies are very good eaten hot, something you are more likely to find as you travel north.

Veal and ham pie: this raised pie is usually oblong, having been baked in bread tins. It is properly constructed of layers of chopped veal and about half its weight or less of chopped uncooked ham or gammon. Hard boiled eggs are always snuggled into the middle. The addition of lemon zest and parsley add extra savouriness and help make this a lighter thing altogether than pork pies. Finer forcemeat may be used instead of chopped veal, and mushrooms, mushroom ketchup, pickled walnuts and pistachio nuts are all traditional additions.

OTHER TRADITIONAL PIES

Cottage and shepherd pies: easily confused even though only a moment's thought indicates beef goes into the first and sheep into the latter – originally it would be stronger tasting mutton but we must make do with lamb. Another old distinction is that the beef for cottage pie was always minced, whereas the lamb for shepherd's pie was coarsely chopped or sliced. For both, the inclusion of a good strong meat stock and some Worcestershire sauce (or a homemade spiced ketchup) were essential.

Fidget pie: a rarer relation of the squab pie – shortcrust containing bacon, apple and onion or bacon, potato, apple and onion which might sometimes also have included a little lamb or mutton if times were good. It was served with sugar in some counties and usually accompanied by cheese, the more common rural protein source. Well made, with far more apples than potato, with very little onion and some fresh thyme (no mixed herbs *please*) this is well worth resurrecting.

Pasty: the true Cornish pasty or pastie should be made with a lard pastry or you are already letting down the side. The raw beef, potato and swede (yellow turnip to Scots) should all be in thin flakes, not minced or chopped, although the latter is not an absolute heresy: if onion is added, it should be very finely chopped indeed to ensure it melts into the filling and sweetens it, but is not independently detectable.

QUICHE AND SAVOURY FLANS

Quiche has gone into the English language and onto the table faster than spaghetti or kebabs ever did. But how woeful most of them are, and how few are quiche at all.

True quiche, the quiche lorraine, is a light, slightly savoury egg custard in short pastry with perhaps some little amount of green bacon and only a scattering of finely sliced leek or onion. At least, that is what it has become.

It seems the quiche may well once have been made with puff pastry, for it was the painter who took the name Lorraine (he came from the area) who is said to have brought this style of pastry back from Italy. Mixtures which included cheese, onions and the like were originally baked on bread and called *féouses*. The pastry is always pre-baked and the quiche should be eaten warm and quivering – not hot, not cold, but warm.

There are some French and German cousins of quiche, absolutely stuffed with bacon or packed with onion. Some do include cheese, it is true. I've had some flavoured with smoked salmon which were good and, like most people, have suffered countless spinach 'quiches' which swam about in a pool of their own juices because no one had taught anyone how to drain spinach. But, no matter how good, they are not quiches and each diminishes the reputation of the real thing.

What is wrong with calling them savoury flans, the way they used to be?

The inclusion of carrot is generally thought pretty bad form, but as the pasty is such a basic and homely thing, individual preference and general availability have always overcome the views of others.

Squab pie: this should be made with young pigeon, as are many of the greatest pies of the Middle East, but these days lamb or mutton is substituted. The importance of this pie is its closeness to the Arab-influenced style of British food, mixing meat with fruit and spices, which dominated our kitchens longer than any other style, from the Crusades on; spices are a much more British things than herbs. Thus it is proper to expect the lamb to appear with apples, onions and sweet spices, and it will be even better if there are also currants and prunes; a little honey helps blend the flavours considerably.

By now you have gathered a squab pie of lamb, apple, onion and the dead hand of mixed herbs (eek, spit, horror!), should be sent back to the chef. Unless squab pie takes your breath away with bravado flavour and sweet-savoury contrast, it is not a squab pie worthy of the name.

PÂTÉS, TERRINES AND GALANTINES

Well done you if you think pâtés are sausages without skins; you are right. Pâtés and terrines are based on chopped or minced pork in combination with liver and, sometimes, salt pork or bacon. They were originally a method of preserving miscellaneous parts of the pig by first sterilizing (baking) and then sealing (with fat).

The difference between pâtés and terrines is now largely eroded and either name is applied arbitrarily by those who manufacture them. Originally pâtés were the ones that might be turned from the containers in which they were baked and terrines stayed in their earthenware bowls.

A well made and matured pâté or terrine remains one of the finest draws to a delicatessen shop and one of the greatest centrepieces of a buffet table. Yet they are clearly on the decrease. This is partly due to a suspicion of their high fat content, essential for flavour and for their keeping quality, but also I suspect, because there has been so much overextended, over-fatted product on the market which did not deliver the individual flavour promised on the label. In the large continental pâté factories you can explain if not forgive this, but when the small kitchens of decent hotels and restaurants can't get it right either, there is clearly a problem.

I spent many years investigating the point, and decided this: you cannot expect the roasted breast flesh plus the minimal, minced dark meat of game birds to flavour many times their bulk of fatty pork-based farce, but that is the blindly followed classic method of making pâté

A PÂTÉ RECIPE PRIMER

Regard these as the most elementary guide to proportion and flavouring, and then do it your way. The first recipe does not necessarily include liver, the second always does. You can change the proportion of pork to veal or leave out the veal. Different degrees of mincing give different textures. Chicken liver can be used instead of pig. And so on.

PORK AND VEAL PÂTÉ

The dried breadcrumbs are good home-cookery practice, as they mean both that the tasty juices are retained where they do most good, and you do without the bore of pressing to get a decent slicing texture.

Makes about 1kg/2lbs

500g/1lb minced fatty pork   500g/1lb minced lean veal
250g/8oz smoked streaky bacon, minced finely
150ml/¼pt dry white wine   2 large cloves garlic, chopped
1 tsp dried thyme   1 tsp dried rosemary
3 tbsp chopped parsley   2 tbsp dried white breadcrumbs
½ tsp ground nutmeg   black or white pepper
To finish:
150ml/¼pt white wine or stock   2 bay leaves

First mix together the meats and bacon evenly and then add all the flavourings: it is best to do this with your fingers as stirring tends to break up the meat. If you can, leave to stand at room temperature for a few hours or covered in the refrigerator overnight. Put into a 1kg/2lb loaf tin or two 500g/1lb tins. Crush the bay leaves and sprinkle over the top and then pour on the extra wine or stock.

Stand in a bain marie and bake at 160°C/325°F/Gas Mark 3 for 1½ hours for the large pâté and 1 hour for two smaller ones: if the mixture was refrigerated add 15 minutes. Leave 24 hours before cutting.

Variations: some of the wine could be cognac, of course. Strips of streaky bacon stretched with the back of a knife can be folded over the mixture and tucked down the sides – looks good but does increase both the cost and fat content. Puréed chicken or pig's liver can be added to this mixture, about 250g/8oz is right, and as

and the reverse is the usual result – the game ends up tasting of pork and the pâté's flavour is therefore disappointing.

The only absolute way to garner and extend the savour of roasted birds is by

well as adding flavour this also gives a firmer set: or you can replace the veal with liver. For a gamier flavour, add six crushed juniper berries and a ½tsp of ground cloves.

PORK LIVER PÂTÉ

To tranquillize the sometimes strong flavour of pork liver, I use sweeter back bacon, fresh pork and minimal onion: too much bacon or onion emphasizes the liver flavour. The classic country trick of soaking liver in milk for an hour also helps. You could also substitute chicken or turkey livers, of course. The long slow cooking also encourages a gentler and more comforting flavour.

Makes about 750g/1½lb

500g/1lb pig's liver	25g/1oz onion
1 large garlic clove	250g/8oz back bacon, minced
½ tsp dried thyme	½ dried bay leaf, finely crushed
1 tsp ground nutmeg	2 tbsp white wine
2 tbsp cognac	freshly ground black pepper

Make a fine purée of the liver, onion and garlic. Mix with the remaining ingredients, season with pepper and spoon into a suitable loaf tin. Seal tightly with foil and bake in a bain marie for 2-2½ hours.

GAME PÂTÉ

If you wish to extend the pleasure of shooting or buying a game bird or two, the pork and veal pâté mixture is a very good basis. Casserole a pheasant from which you have removed all possible traces of feathers (or two grouse or three pigeons), in robust red wine with the zest of an orange, a couple of bay leaves, six juniper berries and some mace blades until it falls from the bone. Retrieve all the flesh, skin and so on possible then return the bones to the cooking liquid and reduce until only six tablespoons remain. Strain and reserve. Keep any decent pieces of breast meat and purée the rest with the reserved liquid. Mix that into the basic pâté mixture and layer the breast in the middle, perhaps with extra cognac dribbled generously upon them.

For firmer slicing, I should also add an extra tablespoon of dried white breadcrumbs.

potting, that is making a smooth or rough purée with butter, perhaps with cognac, rum or calvados and such spice as mace or nutmeg. Delicious at home, but hardly producing a yield which would support a commercial operation.

What is missing from both the classic (French) pâté method and from potting is the flavour obtained from the bones. Thus when I made pâtés for my shop, I casseroled game birds, venison or duck, with wine, herbs, spices and finely chopped bacon – this so its fat was rendered and could be thoroughly emulsified into the subsequent mixture.

Once the birds were cooked, the flesh was removed and mixed with the usual farce of liver and pork belly. Then, and this was the most important trick, the cooking liquid was reduced, strained and also added. Thus a couple of grouse would highly flavour a kilo or more of basic mixture; baked gently and left for at least two days before cutting, the pâtés clearly smelt and tasted more of grouse than of pork, even though their presence was minimal.

There is a second reason for using bacon at the very start of the pâté making process. The saltpetre content of the bacon permeates all the other flesh and although infinitesimal in proportion, nevertheless encourages a delicious pinkness in the meat when the pâté is cut; without the saltpetre all would be remorselessly grey and that is generally perceived negatively, whatever the flavour.

Today, we tend to make terrines and pâtés with a low fat content, and this has changed flavours and storage techniques; a properly made traditional pâté keeps uncut for months under its layer of fat in a cool cellar, whereas many modern producers become uneasy after much shorter storage. On the other hand most commercial pâtés are so preserved as to be almost indestructible, far more likely to damage you than themselves. In fact most of the huge range that has flooded the market over the last decade is everything *but* what it claims to be – traditional. Most are liquidized then stabilized with thickening agents, extended with cellulose or soy, coloured by the roseate action of nitrites, flavoured with herb oils rather than the real thing, enriched with soya flour or milk powder and overloaded with monosodium glutamate to overstimulate your tastebuds into recognizing what little meat is contained. The effect is such that they can be transported over hundreds of miles, stored for weeks and still look fresh ages after they have finally been broken from their vacuum wrappings. Wonders of modern science or the home economist they might be – wholesome, honest and simple they are not.

If you have a food processor, pâtés and terrines are exceptionally simple to make and very satisfying. The ingredients are cheap and easy to obtain. Ignore absolutely those recipes with zillions of ingredients or amazing ideas. I even know someone who wanted to put choux pastry into chicken liver pâté, saying this is what he was taught at a well known catering college.

Galantines are those multi-coloured, large sausages with strips and stripes of brightly-coloured meats and vegetables in a finely textured pâté, held together by a wrapping of fat. Originally the container was the whole skin of a fowl or it was the boned carcass of this or some other bird. Some are available commercially, but I implore you to taste them first for the ones which looked best to me turned out to have the least flavour. It seems the flavour of too many commercial pâtés, terrines and galantines is contributed by the additives rather than the animal upon which the product is based.

Storing: it is better to treat all charcuterie products, including pies, pâtés and terrines, as if they were fresh produce; keep them well wrapped and well chilled. Those which contain a lot of onion are more likely to go sour.

VEGETABLE PATCH PÂTÉ

The much vaunted terrines of vegetable presented as the star turn of many a modern chef have always disappointed me. Somehow it seemed a swizz to call them terrines of vegetable when the vegetables were held together with a mousse of ham or tongue or some other part of an animal. I therefore determined to make a terrine entirely of vegetables and used the techniques behind my savoury flans as the basis.

This recipe makes a large party pâté, so you might halve the quantity to make something for a dinner party; it will keep in the refrigerator for over a week.

Serves 15-20

900g/2lb parsnips	8 eggs
425ml/¾pt milk or single cream	4tbsp lemon juice
50g/2oz butter	900g/2lb vegetables, in thin strips
225g/8 oz curd or cream cheese	vine leaves, as required

Scrub the parsnips well and cut them up roughly, but do not peel them. Poach until tender in creamy milk or single cream, together with the butter. Liquidize and strain, then let cool before beating in the cheese, eggs and lemon juice. If you do this when the parsnip purée is hot you will deflate the cheese, and the mixture will not be able to support the vegetables.

The variety of vegetables with which you dramatize the basic pâté should be chosen for a contrast of colour, texture and taste, and three or four will be enough. None needs to be pre-cooked but all must be in long strips or cubes and each must be independently seasoned. Green beans (I use frozen haricot beans), strips of carrot or of turnip can be smothered in finely chopped parsley or sprinkled well with nutmeg. Equally, the beans or celeriac or fennel could be drenched in garlic, the turnip could be smeared in mustard, sliced artichoke bottoms bathed in tarragon vinegar or tossed in chopped fresh mint, thyme or rosemary. Peas can be avoided.

Once you have your purée ready and your vegetables prepared, liberally oil a 1.7lt/3pt loaf tin then line with overlapping vine leaves, shiny sides outermost, leaving a border hanging over the top of the tin.

Pour in a shallow layer of parsnip then arrange your heaviest vegetable in lines lengthwise along the tin. Add more purée and then another vegetable and so on until everything is used up and the tin is filled. Top with vine leaves and interweave those with the excess from the sides to make a neat parcel. Stand in boiling water in a roasting tray and cover the pâté with a dome of foil, tightly sealed around the loaf tin's edges. Bake 1¼ hours in a preheated oven at 180°C/350°F/Gas 4. Let stand 15 minutes then invert onto a large platter, simply to check it will emerge. If not you will have to do a little scalpel work, but remember, it is only the vine leaves you are dissecting. Then line the loaf tin with clingfilm or foil and replace the pâté so it stays firmly in shape whilst it is cooling. Place in a refrigerator so it chills thoroughly.

Options: instead of parsnips you might choose to use celeriac or carrot, but ensure the latter is well flavoured – it would be a waste of effort to use sweet new carrots. If you have a garden full of herbs, then scatter through a layer of chopped mixed herbs. Those with an artistic bent could soft-boil and shell some quails' eggs and arrange them in strips along the pâté.

A somewhat misused term, game. Game properly meant animals or birds which had to be hunted and killed before you could eat them. You might still do this to grouse and pheasant, even to venison if you are rich enough – or poor enough to live in suitably remote areas. But generally a happy combination of greed and sense means most such animals are now farmed. There will certainly be some compromise on taste and perhaps size, but generally greater availability outweighs that in most cases.

The most important thing for the serious cook and eater to remember is that farmed game animals will almost always be blander in flavour, not necessarily a bad thing, but meaning the old fashioned, strongly flavoured marinades are neither needed nor necessary. This is particularly true with venison.

Generally, young birds may be served roasted but older ones should be casseroled or braised.

The best use of game in the delicatessen and specialty food store is probably in pâtés and pies, especially Britain's famed raised pies. Or so the theory goes. The practice is that we regularly find there is more presence of the pheasant or partridge or pigeon on the label than on the palate, and thus the premium we have paid has been obtained by false pretence. The solution is explained in the chapter _Pies, Pâtés and Terrines_.

Yet as the taste grows for more interesting food, I expect the traditional countryside flavours of the past will come more and more to the fore: already pigeon and Barbary duck, rabbit and hare are regularly featured in the national supermarkets and they are bound to work their way into more and more produce. It is as well you know what they should taste like before you are persuaded otherwise.

Barbary duck and magret: this comparatively huge duck gives thick and long breast meat portions which are positively steak-like: indeed before the word magret came into fashion they would be seen on menus as _steak de canard_. The breast meat is increasingly found available as an independent purchase and makes a terrific change from steak for those who like red meat. Generally the cooking instructions are grotesquely wrong – suggesting 40 minutes cooking for something which requires ten at the most. The best way is to score the fat in a deep criss-cross and then to cook at very high heat in a non-stick pan, fat side down for 4-6 minutes depending on how well cooked you like duck. Then pour away the fat, turn the meat and cook the same amount of time. If you eat this now it will be tougher than boots, new or old. They must, absolutely must, rest for another ten minutes, during which they tenderize and the colour evens, but they won't get cold, I promise you. They may also be grilled for about the same overall time.

But are these breasts magrets? Not if you wish to be accurate. A true magret is properly only the very lean breast of a Muscovy duck which has been force-fed to make _foie gras de canard_. This simply isn't the case with Barbary duck breasts, but the name seems to be sticking.

Bison/buffalo: don't blame Kevin Costner. America had rediscovered its great native mammal some time before he took sides with native Americans. Both in the United States and in Canada the animal is being successfully farmed for the gourmet. It tastes like beef but behaves like venison: it has very little fat and thus overcooks and toughens very easily. When it is good it is exceptionally good. So too is the much rarer and smaller musk ox of the Northern Territories, also being marketed now the species is on the increase. But so far the Inuit language names they use for it prove even more off-putting than calling it musk ox.

Chickens: at last, someone has listened and chicken is getting decidedly better to eat. To be fair much criticism was unfairly based; chickens did not taste fishy because they were fed with fishmeal, for this is expensive and would have put the price up. Like so many criticized foods, there has been and is enormous scope for improvement in standards and

POULTRY CATEGORIES

Check the label on your chicken. It may not have ranged as freely as you thought.

Barn Reared: also known as 'extensive indoor'. There will be up to 12 birds or 25kgs live weight per square metre of floor space. Chickens, geese, guinea fowls, turkeys and both Peking and Muscovy ducks are included in the category and must be a certain number of days old before slaughter. There are regulations about feed, but not quite enough, many would think.

Free Range: the birds must have continuous daytime access to open-air runs for at least half their lifetime. That area must be covered by vegetation (grass) and each chicken must have at least a square metre to call its own. Ducks have twice that space, turkeys four times, and all must be fed 70 per cent cereal during their final fattening period. The poultry house for chickens must provide continuous access with pop-holes equal in length or greater than that of the longest

flavour, but minor shortcomings in basically decent produce were more often exacerbated by dreadful cooking advice on labels and packets from the very people who should know better – *(see COOKING BIRDS)*. It is these 'recipe developers' rather than the producers who should be shot.

Today we have an increasingly excellent choice of poultry available, including corn-fed, free range and a few less well know varieties, such as the black legged Poulet Noir, and there are imports from France, too. In Britain, a tremendous effort is being made in Northern Ireland. Petits Poussins, what we would call baby chickens, are increasingly heavily marketed. They look good, especially at picnics or when you are eating with your hands. But because they are so young they offer precious little flavour and so you should resist any temptation to be too clever with herbs and spices, or they will be all that you taste.

Needless to say the EC has issued very clear directives on what may be called what, based partly on stocking rates and partly on what the birds are fed. The way really to discover the difference in flavour is to make a stock from the bones of a corn-fed, free range chicken, a revelation to the young, a nostalgic leap backwards for those of us who grew up watching grandfathers wring the neck of backyard chickens which had scratched free and dined only on grain and household scraps.

Foie gras: means fat liver, and that's what it is, the livers of geese or Muscovy duck which have been force-fed to such a degree the livers bloat with fat, for this is

side of the house.
Traditional Free Range: you would expect this to be simpler, but it is terribly complicated, yet worth knowing. First, the overall maximum capacity and raising area per farm is restricted, and the outdoor area of vegetation must be twice as big, on average. Daytime access must be continuous from at least six weeks old for chickens, eight weeks for most other birds. Grain must compromise 70 per cent of the fattening feed and the birds must be of a recognized slow-growing breed. There are minimum ages for slaughter, eg 81 days for chickens.
Free Range – Total Freedom: essentially as above, but the open-air runs to which the birds have continuous daytime access must be unlimited, ie they can run wild wherever they like.
Corn-fed: theoretically any of the above can also be corn-fed, which essentially means that the fattening grain used will be maize, giving notable flavour and colour.

where it collects rather than under the skin: force-fed ducks are otherwise surprisingly lean – *(see MAGRET)*. The process is seen by many as exceptionally cruel; others reckon both geese and ducks are so contrary and bad tempered you couldn't get them to do anything they do not want. You must make up your own mind.

In the past decade foie gras from ducks, *foie gras de canard*, has become very much more common. It most usually comes from the south west of France, notably Gascony, where the sudden leap of availability is put down to the simple ploy of shading the ducks during summer, keeping them happier and healthier. Foie gras de canard is cheaper than that from geese and many think it much better value, for it is less likely to explode into pools of melted fat thus further frustrating the gourmet, who must already only make do with just 15 per cent of the foie gras produced – the remainder is unsuited to use whole and must be made into mousses and other commercial products. Some think goose foie gras is more finely flavoured and it probably is, but I belong to the ranks who think the flavour of foie gras de canard is more complicated and thus more gratifying. The EC regulations state that a fattened duck liver should weigh at least 250g and that of a geese 400g.

Fattened livers are nothing new, for the Ancient Greeks and Romans adored them and Ancient Egyptians seemed to have force-fed their geese with figs. It was probably the Romans who brought the idea to France. Foie gras of both kinds are generally associated with Perigord but they are also a specialty of the Landes, Gascony and Alsace. Interestingly, its presence is usually associated with traditional centres of Jewry (they wanted the fat for cooking) and of ancient poverty: poor areas couldn't afford salt and thus fattened geese so they could use the fat as a winter preservative. Geese convert what food there is into flesh and fat more efficiently than almost any other animal and so the bloated liver was pretty much a bonus rather than the goal.

Until the Second World War foie gras was produced widely all along the Danube, again mainly by Middle-Europe's Jewish centres; Hungary and Czechoslovakia used to export their livers to France and have started to do so again. Poland is producing them again and, continuing the Jewish connection, Israel has become a major exporter.

Fresh foie gras is available in Britain, vacuum packed. It is commonly sliced and cooked quickly in a non-stick pan, a few minutes a side at the most; although served pinkish rather a lot, there is a school which thinks this idiotically dangerous. But even baked terrines of foie gras are cooked at such a low temperature any bacteria included would think they were being encouraged to multiply rather than to die. More surprising, some chefs in Gascony serve it raw, having merely salted it overnight and they seem not to be in cahoots with the local doctor or undertaker. I expect they are relying on the fat to be a safe preservative...

It is important to understand with absolute clarity the difference between *foie gras d'oie* or *foie gras de canard* (sometimes *terrine de foie gras* or *foie gras de canard*) and *pâté de foie gras*. The first two are solid liver and however they are cooked, whether sliced and fried or baked in terrines, they are never referred to as a pâté de foie gras. And neither is any of the foie gras which comes in cans, although this is pretty much what they are. They are foie gras in greater or lesser union with pork and other ingredients, the mousses and so forth to which unsuitable livers go. Once you have tasted the real thing you will find these quite a different product and not always easy to tell from lesser meat pastes at much less cost. They usually have speckles which are supposed to be truffles, and indeed may be, but I have yet to taste the effect on anything but the pocket.

Pâté de foie gras, the real thing, was created in the late 18th century by Jean-Pierre Clause for the table of le Marechal de Contudes, governor of Alsace, who sent some to Louis XVI. One M. Doyen is supposed to have perfected it, adding truffles. It is properly whole foie gras wrapped in a farce of pork and baked in pastry. Unless made with exceptional skill the farce will dilute the flavour of the foie gras; thus unless you buy from a traiteur or restaurateur who comes highly recommended you are better off going for nothing but foie gras itself. That of Alsace will have been lightly kneaded and slightly spiced, whereas that from the south west of France will have been layered pretty much the way the lobes came, with just a little cognac or armagnac.

If you are lucky enough to get whole foie gras, it is traditionally served chilled as a first course with an excellent wine – some say the best accompaniment is a chilled sweet sauterne and certainly something with a hint of fruit and sweetness is good. A Verdelho madeira or the rare Palo Cortado sherry would be my other choices.

The labelling on cans containing foie gras is complicated. When French products are made only with goose liver, they need only say *Foie Gras*; if they are made from duck they then need to say *Foie Gras de Canard*.

Semi-cooked or semi preserved foie gras: this is considered the finest way of keeping livers. They are cooked gently with little extra seasoning in a tightly closed container. The juices which come out during cooking are soaked back into the liver: nothing is lost, nothing gained. Provided the seal is not broken, and the liver; has been cooked right through, and it is kept between 0°C and 5°C, it may last six to eight months, but it is not fully sterilized. Not normally available commercially.

Presented foie gras: a fancy way of saying tinned whole foie gras. Fully sterilized in the usual way of canning and probably the way it is most seen. It is important that the preserved liver is allowed to mature after processing – it needs six to eight months at least.

Natural: this indicates the content of the tin will be foie gras in one or several pieces. If there is a marinade or seasoning, that will be shown on the label.

Block, lingot, tombeau, massif, terrine, roll or pâté: any of these used as adjectives preceding foie gras means a minimum of 75 per cent foie gras with pork, veal or poultry meat added.

Purée, mousse or cream: these adjectives indicate a minimum of 75 per cent foie gras, plus pork, veal, or poultry plus eggs, milk, wheat or cornflour up to a maximum of three per cent.

Mousse – foie d'oie: the trick is to notice that it is foie d'oie not foie gras. It is ordinary goose liver and the mousse need only contain 50 per cent of it. Most foie gras products include truffles, but I'm still not sure they add anything other than expense. The purées and mousses are mainly used as pâtés, spread on toast, but are often used in scoops or slices as garnish and should be cold.

Grouse: it's not been a good time for the grouse moors in the past few years: in 1993 only one in 50 moors was shooting on the Glorious 12th. But persevere, for few wild things are as rewarding as the red grouse.

First, it is one of the few which can be eaten the moment it drops from the sky, and will be fabulously tender and sweet. Yet let it hang until whiffy and it becomes something different but equally worth your attention.

At its higher flavour level grouse is one of the very best of all flavouring ingredients for pies and pâtés, but not if you follow the 'traditional' method of expecting only the roasted flesh of a bird to flavour layers of fatty farce – *(see COOKING BIRDS)*. Best cooked dead plain in my view, and served with earthy celeriac purée, parsnip chips and watercress rather than the fatty palaver of game chips, bland bread sauce, bacon and such, all of which so coat the palate you have precious little chance of tasting all for which you have so heavily paid.

Cold grouse is perhaps the best breakfast I have eaten, in turn the only possible reason for subjecting myself to cooking for 14 in a remote Scottish farmhouse in August. But that is another story…

Guinea fowl: increasingly seen, the oven-ready guinea fowl looks rather like a sick chicken with a pigeon chest. They have less fat than chickens and thus require more careful cooking or they will be dry. The taste is like, well, like chicken, but with subtle overtones of smokiness and farminess. A nice change if only for the sake of some new table talk.

Hare: dark, red and delicious, the hare is always wild. Like rabbit, the saddle will be tender and everywhere else a bit of a gamble. Best cooked on the bone so the meat does not shrink and an excellent ingredient in game pies and stews. Spices help a lot, and thus so does a little dark chocolate to finish the sauce. Either that or blood – its, not yours.

Mallard: the biggest of the wild ducks, and possessor of a wonderfully fine and refined flavour that is duckier than duck. The habit of singeing the down which sits under the feathers can taint the flesh flavour, particularly when the plucking is inadequate and then the base of the feathers are also burned and carry the flavour into the flesh. If you shoot or buy mallard from estuaries there is the chance of a fishy flavour, but I have never experienced this in 30 years of being a mallard fan. They say cooking with a potato in the cavity helps.

Mallard have precious little fat and particularly benefit from being cooked on their breasts. Rest them well before serving.

Ostrich: yes, you may well gasp. But the ostrich farms already in Britain do not have only the sale of feathers in their mission statements. They want to sell you ostrich steaks. And they will. Well, if not them, the South Africans. Gamey turkey, pallid venison – just some of the descriptions I have heard, but everyone loved it. They said.

In Australia they now farm emu to the same culinary end; apparently the flavour is very similar and some airlines flying to Australia include it on their business class menus for passengers prepared to worry about cholesterol levels – like most game meats it has exceptionally low levels and is thus considered healthier.

Partridge: perhaps my favourite game bird, just right for one person's treat, and a half bird makes a delicious first course, hot or cold. Partridge flesh is

COOKING BIRDS

For anyone with experience of it, spit-roasting is the only way to cook birds. As they constantly turn, the juices stay inside; any basting juices become true drippings, collected in a pan on the floor. These are what were once thickened with almonds if you were rich, with bread if you were poor. It was only when closed ovens became the norm in households that we began cooking birds flat on their backs and then had to put the bread inside them, both of which contribute to dry birds or those not cooked enough, so that dangerous salmonella remains on their bones.

To get as close as possible to the effects of spit-roasting, all birds should be cooked on their breast or on their sides, in which case they should be turned from time to time. Any stuffing inside the bird should be minimal and based on anything which will create steam and mixture – apples, oranges, onions if you must. Butter or pork-based forcemeat may be pushed between the skin and breast of bigger birds, which may then be spared cooking on their breasts, as the fat will drip through the flesh and keep it moist and flavoursome. Forcemeat or stuffing which contains bread should never be put inside a bird, for it absorbs the juices which should remain in the flesh; instead it must be rolled into balls and cooked around the bird, where it will absorb fats and cooking juices that have been exuded. Interestingly the United States, which we do not always credit with much cooking style, generally follows this practice.

During cooking, basting is pointless, other than to brown the skin. It does not give moister flesh, for how do the juices get through the skin? Basting takes time, continuously reduces the oven temperature and thus affects cooking time

whiter, finer, sweeter and altogether more elegant than its competitors, and thus deserves to be cooked very plainly, with only a little butter rubbed into the skin before roasting. Should you wish to extend the pleasure of a partridge, pot the

calculations, but contrary to what you may have thought, it has absolutely no effect on the end eating result.

More important is to rest birds before they are carved, and to do this on the bird's breast, so that loose juice seeps into the flesh rather than into the body cavity. If the bird is so big its weight would put the breast out of shape, either take the weight in a gentlemanly way by putting uncooked potatoes under its wings, or rest it on alternate sides.

A chicken should rest at least 15 minutes, a turkey at least 30 minutes; such small birds as grouse, petits poussins, partridge and the like are best cooked entirely on their breast with only a brief flash for browning, if that is important to you, and then rested on their breast for five to ten minutes. Please, please do not wrap cooked birds in foil, a horrid and unthinking modern habit with no authentic provenance and less contemporary reason. The foil traps steam which risks toughening the flesh in the same way a grilled or fried steak will toughen if you add liquid. Successful oven baking is actually a gradual concentration of the flesh juices and this must continue when the bird is not in the oven.

In any case, if it is not cut, any bird will remain piping hot for a very long time in even a moderately warm kitchen, just as it did for all those zillions of centuries before aluminium foil was forced onto us. Early carving, slow or inexpert carving and cold plates do far more to chill roasted birds than resting uncovered ever will: hot plates and a sauce or gravy quickly restore what might be lost during serving, and it will be juicier and more tender. As is ever the case with good basic foods, less mucking about always gives more pleasure.

puréed or finely chopped roasted flesh with unsalted butter, ground almonds and mace and then serve with lightly chilled muscatel grapes. Or with pears if it is Christmas, I suppose.

Pheasant: a combination of farmed and wild. They are most likely to have been bred in captivity and then released to fatten naturally before being hunted. At least this is so in Britain. In the United States where almost no truly wild game may be offered commercially, fully farmed pheasant seems to have less flavour than a battery chicken. But this might also be because they have not been hung for any length of time.

Pheasant needs to be hung as it is naturally a dry-fleshed bird and decomposition (let's not mince words) tenderizes it, so making it edible. There is a concomitant increase of flavour which beyond a certain point becomes very much a matter of personal taste. Those who insist on hanging birds until they drop to the ground are increasingly rare, a sign the world is becoming more sophisticated. Too much gaminess means you do not taste the pheasant and the exercise thus seems pointless. But once you are convinced the game smell is what actually converts to sensational sweetness when cooked, you will want to find the perfect balance. For me this means pretty high smelling legs, but a breast which is still fresh seeming.

The smaller hen is sweeter than the cock bird, and whoever reckons you can feed four people off a single bird is a rotten host. Two birds might serve six people. Leave off the nonsense of bacon on the breast, which also hijacks the natural flavours, but do cook the birds only on their sides or breasts and leave them to rest well in this position after roasting; those are the ways to ensure moistness.

Pigeon: now corn-fed farmed pigeon are competing with the more rugged and darker fleshed wild bird, the pigeon is fast climbing the culinary ladder. The scourge of Trafalgar Square sits comfortably with truffled cabbage and foie gras at banquets.

There are a few tricks worth knowing about pigeon. Should you think it smart to remove the breasts before pan-frying, think again. They will shrink so alarmingly your thoughts will only be to leave by the back door or to change the menu. It is always best to roast or grill pigeon as whole birds and then to butcher them when they have rested (on their breasts) until luke-warm, when they will taste better anyway.

Even if you are more inclined to braise than roast, know that most pigeons are ruined by cooks waiting for the legs to cook and thus over-cooking the breast. Judge cooking time only on the breast and whilst that is resting, remove the legs and sauté them to finish; or remove them first and stew them in the liquid over which you braise the resultant heart-shaped breast and rib cage. For casseroles, cut the back bone out of whole birds and then cook as halves with wing and leg attached.

GAME SEASONS

Although prosecution is rare unless someone has transgressed the rules which protect some birds year round, there are nonetheless quite clear restrictions about which game may be sold when. The least regarded, most broken rule is that no distinction is made between fresh and frozen game, neither of which is supposed to be sold later than ten days after the open season is finished; the exception is game imported dead into this country.

Pigeon is actually classified as vermin rather than game and thus has no closed season, but it would have if your customers knew this.

GAME BIRD SEASONS

Black game: *August 20th to December 10th (in Somerset, Devon and the New Forest September 1st to December 1st)*
Grouse: *August 12th to December 10th*
Partridge: *September 1st to February 1st*

Quail: almost everyday now. These small birds have more flesh on their deep breasts than you expect. They are sweet and juicy and have a flavour rather like the dark meat of chicken. Considering quail hens lay an egg a day, and that quails' eggs are commonplace, it seems surprising they are so expensive. There are those who bone them and stuff them. It's a jolly good wheeze and excellent to eat, but unless you are a boning boffin, life really is too short. For special occasions, roasted quails are a terrific first course, when one per person is quite enough; they are commonly served with peeled grapes, which I used to call Quails Beulah, but so few have now seen the incomparable Mae West telling her maid Beulah to peel her a grape... For a main course, two or even three would be the norm. The simplest way to cope with the cooking is to spatchcock, a term often thought to mean a small chicken or pigeon, but actually meaning the following technique: split each bird through the back, open flat and then push bamboo skewers through them to keep them prone, after which they are simply grilled or barbecued. For roasting, vine leaves make an excellent wrapping.

Rabbit: if you buy this ready prepared it will probably be frozen and invariably

Pheasant: *October 1st to February 1st*
Ptarmigan: *August 12th to December 10th*
Wild duck, including mallard, teal and widgeon: *September 1st to February 20th, but thought best from October to December*

WILD VENISON SEASONS

England and Wales

Red and Sika: stags *August 1st to April 30,* hinds *November 1st to February 28th*
Fallow: *as red and sika*
Roe: bucks *October 31st to April 1st,* does *November 1st to April 30th*

Scotland

Sika: stags *July 1st to October 20,* hinds *October 21st to February 15th*
Red/sika hybrids: *as sika*
Roe: bucks *April 1st to October 20th,* does *October 21st to March 31st*
Fallow: bucks *August 1st to April 30th,* does *October 21st to February 15th*
Red: *as sika*

from China. Not that tasty, but invaluable for bulking out game pies and stews and such. Wild rabbits make excellent if scant eating, but you cannot cook the meaty legs and tender saddle meat the same way or for the same time; braise the legs and grill the saddle, having marinaded both, is my answer.

Snails/Escargot: usually from France, snails are available two ways, in cans or frozen. The canned ones sometimes also come presented with empty shells.

The best are said to be fed upon vine leaves. I've heard them compared to oysters and chicken, and as they are cultivated we may be stretching the definition to include them in *Poultry & Game,* but where would you put them? Polite answers on a postcard please.

If you think carefully, it is not the snails you enjoy but the butter, usually redolent of garlic, so the bother of stuffing snails back into their shells, then pulling them out again with special and expensive instruments seems a bit silly. Snails are even nicer (or the butter is) on little beds of pastry or in tiny vol-au-vents.

Other people serve them other ways and the most interesting alternative is a red wine sauce flavoured with anise – either the seed or some suitable alcohol; fennel seed can also be used, and I believe these ideas come from Sicily.

Snails are now being bred for the table in England once more, in the Mendips, as they were by the Romans, but they seem rather small.

In case you were wondering, snails have little food value.

Venison: it is a mystery to me why farmed venison is not on everyone's table every week. It is thought by many to be the world's healthiest red meat, very high in protein, low in saturated fats and very delicious indeed. The Bambi factor is partly to blame, I know. So is the lack of a united marketing front internationally by producers, which keeps the prices high. And then there is the stupidity of chefs and, sad to say, the cooking recommendations of some producers who continuously misunderstand the place of marinades.

Wild venison often needed to soak in strongly flavoured marinades for two good reasons. First, it may have been tough, an enzymatic reaction within the flesh triggered by trauma if hunted; the acid in the marinade counteracted that and tenderized the meat. But almost more important was the big, often rank and tainted flavour of the flesh, sometimes only a natural reflection of what fodder had been eaten, but which had to be diluted, masked, or both. Farmed venison is neither endemically tough nor highly or unsuitably flavoured.

The flavour to expect of decent cuts of farmed venison is that of fine fillet steak, delicate, subtly sweet, beef-like. The flesh is somehow silken in texture too, helping create the privileged sense of elegance and superiority. Light marinades of superior subtle wines, sweet fruit juices and citrus zests, herbs and spices are a good thing, only if they add supportive new dimensions rather than mask what is there. Harsh rough wine, large amounts of acidic raw onions, too much garlic, citrus juice, vinegars and the like have no place in marinades for farmed venison.

Venison may be hung for added flavour, indeed some hanging is essential, and those who are interested in buying venison to turn into other products would be best advised to choose meat which has developed deeper flavour than that which might be simply roasted and served.

Smoking has become a popular way to finish venison, especially in prepacks, but for my taste it is usually wildly overdone. Venison sausages are generally a very good buy, for they will use the 'umbles, the internal organs; venison liver is considered one of the best types possible and should you see anything which says it includes this cut, and think the manufacturers likely to have used enough to taste, it would be well worth exploration.

LABEL ROUGE

Red label foods from France fairly much guarantee anything carrying one is made to strict standards. Of course, with the relish food writers have for scandal there is always a whisper that this or that is not quite right. But if any shoddiness affects the quality, goodness or flavour of what you buy, the numbered label enables the producer to be knobbled and thus deceit is less likely than with something not sporting a Label Rouge. If nothing else, they make shopping in France much easier if you don't speak the language, and justify the higher price they will command, both there and abroad. All in all, over 100 products have the right to carry a Label Rouge, including vegetables, olives, apples and pears, beef and veal, but in this country the most widely known and available is free range poultry.

POULTRY: ninety per cent of Label Rouge poultry is chicken, with duck, guinea fowl and turkey making up the rest. If such chickens are raised outdoors with at least two square metres of their own, they may also be labelled *fermier*. Otherwise they will have been confined, but in controlled conditions and limited numbers. Their diet will have been 70 per cent cereal, rising higher for their final fortnight; some will be fed exclusively on wheat or corn for their last week and it will say so on the pack. Chickens will be at least 81 days old, guinea fowl 94 days, Christmas turkey 140 days and Barbary ducks 84 days.

The labels for poultry are more complicated than others, but worth studying so you know precisely what you are buying. Reading from the top they tell you:

Wild boar: one of the newest of traditional products to return to our table. It became extinct in Britain about three centuries ago, but had been a regular on the table. The wild boar is immediately identifiable for its extraordinary narrow body tapering behind a big, brutish head and neck (which carries most of its fat), black

Duree d'elevage: how long they were alive

Alimentation: what they were fed

Date limite de vente: last day of sale – seven days after slaughter for chickens

Type d'elevage: method of raising, ie fermier or otherwise

Provenance: producer and area

No. de l'etiquette: production number.

COOKED HAM – jambon cuit: only hind-quarter meat may be used, and only full muscles and meat from one animal (nothing tumbled or reconstituted). These hams contains no phosphates.

RAW HAM – jambon sec or cru: only dry-salting allowed in processing and regulated times of salting and curing.

PÂTÉS: guaranteed percentages of the major product featured – 25 per cent pork liver in a pâté de foie, for instance. In fact it is a brave exposé of how intrinsically dishonest most pâté labelling is. I should have expected the percentage to be at least 50 per cent, wouldn't you?

SAUCISSONS: French air-cured sausages (the equivalent of salami) which sport a Label Rouge will only be made from noble cuts and contain a maximum 25 per cent fat, all of which must be hard fats. The texture will always be coarse so the quality of the meat and fat can be appreciated at a glance. No colouring or phosphates and regulated methods and times of curing.

EMMENTAL GRAND CRU: Cheese made in all the eastern departments of France, but only from grass and hay (no silage), and aged at least ten weeks. Shape, flavour, smell and everything else are controlled, but no matter how good, it must not be confused with Emmental *qv*, the Swiss cheese which is aged from six to twelve months.

hairiness and spindly legs, all a help to skittering through bush and brush I suppose. They are slow growers but their flight or fight genes produce red protein flesh rather than the pallid white protein of domesticated pigs. The meat is tender if cooked properly but will always appear more textured and grainy than pork.

Most producers in Britain claim not to interfere in their natural growth with hormones and the like, and although some animals are also claimed to feed absolutely naturally, others will be offered supplements.

In reality, the perceived pleasure of eating wild boar can be rather cerebral. In the first place it should not taste like pork, and if it does it means you are eating a cross-bred animal: the in-built possibilities for disappointment are thus enormous. Neither should there be the strong or gamey flavour found in wild venison; indeed even producers find it difficult to describe what we should expect – a veal-like flavour between rabbit and hare was thought to be accurate. To add to the confusion, it is not just the boar which is eaten, but both sexes, usually killed at about 12 months.

Products on offer, apart from such cuts as haunches and saddles, include wild boar sausages, dry-cured hams and smoked shoulder. I have also tasted pâtés and pies and everything else you would expect. In many cases the marinade overpowered the taste of the flesh and thus one could be forgiven for wondering why the fuss. But I'm sure this will all work out and I welcome the pioneers and thank them for reintroducing the wild boar to our table, in whatever form they can and will.

Put simply, an oil is a fat which is liquid at normal temperatures. Although earliest man in northern Europe relied on animals for fat, the rest of the world looked to vegetable oils. The type varied according to locality. In Mesopotamia sesame seed oil was used and records survive of the 'best quality' being bought for Nebuchadnezzar's palace. In Anatolia it was almond oil; in the Americas oil from the peanut, maize and sunflower; in China and south-east Asia they used soya and coconuts. Before the introduction of the olive, you would have used radish seed oil in Egypt, walnut and poppy seed oil in Greece. Poppies of a different type were used in northern Europe, as well as oil from flax and the cameline.

Not all these oils were used exclusively for cooking, nor are they now. Pliny gives an explanatory quote which I vote the most tantalizing of any. He said: 'There are two liquids especially agreeable to the human body, wine inside and oil outside.' And I shouldn't think he was speaking of salads al fresco...

The Egyptians used olive oil (and buttermilk incidentally) as a lubricant for moving heavy building materials. Homer mentions it as an aid to weaving and it has been used to make soap since the days of ancient Rome, where it also powered lamps. In Minoan Crete, oil was considered part of the king's treasure and an important commodity for earning foreign exchange.

Oils were also used as protective agents on ships' hulls and in painting. Modern emulsion paints, which are now water soluble, are descendants of tempera, an emulsion in water of oil and pigments stabilized with vegetable gums or egg yolks.

Oil's uses pharmacologically are manifold, and far more sophisticated than the purgative spoonful of castor oil. This perhaps is the time to simplify the vexed question of saturated and unsaturated fats and all that.

Animal fats have a high level of so-called saturated fats. These are solid at normal temperature and are believed to increase blood cholesterol, leading to hardening of the arteries and heart problems. Vegetable oils mainly contain polyunsaturated fats, which are always liquid unless specially treated. They in turn contain something called linoleic acid which when eaten with food helps lower the cholesterol level and aids the burning up of carbohydrate, preventing its conversion into fat. This is not to say you must throw your butter out the window, but rather, as in most dietary matters, try to strike a balance of what you like, what makes you fat, and what might help prolong your life. Butter is not an assassin, nor is safflower oil an elixir of everlasting life.

The major uses of vegetable oils are for cooking, and as the basis of margarine; they also go into cooking fats, salad dressings and ice cream.

OLIVE OIL

We have the message, thank you very much and we agree. Olive oil does taste terrific and does do us good and we are all using it like mad. Except that some people are insane, quite missing the point of virginity and ignoring the qualities of other oils.

Any cook who understands oil has at least three in the cupboard: an extra virgin olive oil to use as is, a lesser virgin olive oil or a plain olive oil for cooking or frying and a plain olive oil for basics or when a full olive oil flavour is unwanted – unless it is for mayonnaise, a vegetable oil might substitute for the last of these. To these basics I would add walnut or hazelnut oil, for a delicious change, and sesame oil for finishing oriental dishes. Those who buy only extra virgin olive oil and use it for all their culinary chores are either pretentious, which is sadly common, or have been misled by ill-informed writing, which is depressing.

In case you have not kept up, olive oil is considered important in balanced diets, its monounsaturate content positively helping to control and reduce the destructive inroads of the bad type of cholesterol. It tas-

TYPES OF OLIVE OIL

The classification of olive oil is vexing, for it is based on a combination of objective scientific principles and the Panel Test, a rather more subjective assessment of organoleptic characteristics; in 1992 these new EC tests meant 60 per cent of Italian oils risked being downgraded – they had the acid level of a higher grade but not the standards of flavour or authenticity.

The basic classification is virgin olive oil, and that has been defined by The International Olive Oil Council as oil: *'obtained solely by mechanical or other physical means under conditions, and particularly thermal conditions, that do not lead to the deterioration of the oil, and which has not undergone any treatment other than washing, decantation, centrifugation and filtration... virgin olive oil* (must thus be) *fit for consumption as it is ...'*

Virgin olive oil is thus made by a traditional mill's first cold pressing or by the modern, more common and greater yielding hydraulic press and centrifuge, each process without heating or chemical assistance. The lower an oil's acidity, the more care has been taken with every aspect of the growing, harvesting and oil making: perhaps equally important, low acid oils will keep their integrity, flavour and appearance longer. There are several categories, but to use the name virgin for an oil which may be eaten as it comes from the press, it must have no more than 3.3 per cent acidity and at least a 3.5 score on the organoleptic scale.

As you shop and travel you will see variations of names and grades. This is because there has been monumental confusion for some years, and even though regulations are now firm, some areas have no working taste panels and some distributors are simply getting away with what they can. Don't forget that your own tastebuds can help you select a good olive oil.

tes wonderful too, an ingredient to choose and use as a flavouring rather than as mere emollient in salads or as a medium for frying. Beyond that, olive oil becomes inordinately complicated and, anyway, like many good things, contains a good chunk of calories. You know where they might spend the next month...

Extra virgin is certainly no guarantee that the oil has been extracted traditionally, first crushed into a paste which is pressed between fibre mats. These days mechanical methods prevail, first to chop the olives and then using hydraulic presses and centrifugal force so every skerrick of decent oil is extracted in a single process, which goes some way to explain the sudden increase in virginity on the shelves.

The United States has also recognized that acid content can be reduced by chemical means which means a lesser oil might easily be promoted if judged only by

Virgin olive oil fit for consumption as is

Extra virgin olive oil: they must reach a score of 6.5 or more on the organoleptic scale and have a maximum acidity of 1 per cent, but most are about 0.5 per cent. Thus they will be impeccable in every way.

Virgin olive oil: organoleptic rating of 5.5 or more and maximum 1.5 per cent acidity. Probably indistinguishable from extra virgin to most of us.

Ordinary virgin olive oil: organoleptic rating of 3.5 or more and acidity up to 3.3 per cent. Not commonly seen in the retail trade. All the above may properly be described as natural.

Virgin olive oil not fit for consumption as is

Lampante virgin olive oil: organoleptic rating of less than 3.5 and/or acidity of more than 3.3 per cent: it is fated to become one of the following after treatment to reduce acidity and improve, which generally means lessen, its flavour.

Refined Olive Oil

The result of refining virgin olive oil which was not fit for consumption as it was. It is likely to be rather colourless, flavourless and characterless.

Olive Oil

A combination of refined olive oil and one of the top three grades of virgin olive oil to give character and flavour. It will have an acidity no higher than 1.5 per cent. This used to be called Pure Olive Oil but this phrase is no longer allowed: the word pure or the term 100 per cent pure may only be used as a description of the quality of the oil. The best of these are very good oils, and their general economy and light flavour make them an outstanding choice for mayonnaise, for basic cooking and to introduce those whose commitment to olive oil is less than total.

acidity. There, the top quality must be an unequivocally guaranteed 'first press' which also has the proper minimal acidity; they've dug a bit of a hole for themselves as modern mechanics mean almost all oil is first press these days, and they will probably come around to adopting the EC categorization. Should you find yourself on a Californian wine tasting tour, keep an eye out for local olive oils too, often sold by variety of olive.

It is an absolute fact that there are few rules guaranteeing the origination of olive oil. There is huge international trade; the south of France has always been a net importer from North Africa and Italy cannot exist without oils from Spain. This is not necessarily criticism, for consistency of flavour and style within a commercial label is important. It is merely a caveat, and should you find a cheaper olive oil you like, which does not have fancy packing or famous names, you are more likely to be paying for what is in the bottle rather than what's on it. It's just that none of it may have come from where you might expect.

Olives are contrary and complicated. There are hundreds of varieties, each of which, like grapes, give different results in different soils and from year to year. The south of France still has thousands of small local olive mills and it was there I was taught that each day's pressing will taste different, sometimes because of the varieties harvested that day, other times because of the temperature and humidity. Most countries have pretty strict rules about how long olives may wait before they are pressed; too long or too warm and the flavour changes and acidity rises alarmingly. If you speak a local language and can be at a small olive press when others are not, it is an educative treat beyond compare to be able to taste the storage tanks which hold individual pressings, first comparing these and then those from a previous year, probably bottled by then. It quickly makes nonsense of any belief that there is such a thing as very particular flavours produced in an area; if there is consistency it is almost always due to blending, as with champagne.

Although I concentrate here on the four major producing countries you will know, olive oil is produced in dozens of countries, including every one with Mediterranean shores. Australia produces small amounts of outstandingly good oil, and the trees thrive in Mexico and in California, so nothing should surprise you when you read the label.

Broadly speaking olives are sweeter and gentler in France, get stronger in Spain and become increasingly robust as you move eastwards across the Mediterranean, or southwards in a Mediterranean country. Thus an extra virgin oil from Spain or Provençe may seem positively honeyed and vinous compared to the same quality from Italy which can be distinctly biting and peppery or from Greece which will be altogether thicker and throatier, except this will depend on whereabouts in Italy or Greece. And the year of course, (now I see that some of the better suppliers put the harvest months on the label of their finer products), is a really useful tool if you are an olive oil freak.

Today, the popularity of olive oil is such that we can spend large sums on small bottles from single estates, and like great vintage wines some are sensational, some eccentric beyond belief. Tuscany was a pioneer in 'boutique' oils, making much of its tradition of Michelangelo-designed palaces and great and ancient titled family names on eccentrically shaped bottles. And yet... to my palate, Tuscan oils can be so peppery you would think they had been sitting about with fresh chillies, and that bite camouflages any delicacy of its own and transforms into brutishness any delicate food upon which it falls. Not for me, not at those prices. And anyway, the sums do not always add up. How does the supposedly artisan production of a single small estate become a year-round best-seller in a national supermarket chain? Olive oil must beware it is not lubricating its own dead-end, as did own-label champagnes, which first created a new market and then betrayed it with ever less good produce.

Time, taste and budget are all necessary partners to finding the olive oil you most like. What follows is a mixture of personal experience, the advice of respected specialist oil importers, and of Anne Dolamore's *The Essential Oil Companion*. I specially like that book because her palate seems to be exactly the same as mine. Yet, do not fear to disagree, for exchange of opinion is the greatest flavouring of food.

France: the provinces with a Mediterranean coastline all produce olive oil, and as with all horticulture down there, little of it is mechanized or even produced by large co-operatives. Instead thousands of small olive mills continue to press local produce and make truly individual oils of finesse and delicacy. In broad terms the expression *Huile de Provençe* is generally a guarantee of decent standards.

In Provençe, Nyons is the great olive centre, relying heavily for eating and for oil olives on the invaluable *tanche*, a small black olive introduced by the Romans; it adds terrific sweetness and fruit to oils. In the village of Mirabel the Farnoux family produces Le Vieux Moulin oil only from these olives. *Huile d'olives Nyons* is one of the French products guaranteed by the rigid AOC regulations.

Because France produces relatively small amounts of her own olive oil you don't easily find it available. But if you are travelling in the south an olive oil tasting and buying expedition is great fun. There are five olive mills just north of Marseilles on either side of the A7; here local varieties *aglandaus* and *saurines* make very individual oils. Head also for Mausannes-les-Alpilles, Mouries, Beaumes-de-Venise, and the famed Les Barronnies, also at Nyons. The oils of La Lucques in Languedoc are considered quite the equal of Provençal oil, if not better, which will give you something to argue.

Portugal: I rather like what I have tasted of these rather uncommon oils, which often have a fresh taste of apples, a much better way to balance unctuousness than pepperiness. The oil of Conservas Rainha Santa from Estremoz is available in Britain and I find it wonderfully supple, clear and gratifying in the mouth.

Spain: two surprises for most people here. Spain is the world's largest olive oil producer and exporter (especially to Italy it should be noted) and was also the first to declare officially guaranteed areas of origin and production standards for olive oils, their DO or Denominacion de Origen system.

To my taste, many Spanish oils have it just right, elegant and individual without being assertive or show-offs, the way one hopes those at one's table will behave.

Borjas blancas: an area in southern Catalonia, not far from Barcelona. The most important olive here, by decree, is the *arbequina*. If you are in the area, the olives are picked between November 10th and early February – the green ones make a fruity but green and sharpish Early Harvest oil and the remainder are picked and pressed each day as they turn to yellow and purple and then black, which makes a noticeably yellower and more mellow oil.

A well-liked example is Lerida. In this case the makers blend early and late harvest oils to give a consistent standard and luscious flavour. You can taste the care and concern, I promise you.

Siurana: actually two areas in Tarragona – the foothills of the Sierra Montsant and the Campo de Tarragona, closer to the coast. Here the arbequina is joined by the *rojal* and *morrut* olive. The flavours and appearance have a slightly harder edge and fullness than the previous area. Again they make a green Early Harvest oil and a fuller, yellow Main Harvest oil.

Sierra de segura: the north east of the province of Jaen in Andalucia. It's particularly rugged and thus manual harvesting is unlikely ever to be superseded, which explains why the cost can creep up. The *picula* olive gives big fruitiness and body but also a bitterness which should not be intrusive or unpleasant. Definitely a rural, peasanty flavour.

Baena: south of the province of Cordoba. As you might expect, the oils of this area have a hotter, fuller body but are as fragrant and complicated as the gardens the Moors left behind. They are essentially yellow but some have green and purple or violet tinges. Nunez de Prado is very unusual, a 'flower of oil' and pressed from only the flesh of olives – it takes 11kgs of them to make one litre and yet it is not more expensive than other extra virgin Spanish oils.

Italy: this is where I start to get into trouble. Of course I have enjoyed truly wonderful oils throughout the country, but there is an awful lot of hype. Lucca oil? Yes, jolly nice, luscious even, but most of it is merely bottled in Lucca rather than produced there. Tuscan? Yes, it is wonderful to enjoy single estate oils with houses designed by Michelangelo and more ancient titles on a label than an entire issue of *Hello!*. But the *frantoio* and *moraiolo* olives sometimes give such a chilli-type pepperiness I find it difficult to enjoy either the oils or the foods onto which they might be sprinkled. Tuscan cooking is remarkably straightforward and unseasoned; even so I suspect a lesser oil and freshly ground black pepper would be kinder and more fragrant. And they are terribly expensive oils, too. This is partly because the frosts of winter 1984/85 wiped out much production for many seasons. Laudemio is a consortium of Tuscany's greatest and oldest producers, who market individually to exceptionally high and rigidly controlled standards. The shape of the bottle and Laudemio trademark are universal but the name of the producer will change. That of the Marchesi de Frescobaldi has been softened a little with *leccino* olives and I have also enjoyed that of Marchese Antinori: the independently marketed Ornellaia of Marchese Lodovico Antinori, produced on a maritime estate not affected by the infamous frosts, is deliciously full and *un*peppery.

Much of Tuscan oil is made by the same estates which make Chianti Classico and the tall, green, square bottles of Badia a Coltibuono are a prime example; very robust and a balanced amount of the expected peppery aftertaste.

Umbria, next door to Tuscany, uses the same olives to produce the same sort of effect, but generally less so: they are often grown in association with the grapes for Orvieto wines.

The Molise region of Central Italy makes tremendously rich oils with a clean grassiness. The estate of Prince Colonna uses a blend of four olives: the *ascolera tenera* is a green eating olive which adds delicate fruitiness; the black eater *leccino* adds sweetness, the *coratino* (actually from Apulia) keeps its rich fruitiness for a long time and the *nocellara Etnea* from eastern Sicily gives a deep greeney-gold colour and a distinct perfume.

Apulia in the south is the country's largest producer, mainly from the *coratina*; when pressed, even Italians from other areas will probably agree most of the time that this is Italy's best, with a full olive flavour that is balanced and has a clean aftertaste but no pepperiness.

Ravida oils from Sicily's southern coast are highly rated, light but flavoury oils and made from three varieties: the *cerasuola* olive is picked when changing from green to violet and gives a hearty full oil; the *biancolilla* offers a silky texture and light green tint; *nocellara del belice* have a distinct olive taste and are used green for oil and ripe for eating.

There are many excellent commercial extra virgin oils marketed by Italian companies, which have all the appeal and none of the eccentricity of estate oils. This may be because they come from Spain...

Greece: no one can accuse these oils of delicacy. But the generally robust, straightforward flavour can be neat and clean behind a full, flavoury body – and they have probably been making them longer than most, too. The two main areas of production are the Peloponnese (which includes Kalamata) and the island of Crete, where olive trees cover more than half the cultivated land.

You will find organic oils made in remote areas, and a Cretan oil pressed from a particularly small variety of olive with negligible acid content. Kalamata oils are outstanding, but not what you might think. They are not made from the exceptional *kalamata* olive but produced in the Kalamata area from the major Greek oil olive, the *koroneiki*, but then so are most mainland oils, whatever they are called.

Cooking: the single great culinary immutable of extra virgin olive oils is that none should be used for cooking, ever. Heat destroys the very complexity you have paid to enjoy. But once the cooking is complete nothing is quite so engaging as a spoonful of extra virgin olive oil poured over food as a condiment, in vegetable soups, thick or thin, on simply cooked vegetables, on grilled fish, on fowl or decent bits of an animal, in a small bowl for dunking bread, or a salad, of course. Long-baked potatoes drizzled with olive oil, a minor squeeze of garlic and plenty of parsley are almost too good to eat, rather like the current fashion for potatoes mashed with olive oil – but don't stop there. Rich butternut squash mashed with olive oil and brightened with sweet paprika made a Michelin-star chef sit up at my table; that's rather Moroccan. For a flavour from further down the Mediterranean, cook sliced white turnips with a tiny amount of chopped onion and garlic over olive oil, butter and orange juice until the liquids are reduced to a thick emulsified syrup; finish with fresh dates, parsley and cinnamon.

For Mediterranean or new-fangled British cooking buy olive oils that are less than extra virgin or choose one of the excellent cheaper mixtures of olive and vegetable oil, sometimes labelled as green oil. These lesser oils are also marvellous to flavour by storing with sprigs of rosemary and thyme, crushed garlic cloves, coriander seeds and pepper; a month in a warm but not too light place is usually enough and I find it good to remove the flavouring and replace with just a small amount of fresh, which adds an edge to the flavour. Use these flavoured oils to marinate a leg of lamb or, say, cod steaks before grilling, to make a potato salad or to fry eggs. With chilli and oregano you concoct a wonderful oil for sprinkling on pizza, both before and after cooking.

I don't hold with the school that olive oil should be used only for Mediterranean dishes; eggs and chips fried in olive oil are fabulous, British salads of beetroot or cucumber a revelation, and frozen peas dressed with oil rather than butter worth eating by themselves. But when you use olive oil you must want its flavour to make a recognizable and tasty contribution. The silly home economist who sent me recipes for a curry using two tablespoons of extra virgin olive oil should be stripped of her undoubtedly neat aprons and boiled alive.

Storing: virgin olive oils easily deteriorate through oxidation after exposure to light and air. Thus cans and green glass are better than clear glass and storage should be in a cool, dark larder or the refrigerator, except in the latter oils will cloud and thicken unpleasantly and there is always the risk of picking up off flavours. The neck and pouring mouth should be kept clean as drops will acidify. Oil left exposed to air should never be poured back into the bottle.

OTHER TYPES OF OIL

Cottonseed: widely used in vegetable oil mixtures and in oleo margarines, especially in the United States. In these products it has usually been bleached but when used to pack seafood (especially from Japan) it has slight colour and, to me, a rather unpleasant taste and texture, some of which I think remains in the butter substitutes. It is the second most important seed oil, produced mainly in Russia, the United States and China.

Grapeseed: some say delicate, some say dull, but as it is not commonly seen this may not matter. Used for margarine or for salads, but I can't think why.

Hazelnut, huile de noisettes: Less common than walnut oil, but worth every centime – it usually comes from France. It has an affinity with tomatoes, although not as strong as that of walnut oil. Heat ruins it and so it is not a good plan to cook with it; better pretend it is an extra virgin olive oil and pour it lightly over, say, grilled rabbit or game, onto warm artichokes with soft-boiled eggs or green beans into which you have stirred roasted hazelnuts and garlic – that sort of thing. If this seems too extreme, try flavouring a traditional bread sauce with the oil rather than butter.

Hazelnut oil is considered coarser than walnut oil and more strident, and thus it is usually diluted, with vegetable oil, a lesser olive oil, or, as a sauce, melted butter. Not unexpectedly it works very well with berry fruits and thus with such fruit vinegars as raspberry, especially. I usually include some when I make a fruit vinaigrette, by puréeing soft fruits with a touch of mustard, oil and a suitable vinegar. Hazelnut oil adds a perfect finishing touch. Made with blackberries, even those from a freezer, such a vinaigrette is sensational with quickly seared scallops scattered over a salad of autumnal-tinted lettuce leaves; keep the vinegar or acid level minimal. The oil must be kept cool and dark once opened as it oxidizes very quickly. In extremis I should refrigerate it, even though it thickens and clouds.

Palm and palm kernel oil: the oil palm is native to West Africa and although its existence is barely even suspected by most Europeans it is a most important part of our diet... especially if you like ice cream products.

The brilliant red fruit of the oil palm grows in bunches averaging 13-18kg/26-32lb in weight and if properly cultivated the tree produces a higher yield than any other oil-producing plant per acre. Each palm fruit is built up like a miniature coconut with a thick fibrous pulp on the outside and a hard kernel inside. Palm oil is obtained from its outer layer and this red substance is an essential ingredient to the food of Brazil and Nigeria. But it adds a flavour not readily appreciated by others, ie non-natives. More refined palm oils are staples in India and Asia and some edible fats include refined palm oil.

Kernel oil is an altogether harder oil, rather like that of the coconut, and it has two uses that some would say are indistinguishable, and others would argue are poles apart. One use is in soap, as Hollywood stars constantly remind us in return for huge fees. If the name is honest, there is olive oil in this soap, too. The other use, as *no one* reminds you, is as a major substitute for milk, butter and cream in 'non-dairy fat' foods. Palm kernel oil, after suitable treatment, can be whipped and frozen into believing it is cream and subsequently ice cream. It is the major fat used in ice creams in this country and the basis for the pareve (dairy-free kosher) whips, creams and ice creams.

Peanut (groundnut) oil: the nut has an oil content of 45-50 per cent, which is used in fats, ice cream and margarine. Especially important in the catering trade for, as well as having no taste, it can be used to fry at an extremely high temperature without unpleasant smoking or other side effects. The combination of high temperature and lack of taste means you get crisper food faster and that the fat has had no opportunity to penetrate. By far the best oil for deep-frying and for wok cooking.

Poppyseed oil: another oil popular simply for its lack of taste, an asset in some sorts of cooking. It is sold as *huile blanche* (white oil) in northern France and Paris, where it enjoys greatest popularity.

Pumpkin seed oil: an initial belief in some relationship with motor oil is not unnatural. It is thick, turgid and terribly brown. But it does have an astonishingly rich, nutty flavour – too much to use by itself unless flavouring a soup or a mash. For salads it very much needs to be diluted with a vegetable oil. It is said to be very popular in Austria, and so when you are there you might find out what they use it for and tell the rest of us.

Rape seed oil: oil-seed rape is now one of Europe's biggest crops and responsible for those sensational blankets of mustard yellow which are not mustard in spring. It is a mixed blessing to say the least. The powdery, musky scent from these fields causes untold agonies of allergy, no laughing matter if you are driving on a motorway. The bitterness of its nectar permeates, and to some palates, ruins honey and its oil must be radically purified and refined to make it useful. Yet, if you buy or use something called mere vegetable oil, this is what it is likely to be, and why it is taking over Britain's fields.

Safflower oil: safflower, seeds of which have been found in Egyptian tombs of 2000 BC, was originally grown for the colour of its florets, which give a cheap imitation of saffron. When synthetic dyes began to displace safflower it seemed doomed, but then it was discovered that the oil obtained from the same florets and their seeds has the highest percentage of polyunsaturated oil known – 78 per cent. The major producers are now Mexico and the United States who between them produce over half a million tons of seeds each year.

Sesame seed oil: a very ancient oil, used as much for flavouring as anything

---

FLAVOURED OILS

One of the greatest contributions to safe sensuality in public places is the recent marketing of truffle flavoured oils, especially *white truffle oil*. It would be nice to think that some altruistic manufacturer decided to soak a few of his breath-arrestingly expensive white Alba truffles in oil for our benefit. He didn't. Not to make the commercial ones anyway. They are generally made by adding a nature identical flavouring, which in this case is exceptionally good.

Thus instead of shaving white truffles over your risotto or onto your brioche, the two great ways of enjoying them, you simply sprinkle a little of the oil onto the completed thing; in the same way you never cook with white truffles you should not cook with white truffle oil.

Once hooked you will find zillions of ways to use it, but beware: many people are utterly phased by the scent and flavour which invasively reeks of every forbidden vice, and then some. When I once had a suitcase full of them in the BBC Breakfast Time television studio a Labour MP was so outraged to be in the presence of such expense he threatened it was either him or them on the programme. But I bet the unsettling odour had reminded him of what he would rather be doing at that hour of the morning, where and with what. A little bottle of white truffle oil at home is much safer.

---

else. It can be dark or a nice reddish brown depending on whether the seeds have been toasted or not. Marco Polo was impressed enough to write about it and it is still widely used in India and the Orient, especially in confectionery and bakery. Add a few drops only when deep-frying tempura or anything else in batter. Add to marinades, especially for microwaving, or sprinkle onto almost anything to which you would add sesame seeds: prawns, green beans, pumpkin purée, chicken joints, baked hams...

Soybean oil: although used in China for the past 4,000 years, the first shipment did not arrive in the United Kingdom until 1908. It is one of the top four in the polyunsaturated league and is an extremely good keeper. Soybean oil also has quite a high smoking point, which means it will fry or deep fry at a temperature high

Black truffle oil is less immediate but does have that earthy bacon-like flavour which the late food writer Jeremy Round bravely described as scrotal. It is also best used without exposure to direct heat, but may be whisked into warm sauces or mashed potatoes, poured into eggs just before they scramble, sprinkled onto smoked salmon or worked into whipped cream or butter for almost anything.

Porcini oil is pretty good too, but I make my own with dried porcini (ceps). It keeps its flavour rather well in gentle cooking.

The other commercially available flavoured oils worth considering are those flavoured with Oriental ingredients for wok cooking. But honestly, why pay others to do what is so easily obtained at home? Make oils just the same way as you would a flavoured vinegar, by macerating. Unwaxed lemon zest, garlic, chillies, fresh herbs, black or green peppers or whatever combinations you choose: fresh lime and chillies; orange and juniper berries; rosemary and thyme; lavender and rose petals with roasted black peppercorns; or toast some nuts and make your own toasted nut oils too. Needless to say you use an almost flavourless vegetable oil to start, keep them warm but not in sunlight for a few weeks and then test regularly to ensure they are not too strong or need to be strained off and made stronger by adding a fresh batch.

enough to ensure it will not pass what little flavour it has onto the food. As well as margarines and cooking fats the oil is used in paint, printing ink, soap, cosmetics, varnishes and insecticides.

Sunflower oil: the very high percentage of polyunsaturates in this oil make it very important indeed, and it is widely used as an oil for salads, cooking, fats and margarine. It is very good for frying also but perhaps a little expensive for this use on a regular basis. The sunflower is a native of Mexico but grown in many parts of the world, particularly south Russia. China, Hungary and South Africa also grow enough to be useful but Great Britain, although it has an eminently suitable climate, produces a very small crop indeed. New varieties developed in the old Soviet Union have increased the oil content of seed from 20 to 40 per cent.

Walnut oil, huile de noix: Perigueux, that was the place, on a warm stone wall on the corner of a hot cobbled street. There I first discovered the God-given affinity of tomatoes and walnuts when I poured walnut oil onto a sun-toasted tomato. Bacon and eggs, gin and tonic, fish and chips? Such are as nothing in comparison to this combination, and, just as few additions can improve those, you need little else when you have tomatoes and walnut oil. Perhaps some parsley, that's very good, and maybe a little salt and pepper. But no vinegar, no herbs, no garlic or chives, no million-and-one ingredients, clear-out-the-fridge salad. Just two ingredients which work together to make something bigger and better than either. But there's more to walnut oil. It keeps the slight bite of fresh walnuts and together with its inherent sweetness thus both complements and extends the flavours of light meats, from grilled pork chops to pan-seared pheasant breasts. It's terribly good with fruit as you might expect, so grilled peach halves dribbled with walnut oil become a much faster and better tasting accompaniment than grilled stuffed peaches, especially with hot or cold ham. Walnut oil goes well with green salads of course, or add it to mayonnaise made with bland vegetable oil.

OIL, VINEGAR AND STORE-CUPBOARD MAYONNAISE

In the same way olive oil is used to give flavour and sumptuousness to mayonnaise made with cheaper blander oils, you should consider using some of the rarer nut oils to give individuality. The magical affinity of tomatoes and walnuts is enhanced by serving them topped with mayonnaise flavoured with walnut oil, and perhaps stirring in some very finely chopped nuts. Hazelnut oil and virgin-pressed almond oil can also give an extraordinary but subtle lift to a mayonnaise even if served with something as simple as cold French beans, artichoke or asparagus.

Remember when you are making mayonnaise you can increase the quantity dramatically by diluting with water or vinegar or wine as you proceed; when the mayonnaise is very thick, keep beating, but dribble in water until it is much softer, then, if you like, add a little flavoured vinegar or citrus juice. Proceed with more oil. There is no reason why you should not substitute wine, vermouth or some spirit or liqueur, or a balanced mixture, for the water.

It is extraordinarily simple to flavour mayonnaise with spices or herbs, but ensure you first heat the spices to develop the flavours and that you leave herb combinations to blend for some hours, preferably out of the fridge. To start you off on this exciting road, I suggest an eastern Mediterranean combination of equal parts of ground cumin, coriander and cinnamon, which is also a revelation upon hard-boiled eggs.

WALNUT MAYONNAISE

150ml/¼pt mayonnaise
1 tbsp vinegar (see method)
50g/2oz ground walnuts
1 medium-sized garlic clove
2 tbsp walnut oil

Fold into the mayonnaise the ground walnuts, walnut oil, a sympathetic vinegar (say, tarragon, cider or raspberry), plus the juice of the medium clove of garlic.

Although wonderful with veal or chicken, one of my experimenters found it specially good on cold cooked vegetables, particularly cold sliced fennel. I imagine it is quite as good on the raw ones. I also think this would be nice with the addition of some grated orange rind.

WALDORF MAYONNAISE

150ml/¼pt mayonnaise
2 tbsp walnut oil
225g/8oz Bramley apples, trimmed, cored and peeled
1 tbsp water
sugar
1 tbsp fresh mint leaves, chopped

Cook Bramley apples with the water and walnut oil until soft and fairly dry. Strain, then add up to one dstsp of sugar, if you think this is necessary. Mix with the chopped mint leaves and fold into the thick mayonnaise.

Very good with cold poultry, especially turkey. Some toasted, flaked almonds would be a good garnish.

Don't cook with it, as most of the flavour goes, and that's a waste of money, but sprinkle it onto cooked foods as you would a virgin olive oil. If you have masses of it and are prepared to experiment, it can be jolly good in breads and scones, but use some of the nuts too, or you might find the flavour so fugitive you will curse. Keep the oil dark and cool, refrigerated in summer or in centrally heated winter kitchens if you are not using it up quickly, even though it goes thick and cloudy. But most of all, be constantly on the alert for really ripe tomatoes…

Other nuts: no, not people I know, but rarer nut oils. **Almond oil** is best known as a beauty treatment, but edible varieties are bottled and sold, mainly in France. It is pallid in colour and exceptionally fragile in flavour, but if you wait it gradually titillates the mouth with a slight milky greenness, the same after-effects as eating fresh green almonds. Quite what sort of food will stand up to this I do not know, except that its very gentility makes it a good thing to grease baking trays, moisten your hands when moulding sugar, lubricate molds and so on. Perhaps it is more pleasing outside than inside one…

Two others you are likely to find, but only in such rarified stores as Fauchon or Hediard on the Place de la Madeleine in Paris, are **pistachio** *(pistache)* or **pine nut** *(pignole)*. The pistachio oil is almost fluorescent, a wonderful colour and perfectly but lightly pistachio flavoured: it is such a rare treat I would fain confuse its appeal and dribble it only onto a guaranteed friend, excellent lettuce or other saladings, perhaps with some edible flowers; segments of room temperature blood oranges to accompany duck scattered with roasted pistachios; or on perfectly poached slices of salmon served just below room temperature. Or on a warm brioche, in which case I might just have whipped some into an unsalted *beurre cru*, a pretty good idea with all the nut oils incidentally. A minuscule amount of garlic is very good.

Pine nut oil is a little less immediate in flavour, and so must be used in greater quantity but with greater restraint and discretion as the slight resinous taste is not to everyone's taste, no matter how often they scatter the nuts onto their creations. It is good on lightly chilled poached poultry breasts or on salmon, with perfect tomatoes, perhaps dribbled onto small warm rolls to serve with fragrant Moroccan dishes… maybe to finish a Provençal tian of spinach or chard with pine nuts.

CIDER
VINEGAR

250ml

VINAGRE
XERES

The basis of vinegar is acetic acid, and thus a vinegar-like flavour can be obtained by diluting man-made acetic acid with water. But it would be of little culinary use, for real vinegars can be as complicated of flavour as the finest wines or ales, from which they should be made. The souring of wine or ale is a natural process and is the result of the oxidizing of alcohol to form natural acetic acid, which will happen to any alcoholic liquid with less than 18 per cent alcohol when exposed to air. But it is not enough simply to open a bottle of wine or ale and wait for vinegar. The process must be controlled of speed and temperature, or the original liquid will go off in its own direction losing flavour or picking up others before the acetic acid level is high enough to inhibit any further bacterial action of flavour change.

Modern techniques make modern vinegars in less than 24 hours. But the best vinegars, wine vinegars that is, are made by the Orléans process. First wine is converted to basic vinegar over three weeks or so, which promotes the development of bouquet and perfume. It is then drawn off to mature in oaken casks for three or four months. Look for some indication that the Orléans process has been used on the label; if you find it and compare the contents with ordinary wine vinegar you'll taste a very sharp difference indeed.

Balsamic: balsamic vinegar became a buzz word of the greedy, flash 80s. Certainly, if it was the real thing you had to flash plenty of cash, for that can cost £100 or more for quite a small bottle. Other stuff called balsamic vinegar sells for just a few pounds in supermarkets.

The real thing must say *Balsamico di Modena tradizionale* on the label. This is as much a guarantee as you can expect, for there are no national food guides in Italy, like the French AOC or the Spanish DO. Such a label guarantees what is in the bottle will have been made only in Modena by an extraordinary method and be at least ten years old. It is not a true vinegar but made with the cooked must, pressed juice, of the white trebbiano grape. This is aged in fragrant wooden vessels, sometimes just of juniper or oak, sometimes a progression of different woods also including cherry, mulberry, birch and others. It thus becomes progressively more deeply flavoured, deeply coloured and concentrated, but may not be sold for a decade – often it will be many decades old. Its appeal is a balance of sour and sweet, a complex richness to enjoy just by itself, with only minimal intrusion of oils, salt and pepper.

It is credited with magical restorative properties and certainly has the same ability as very ancient sherry, a tiny amount of which transforms huge quantities of younger stuff in the solera system. Thus you need use only small amounts on food. Or so I thought until I spoke to a manufacturer. 'No no,' he said, 'we only use it in small amounts because it is so expensive – it is wonderful when you use lots of it!'

I suppose that is why other companies make cheaper non-traditional balsamic vinegars all over Italy. They use the same trebbiano must and the colour is as likely to be caramel. Yet it has great gulping helpings of the flavour of its grander relation and is a much more useful thing for general salading and cooking. And yet...

FLAVOURED VINEGARS

We are most likely to buy red or white wine vinegar that has been flavoured after manufacture with a variety of herbs, petals, or fruit. Best known, and most useful, is tarragon vinegar, but you can easily buy dill, shallot, chilli and garlic varieties. Less known are basil and lemon vinegars.

All these varieties are made easily at home by infusing any of the above ingredients in a bottle of vinegar in a warm place for several days.

Vinegars flavoured with raspberries, strawberries, blackcurrants or blackberries were once the basis of sweetened summer drinks, when diluted with iced soda water, and very good they were too. But now unsweetened fruit vinegars are back on the market and making a mark in restaurants. Raspberry vinegar is a sensation on beans, cauliflower or raw spinach and blackcurrant vinegar is excellent with liver.

All these can be made, if you have the fruit, by soaking say ½kg/1lb of raspberries in 600ml/1pt vinegar for five days on a warm window ledge, removing the fruit and replacing with another ½kg/1lb and leaving another week. Strain and store in a cool place. You could add more raspberries and you may also sweeten it somewhat. I used this vinegar, together with some of the pickled raspberries and some fresh, to make duck with sweet and sour raspberry sauce for His Excellency the Chinese Ambassador when he visited a house at which I was cooking in Scotland during the summer of 1981. He asked if I had learned to cook in Peking, his home town, which I thought a compliment. It did look – and taste – exceptional.

frankly, I find a sherry vinegar far more fascinating and much greater value for money. So are some of the truly wonderful red and black vinegars of China. Will I ever be able to show my face in Modena again?

Chinese: Chinese vinegars are usually based on rice wine and have a great spectrum of flavour from very mild to defiant pungency, but divide into four main groups. Many are aged in wood and the best are often compared to Italian balsamic vinegar. Those from the northern provinces, where vinegar is very extensively used in cooking, are considered China's finest.

White: very much milder than any western vinegar so if you are substituting with white wine or brewed vinegar you must dilute.

Red: the best known is Chinkiang, made from glutinous rice and malt. It is powerful but aromatic and very dark red or brown. Specially used in the Chiu Chow and Hakka kitchens of Cantonese cooking and particularly good with seafood. Yan-Kit So likens it to a lesser balsamic vinegar which explains its frequent use as a condiment. Red wine vinegar would be a sad substitute, even though regularly recommended; I think sherry vinegar would be closer.

Black: very dark and deeply flavoured, these may be made from rice or from sorghum: but like white vinegars, some may be diluted so shop with care.

Sweet: this is the richest style of black vinegar and is used for braising and stewing, to balance and enhance the fattiness.

Cider: people are drinking it, prescribing it – almost worshipping it. If you would believe only half of what people – especially Americans – say, it is the elixir of life. Well… some people don't even like the flavour and generally I find it a little intrusive, appley and honey-like, which is not unexpected I suppose. But it does come into its own when you are pickling fruit – peaches, pears, plums and so on. Then it is wonderful. It is made, of course, from soured cider.

Malt: this is made from soured ale, that is an unhopped beer. Brown malt vinegar is coloured, usually with caramel. It is actually less sharp than wine vinegars but does not carry with it the advantages of other aromas and flavours. It is usually distilled to increase its strength. Spirit vinegar and distilled vinegar are almost always made from malt vinegar and are the same thing. White malt vinegar, distilled or otherwise, has simply been decolourized by a charcoal process.

Sherry: one of the wonders of the world, much more reasonably priced than a decent balsamic and easier to buy than Chinese varieties. Sherry vinegar is a rich, full golden brown, and when you pull the cork of the bottle a balloon of truly mellow fruitfulness makes the senses swoon. Well, it does mine, anyway.

Sherry is made from wines which are not very drinkable in their young and unfortified state. Some are too acidic even for the mellowing sherry process, and it is these which are made into vinegar. The unique part of the process is their aging in oaken sherry casks, which give much of the vinegars' culinary appeal.

The rich, full flavour of sherry vinegar means you need comparatively little, and I often use it unassailed by the temperance of oil, on tomatoes or on buffalo milk Mozzarella for instance. But whether solo or with oil, sherry vinegar clearly exposes the shallow wickedness of making salad dressings which contain mustard and sugar and such excess. Use decent ingredients and additions are unnecessary. Oh yes, and you can also throw away the dratted jam jar in which such concoctions are traditionally shaken, and jolly good riddance too.

Wine: do not take it for granted that all wine vinegar will reward you with a kaleidoscope of wondrous flavour. It will only be as good as the wine from which it was made, and only if it was also made by the slow, expensive Orléans process, which protects all the natural aromas of the wine. Most wine vinegar is *not* made this way; like most ingredients of excellence, Orléans vinegar costs more. It really is worth buying Orléans vinega if you care about your food, and want a wine vinegar.

Champagne vinegar: as with sherry, the basic wines of Champagne are close to undrinkable in their natural state. So the most difficult are encouraged to become vinegar. Champagne vinegar has a fresh, clean taste which is lost if combined with strong oils, and can be used by itself, but in small quantities of course.

Cooking: very reduced vinegars, especially the flavoured ones, are the key to many added, say, to the cooking juices of some quickly fried liver or fish. Sweet and sour sauces are nothing without vinegar; but they are improved if you use a good quality one. The merest whisper of vinegar can miraculously transform the flavour of a lifeless casserole, especially if it is a rather fatty one. The use of vinegar in bread dough is a cheat's way to emulate the flavour of real sourdough. You only need 25ml/1fl oz of cider vinegar for ½kg/1lb of flour. But can anyone explain to me why the English put vinegar, *malt* vinegar, on fish and chips?

Pure sugar is sucrose, a white carbohydrate ($C_{12}H_{22}O_{11}$) with a sweet flavour, obtained mainly from sugar cane and the sugar beet but some countries obtain sugars from palm trees, maple trees and from sorghum, a type of millet. Before such sugar was discovered by the western world, honey, fruit and such vegetables as parsnip and carrot were the major sources of sweetness.

From a dietary point of view extra sugar (including honey) is unnecessary in an otherwise balanced diet. Enough 'energy fuel' can be obtained from the starch of cereals or from the galactose and fructose of vegetables and fruits respectively, and the advantage of using such sources of sugar is that they are ingested with other vitamins and minerals.

The one thing to be certain of is that sugar is not a poison, and does not cause disease, no, not even a single one. Impeccable research all round the world has shown that the only direct connection sugar has with any negative change to our body is a potential to cause tooth decay. Other than that, an excess of sugar can certainly lead to obesity which in turn causes many a problem – but eating too much of anything or drinking too much alcohol can also make you fat. Sugar is not the enemy.

And don't be fooled by honey. Its sweetness is only sucrose which has been broken down into invert or simpler sugars; the minimal amount of other good things honey contains in no way compensates for the possible damage done to teeth and health by eating more sugar than you really need. Honey is not a substitute for sugar – it is an alternative source of something you shouldn't need. But, having said that, I also know few people, myself included, can live without either the flavour or the silken texture sugar adds to food. So I'd better stop lecturing and start explaining.

CANE SUGAR

Once the white gold of merchants, for whom one cargo load of just 100 tonnes would be worth £1 million, sugar is now simply the world's most common sweetener.

Whence the cane from which it is extracted came, no one is quite certain, but it is likely that it was the Solomon Islands in the South Pacific. Different cultures produce different sugar-related mythologies, the most titillating of which hails from India. It is said a King Subandu found a sugar cane growing in his bedroom, from which issued a Prince Ilshvaku, reputedly a direct ancestor of the Budda. I've heard some fine excuses for being found with a sweet young thing in your bedroom, but *really...*

As they seem to have been refining sugar since as long ago as 3000 BC, Indian communities also seem to have been the first to have cultivated it on any scale. The knowledge spread slowly east to Indo-China and later ebbed west into Arabia and Europe. By the 5th century BC the Persians could both refine sugar and form it into loaves but jealously protected their techniques. Alexander the Great's General Nearchus commented in the 4th century BC on a reed that produced honey without bees and the Arab Conquests carried sugar further westwards so that by the 8th century it was being grown and processed in Spain and southern France. But it was not officially mentioned in England until the 12th century, when it was referred to in the Court Rolls. By 1544 there were two refineries in London.

Early sugars had charming names; one was *Zucchero Muccho,* flavoured with musk. This sugar was the highest Egyptian quality and generally available only in the Middle East. *Candi* was, as you might guess, like rock candy – clear chunks made by boiling sugar syrup; five types might be found in the apothecary's shop: simple (unflavoured), rose, violet, lemon and red gooseberry. *Montreal Mill* came not from Canada but from a Syrian town to the south of the Dead Sea. *Caffetin* came from Caffa in the Crimea and was wrapped in palm leaves, which explains its 17th century name, palm sugar (this term is now used for something else, see page 343).

During much of its history, sugar was used as a medicine, for it was far too expensive to use as a food or sweetener. As late as 1736 it was listed alongside the precious gems among the wedding gifts of Maria-Theresa, later queen of Austria and Hungary.

For a long time Venice controlled the sugar trade, but the discovery of the New World radically altered this. In the days of Christopher Columbus, sugar cost at least £20 per lb in modern terms, so on his second voyage west Columbus experimented with growing the cane on Santo Domingo in the Caribbean and found it grew faster and better there than anywhere else. The European crowns fought long, hard and expensively for the new sugar producing areas. At the end of the Seven Years' War in 1763, England had a difficult choice over which French colonies to keep as indemnity, the tiny sugar islands of Martinique and Guadaloupe – or unmeasured Canada. She plumped for the latter only because she was certain she already had the better sugar islands.

In England, rapidly becoming the new hub of the sugar trade, technical developments in refining pre-dated the Industrial Revolution. By 1750 there were more than 150 factories producing over 30,000 tons of white sugar a year, which at an average of something over 15g/½oz per cup would sweeten 63 million servings of tea.

By the 18th century you usually bought loaf sugar which was refined sugar pressed with syrup into a very hard lump and then shaped into a loaf or cone. It was used with great care, for it was both expensive and highly taxed. In the kitchen books of Mary Senhouse, my grandmother of nine generations ago, you carefully annotated when a loaf was bought, how much was used and when. Sugar didn't come into general use until 1874, when Gladstone removed the tax, a blessing about which dentists have had mixed feelings ever since.

The 3-8m/10-24ft high sugar canes are harvested in tropical sun in ghastly conditions, as any reader of the Australian novel *The Thornbirds* will know; but now this is increasingly done by machine.

The root of each cane is left in the ground to sprout again, a technique known as ratooning and which can be repeated for up to six years. The freshly picked cane deteriorates rapidly, so is processed as quickly as possible.

First the cane is cleaned and shredded to expose the inner core. It is then crushed and sprayed with hot water to form a free running juice. The separated fibres are recycled to fuel the boilers essential to the subsequent process: in Mauritius there is so much of the stuff it feeds local electricity stations, too. Clarification comes next. A range of ingredients must be added to the liquid to encourage pitching of impurities which can then be collected and removed; this sediment is filtered out under vacuum and used as fertilizer in the fields.

Now the process starts in earnest. The clarified liquid is reduced by evaporation and the condensed liquid, a type of treacle or sugar-containing molasses, is seeded to encourage the formation of sugar crystals, which are then extracted by centrifuge. This first extraction gives the biggest crystals, and at this stage they will contain both residual impurities and molasses and also have a very light coating of molasses; this will be golden sugar and demerara. Two more stages of processing and centrifuges result in the extraction of the remaining sucrose in increasingly smaller crystals which are darkened by greater concentrations of molasses – muscavado and molasses sugars. Eventually, with almost all the available sucrose extracted, only blackstrap molasses are left.

White sugar is obtained by chemically treating and bleaching the original sucrose-rich syrup, and it is this process which is generally called refining.

BEET SUGAR

The other source of refined white sugar is the sugar beet, and from the outset you can be assured that the sugar from both is exactly the same thing – pure sucrose. Any differences in taste are the result of the processing technique used – or of imagination. Used as animal fodder and a table vegetable as far back as Roman times, the sugar beet didn't begin to be taken seriously as a sweetening source until the 18th century. In 1575 Olivier de Serres had ascertained beet sugar syrup to be 'very beautiful to see because of its vermilion colour', but he did nothing other than look at it. In 1747 the German Andreas Marggraf extracted sugar from beet and made it solid for the first time and then in 1802 one of his pupils, Achard, set up a sugar factory in Silesia with the help of the King of Prussia; but the quality was low and the price high.

It was Napoleon who finally put beet sugar on the table. Suffering from the British blockade he enlisted the aid of the French Academy of Sciences, and the chemist Delassert finally made sugar from beet into a viable commercial proposition. Nowadays sugar beet is Europe's principal source of sugar. Much of England's comes from Norfolk and thereabouts, and experiments continue to produce better strains that can be grown in more parts of the world more easily.

The sugar beet arrive at the factory to be washed and cut into 'V' shapes, called cosettes. Together with hot water the cosettes are fed into a tower or slowly rotating drum so that the sugar can dissolve into the water. Then in other tanks this syrup has lime added to it and then carbon dioxide is bubbled through which forms a precipitate to carry out the impurities. More careful filtration follows, then a sulphur dioxide treatment and then concentration until you have the final syrup which can be crystallized in the same way as sucrose from cane.

Be assured that only white sugar can be obtained from beet which is thus by definition refined. Beet sugar accounts for over half of all the sugar eaten and any coloured sugars made from it have had the extra colour and flavour added by spraying.

CANE SUGAR PRODUCTS
Molasses sugar, Black Barbados, Demerara molasses: this is fairly difficult to find outside sugar cane processing areas. It is a very strong tasting sugar with a high molasses content and a rich, almost black colour. The sticky texture and taste are similar to good treacle toffee.

Muscovado or Barbados sugar: the most common naturally-dark sugar, this is extracted after the mother liquor has made three trips through the centrifuge. It is the last time the producer can extract sugar from the almost exhausted source. Thus the crystals are very small and one-seventh of their weight is molasses, which forms a coating on each crystal.

The rich flavour is very similar to that of dark rum and can substitute for it. One of the best ways to use this is on Dusky Virgins, a simple, delicious and quick way to make something as good as crème brûlée in minutes. Mix equal volumes of plain yoghurt and whipped cream together and pile into ramekins, over fresh fruit if you like. The acidity of the yoghurt will stiffen and set the cream. On top of each, sprinkle muscovado sugar and leave to chill for several hours, during which time the sugar will melt, looking like a crust of caramelized white sugar but tasting very much better.

Light muscovado: is a creamier-coloured muscovado with a lower molasses content than true muscovado. It is ideal for cakes and puddings where you want extra flavour; the darker sugars aren't generally recommended for cake making.

Demerara sugar: this highly important and delicious natural brown sugar is crystallized from syrup that has been only partly discolourized and filtered during boiling. The large, sparkling, yellow crystals are about 98 per cent pure sucrose and two per cent molasses and thus quite refined, but at least give you some minerals. It takes its name from the county in Guyana where it was first produced. But now there are other types of 'dem' as it is affectionately known, and it can be made by adding cane molasses to refined white sugar, which could thus be beet sugar. It will have exactly the same qualities and you will always know if it has been made for its name must be qualified. Demerara on a packet means it was made from cane sugar in the country in which the cane was grown. Other types, such as London Demerara indicate that it has been artificially made and the qualifying adjective usually indicates this was done in a refinery closer to the point of consumption.

There is almost no nutritional difference between muscovado and demerara sugar.

Demerara is excellent for flavouring cooked or new fruits, and for cereals. It is traditionally used to sprinkle on fruitcakes and biscuits before baking, to give a crunchy topping. It can replace white sugar in virtually every recipe where you do not mind the addition of a little colour.

Turbinado: a raw sugar which has been steam cleaned and is thus lighter in colour and flavour. A term found rather more often in the United States where true raw sugar is considered unfit for human consumption because of its impurities, turbinado falls somewhere between light muscovado and demerara in appearance and flavour and thus either of these or light soft brown sugar may be substituted when you are using American cookbooks.

Molasses, Blackstrap molasses: this is the rich concentrated syrup remaining after cane sugar syrup has been through the several boiling and separating processes necessary to extract almost all the pure sucrose. It contains some sucrose and other types of sugar as well as everything that refined white sugar is missing; in fact 8-10 per cent of molasses is vital minerals including iron, copper, calcium, magnesium, chromium, phosphorous, potassium and zinc.

There are various colours and grades, depending on how much sugar is left in the liquid. The darker the molasses the less sugar it contains. All types can also contain sulphur, which is used in some refineries – unsulphured molasses is usually light coloured and better flavoured. Some cane growing areas will simply reduce cane syrup over heat and call this sweet golden liquid molasses; but this is never sold commercially that I know of. Molasses is mainly used these days to flavour baking, in Creole cooking and to add flavour to the water when boiling hams.

Treacle: this is much sweeter than molasses for it is actually the full syrup that has only had a proportion of the sucrose removed from it, and again can only be made from cane sugar although golden syrup might also be added to it – the label will tell you. Used mainly for puddings.

Other than those natural brown sugars from the cane, it's all sweetness and white, for further refining produces a crystal that is practically 100 per cent pure sucrose, and it is this white granulated sugar which is usually demanded and to which the refineries and factories are basically geared. There is no proof that refined white sugar is in itself more fattening than the natural brown sugars, but the latter are nutritionally more valuable and balanced, *relatively*.

WHITE SUGARS

These are classified according to grain size, and may be made from cane or beet.

Rock or Candy sugar: huge sugar crystals, often strung together. It is used for sweet making as it does not burn easily.

Granulated sugar: although varying from country to country each grain is usually about 1mm.

Caster sugar: useful for cake making, drinks and decorating where the smaller grain either dissolves faster or looks prettier. Usually under .25mm in Britain. In the United States the grain is even smaller and called superfine or Baker's Special;

one can be substituted for the other.

Icing sugar: called confectioner's sugar in the United States, this is made by grinding small crystals, and cornflour is usually added to prevent caking.

Cube sugar: this is produced by moulding and pressing selected granulated sugar with sugar syrup which cements the crystal. On drying, it is very hard and this is presumably based on the process which formed loaf sugar.

Jam sugar: a useful, relatively new product which blends granulated sugar with apple pectin and citric acid and thus guarantees a good set when making preserves.

Preserving sugar: specially suited to such work as its large crystals dissolve slowly and do not settle in a dense layer on the bottom of the pan – therefore there is less stirring and less chance of your jam burning.

BROWN SUGARS

Light brown and dark brown soft sugars are usually granulated white beet sugar which has been coloured and flavoured with sugar cane molasses. If you hold these sugars under running water the applied coating will be seen to dissolve. They are not artificially created alternatives to demerara or muscovado sugars but have been carefully planned to have very specific culinary uses.

Light brown: this is rather fine grained, designed to dissolve easily, and specially recommended for creaming with butter (or margarine if you must) for cake making or for making brown sugar meringues. It will give marginally more flavour and a little more colour than white sugar.

Dark brown: also planned with baking in mind, when rich colour and dark flavour is wanted, in ginger breads, rich fruit cakes or other mixtures containing vine fruits. Like muscovado sugars, you can almost pretend it is dark rum you have used.

Cassonade: few French people believe it but this is white beet sugar coloured and flavoured with sugar cane molasses as explained above. The molasses equivalent of sugar beet is utterly inedible.

GOLDEN SUGARS

Golden sugars are made in Mauritius and sit in a culinary oasis of their own between white sugar and demerara. They may be sold as unrefined because the crystals naturally contain a slight amount of molasses and thus offer a certain amount of the original vitamins and minerals; at the same time there is little molasses flavour and they may be used as though white sugar, even in tea. Essentially, steam cleaning and careful manipulation of the processing cleverly leaves less molasses in the crystals than in a demerara, but has stopped short of complete refining.

Golden sugars tend to create anything but sweetness in the mouths of white sugar refiners who say any sugar which has been processed in some way is by definition a refined sugar and that it is deceptive of the producers to say these are unrefined. In the end, it matters little. The difference in nutrition, colour and flavour is minimal unless you are eating sugars by the spoonful, in which case you are unlikely to care anyway.

GOLDEN SYRUP

Terribly popular but, like 'brown sugars', a little dishonest. It is a syrup of refined sugar plus something called invert sugar plus colouring from the original sugar syrup. Invert sugar is sucrose (a complicated sugar) broken down into its components, the two simple sugars called dextrose and laevulose. If you must have a syrup, treacle is probably a marginally better choice; but I wouldn't put anybody off a golden-syrup flavoured steamed pudding.

If you are American you cannot buy golden syrup so you must use corn syrup and, if you like, colour it with some brown sugar of one kind or another.

COFFEE CRYSTALS

These stupid, over expensive, maddening things, thought to be the height of sophistication in far too many restaurants and houses, seem carefully planned to ensure you either enjoy the complete cup of coffee in all its bitterness before the crystals begin to melt, or that you drink it stone-cold, by which time some of the crystals might have melted. I can't think why anybody buys them.

FLAVOURED SUGARS

Perhaps the most useful sweet flavouring in any kitchen is vanilla sugar, caster sugar which has been stored with vanilla beans in a screw-top jar. The beans may also be removed and used several times for flavouring sauces etc, simply being dried properly before returning to the sugar; and the sugar can be topped up as it is used. But there are many other flavoured sugars you might find useful to make and use. They should be allowed to sit for at least two weeks in a cool dark place before you can expect the flavours to have been absorbed. Even quite small amounts make nice gifts when prettily presented.

Citrus sugar: wonderful on fruit, in cream or sprinkled over hot or cold puddings of almost any type. This may be flavoured with lemon, lime, bitter (Seville) or sweet oranges, tangerines or any of the new styles marketed. Rub the zest with sugar lumps, but stop before you get to the bitter pith. As the outer layer of the cube collects the zest and oils and thus slightly dissolves, scrape it off onto a plate. When you have enough, dry the flavoured sugar and zest residue very gently in a low oven, and then crush it and store in an air tight jar. You might find it easier to mix a few tablespoons of finely grated zest with each 250g/8oz of granulated sugar and dry that before storing. Do the grating directly over the sugar or you will lose the zest, and rub sugar over the inside of the grater to collect the zest there: even so it will not be as elegantly flavoured as the cube method.

Floral sugar: rose petals, jasmine flowers, rose geranium, lavender and orange blossom are the best. Violet is a terrific idea too, but where can you find strongly scented ones these days? The flowers should be perfectly dry and used in quite large amounts. Take extra special care to store away from heat and light and use on berry fruits, or in cream cheeses, yoghurts, whipped cream, sponges and the like.

Spice sugars: cinnamon, ginger, aniseed, cardamom, clove or mixed spice sugars are suddenly invaluable once you have them, for pancakes and batters, toast, yoghurts, cake toppings or flavourings, fruit pies, hot chocolate and coffee or the whipped cream which might top them. Use very freshly ground spices and about two tablespoons per 250g/8oz.

Cooking: the most important contributions to cooking made by sugar are its preserving qualities and its lightening of cake mixtures.

Sugar's preservative qualities give us jams, jellies and preserves, for a high sugar level prevents the growth of bacteria or the action of enzymes. It is important that sugar is used when freezing fresh fruits and some vegetables, as the temperatures of a freezer are not low enough to kill or dissuade the attentions of enzymic actions which putrefy such goods. In addition the presence of sugar or sugar syrup in frozen soft fruits or berries prevents the formation of ice particles which break up the structure of the fruit and cause them to disintegrate when defrosted. Cream, butter and egg yolks all freeze better if sugar is added and cakes and biscuits will freeze well if they have a high sugar content.

Sugar in a cake mixture helps keep the gluten of the flour soft and pliable, allowing it to expand thereby giving volume and lightness.

I know it is popular but I cannot bring myself to use sugar when cooking peas or tomatoes. If you need sugar either you have been soaking the peas, which removes their own sugar, or are using unripe or English salad tomatoes, for which there is no cure – or perhaps you have used too much salt...

> **WATCH THE LABELS**
> Manufacturers have got cagey about spelling out sugar contents, and often disguise the sweetness of products by using almost anything but pure sucrose. But the information is there if you know that glucose, laevulose, maltose and fructose (fruit sugar) are all sugars. Invert sugar is a mixture of glucose and laevulose obtained by breaking down sucrose into these simpler sugars. Corn syrup and sorghum syrup are also sweeteners and often used in soft drinks and frozen products.

OTHER SWEETENERS

The usual substitute for sugar is honey, another natural sweetener which was replaced by refined sugar when it became generally available. However you are also likely to find these in shops and recipes:

Corn syrup: made by hydrolysis of the corn starch, that is, a chemical splitting into component sugars together with the addition of water. Often used in the United States. If you find a recipe that calls for corn syrup, you can replace it with golden syrup, but remember that it will give added colour, for corn syrup is colourless.

Sorghum syrup: a relatively natural product made by concentrating the stalk juice of sorghum, which is a type of millet. Less common nowadays.

Maple syrup: the reduced, sweet sap of the North American sugar maple (*Acer saccharum*) varies in sweetness, colour and flavour depending on how much it is boiled. Use hot, especially on pancakes and waffles or with bacon; otherwise as a flavouring for ices, sauces, icings and baking. Sometimes crystallized to make maple sugar.

Palm sugar: also known as jaggery, this is made from the boiled sap of a number of varieties of palm tree. Moist and tawny and only slightly crystalline, it has a truly delicious fudgy flavour which is less sweet than cane and beet sugars. Available packed in many forms, including frozen, it easily picks up moisture and becomes liquid. In Sri Lanka it is melted over heat, lightly spiced and then thickened with dessicated coconut as a stuffing for small sweet pancakes, but is always a sensation when used instead of cane or beet sugars. Baked apples, pears and peaches are transformed, baked bananas double their ambrosial appeal and a mixture of toasted nuts and warmed palm sugar on ice cream is almost too good to eat. Almost...

HONEY

You may safely dismiss most claims made for honey as mere sweet nothings. Honey is essentially a concentrated solution of water and sucrose which has been predigested into simpler sugars, laevulose and dextrose, which will make up 75 per cent of the bulk. To be stored and sold in the retail market honey has been strained to take from the solution of sugar all traces of wax debris, but leaving pollen and other minutiae including colloids. It is only these minimal ingredients which could remotely give honey magical qualities. There do seem to be substantiated claims that it helps wounds to heal, but essentially, honey is sugar and sugar is calories.

Even without claims for it as an elixir of life, honey has long been one of the world's most important foods. Together with the lowly parsnip and carrot it was the world's main sweetener until sugar dropped in price to become more universally available in the late 19th century. It is recognizable in Egyptian pyramid burials at least 5,000 years old and has been relied upon, as sugar syrup is today, as a preservative. But it is not entirely safe or as sterile as so commonly believed; untreated honey contains many spores including that of fatally dangerous botulism. The exact strain is weak enough to be destroyed internally by children and adults but babies under a year old should not be fed untreated honey, which includes all honeycombs.

The greatest marvel of honey is the extraordinary industry which goes into its manufacture: to call bees busy is a phenomenal understatement. It all starts with nectar, the sugary syrup which collects in the base of flowers. In some cases – the Australian eucalyptus for instance – a bee might obtain a full load of nectar from one blossom but it is more usual to have to visit up to 1500! It takes 300 bees up to a month to make 450g/1lb of honey from the nectar.

First they store it in a special nectar stomach, whence the bee can siphon off supplies to keep it going; the bee is so well designed it can carry its own weight whereas jets have to settle for a 25 per cent payload. It has been estimated the bee is efficient enough to fly four million miles at a steady 7 mph on a gallon of nectar.

Back at the hive the nectar is transferred from mouth to mouth of worker bees. This digests the original complicated sugars to simple invert sugar (that combination of laevulose and dextrose) and reduces the moisture content from 70 per cent to between 15 and 20 per cent: because the hive is kept at a constant 32°C further reduction is unavoidable. The point of the effort is to give the bees food for winter. It is sometimes said cheap honey is made by feeding bees sugar syrup which they convert into lesser honey but this is incorrect. Because the bees' natural food has been taken from them, bee keepers must artificially feed the bees during winter. None of the sugar syrup is converted and stored as honey.

Once the honeycombs are harvested the cells are decapped, usually by a heat process, and the honey extracted by centrifugal force. If the solid particles of wax and pollen are not removed, crystallization will begin more quickly than required. Sometimes new honeys are stored unstrained or part-refined and later heated to 52°C for several days to liquidize them before further treatment. Once bottled, the honey is usually heated again which helps promote a shelf life of 6-9 months.

Even such strained and pasteurized honey will contain enough oils and essences from its origins to present an enormous range of flavours and styles. This is the real point of honey today, spectacular natural flavours in a natural product.

Most commercial honeys are blended for uniformity and from year to year will contain honey from a number of countries. China is a major source, and so is America, Russia, Australia and Africa, some giving colour, some fragrance, some texture and some sheer economy.

The aristocrats are honeys made from the nectar of a single flower and the rarer the flower the more expensive the honey. Like good olive oils, these should never be used in cooking but enjoyed solo.

If you like a medium richness and fullness of flavour, clover honey is a marvellous middle-range choice but even this will vary according to the country. Generally, the hotter the country the richer the flavour of any honey and thus Australian clover honey will be more robust than an English one.

The queen of honeys is generally thought to be Greek Hymettus, flavoured with the nectar of wild thyme from the mountain of that name; others argue that Middle European acacia honey is better.

The range of single flower honeys increases every year and some shippers will be able to offer specials on a once only basis. There is a huge choice – over 300 single flower honeys in the United States alone – with some of the best coming from the Balkans and Mediterranean; lavender honey and rosemary honey have their addicts and there are supposed to be rose and raspberry blossom honeys but I have never yet spotted them. My absolute favourite is orange blossom honey, and it is a lifetime of pleasure to compare those of each country which makes it, which includes Central American countries as well as the Middle East. Linden (usually called lime) blossom honey is also exceptionally delicious.

English honey is properly famed for its elegance but single flower varieties are terribly expensive, presumably because there is so little harvest in most summers. Scottish heather honey is an exception to the hot weather/robust honey rule for in this, the cool moors have produced a very tasty, rather direct honey which is particularly well thought of for desserts and cooking in general. A great deal of British and European honey making is blighted by the ever-increasing acreage of rape, the nectar of which gives an overbearing muskiness and bitterness which many find destroys their enjoyment of honey, even when in minute quantities.

New Zealand supplies some outstandingly individual honey from its native trees, many of which have supportable claims to being truly organic. Manuka (or ti-tree) is a dark, full, sharpish honey; pohutukawa honey is made from the gorgeous red flowers of a tree which lines the beaches and blooms at Christmas time.

New on the market is New Zealand Honeydew, not really a honey in that it is not made by bees but by aphids which live on the bark of black beech trees in the country's virgin Southern Alps: it is untreated and also guaranteed organic. It has a slightly yeasty nose and flavour with a stunning aftertaste of orange flower water.

Comb honey: if you can bear to chew the wax, this is the most nutritious of honeys, and, being complete, is more likely to contain whatever is said to be one of life's elixirs. But don't make the mistake of storing comb honey lying down. The bees don't. Examine a comb closely and you will see each cell slopes down slightly, so it can stand upright without leakages. This is how you should keep it too. It is always untreated and increasingly expensive. Generally you find you buy a square cut from a larger comb, but sometimes the bees have been persuaded to make combs in smaller, plastic squares – an expensive but practical ploy.

Clear honey: even the most carefully refined and pasteurized honey will crystallize eventually. It depends very much on the type and some heather honeys may not begin for up to two years. If you have honey which is crystallized and you prefer it not to be, stand the sealed pot in cold water and slowly bring it to a temperature into which you can just put your fingertips. Keep the water at this temperature until the honey is clear. Do not think of clear honey which is crystallized as 'off'.

Set honey: the real term is crystallized honey, an effect which is perfectly natural, but which can be helped by stirring or whipping clear honey.

Cooking: the individual oils and perfumes of specialist honeys are lost in baking, so it is pointless using anything but the most basic blends. Indeed if you want the best of honey flavour in cooking it is far better to add it to cooked fruits, exotic sweetmeats and pastries after they are cooked. For the latter, typically in Greek and Middle Eastern pastries using filo pastry, diluted honey is much better than syrup, but you must always use a cold honey or syrup on hot pastry: hot syrup on hot pastry, or cold on cold or hot on cold will always give sogginess.

To convert recipes using sugar, calculate that sugar and honey have the same sweetening capacity weight for weight. But by volume honey is almost twice as sweet; one tablespoon of honey is as sweet as two tablespoons of sugar. You must also use slightly less liquid to mix the original recipe.

Storing: like most natural products, honey does not stand up to light and heat. It also frosts in very cold conditions, caused by bubbles of air being forced out as the honey shrinks. When it expands again on reheating the bubbles remain and are virtually impossible to remove.

PRODUCTS OF DESIGNATED ORIGIN AND QUALITY

FRENCH AOC
The Appellation d'Origine Contrôlée (AOC) of France, currently recognises and strictly controls the following food products, giving them the status of national treasures.

Blackcurrants:	Cassis de Dijon
Black Truffles:	Truffe Noire du Tricastin
Butters:	Beurre Charente Poitou
	Beurre des Charentes
	Beurre des Deux-sevres
	Beurre d'Isigny
Carrots:	Carrottes de Creance
Cheeses:	Abondance (usually Tomme d'Abondance)
	Beaufort
	Bleu d'Auvergne
	Bleu des Causses
	Bleu du Haut-Jura (Bleu de Gex or Bleu de Septmoncel)
	Brie de Meaux
	Brie de Melun
	Broccio Corse (or Brucciu)
	Camembert de Normandie
	Cantal (Fourme de Cantal or Salers)
	Chabichou du Poitu
	Chaource
	Comté
	Crottins de Chavignol
	Fourme d'Ambert (or Fourme de Montbrison)
	Lagiuole
	Livarot
	Maroilles or Marolles
	Mont d'Or (or Vacherin du Haut Doubs)
	Munster (or Munster Géromé)
	Neufchâtel
	Ossau-Iraty Brebis Pyrénées (or
	Petites Ossau-Iraty-Brebis Pyrénées)
	Picodon de l'Ardeche (or Picodon de la Drôme)
	Pouligny-Saint-Pierre
	Pont l'Evêque
	Reblochon (or Petit Reblochon)
	Roquefort
	Saint-Nectaire

	Sainte-Maure de Touraine
	Selles-sur-Cher
Chicken:	Poulets du Bourbonnais
	Volailles de Bresse
Cream:	Creme d'Isigny
Grapes:	Chasselas de Moissac
Green Lentils:	Lentilles Vertes du Puy
Guinea Fowl:	Pintadeaux de la Drôme
Hay:	Foin de Crau
Honey:	Miel de Lorraine
	Miel des Vosges
Olives:	Olives de Nyons
Olive Oil:	Huile d'Olive de Nyons
Oysters:	Huitres de Belon
Ravioli:	Raviole du Dauphine
Turkey:	Dinde Fermiere de Bresse
Vermouth:	Vermouth de Chambery
Walnuts:	Noix de Grenoble

SPAIN DOC

Spain has a limited Denominaciones de Origen (DO) system to supervise and guarantee the standards of its most esteemed foods. As standards improve or regulations are refined, products can move precise categories, but those you should seek with confidence are:

Asparagus:	Esparrago de Navarra
Cheeses:	Cabrales
	Cantabria
	Idiazabal
	Liebana cheeses
	Manchego
	Mahon
	Roncal
Hams:	Jamon de Guijuelo
	Jamon de Teruel
Peppers:	Pimiento del Piquillo de Lodosa
Rice:	Arroz de Calasparra

USEFUL ADDRESSES

CHEESES FROM SWITZERLAND
Swiss Cheese Union Information Centre, 2 Haslemere Way, Banbury, Oxon OX16 8TY.

GOOD FOOD RETAILING
Stanstead Publications, 177 Stanstead Road, Caterham, Surrey CR3 6AJ.

ACCORD SERVICES LIMITED (FINE TEAS)
Infusion House, Rougham Industrial Estate, Bury St Edmunds, Suffolk IP30 9ND.

ANDRONICAS COFFEE COMPANY LIMITED
328 Blucher Road, London SE5 0LH.

BRITISH DEER FARMERS' ASSOCIATION
Holly Lodge, Spencers Lane, Berkswell, Coventry CV7 7BZ.

BRITISH EGG INFORMATION SERVICE
Bury House, 126-128 Cromwell Road, London SW7 4ET.

BRITISH HONEY IMPORTERS' ASSOCIATION
PR Connection, 47-48 Westminster Palace Gardens, Artillery Row, London SW1P 1RR.

BRITISH INDEPENDENT GROCERS' ASSOCIATION
Federation House, 17 Farnborough Street, Farnborough, Hampshire GU14 8AG.

BRITISH VINEGAR BREWERS' FEDERATION
PR Connection, 47-48 Westminster Palace Gardens, Artillery Row, London SW1P 1RR.

THE CHOCOLATE SOCIETY
Norwood Bottom Farm, Norwood Bottom, Near Otley, West Yorkshire LS21 2RA.

CHOCOLATERIE VALRHONA
26600 Tain-L'Hermitage, France.

CMA (German food and drink marketing organisation)
CMA House, 17a Church Road, Wimbledon, London SW19 5DQ.

FARMHOUSE CHEESEMAKERS LIMITED
23 Union Street, Wells, Somerset BA5 2PU.

FOOD AND WINE FROM FRANCE
41 Piccadilly, London W1V 9AJ.

FOOD FROM BRITAIN
Market Towers, New Covent Garden, Nine Elms Lane, London SW8 5NU.

FOODS FROM SPAIN
Spanish Embassy Commercial Office, Chiltern Street, London W1M 1PR.

FOX'S SPICES LIMITED
Mason Road Industrial Estate, Stratford-upon-Avon, Warwickshire CV37 9NF.

THE IRISH TRADE BOARD
Ireland House, 150-151 New Bond Street, London W1Y 0HD.

THE ITALIAN TRADE CENTRE
37 Sackville Street, London W1X 2DQ.

NATIONAL DAIRY COUNCIL
5-7 John Princes Street, London W1M 0AP.

SCOTTISH SALMON SMOKERS' ASSOCIATION
33 Melville Street, Edinburgh EH3 7JH.

THE SPECIALIST CHEESEMAKERS' ASSOCIATION
PO Box 256A, Thames Ditton, Surrey KT7 0HR.

STILTON CHEESEMAKERS' ASSOCIATION INFORMATION BUREAU
PO Box 11, Buxton, Derbyshire SK17 6DD.

THE UNITED KINGDOM CHEESE GUILD
177 Stanstead Road, Caterham, Surrey CR3 6AJ.